Heroes, Saints, &
Ordinary Morality

MORAL TRADITIONS SERIES
James F. Keenan, S.J., Editor

Heroes, Saints, &
Ordinary Morality

ANDREW MICHAEL FLESCHER

Georgetown University Press
Washington, D.C.

Georgetown University Press, Washington, D.C.
© 2003 by Georgetown University Press. All rights reserved.
Printed in the United States of America

10 9 8 7 6 5 4 3 2 1   2003

Library of Congress Cataloging-in-Publication Data

Flescher, Andrew Michael, 1969–
    Heroes, saints, and ordinary morality / Andrew Michael Flescher.
       p. cm. — (Moral traditions series)
Includes bibliographical references and index.
    ISBN 0-87840-137-7 (cloth : alk. paper)
    1. Duty. 2. Supererogation. 3. Moral development. 4. Religious
ethics.   I. Title. II. Series.
    BJ1451.F58   2003
    170—dc21
                                              2003004569

Contents

Acknowledgments

I am grateful for the financial assistance, encouragement, and advice of those whose generosity made possible the preparation of this project. I am blessed with having had the opportunity to learn from such caring mentors and colleagues. I want to thank them, as well as the many probing, energetic students of mine over the past few years for pressing me to think so hard.

My ability to research and write this book was facilitated by three grants I received between June 2001 and December 2002 from California State University, Chico, and by the Reverend William Ellery Arnold Memorial Dissertation Fellowship and the Richardson Dissertation Fellowship, which I received between January 1999 and May 2000 at Brown University. It is through countless conversations on the topics of obligation and benevolence with Jock Reeder, my advisor at Brown, that I began to think about heroes, saints, and the concepts of duty and supererogation in a new way. I am overwhelmed by the sheer amount of effort and time Jock put into helping me to conceive and then articulate my ideas, and by the eagerness and warmth with which he conveyed to me his input. He embodies the intellectual and moral virtues that I can only hope to cultivate and pass on to my students.

My experience with Georgetown Press has been wonderful. I am deeply grateful to Richard Brown and Jim Keenan, who assisted me in the organization of the manuscript and stimulated me to connect my insights to a broader readership. I was continually impressed by their professionalism and razor-sharp insights.

I could not have asked for a more meticulous, competent, patient, supportive, and critical reader than Saundra Wright. Her careful eye and organizational sense were indispensable to the process of writing. In addition to those mentioned so far, I have benefited from the thoughtful guidance of colleagues who helped me to formulate and refine my thoughts at various stages, in particular Barney Twiss, Wendell Dietrich, Giles Milhaven,

Jung Lee, Melanie Gustin, Steve Lubkemann, Lucas Swaine, Bruce Grelle, and Robert Burton. I would like, above all, to thank my family, in particular my father and mother, Robert and Joyce Flescher, and my sister and brother in law, Ellen and Ethan Foxman. Their support does not now, and never did, have any limits.

Finally, aside from Jock, there are two other mentors to whom I would like to call special attention for providing me with the inspiration for writing this book: Kalman Bland and Jerry Trecker. These three, like the heroes and saints whom I discuss within, gave of themselves beyond even the most ambitious description of their roles. This book is about the human interaction that takes place between mentors and those who aspire to become more like them. In my own case, I could not have been more fortunate.

The Morally Ordinary and the Morally Extraordinary

> I feel that I have done nothing well. But I have done what I could.
> —Dorothy Day, *The Long Loneliness*

In this book I ask a commonplace question, but it is one that, if successfully answered, will have profound implications for those who wish to live and conduct themselves in a deliberate, reflective, and morally honest fashion. The question is this: What ought we to expect ordinary people to do for others who need their help? This is a slightly more complicated question than it appears, for I am really asking both *how much* we ought to expect ordinary people to give of themselves and what *attitude* we ought to expect them to have with respect to their giving. Perhaps, though, the question could be put even more simply: What is morally required of an ordinary person in order to be considered a "good" person? This question, albeit basic, goes to the heart of a lifestyle that we take for granted. It forces us to reexamine our most routine habits and leads us to ponder a kind of interaction with others that is likely different from the one to which we have become accustomed in present-day society.

My inquiry is undertaken in light of the moral reality of my own secular, contemporary culture, a culture in which most people do less, or as much as, but rarely more than what they perceive to be expected of them. In my encounters with friends, acquaintances, and students—and in my own self-examination—I have discovered that even by initiating an inquiry such as mine, one risks incurring the resentment of the person questioned, for that person frequently feels as though the questioner has been intrusive. Some read into the inquiry an idealism or self-righteousness that they find unbecoming. When one raises questions about the specific issue of world hunger, for example, many respond: "Who are you to decide for me what of mine I should give away? And on what basis do you hope to persuade me that I should in the first place make sacrifices for a perfect stranger?" Thus, I also ask the question, "What ought to be expected of ordinary people?" in the face of an objection that takes the form of a pragmatic appeal to individual and civil liberties, liberties which in the United States we tend to regard as fundamental to our very freedom and well-being.

This objection is one with which I have been confronted regularly in casual discussion, in the classroom, and in scholarly exchanges with colleagues. When I hear it, I take it seriously. I then ask myself whether or not a secular society such as ours has the resources to induce its inhabitants to become, or even to want to become, better people than they currently are. This reflection leads to even more basic considerations. *Ought* we to expect ordinary people to become more caring toward others in their midst, to sacrifice their own self-interest, if such is required, in order to attend to the one in need? *Ought* we at least to expect ordinary people to lament that they do not do more for others than they usually do, to feel a sense of contrition that they rarely, if ever, exceed the minimum? If so, on what basis might we make these claims? Alternatively, are these maxims too much to expect of ordinary people—in particular, ordinary people who live in a society such as ours?

The majority of those whom I have asked do, in fact, believe that "becoming better" is for the most part too much to ask of the ordinary person. What makes someone morally "ordinary," they usually reply, is precisely that one does *not* go above and beyond, or does so only on an exceptional basis, at which time we sometimes refer to one's conduct as "heroic" or "saintly." According to this view, it is considered praiseworthy for the morally ordinary person merely to avoid falling below the minimum on a consistent basis. On the other hand, we can expect morally *extraordinary* people, such as heroes and saints, to do the very most they can to help whomever they can, owing to their extraordinarily courageous and loving natures. As such, according to the typical view, we ought to hold heroes and saints in our highest esteem without at the same time deluding ourselves into thinking that we have the ability to do as they do. Heroes and saints are exceptional. They stand in relation to us as exemplary ideals. Their deeds and lives we may behold. However, their moral outlooks are relevant to ours only as points of contrast. Heroic or saintly morality does not reflect what is ordinarily expected of us. According to this view, to scrutinize the conduct, character, and habits of heroes and saints, while of significant academic interest, will not be very helpful in clarifying for us what is to be morally expected of ordinary people. In my experience, I have found that discussions about heroes and saints frequently complement the development of a two-tiered morality of duty and supererogation. Accordingly, two separate systems of norms are thought to apply to two categories of people: morally ordinary people and morally extraordinary people.

In this book, I hope to refute this intuitive proposition about the relation between "ordinary" and "extraordinary" people and thus undo the two-tiered model of "duty" and "above and beyond" that we normally presuppose applies to ourselves in relation to those whose particular moral capacities exceed the ordinary standard. I attempt to do this through reference to the testimony of morally extraordinary people themselves.

Even though I have been referring to them together, it bears remarking that heroes and saints are different categories. This difference will emerge in the course of this book. Both heroes and saints, however, can be characterized as morally extraordinarily people. Sometimes such people contradict one of our most fundamental characterizations of their conduct. They do this when they deny what we tend to take for granted, namely, that they go above and beyond the call of duty. In their denials, they sometimes provoke us to reconsider our conception of how we, as ordinary people, stand in relation to them. One example of this comes from Dorothy Day, cofounder of the Catholic Worker movement. The following passage is one I like to discuss with my students:

> Through voluntary poverty we have the means to help our brothers. We cannot even see our brothers in need without first stripping ourselves. It is the only way we have of showing our love.
>
> Poverty is a strange and elusive thing. I have tried to write about it for years now; I could probably write about it for another twenty years without conveying what I feel about it as well as I would like. I condemn poverty *and I advocate it*; poverty is simple and complex at once; it is a social phenomenon and a personal matter. It is a paradox....
>
> In front of me as I write is Fritz Eichenberg's picture of St. Vincent de Paul. He holds a chubby child in his arms and a thin pale child clinging to him. Yes, the poor are always going to be with us—our Lord told us that—and there will always be a need for our sharing, for stripping ourselves to help others. It will always be a lifetime job.[1]

In this passage the author makes abundantly clear that she endorses the strongest possible sense of other-regard. She acknowledges no limits to the costs she may be asked to endure in the course of helping others worse off than she. Such costs—which include becoming poor oneself—are to be embraced. Moreover, she asserts that the responsibility to attend to the amelioration of the impoverished remains a project to which one is bound over the course of a lifetime. One does not simply fulfill this responsibility and then turn to something else. Finally, this responsibility to the poor, even though Day refers to it as "voluntary poverty," is in a very important sense morally obligatory. It is both cognitively necessary—without becoming poor ourselves we cannot empathize with the plight of the impoverished—and, according to Day, a condition of one's fulfillment of the command to love one's neighbor. While such a demanding view of moral requirement is, of course, the product of the deep religious convictions that Day developed as a devout Catholic (that we have business with the poor, and vice versa, is the crux of what it means to remain faithful to one's discipleship), the foregoing passage can also be read as a broad endorsement for morality in general. In advocating poverty, Day is not holding herself to a higher standard. Rather, she is exhorting us not to fall below that which is minimally morally required of ourselves, at least if we are to acknowledge genuinely that poverty is, in fact, a problem in need of a remedy.

This is a controversial and perhaps counterintuitive feature of Dorothy Day's message. When I discuss Day with my students, they are ambivalent about the extent to which she is, as she claims, no different from anyone else. The controversy can be posed as a question: Is a figure like Day to be emulated or merely admired? It is certainly easier to admire her, for it is pleasurable to reflect upon how much better off the world is that we have people like Day in it, and it comes as a relief to tell ourselves that what she does is not realistically possible for us to do as well. Should we, then, understand Day's impassioned plea to enter a life of poverty as merely descriptive of what a morally noble, or superior, way of life might look like? According to Day herself, the answer is, of course, no. She intends to *involve* us in her plight. To claim an appreciation for Day and then fail to look inward is to engage in a moral evasion. We might be inclined to disagree with the maximally demanding view of morality that Day endorses, but it is difficult to read her in a positive light and simultaneously not perceive her indicting herself and others for not doing enough. To read her literally is in part to feel the force of this character assault.

In my experience teaching her, I have found that the literal reading of Day is a particularly difficult interpretation for students to accept. So many of them are immediately attracted to this woman's earnest hunger for God and desire to escape her "long loneliness." However, they are attracted to her integrity and moral courage, not to her life itself, which, they are quick to point out, is well beyond their own reach. When they articulate as much, I often respond by asking them how this reading of Day squares with the instructional tone that she takes with the reader. How can we plausibly admire Day without emulating her, in light of what she herself actually has to say?

Some students propose a clever way out of the dilemma. We can admire the life of this remarkable woman, who is to be extolled for being consistent in word and deed, while reading her exhortations to us *rhetorically*. According to this solution, either (1) Day does not really intend for us to strip ourselves of our possessions in order to combat poverty, although she realizes that this is what she must say if she is to have any chance of convincing us to do more for the poor than we are currently doing; or (2) Day does intend this morally demanding response on our part, but, amid her passion for the cause, overshoots the mark and ends up requiring too much of us. In either case, Day errs, either deliberately or unwittingly, in her understanding of what is morally required of us, although we prize her all the more for her error. She would not be Dorothy Day, protest the defenders of this "rhetorical" reading, if she did not articulate in earnest that the level of other-regard to which she subscribes is morally appropriate for everyone. The problem with this solution, however, is that it makes a virtue out of an error in judgment. Worse, it fails to acknowledge sufficiently the nature of Dorothy Day's virtuous character, which surely consists of moral *insight*, along with moral *fortitude*. If we extol Day for her views on poverty, and we deem that she has the moral fortitude to act accordingly in her own life, then wouldn't it be disingenuous for us to fail to assume that as a moral authority, she has credibility? Is it consistent to praise her for what she does without trusting her when she tells us what to do?

When I raise this objection, my students often respond that we are for the most part not capable of the things of which Day is capable, and so we are not required to be like her, even though she herself claims otherwise. But, they press further, why should this preclude us from holding her in high moral esteem? Indeed, isn't it the case that I have them read her works in order to show them a picture of a particular—religious— way of life, one that is inspirational even if not completely realistic for the rest of us? And isn't that, after all, the point of studying other great figures from the world's religious traditions: to give us a sense of the remarkable, a sense of the awesome? Would I not be undermining my pedagogical goals if I were to construe an inspirational figure such as Day as ordinary, as not terribly different from everyone else?

I am sympathetic to these responses to my objection. I recognize that there is a difference between figures like Day and the rest of us, and that this difference is, furthermore, what prompts me to include such figures on my syllabi in the first place. *We* are not heroes or saints. On those occasions when we *do* struggle to be altruistic, the endeavor remains just that, a struggle. By contrast, heroes and saints mark themselves as heroic and saintly insofar as they possess the ability to stretch to the limit their human capacity to give. We marvel at this ability. That heroes and saints embody the ideal, and not the norm, is a significant part of what constitutes their appeal.

On the other hand, an equally important objective in having my students read Dorothy Day is that it serves as an excellent way of provoking an important type of introspection. Studying figures like Day serves to undermine a moral complacency that we might exhibit by prompting us to engage in healthy self-criticism. Such complacency often manifests itself in a common, two-part claim. This is the claim that (1) while some people are born with an especially developed tendency for altruism (we use terms like "heroes" and "saints" to describe them), most others are not; and (2) consequently, it is futile to make any kind of attempt to become "heroic" or "saintly" if we are not heroic or saintly already. In rejecting the stark dichotomy between ordinary persons and heroic or saintly persons, as Day herself does so eloquently, sweeping assumptions about the extent to which we can (or cannot) "become otherwise"[2] are held under close scrutiny.

Could we realistically choose "voluntary poverty" if we wished? Could we at least choose it for a sustained period of time? One advantage to reading Day is that the accessibility of an impoverished lifestyle becomes a vivid possibility for us in a way it previously had not been. To be sure, the selections I have students scrutinize from her writings read more like a manual for the altruist-in-training than like a testament chronicling the deeds of the exemplar beyond reproach. The value of such literature is that it helps us to reframe in our own minds exactly what *is* "possible" or "realistic" in terms of setting standards for our responsibilities to others.

There is a tension here in the way we interpret the deeds of extraordinary altruists on the one hand, and in the way we interpret their words on the other. Because we are to a large degree disposed to safeguard our own self-interest when it comes into conflict with the interest of others, we cannot immediately do what the thoroughgoing altruist does. Day tells us that we ought to take responsibility for the poor the way nurses do their patients and the way mothers do their children.[3] In order to remain psychologically honest about what we are capable of morally achieving, however, we tend to dismiss claims like this one as well-intended hyperbole. In making this judgment, we assume that what is of primary value in examining Day is neither her words nor her normative vision, but rather her life viewed as a whole. If this is so, as many of my students suggest, then we are, after all, justified in extolling a figure like Day without emulating her. According to this view, we are not morally obligated to participate in the "permanent revolution" of which she speaks, though we may recognize that we are at times urged to contribute.[4] Day is in this sense an exemplar whose talents exceed ours, and next to whom we may place ourselves for inspiration, but only briefly. On this understanding, we are to her much like the person who runs a mile or so alongside a marathoner and then, as expected, falls away during the course of the race. The problem is that this is not how Day sees herself in relation to others. She claims that it is always possible for us to become marathoners ourselves, "little by little." Thus, students who admire Day's deeds often find themselves confronted by her words. They want to hold her in esteem for the works of mercy that she regularly performs, but they do not see, as she sees so vividly, how the kind of self-transformation that would enable them to become likewise is for them realistic or even possible. The more seriously students take her words, the more they feel indicted for not exploring the possible, and the more the tension that already exists between word and deed increases.

THE TREACHEROUS JOURNEY FROM WORD TO DEED

Getting to the heart of this tension remains one of the most intriguing issues for those interested in ethics, religion, and the intersection of these related fields of inquiry. How can we account for the conflicting—and potentially contradictory—attitude that we, as ordinary persons, tend to adopt toward figures like Dorothy Day? On the one hand, we typically admire and extol them for the altruistic sacrifices that they make. On the other, we do not fully trust them as moral authorities, for when we hear them exhort us in earnest to follow them, we tend to decline their offer. We do this by reinterpreting their exhortations as "ideals," ones that constitute a standard of other-regard appropriate for the exhorter, but not for the one exhorted. When, for example, Day tells us to strip ourselves of our possessions, we may praise her for her selflessness. However, we find it hard to believe that we are strictly morally bound to "advocate" poverty, as she sees herself to be bound. We may cast her mistake in a positive light. We may interpret her exhorting tone as indicative of an optimism, one that places great faith in humanity and the human capacity to be for-the-other. But we find it dangerous to *believe* what she actually says, lest we overestimate our capacity to engage in a maximally demanding life of altruism.

Looked at from a realistic, commonsense perspective, there are arguably dangers to society's adoption of a heroic or saintly ethic. By failing to distinguish between what is required of heroes or saints on the one hand, and the rest of us on the other, there is the concern that morality itself might come to ask too much of us. This worries the defender of commonsense morality, who theorizes that the more morality is perceived as a burden, the more we will get used to the notion that we will fall short of its demands. As a matter of course, we will lose respect for all of morality, and morality as a whole will fall into wide neglect.[5] On this view, a society whose rules were based on what Edith Wyschogrod has called the "ethics of excess,"[6] would not be efficacious. To be guided by the *literal* meaning of heroic or saintly instruction, when heroes and saints enjoin us to walk with them, is possibly to open ourselves up to exploitation, exhaustion, and perhaps permanent corporeal bankruptcy. To follow the hero or saint, who is presumably more psychologically equipped to endure suffering than we are, is to place ourselves in even graver danger than the hero or saint places him or herself.

It would seem, then, that interpreting heroic or saintly exhortations rhetorically, and not literally, is one tenable way to continue to hold heroes or saints in high moral esteem but not hold ourselves accountable to an unreasonably demanding standard of moral requirement. This solution has important consequences for answering the ethicist's question "Why read about heroes and saints?" We do so, claim defenders of the "rhetorical" reading, in order to acquaint ourselves with pictures of virtuous living, but not in order to attain moral insight that is relevant to *our* predicament. Extraordinarily virtuous persons, like Day, inspire, and they sometimes awe. Their stories remain for us a topic of interest in the way that the most talented representatives of any vocation remain a topic of interest. We interpret their overriding disposition to love the neighbor as a gift that we ourselves lack, and, we assume, one that we are unlikely to come to possess. For this reason, we think that learning about heroes and saints will not help us to construct workable notions of what our moral responsibility to others entails. We note that the world is better off with heroes and saints in it. We appreciate their contributions. At the same time, we acknowledge that we are better off if we recognize how very different we are from them. We acknowledge this in spite of what heroes and saints themselves may have to say about the nature of our relation to them.

In this book, I attempt to provide a different answer to the question "Why read about heroes and saints?" I hypothesize that we ought to read about heroes and saints because they, who were once not so heroic or saintly, have struggled just as we have but have subsequently learned to lead a virtuous life. This is a life, I suggest, that we should all want to lead, and a life that, at least in varying degrees, we *can* lead. We ought to read about heroes and saints because of their potential to serve as mentors for those interested in living a virtuous life. As opposed to the majority of interpreters, I do not assume that heroic or saintly exhortations are instances of well-intended hyperbole. Rather, I interpret such exhortations as instructions for virtuous living, albeit instructions that are meant to be followed flexibly according to our particular capacities for moral development over time.

Heroes and saints urge us to regard morality not in terms of avoiding wrongdoing, but in terms of doing what good we can for those who need our help. Reading about heroes and saints is important for alerting us to the proactive nature of morality. To suggest as much is not to fail to acknowledge that there is a gap between how we are now and how we would be were we not so selfishly inclined. We cannot simply will ourselves immediately to become heroes or saints. However, this gap, which John Hare has called the "moral gap,"[7] while unbridgeable for many, does not have to stay as wide as it is at the moment we first recognize it. Over time, we can struggle to decrease it. This is a struggle that involves failure. Virtue is elusive. It is hard to dispose ourselves to be altruistic, and even when we have so disposed ourselves, our greatest efforts to help others can still fall short of what is required to remedy those who stand in need. When we read about heroes and saints, I hope to show, we recognize our own human plight.

HEROES, SAINTS, AND SUPEREROGATION

An advantage to interpreting the words of heroes and saints literally is that it attempts to be faithful to how such figures actually see themselves and to how they see us. When questioned about their self-sacrificial altruistic acts, they tend to assert—adamantly—that they do what would be required of anyone who stood in their shoes. This is an assertion made with confidence, and it is one made by prominent moral exemplars. For this reason, it compels the reflective ethicist to reexamine traditional assumptions about what constitutes an act done above and beyond the call of duty, or an act of "supererogation." Should works of supererogation be defined according to the acts themselves, or should their classification be dependent on the person performing them? We normally assume that one who exceeds one's moral duty does so optionally, is deserving of moral praise, and would not be deserving of moral censure for declining to so act. We determine whether or not one exceeds one's duty, furthermore, by appraising the level of cost involved in the action being performed. We assume that heroes and saints, whose altruistic sacrifices range from especially demanding to maximally costly, go above and beyond the call of duty every time they perform their heroic and saintly acts. So understood, the traditional interpretation allows no sense in which heroic and saintly acts can ever be regarded as morally required, either for ordinary persons or for heroes and saints themselves. The cost one incurs when one risks the lives of oneself and one's loved ones in order to shelter another, for example, is presumed to be too great to regard such an act as morally required. However, in light of the compelling testimony of actual altruists (such as the example of Holocaust rescuers that I take up later in the book) I am inclined to question whether the concept of supererogation is

this cut and dry. Might there be another way of understanding the concept of supererogation that is more consistent with how especially sacrificing persons see their own acts of altruism?

Reworking traditional notions of the concept of supererogation constitutes another important aim of this book. In the pages that follow, I dissent both from the traditional understanding of supererogation, by which
the concept is identified strictly according to the *actions* that exemplify it,
as well as from the corresponding notion that "heroes" and "saints" are
necessarily supererogatory because of the actions they perform. While recognizing that it is possible to exceed the bounds of moral requirement,
and therefore acknowledging the importance of distinguishing duty from
supererogation, I seek to modify the traditional view by arguing that to
fail consistently in one's life to go above and beyond the call of duty is to
betray certain shortcomings of character for which one can be morally
blamed. Stated positively, I argue for a sense in which we ought—i.e., have
a duty—to strive to reach beyond the "call of duty" throughout the course
of our lives, paradoxical though this claim may appear. I suggest that the
maxim to go beyond the call of duty is, in effect, a virtue-based imperative, suggested by various moral and religious traditions, which bids one
to improve one's character over time and thereby to reconceive the nature
and scope of one's first-order moral obligations.[8] Likewise, I argue that
heroes and saints, who already have achieved an extraordinary level of
virtue, have the ability to discern correctly what is morally required of
them. They are not just persons with an unusually high degree of *moral
fortitude*, as defenders of the dominant view readily grant. They are also
credible *moral authorities*, who, precisely because they are more virtuous
than us, can be trusted not to mischaracterize the moral status of their
own actions.

The idea that we should not just admire heroes and saints for their
heroic and saintly conduct but that we should also cultivate their sense of
other-regard has profound implications for what we take moral "duty" to
mean in ethics. For one, it implies that there is a difference between those
duties that represent the minimal moral requirement of everyone and
duty per se. The latter, and not the former, I argue, varies depending on
one's particular level of moral development. In this sense "duty" is tied
to character. Like many ethicists who have over the last couple decades
become dissatisfied with a moral theory that concentrates strictly on principles and proscriptions for deciding what is morally required, I maintain
that the notions of duty and character are inexorably linked, and that we
cannot be sure that we have acted rightly if we have failed to attempt to
live virtuously. To live "virtuously" is to inculcate the character traits necessary for human excellence and flourishing. This is a process that begins

first by *disposing* oneself to think, to feel, and finally to act as a virtuous person would think, feel, and act.[9] In short, it is a process that entails becoming a different kind of person. But just what is it to think, feel, and act virtuously? This question serves as the subject of an important and ongoing debate internal to the virtue ethics camp.[10]

Helpfully, we can find clues as to what living virtuously involves by looking at the words and deeds of virtuous persons themselves. Through examining the lives of heroes and saints, we are able to see that a life of virtue at least entails being courageous in terms of risking self-interest, and being compassionate in terms of desiring the betterment of others in need. Virtuous persons go out of their way to help others. Unlike other virtue ethicists, I suggest, through reference to virtuous exemplars, that while living virtuously is not synonymous with living altruistically, *living altruistically is the kernel of living virtuously*. Along with the majority of virtue theorists, I applaud the recent shift in contemporary secular and religious ethics that focuses less on specific acts performed (or not performed) by an agent and more on enduring character traits possessed by that agent. In this book, I take the further step of arguing for the close connection between virtue and altruism. Such a shift in emphasis involves reexamining the way in which we normally attribute moral praiseworthiness or blameworthiness to particular agents. The virtue ethic that I will endorse maintains that if we do not work on our character development, and thereby fail to dispose ourselves to love the neighbor and subsequently act on behalf of the neighbor to a much larger degree than we currently do, then we can be found morally blameworthy.

While morally demanding, this particular virtue ethic is not "perfectionist" in a strong sense. We are not morally blameworthy if we fail in the present to devote every feeling, thought, and action to the good cause of helping others.[11] Since we are human beings, and not robots, we have projects, desires, and relationships that are in our nature to pursue. Sometimes these aims stand in opposition to the objective of extreme altruism. While for a few, self-sacrifice constitutes nearly the whole of one's life, the majority of us are neither capable of, nor should want to desire, such a thoroughly other-regarding existence. Thus, according to the view for which I shall argue, we are not required to realize the *ideal* of virtuous living in order to escape moral censure. However, we are required always to be looking in that direction. That is, the ideal for us must remain our *telos*, toward which we continually have the ability—and therefore ought—to direct ourselves, however gradually.[12] Thus, the virtue ethic of which I am in favor may, after all, be described as weakly "perfectionist" in the sense that we are encouraged always to have our mind on improving our character.[13] Morally speaking, there is no "down time" or private space into which the virtuously minded agent may retreat. Our character development is a project that permeates every aspect of our life. Even seemingly trivial feelings, thoughts, and actions have ramifications for the agent seriously committed to living the best kind of life.[14] We should regard everything we do as potentially morally relevant. Because we are not now perfect, and are in all likelihood not going to become so, it makes sense that we come to see moral development as an ever-present task, one which entails our coming to cultivate a kind of "moral angst" about our present level of accomplishment. Such an attitude perhaps strikes the reader as unreasonably strenuous. Angst-ridden agents are never to be satisfied. The question arises as to whether or not angst is an appropriate attitude around which to construct a moral framework intended for widespread use in a society such as ours.

VIRTUE, ETHICS, AND RELIGION

It bears remarking that the version of virtue ethics that I have just described in broad strokes, in which the acquisition of virtue is closely connected to moral progress, is one that appears in similar versions among virtue ethicists working out of the sources of their own religious traditions. The last decade has witnessed several ethicists from the Christian tradition, for example, who have argued for the compatibility between Christian morality and virtue ethics.[15] What is more, such thinkers have read into the gospel precisely the kind of dynamic and strenuous moral imperative to become better that is consistent with a virtue ethic that prioritizes disposing oneself to adopt a demanding standard of other-regard. Thomas Ogletree, for example, interprets the Book of Matthew not as recommending a set of "laws and commandments" that function primarily as guiding principles, but rather as offering its audience instructions for how to *be* in every aspect of living, namely, as loving disciples of Jesus.[16] Joseph Kotva makes a similar point in his discussion of Paul's letters, in which he interprets the abundant references to "walking," "transforming," and "progressing" as indicative of a virtue-based imperative to become better, by which Paul means "more loving."[17] Kotva explains that Paul is explicit in his call for moral development, which is indicative of one's maturing faith:

> Paul's vision of the Christian life is not that of a static state of already achieved perfection. There is room for "progress" and an "increase" in faith (Phil 1:25; 2 Cor 10:15). Paul calls for an increase in love "with knowledge and full insight to help you determine what is best" (Phil 1:9–10; cf. 1 Thess 3:12; 4:9–10). The Corinthians, likewise, are chided for

not having become more mature (1 Cor 3:1–2; 2 Cor 6:13; cf. Heb 5:13–6:1) and are challenged to "strive" both for "spiritual gifts" (14:1) and "to excel" (14:14). In short, there is need for growth in the Christian life.[18]

Kotva also reads into the Book of Matthew what I have characterized as that "weaker" sort of perfectionism that summons us forward toward a more robust realization of the good. Echoing Ogletree, Kotva writes:

> There can be little doubt that Matthew also espouses a kind of perfec-
> tionist ethic. The rigorous teaching of the Sermon on the Mount is held
> up "as an ethic disciples are to live." Within the Sermon, Jesus demands
> a "righteousness" exceeding that of the scribes and Pharisees (5:20) and
> calls us to be "perfect" as God is perfect (5:48; cf. 19:21). Outside the Ser-
> mon, we are told that disciples must be willing to give up everything,
> including their families and their lives (10:35–39; 16:24–26). Similarly, the
> parables on watchfulness invoke the parousia to reject a sense of attain-
> ment or self-satisfaction: one must remain "awake" and seek to increase
> his or her "talents" (24:37–25:30).[19]

The sacrifices that Kotva understands Matthew to require of ordinary Christians are reminiscent of the exhortations of Dorothy Day. They pro-voke us in a similar manner. Is a religious life properly characterized as a life lived supererogatorily, as we customarily hold, or is it one in which we would be willing to "give up everything" as part of what is normatively expected of ordinary believers in everyday society? A virtue of Kotva's discussion of these passages from the New Testament is the subtle dis-tinction he makes between a life lived under conditions of the kingdom of heaven having fully arrived and one lived in hopes of that eventuality coming to pass. Since the Gospel is under no illusions about the prospects of the eternal permanently breaking into the present,[20] Kotva concludes that perfectionism is not required of us now; however, this does not give us sanction to stand idle and not strive for the ideal. As the important nineteenth-century Christian theologian Ernst Troeltsch notes, although we have no choice now but to "look through the glass darkly" (1 Corinthi-ans 13:12), we progress from darkness to light, a light which remains con-stantly worthy of our gaze.[21] Even if, according to Troeltsch, we never see the light clearly, we always stand to see it better.

Although Kotva's work is particularly useful because of the explicit con-nection he makes between Christian ethics and virtue theory, the crux of his "weak" perfectionism, namely, that we ought to commit ourselves in everything we do to improving our character, is by no means a novel idea in contemporary religious ethics. Kotva's sense of perfectionism is, for instance, clearly reflected in the thought of the early–twentieth-century Christian theologian R. N. Flew. Flew's *The Idea of Perfection in Christian Theology* is a comprehensive interpretation of Christian ethics as promulgated by Jesus, right on down through those whom Flew subsequently identifies as the most significant Christian thinkers over the last two thousand years.[22] Flew's goal in the work is to understand the strategy of the cross in such a fashion that does not "water down" its central normative message. Thus, while he stipulates that "perfectionism" is not synonymous with "sinlessness," a state that is impossible to achieve save by means of divine intervention for a few, especially graced individuals, he does insist that it nonetheless ought to be pursued within the relatively limited confines of human existence.[23] Foreshadowing Kotva's exegesis of Matthew's gospel and Paul's letters, Flew remarks:

> On the one hand, we must hold fast the truth that the ideal attainable in this life can never be the Christian's ultimate goal; on the other hand, the words 'perfect' or 'perfection' as applied to a certain degree of attainment in this world are enshrined in the Sermon on the Mount, in the Epistles of St. Paul, in the Epistle to the Hebrews, and have had a long and honourable history. . . .[24]

If the attainment of the ideal itself is impossible in this life, the pursuit of its attainment is not just possible, but required. Perfectionism in this sense comes to imply "as much as we possibly can." It is not an absolute perfection, which is possible for God alone, and in any case would circumvent the kind of human struggle that New Testament ethics is intended to promote. When Flew discusses St. Paul, and especially later when he discusses St. Thomas Aquinas, he develops the idea that love (*caritas*), which is the "bond of perfection," is the key to moral progress and, as Aquinas wrote, "binds the other virtues together in perfect unity."[25] To become virtuous, Flew suggests, is at once to become more loving of the neighbor, which, if one is a Christian, is done through means of letting God's love flow through oneself and redirecting it outward, into the world. Human fulfillment, the pursuit of excellence, and moral development are each the product of acquiring a loving disposition. Clearly, "virtue" has a substantially altruistic component in this account.

The notion that morality is more centrally about "becoming better" than it is about avoiding wrongdoing is similarly present in modern and contemporary Christian theology. Two Catholic thinkers worth mentioning briefly, Josef Fuchs and Klaus Demmer, have written about moral improvement out of sources in the Christian tradition. Fuchs's important essay "On the Theology of Human Progress" argues that human progress, including moral progress, is the primary moral duty of man,[26] while Demmer's volume *Shaping the Moral Life* grounds the "imperative" dimension of man's existence, what one *ought* to do, in the "indicative" dimension, what one *is*, namely, a creature of God with innate capacities, including moral capacities, that seek actualization.[27] Both thinkers stress that we have a duty to become virtuous by developing to the greatest degree we can those traits that we already possess in some measure, and exhibiting them in such a way that will benefit others most. Sensitive to the differences that exist among particular persons, Fuchs characterizes this duty as an ongoing process that each Christian is commanded to take up in a distinctive manner but that, in each case, aims ultimately at the betterment of society as a whole. Thus, he interprets the principle *praecepta affirmativa valent semper sed non pro semper* in the following manner:

> It expresses the precept that one must put into practice the values involved in these commands, but that this putting into practice has to be co-ordinated with the realization of other values, that is to say that the best combination of values must be discovered and put into effect.... [T]here is an absolute duty to put into practice *in the best possible manner* the values indicated in affirmative commands, that is to say with regard to other equally necessary values. This expresses the basic precept of human morality. In this world we have an absolute duty to make the best possible effort towards the realization of (relative) values. What this 'best possible' is, what the best possible realization of the man-world reality can be, today and tomorrow, this mankind has to find out for itself. But this search for the best possible concrete solution itself forms part of the absolute moral precept, to make the best that is possible out of the man-world reality. The principle, *praecepta affirmativa valent semper sed non pro semper*, is therefore to be understood dynamically, and means in the last analysis that man, in building the man-world reality, is bound constantly to build for the betterment of the world, that is, to progress.[28]

Fuchs's Weberian faith in the linear progress of human conduct and technology reflects the optimistic "modern" spirit of the mid-twentieth century, when his essay was written. This view of us as a morally progressing species has since come under attack by a wide variety of contemporary thinkers,[29] ranging from feminists, to postmodernists, even to some virtue ethicists themselves. Still, we might note on its own terms the intuition in this passage pertaining to what, at its base, morality is primarily about, namely, proactive self-realization, which is at once tantamount to human betterment. Morality, according to Fuchs, is not a private affair in which we maintain responsibility primarily for ourselves. Its trajectory is inherently outward. According to Fuchs, God puts us in a specific situation, our "man-world reality," not to remain static, but to make a positive impact on those who stand to benefit from our influence.

While addressing the same theme as Fuchs, namely, that morality requires one always to be becoming a person who will impact the world in a positive way, Klaus Demmer affirms the importance of "virtue ethics" as the appropriate model for purposes of explaining this underlying imperative. Demmer, a Catholic theologian, enlists a Thomistic understanding of virtue to make the point. Writes Demmer:

> One of Aquinas's definitions of virtue is *habitus operatives boni* (an operative habit to do the good); virtue consists in a willful disposition to do the good *prompte, faciliter, delectabiliter* (readily, easily, and delightfully). One of Aquinas's interpreters, German philosopher Josef Pieper, reframes the Thomistic definition of virtue as a way of "being on alert" (*Auf-dem-Spring-liegen*) in the realization of the good. Virtue provides action with the certainty of constant disposition so that particular decisions are already prepared, in a sense, by a kind of pre-decision.
>
> Another of Aquinas's important contributions to the definition of virtue is his notion of virtue as *ultimum potentiae* (the final potency). In the virtues, moral commitment reaches its peak; the attitude of the virtuous person is anything but lukewarm mediocrity. Virtues bring forth the best in a person, and to this end, all the moral strength available to her or him is required. The task associated with the virtues can be accomplished only with an entire life of dedication to the moral truth. The virtuous person knows that in the same way she or he responds to the fascination of the goods, she or he enables others, who may live a life of mediocrity, to follow the attraction of the good.[30]

Virtue ethics, according to this Thomistic reading, is conducive to producing a vigilant moral agent, one concerned both with his or her own moral preparation and development and with the improvement of the situation of others. An underlying duty of character to become more virtuous serves as a remedy for our tendency to be morally mediocre. This is an advantage that is noticeably not present in other contemporary normative models that give primacy to actions, abstract principles, and proscriptions. The morally righteous person, according to the latter, is required merely to stay within the right. In the former, Thomistic model, he or she is enjoined to produce good. The Thomistic model is more demanding, which is one reason, Demmer notes, that Aquinas frames his discussion *theologically*. Human beings have the capacity both to know the virtues and to know how to inculcate them when they stand in relation to God, from whom the four moral and intellectual "cardinal" virtues (prudence, justice, fortitude, and temperance) emanate, as well as through whom we gain access to the "theological" virtues of faith, hope, and love.[31] In standing in relation to God, and in standing in relation to virtuous exemplars who themselves stand in closer relation to God, we give ourselves the best chance of meeting the demands of the imperative to better ourselves and thereby of living a fruitful, authentic life.

Demmer's association of virtue with alertness, potency, excellence, and ultimately the love of others, is, like Fuchs's, indicative of a specific kind of virtue ethic, namely, one that is forward looking, highly morally demanding, and finally other-regarding. In this book, I shall argue for this kind of virtue ethic out of more secular sources, but not without keeping a watchful eye toward religious traditions, in particular Christianity and Judaism. It is my hope that contemporary ethicists working from within these religious traditions may come to see themselves as allies of those who defend a certain sort of secular view. Certainly, I have benefited from my engagement with them. Not only do I regard the insights of ethicists working from within religious traditions as valuable resources for my own view, but the heroes and saints whom I examine are also often themselves the products of their religious traditions. Because the views and values espoused by heroes and saints cannot be severed from the worldview that has informed them, that worldview must be considered relevant to the "heroic" and "saintly" understandings of the concepts of "duty," "supererogation," and "responsibility" upon which my own view comes to rely so heavily. In this way, religious ethics proves to be an indispensable resource for secular ethics. We cannot broadly discuss "heroic" or "saintly" actions—and we certainly cannot assume that they are by definition supererogatory—without investigating who heroes and saints are and what motivates them.

Thus, the duty to become a better person, for the existence of which I hope to argue afresh from within a secular context, is, theologically speaking, already alive and well. Ethicists working out of primarily secular sources have much to gain by consulting ethicists who are more theologically oriented. One example of how secular ethics can benefit from theological ethics involves our understanding of the fundamental normative concepts of duty and virtue. According to the Christian thinkers discussed above, the idea that we *ought* to improve our character does not entail a use of essentially incompatible terms. In secular ethics, by contrast, "duty" and "virtue" often comprise separate if not irreconcilable conceptual avenues for depicting the moral life. While the resurgence of virtue theory has made an enormous impact in contemporary normative ethics, it has yet to establish how terms like "duty" and "supererogation" might be interpreted according to the new model. One of the reasons for this is that some virtue ethicists themselves have seen fit to downplay the importance of such "deontic" terms altogether.[32] A problem with this solution, however, is that it fails to do justice to the crucial role the notions of obligation and moral requirement have played in the thinking of especially virtuous persons. Since heroes and saints, exemplary virtuous agents, speak clearly of their duty and of ours, it behooves us not to take the liberty of dismissing or even marginalizing the concept of a "duty" within the overall framework of a virtue ethic. As the Christian thinkers discussed above observe, an important advantage to not dispensing with deontic language entirely is that it enables us to describe the moral force behind the imperative to become virtuous—hence their acknowledgment of the profound connection between Christian ethics and the virtue-based maxim to improve our character. In connecting the concept of duty to the concept of virtue, I seek to forge a symbiosis between religious ethics and a certain kind of secular ethic.[33] If successful, I will have developed a new way of understanding "duty" and "supererogation" within a virtue-based ethics that on the one hand does not dispense with the importance of these terms for ethics generally, and on the other may give a more solid basis for religious thinkers to read into such a maxim—which they identify independently out of sources from within their respective traditions— a significant and pervasive presence that extends beyond their traditions into society as a whole.

ORGANIZATION, SOURCES, AND ARGUMENT

Where does the virtue-based imperative to become a better person come from? Furthermore, how can such a maxim be explained within the language of "duty" and "supererogation"? While I have said something about how these questions might be answered from a theological perspective, I have not yet outlined how I plan to discuss them from within a secular context, nor have I said much about the particular secular tradition that I intend to modify in the process.

The concept of supererogation and its relation to duty did not receive much attention in ethics until nearly half a century ago, when, in 1958, J. O. Urmson wrote his pioneering essay "Saints and Heroes."[34] It is with this essay that my discussion of duty and going above and beyond the call of duty begins. Urmson's essay is significant because it contains the still prevailing understanding of the concept of supererogation in contemporary moral theory as referring to actions considered morally praiseworthy but, due to their characteristic costliness, not obligatory. Urmson's essay was attractive to ethicists largely because of its appeal to common sense. Certain self-sacrificial acts of altruism were obviously morally good, and arguably morally laudable, but, due to their objectively demanding nature, could not be considered morally required, regardless of who was performing them.

No sooner had Urmson argued for the significance of the category of the supererogatory than did its descriptive utility and normative desirability become fiercely contested. In this book I defend Urmson's insights about the value of the concept of supererogation for moral theory while challenging his restrictive understanding of how the concept functions within it. I contest both Urmson's assumption that what is deemed supererogatory is the same for all agents and the derivative idea that a specific act of supererogation retains its supererogatory status throughout the course of a particular agent's life. I do this by making reference to virtue ethics, where I suggest that not to revise over time what one considers required on the one hand, and above and beyond on the other, is to live poorly. My thesis is that our sense of duty ought to expand over time, that we should strive to dispose ourselves to go above and beyond duty when possible, and that the scope of what we consider to be supererogatory correspondingly ought to diminish as we acquire an expanded sense of duty and cultivate the disposition to go above and beyond. The burden of my thesis will be to show how it might be possible to interpret a sense in which we "ought" to go beyond the call of duty, without collapsing that "ought" back into duty and thereby dispensing with the category of supererogation altogether. In this sense, my treatment of Urmson and those who followed him is intended more as an expansion of their work than as a criticism of it.

Can the notion of supererogation sustain its conceptual distinction from the notion of duty while still accommodating the insight that the fully moral life entails doing more than what is considered strictly morally required at any particular moment in time? To answer this question in the affirmative, it is essential to show that morality is a process of *becoming* a certain sort of person, and not simply an exact method for determining the moral status of specific acts at snapshots in time. The defender of the revised notion of supererogation needs to show that morality is about the sort of person someone is and not merely about what he or she does. The claim that more moral significance should be attributed to character than to the actions we perform is becoming increasingly familiar in theological and secular circles of thought. It is one uniformly made by virtue ethicists with disparate orientations and divergent methodological and ideological commitments. It is also one that Urmson and his followers, whose deontic view of morality is notably act-based, do not embrace.

What are the advantages to characterizing terms like "duty" and "super-erogation" within a moral framework that prioritizes character? Any defender of a paradigm shift must explain why the new model is better than the old. While in the last two decades plenty of virtue ethicists have undertaken the task of replacing deontic vocabulary with the language of character, I have encountered no comprehensive argument that attempts to understand the terms "duty" and "supererogation" within the context of a virtue ethic. Proceeding from Urmson's essay, expanding and in some cases revising his own innovative use of the concept of supererogation, I hope by the end of this book to have provided such an account. It makes sense, then, to begin with Urmson himself, since he is the one who first brought the concept of supererogation to prominence in contemporary moral theory.

In part I, chapters 1 and 2, I assess the dominant view of supereroga-tion, introduced by Urmson and developed by his philosophical succes-sors, primarily David Heyd. I focus especially on the portrayal of heroes and saints presented in this view. My primary goal in chapter 1 is not to criticize Urmson and Heyd, but rather to elucidate their historical impor-tance for modern moral philosophy. The now commonsensical notion that we ought to regard heroes and saints as more altruistic than the kind of people we reasonably can hope to become was an Urmsonian innova-tion. The almost universally accepted idea that actions deemed above and beyond are morally optional and, as such, do not beckon censure if not performed was first laid out in a formal theory of "unqualified super-erogation" by David Heyd. In chapter 1, I explain where these intuitive notions, so important to how we tend to think about moral obligation in secular society today, come from. In my treatment of Urmson's essay, I introduce and explain the vocabulary of "heroes" and "saints" in order to formulate a working understanding of the identity of the supererogatory agent. This will later be revised and expanded. Subsequently, I connect Urmson's essay to the dominant view of supererogation that would soon emerge in modern moral philosophy, which held that the omission of supererogatory acts could not, under any circumstances, be considered wrong or warrant sanction of any kind.[35] In chapter 1, then, my task is chiefly interpretive. I attempt to present Urmson and Heyd's views in terms of which they themselves would approve.

While acknowledging with Urmson and Heyd that there exists a pub-licly recognizable moral minimum that constitutes what we are all required to do, as well as agreeing with them that there is such a thing as supererogation, in chapter 2 I question whether the moral minimum ought to be equated with "duty," as if duty were some fixed referent. In my analysis I raise several questions, both about Urmson's characterization of heroes and saints and about Heyd's argument for adopting a theory of "unqualified supererogation." Has Urmson correctly described the nature of the hero or saint's "ought"? Is his interpretation of heroic and saintly testimony in conformity with what heroes and saints say about themselves? Is Heyd correct in asserting the existence of objective, universal criteria for determining the boundary that separates duty from supererogation? What is the relationship between duty and virtue assumed in Urmson and Heyd's view? How do they justify the stark contrast that they draw between the two? Finally, are heroes and saints properly to be construed as the extraordinary "other," as Urmson and Heyd characterize them, or do heroes and saints have more in common with ordinary persons than we initially might be led to believe? I raise some of these issues through reference to historical and theological sources. Part of the problem with Urmson and Heyd's characterization of supererogation is that it does not provide a concrete understanding of the practices and self-understanding of heroes and saints themselves. I attempt to remedy this neglect in part by challenging the exclusively philosophical orientation with which Urmson and Heyd examine the issue. The criticisms I raise in chapter 2 prepare me to speculate about other possible ways of understanding heroes and saints and subsequently lead me to consider a more "qualified" way of thinking about the concept of supererogation.

In chapters 3 and 4, which comprise part II, I utilize the testimony of actual heroes and saints as possible points of contrast to the picture of the supererogatory agent posited by Urmson and Heyd. In chapter 3, I begin my examination by looking at four "heroes" from literature in order to glean from them certain heroic traits that do not seem to be present in the Urmsonian characterization. These exploratory observations prepare the discussion of my primary case study in the chapter. Drawing on the empirical work and in some cases the normative insights of social scientists and historians, I consider examples of real-life altruists. I put special emphasis on Holocaust rescuers, otherwise known as "righteous gentiles," whom I construe as moral heroes, and I ask whether it is appropriate to characterize them as supererogatory agents in light of their own accounts of their behavior. In this chapter, I closely examine the claim that is consistently made by rescuers that their actions ought not to be regarded as special or as deserving of any moral praise. This assessment of the heroes' self-descriptions positions me to explore the senses in which heroes might be said to be both exceptional *and* ordinary. I suggest that what is distinctive about heroes is not so much an innate capacity to be altruistic, but their expanded sense of duty, which may be a function of their individual character development and the influence of the communities in which they live. Against the Urmsonian characterization, I argue that heroes are moral exemplars, worthy not only of our admiration but also of our emulation.

In chapter 4, the data for testing Urmson and Heyd's account of the supererogatory agent changes. It is no longer comprised of the sociological analyses of actual historical figures, but depends on my own treatment of two important political figures in twentieth-century American society: Martin Luther King, Jr., and Dorothy Day. The analysis of these two figures leads to my construction of the contemporary moral category of "saints," which is akin to that introduced by Edith Wyschogrod in her influential work *Saints and Postmodernism.* Wyschogrod refers to a number of postmodern thinkers who converge in their estimation of what the authentic moral life centrally entails, namely, a saintly "ethics of excess." In chapter 4, I ask whether, contrary to what Urmson and Heyd would say, the "ethics of excess" can legitimately be considered required from saints' own perspectives and then ask about the extent to which it can be regarded as a useful (even if not fully realizable) ideal for "ordinary" morality. Informed by Wyschogrod, I characterize saints as persons who are maximally disposed to go beyond even the hero's expanded sense of duty, sacrificing themselves for the sake of others to the very limit of what they can possibly manage.

In part III, chapters 5 and 6, I make my constructive argument, in which I propose a revised understanding of the category of supererogation that plausibly accommodates my findings in part II. In chapter 5, I challenge the exclusively duty-based, or deontic, view of agency that characterizes Urmson and Heyd's approach to ethics, I and modify that view in light of some considerations that emerge from the ethics of virtue. Here I try to defend the claim that supererogation is a useful notion because, in explicitly pointing to altruistic actions that are for the time being "beyond" us, it awakens us to shortcomings in our character, shortcomings that are not revealed as we conform our actions to required minimal norms of conduct. Working from certain passages in Aristotle's *Nicomachean Ethics,* relying in particular on an interpretation of these passages rendered in one strand of neo-Aristotelian thought, I explore the idea that good human living entails both the recognition and the fulfillment of a duty to improve our character over the course of our lives, a duty which in turn prompts us to add to the initial set of universal obligations that are specified by minimal moral requirement. This leads to a detailed discussion of *how* it is possible for us to improve our character throughout our lives, and specifically how it is possible for a beginner to become a more advanced moral agent. Finally, I distinguish my view from more demanding normative approaches in ethics such as strong perfectionism and consequentialism before defending it against criticisms likely to be raised by traditional supererogationists, who endorse the dominant understanding of the concept of supererogation, and antisupererogationists, who object to its use altogether. It is in chapter 5, then, that my argument, which I will call "the thesis of moral development," is formally stated and defended.

In chapter 6, I briefly examine the significance of the idea that there is moral value in ordinary persons' feeling compelled to do that which is defined as being more than required, locating this value within Jewish and Christian sources. I engage in a close textual analysis of some of the ethical writings of Abraham Heschel and Paul Tillich in order to show that the meta-duty of character improvement is not a novel or radical idea in ethics, but one that is already suggested in Jewish and Christian thought, which becomes apparent upon examining what these two thinkers have to say about the nature and purpose of human existence. In these closing pages, then, I aim to move from the possible to the actual. I suggest that the "revised" understanding of the relationship between duty and supererogation first hypothesized in chapter 2, developed through my analyses of heroes and saints in chapters 3 and 4, and finally defended in chapter 5, is one that is already present in at least two contemporary religious traditions, albeit often described rather differently. My concluding hope is that this discovery will add to the important and ongoing exchange under way between thinkers working in secular ethics and ethicists working in Western religious traditions, and that it will promote further dialogue between these two groups.

OTHER-REGARD AND THE STRANGER

I make two major suppositions throughout this book that could easily be, and indeed have been, contested by other ethicists. The first is that morality is primarily about other-regard, and that one of the most important questions facing normative ethicists is, correspondingly, that of just how other-regarding any moral framework ought to be. I assume that a moral emotion, attitude, or action is one that will, constitutively, have an effect on the welfare of others.[36] A morally *good* action, by extension, is one that will have a *positive* effect on the welfare of others. It is this assumption that tells us that sacrificing our own interests in order to help others is a good thing, likely even to be morally praiseworthy, and certainly an activity in which we would want "moral" persons to engage. By contrast, *self-regard* is important only in a secondary sense. Self-regarding actions can be morally good and can even coincide with other-regarding actions. However, self-regard, in the first instance, can never take normative priority over other-regard, or so I assume.

Each of my principal opponents whose arguments I attempt to assess, challenge, and revise in this book make the major assumption just mentioned. Thus, both the thoroughgoing supererogationists (e.g., Urmson and Heyd) *and* antisupererogationists (e.g., Shelly Kagan) with whom I debate take for granted the *moral value* of altruistic actions, as I do; in fact, we maintain that altruism comprises the most valuable kind of moral actions. What we are all interested in discussing is the *moral status* such actions carry, that is, whether and in what sense they can be said to be *required*. There are, of course, several feminists, Aristotelians, and other moral theorists who would strongly disagree with this "alter-centric" way of characterizing morality. Throughout this book, I will occasionally stop to acknowledge where those who might not accept some of my alter-centric claims might be likely to raise objections. However, while I will give them some consideration, I do not mount any formal defense of my other-regarding approach to understanding morality. The question of whether self-regard ought to be given primacy over other-regard, and the related question of the extent to which this move is justified on *moral* grounds, are ones that are outside the scope of this book.

The second major assumption I make is this: while I readily recognize that morality pertains *both* to special relations and to the impersonal other, I assume that when there is a conflict between the two, the latter takes precedence, all other things being equal. This means that unless otherwise stated, I assume that moral claims made on the self by others are claims that typically emanate from the impersonal other, or stranger. Like the first assumption, this is one with which my primary opponents will tend to agree, and one that the feminists and Aristotelians with whom I am not primarily debating are likely to contest. My view is that the nature of the relationship between universal altruism and particular attachments is such that the latter is morally derived from the former.[37] Without introducing extenuating reasons that might be considered in particular cases, I maintain that special relations should never *override* universal altruism when the benefits to each recipient are equal or weigh in favor of the impersonal other. One particularly noteworthy place where this issue arises is in my treatment of Holocaust rescuers. I am concerned primarily with the question of how to characterize their actions: were they morally required or supererogatory? Some, however, would question the common intuition that Holocaust rescuers did something that is morally good in the first place, for they would point out that rescuers placed not only themselves, but also their families, at great risk, and thereby neglected important role duties to their loved ones. In my view, this objection is misguided, for it fundamentally misunderstands the hierarchical ordering of the various kinds of duties to the other required by other-regard. I discuss the objection raised by the proponent of special relations as part of my overall treatment of the righteous gentile phenomenon, and briefly offer some reasons for why I assume what I do. However, I leave the task of rigorously defending my view of special relations to another study, as the constraints of time and space prevent me from sufficiently attending to it here. In any case, I think that the major arguments that I make in support of my thesis, including my argument for adopting the revised understanding of the concept of supererogation, are ones that those concerned with giving primacy to special relations could find acceptable, even though we would disagree about who might be considered the primary objects of other-regard.

It bears mentioning that these two assumptions are generally ones that do not need to be disclosed as disclaimers by the majority of thinkers working in religious ethics. In the case of Christianity, for example, I think it is fair to suggest that any plausible interpretation of the Second Love Commandment yields a positive evaluation of altruism, and most regard aid and assistance to the stranger as the epitome of loving action.[38] Indeed, we would find wanting any characterization of the commandment to love the neighbor that did not advocate deference to the other on the part of the self. What Christian ethicists *do* debate, and continue to do so energetically, is the nature of this deference. Few, for example, read into the Second Love Commandment the mandate to sacrifice oneself so completely as does Anders Nygren.[39] Having said this, I am aware of no Christian ethicist who outright fails to associate the duty to love the neighbor with costs borne by the self for the sake of the other. Upon considering the variety of ways of interpreting the Second Love Commandment, the Christian ethicist is forced to assess just how much the commandment requires of oneself. Perhaps we can safely say that the duty toward the neighbor requires enough to see to the fulfillment of the commandment, but not so much that the fulfiller loses a sense of self entirely, so much so that he or she would be precluded from further developing his or her spiritual and moral capacities. There is thus an inherent justification for acting on behalf of ourselves in those instances when the work of love strikes us as particularly demanding. Still, when we *do* err on the side of ourselves in the face of such a dilemma, then, from the point of view of Christian ethics, there is always a burden to shoulder. This burden takes the form of the anxious feeling that we have not done as much as we could for the other in need, even when we have done as much as we think we can on any particular occasion. As Kotva, Fuchs, and Demmer each suggest, the *ethical* Christian never has the luxury of being morally complacent. Heroes and saints, who push themselves as much as is humanly possible, warrant our serious consideration from a theological point of view because of their excellent track record with respect to overcoming complacency.

While in a sense dominant religious symbols such as the cross do not belong to the secular world, and indeed gain their influential power precisely because of the alternative they are meant to provide, it is a disadvantage of secular ethics that it affords the agent much more leeway with respect to interpreting the relative importance of other-regard and its representative object, the stranger. The free and autonomous agent whose rights we are committed to protecting in our society is presumed to be under no urgent moral duress to respond to the needs of those who need his or her help. As a result, I would suggest that such an agent is susceptible to facing the predicament shared by Camus's Parisian lawyer in *The Fall*, Jean Baptiste, who tries to avoid personal judgment by using society's conventional standards for distinguishing right from wrong and by avoiding any situation demanding moral action on his part.[40] When Jean Baptiste passes by a drowning woman who calls out for help, his failure to act precludes him from winning his self-esteem and ultimately elicits his self-condemnation.

Most of us are not even as honest as Camus's character. We tend to stand by when the needy suffer and then look to excuse our idleness by making reference to the weak standards of society as a whole. We address situations that would otherwise require a morally demanding response on our part by appealing to the moral complacency of others. As a result, all too often, we do not blame ourselves when we *should* blame ourselves. In the United States, we earn the moral praise of others if we sign up as organ donors when we get our driver's licenses; if we spontaneously give to charities; even if we donate blood during a local blood drive. Rarely do we consider these things to be morally required. We tend to assume that the individual and civil liberties to which we are entitled preclude us from being compelled to act altruistically. By contrast, the idea that we should be altruistic, and that we should feel a sense of contrition when we are not, is one that is seldom questioned by ethicists whose views are informed by their religious convictions. In this book, I ask whether it is possible to lay the grounds within a parallel secular framework for claiming that we ought to be more compassionate than our society currently requires us to be.[41] It is now generally agreed that utilitarians and Kantians who attempted to answer this question in the affirmative during the latter half of the twentieth century fell short of achieving their goal because their approach was not psychologically realistic enough; it was not sufficiently attuned to the limits posed by human nature. The turn to the ethics of virtue provides a promising remedy to this shortcoming while remaining faithful to the fundamental ambition—overcoming moral complacency—that motivated their projects in the first place.

NOTES

1. Dorothy Day, *By Little and by Little: Selected Writings of Dorothy Day*, ed. Robert Ellsberg (New York: Orbis Books, 1992), 109–11 (emphasis mine).

2. My use of this phrase is somewhat technical. Like many other contemporary ethicists, my thinking has been heavily influenced by the contrast that Emmanuel Levinas draws between being-for-oneself and "being otherwise." See Levinas, *Otherwise Than Being or Beyond Essence*, trans. Alphonso Lingus (The Hague: Martinus Nijhoff, 1974).

3. Day, *Selected Writings*, 110.

4. Day adopted this phrase from Mao Tse-tung. See ibid., 240, 343.

5. The consequentialist Shelly Kagan, in particular, characterizes "commonsense" morality in this manner. See Kagan, *The Limits of Morality* (Oxford: Oxford University Press, 1989), 35.

6. Edith Wyschogrod, *Saints and Postmodernism* (Chicago: University of Chicago Press, 1990), 150.

7. John E. Hare, *The Moral Gap: Kantian Ethics, Human Limits, and God's Assistance* (Oxford: Clarendon Press, 1996).

8. I make no distinction between the terms "obligation" and "duty," although I am aware that they have been distinguished from one another by other ethicists. According to a common contrast, an *obligation* is morally required of an agent fulfilling a specific role, while *duty* is morally required of all generic agents. In using the two terms interchangeably, I do not mean to ignore this contrast; in fact, I acknowledge the difference between role duties and duty as such at points throughout the book.

9. This way of describing what it means to live virtuously, prominent among neo-Aristotelians, can be found in the *Nicomachean Ethics*. See Aristotle, *Nicomachean Ethics*, trans. Terence Irwin (Indianapolis: Hackett Publishing Company, 1985), 1107a1–2.

10. For three excellent articles describing the varieties of virtue ethics and ongoing debates internal to the virtue ethics camp, see Justin Oakley, "Varieties of Virtue Ethics," *Ratio* 9 (1996): 128–52; Lee Yearly, "Recent Work on Virtue," *Religious Studies Review* 16, no. 4 (1990): 1–8; and William Spohn, "The Recovery of Virtue Ethics," *Theological Studies* 53, no. 1 (1992): 60–75.

11. Joseph Kotva calls this strong sense of perfectionism "brittle perfectionism." Joseph Kotva, Jr., *The Christian Case for Virtue Ethics* (Washington, D.C.: Georgetown University Press, 1996), 38.

12. Ibid.

13. Christian virtue ethicists, such as Kotva, might put the point a bit differently by asserting, for example, that we are always required to be putting ourselves in a position to grow in grace. The idea is the same. Regardless of our current

level of moral or spiritual achievement, we cannot rest content and must try continually to become better.

14. Ibid., 37.

15. Three good examples are: L. Gregory Jones, *Transformed Judgment: Toward
a Trinitarian Account of the Moral Life* (Notre Dame: University of Notre Dame
Press, 1990); James F. Keenan, *Goodness and Rightness in Thomas Aquinas's Summa
Theologiae* (Washington, D.C.: Georgetown University Press, 1992); and Joseph
Kotva's *The Christian Case for Virtue Ethics,* discussed above.

16. Thomas W. Ogletree, *The Use of the Bible in Christian Ethics* (Philadelphia:
Fortress Press, 1983), 90, quoted in Kotva, *The Christian Case for Virtue Ethics,* 117.

17. Kotva, *The Christian Case for Virtue Ethics,* 124.

18. Ibid., 125.

19. Ibid., 106. The "parousia" pertains to the moment of ultimate revelation in
the eschaton (the moment of the second coming).

20. Ibid., 107.

21. Ernst Troeltsch, *The Christian Faith* (Minneapolis: Fortress Press, 1991), 38.

22. R. N. Flew, *The Idea of Perfection in Christian Theology: An Historical Study
of the Ideal for the Present Life* (New York: Humanities Press, 1968).

23. Ibid., xii–xiii.

24. Ibid., xiii.

25. Ibid., 71ff., 214ff., respectively.

26. Josef Fuchs, "On the Theology of Human Progress," *Human Values and
Christian Morality* (Dublin: Gill and MacMillan Ltd., 1970), 178–203.

27. Klaus Demmer, *Shaping the Moral Life: An Approach to Moral Theology,* ed.
James Keenan, trans. Roberto Dell'Oro (Washington, D.C.: Georgetown University Press, 2000), 4ff.

28. Fuchs, "On the Theology of Human Progress," 196. The principle that Fuchs
interprets in this passage can be translated as "Positive duties are always valid, but
not on every occasion."

29. The most comprehensive critique of this view of which I am aware is
Jonathan Glover's wonderful *Humanity: A Moral History of the Twentieth Century*
(New Haven: Yale University Press, 1999). In this volume, Glover chronicles the
brutal record of atrocities witnessed in our most recent century and then attempts
to explain how human beings could have so acted toward other human beings.
While Glover's highly empirical and psychological approach to ethics stands in
contrast to the Weberian view of human progress, he is in the end cautiously optimistic that the development of moral imagination might furnish us with the
resources to combat the urge to cruelty to which human beings are otherwise naturally drawn.

30. Demmer, *Shaping the Moral Life,* 53.

31. Ibid.

32. This approach to virtue ethics, which has been called "eliminatism" by
some, seeks to get rid of principle-based ethics altogether, and as a result to abandon the use of terms like "rights" and "duties." Versions of it have been advanced
even by thinkers as prominent as Elizabeth Anscombe and Alasdair MacIntyre.

See G. E. M. Anscombe, "Modern Moral Philosophy," *Philosophy* 33 (1958): 1–19; and MacIntyre, *After Virtue*, 2d ed. (South Bend: University of Notre Dame Press, 1982): 51–78. Gregory Pence discusses eliminatism and its association with Anscombe and MacIntyre in "Virtue Theory," in *A Companion to Ethics*, ed. Peter Singer (Oxford: Basil Blackwell, 1993), 253–55.

33. The terms "religious ethics" and "secular ethics" have become controversial as of late, particularly because of the increasing tendency for scholars working out of religious traditions to adopt broad definitions of religion. For more on this controversy, see John P. Reeder, Jr., "What Is a Religious Ethic?" *Journal of Religious Ethics* 25, n. 3 (1998): 157–81.

34. J. O. Urmson, "Saints and Heroes," *Essays in Moral Philosophy*, ed. A. I. Melden (Seattle: University of Washington Press), 198–216.

35. David Heyd, *Supererogation* (Cambridge: Cambridge University Press, 1982), 125–26.

36. For a formal articulation of this assumption, see David Little and Sumner B. Twiss, *Comparative Religious Ethics: A New Method* (San Francisco: Harper and Row, 1978), 41.

37. William Werpehowski considers the question of whether we are justified in making this assumption in Christian ethics in "'Agape' and Special Relations," in *The Love Commandments: Essays in Christian Ethics and Moral Philosophy*, ed. Edmund Santurri and William Werpehowski (Washington, D.C.: Georgetown University Press, 1992), 138–56.

38. Stephen Pope is one Christian ethicist who would object to the notion that the stranger represents the paradigmatic "other" to whom the Second Love Commandment directs us to attend. See Pope, *The Evolution of Altruism and the Ordering of Love* (Washington, D.C.: Georgetown University Press, 1994). In this volume Pope looks at recent developments in science and evolutionary theory in order to argue for a reinterpretation of neighbor-love in the Catholic tradition that gives more primacy to kin preference than is given in previous accounts.

39. See Anders Nygren, *Agape and Eros*, trans. Philip S. Watson (Philadelphia: The Westminster Press, 1953).

40. Albert Camus, *The Fall*, trans. Justin O'Brien (New York: Vintage Press, 1991).

41. In his book *The Moral Gap*, John Hare argues that without God's assistance there is no viable means by which we may attempt to close the chasm that spans our natural capacities and the moral demand on us that exceeds them. Hare considers, and rejects, three main strategies that have been advanced in secular ethics in the modern era: (1) the utilitarian's approach of exaggerating our natural capacities; (2) the feminist's and pragmatist's approach of diminishing (through reinterpretation) the moral demand; and (3) the naturalist's attempt to find some substitute for God's assistance. Hare's conclusion is Augustinian: God instructs us beyond our means so that we may know what to seek from him (Hare, *The Moral Gap*, 113). While the pitch Hare makes for God's grace is compelling, and plausible for Christians, in my view he does not sufficiently consider in his analysis of secular strategies an approach that makes virtue theory a focus.

PART I

Heroes, Saints, and Supererogation within the Context of a Duty-Based Morality

The Right of Nature, which writers commonly call *jus naturale*, is the liberty each man hath to use his own power, as he will himself, for the preservation of his own nature, that is to say, of his own life, and consequently of doing anything which, in his own judgment and reason, he shall conceive to be the aptest means thereunto.

—Thomas Hobbes, *Leviathan*

CHAPTER 1

Supererogation, Optional Morality, and the Importance of J. O. Urmson and David Heyd in the History of Ethics

THE ADVENT OF THE CONCEPT OF SUPEREROGATION IN CONTEMPORARY ETHICS

Only the strictest consequentialists contend that moral action exhausts the whole of human action. The rest of us maintain that among the infinite number of things we can do, the majority of these are a matter of personal preference, occurring within a sphere of permissibility. It is by virtue of the existence of permissible acts that morality is not seen to intrude too severely into our own lives. If we are to live as human beings who pursue a variety of goals and projects, rather than as automatons who function within a larger colony, then, we tend to assume tacitly, there must be limits to what we are obligated to do. Moral duty—as a system of rules for governing our interactions with one another—is generally conceived as a necessary though not exhaustive facet of the human condition. It is indispensable as a way of adequately preserving the opportunity for us to choose the kind of life we want to lead, while it alone cannot embody that choice.

Far less acknowledged than this commonplace, secular "liberal" intuition is its source. The category of "permissible" actions, the existence of which has been recognized as long as there has been the concept of duty itself, was not a *focus* for moral theorists until the appearance of J. O. Urmson's "Saints and Heroes" in 1958.[1] It was Urmson who first beckoned the majority of Kantians and utilitarians, prominent among philosophers working in ethics in the mid-twentieth century, to reconsider their then widely held belief that the performance of moral actions could never be considered optional. Urmson adduced saintly and heroic deeds as examples of actions that were morally praiseworthy but which, due to their characteristic costliness, could not be regarded as morally required. In his essay Urmson sought to modify, though not overturn, traditional secular conceptions of duty and moral agency. Like those Kantians and utilitarians against whom he was reacting, he saw human beings as having certain common features that placed them in a uniform moral community, which, in turn, made them subject to the same basic rules for governing their interactions with one another. However, Urmson sought to construct a moral code according to what lay within the capacity of ordinary persons. He thus argued for retaining universal principles of duty, while recognizing a "cut-off" point beyond which certain altruistic deeds would not be regarded as morally compulsory due to their "saintly" or "heroic" nature.

In emphasizing the futility of demanding the performance of costly altruistic conduct beyond what could reasonably be expected of most people, Urmson related human psychology to ethics in a way that Kantians and utilitarians previously had not done. It was Urmson who first stressed that motivations, human ability, and human limitation ought to be relevant to determining the status of moral acts. And it was Urmson who declared, two decades before critics of the Enlightenment project launched their assault on "modern ethics," that any moral theory which failed to take into account "man as he is and as he can be expected to become" was an empty abstraction, perhaps suitable for "perfectly rational persons" or "incorporeal angels," but not for human beings.[2] The extent to which Urmson's own misgivings with Enlightenment and neo-Enlightenment thinking served as a precursor to the paradigm shift that was about to take place in moral philosophy can be established by examining his essay alongside the work of those who, unlike him, called for a full-out revolution in modern ethics.

Alasdair MacIntyre and Charles Taylor serve as perhaps the two best representatives of the vast school of philosophers and moral theorists who, starting in the early 1980s, began to challenge the Kantian and utilitarian modes of thinking that had up to that time dominated the scene in modern moral philosophy. In *After Virtue*, MacIntyre insisted on the failure of a modern ethics based on principles and duty to take into account the "intentions and purposes of man," while Charles Taylor, in *Sources of the Self*, emphasized the anomie that plagues the modern self bereft of life-shaping, self-acknowledged goals.[3] In their view, both kinds of afflictions were the direct result of a post-Enlightenment tendency to define moral identity according to uniform abstract criteria rather than through reference to the things that have the most significance for us. Both MacIntyre and Taylor alerted their readers to a society in crisis, one lacking a sense of itself and a consciousness of its historical context. In response to this crisis, they argued for a return to tradition and societal mores as a means of grounding practical moral reasoning. According to this model, the substance of a moral "ought" would be determined exclusively in reference to a socially established set of rules. Gone would be any legitimate appeals to all-encompassing principles of moral reason or supposed universally justified, "indubitable" or "inalienable" rights, even at the "thinnest," most basic level of consideration.[4]

In their appeals to values, coherence, and self-awareness, MacIntyre and Taylor rightly call our attention to what is wrong with thinking about moral agents as if they are anchorless deliberators, able, through reason, to strip themselves of any former allegiance they might have had to particular ethical traditions from the past. The problem, in short, is that human beings simply do not work in this way. Even if it *could* be shown that in the moral decision-making process abstract universal principles of reason ought to trump appeals to particular practices and customs, there would still be the fundamental problem of human motivation. The defender of the deliberative model retains the burden of demonstrating *why* one would choose to follow reason when it comes into conflict with mores and customs. The critic maintains that notions of moral duty and obligation are at best acknowledged rational maxims that lack any kind of appeal to human emotion or desire, and are at worst unintelligible commands that appear to emanate from a totally foreign source. As such, according to the critic, the moral "ought" in an Enlightenment framework remains unpersuasive to the majority for whom it is intended. Human beings make important decisions, moral or otherwise, in the context of an overarching narrative that renders their life sensible to them. Only through reference to concrete norms of conduct can people come to lead a morally authentic and personally fulfilling life.

Both *After Virtue* and *Sources of the Self* stress the importance of locating moral ambition and human fulfillment within the context of defined communal values and ends. Consequently, in both volumes morality is conceived as a project of becoming what one ought to be in light of who one, at some deep, fundamental level, already is. To use Taylor's language, moral philosophy ought to begin through means of honest consultation of the *sources* of the moral agent, which will vary depending on the particular self in question. Criteria for rational moral theorizing, contends MacIntyre, are historical and "come into existence at particular periods under particular social circumstances," which also means that "they are in no way universal features of the human condition."[5] In suggesting as much, MacIntyre and Taylor seek to overturn the very basis of theorizing in modern moral philosophy, namely, an underlying dependence on those principles thought to guarantee *uniformity* in ethics, principles through reference to which all agents reliably know those actions that are proscribed and those that are required.

Like MacIntyre, Taylor, and a host of others that would soon follow, Urmson was himself already alarmed over two decades earlier by the gap he perceived in ethical theory between human nature and human ideals. However, unlike the neo-Aristotelian critics of the Enlightenment tradition that came after him, Urmson's response was to attempt to remedy the problem without betraying the established mode of theorizing: he would introduce a new criterion for what should qualify as a rule or principle, although rules and principles in general would continue to remain the central concepts from which right action was determined. As a result, the idea of a "duty" remained the pivotal concept in moral theory, although universalizability no longer stood alone as its centrally important feature. To refer to a duty meant also to refer to something that one manageably could *fulfill*. In relating duty to human nature in this fashion, Urmson offered a way of incorporating psychology into ethics without abandoning altogether the priority of the concept of moral obligation. In this sense, Urmson can be considered a reformer of the neo-Enlightenment tradition. His modification to the traditional tripartite classification of actions into morally required, neutral, and prohibited actions—his introduction of the category of supererogation—provided a nonrevolutionary solution to those dissatisfied with modern moral philosophy for its failure to acknowledge sufficiently the limitations posed by human psychology. Like MacIntyre and Taylor, Urmson's approach to ethics was concrete and pragmatic. "Saints and Heroes" offered a way of rescuing modern moral philosophy from charges of abstraction and moral idealism typical of more traditional Kantian and utilitarian modes of moral theorizing. Consequently, just as the critics of the Enlightenment project began to gain wide influence among religious and secular ethicists, so, too, did Urmson's revision to Kantianism and utilitarianism start to be taken seriously by many others committed to defending the traditional, neo-Enlightenment view.[6]

Urmson's reforms to the neo-Enlightenment tradition are today reflected in one of the most basic intuitions of most people in our society. This is the commonsense intuition that moral *accountability* corresponds to strict moral *requirement*. According to the commonsense morality, as long as we satisfy what we are morally bound to uphold, we cannot be judged to be in the wrong. Moral blameworthiness, we assume, results from falling below the manageable threshold of minimal duty. It does not result from failing to go beyond this threshold. At this point, it might be helpful to pause briefly to explain what one means when one refers to the model of "commonsense" morality, if for no other reason than this model represents the primary basis upon which we construct the rules, laws, and mores that form the normative glue of contemporary society.

Commonsense Morality and the "Standard View"

Ever since "Saints and Heroes" was first published in 1958, it has become fashionable to speak of an "ordinary" or "commonsense" morality, which, as its name suggests, conforms to intuitions that the majority is thought to have about how much morality can demand in terms of cost to the self.[7] Commonsense morality acknowledges the imperative to be other-regarding, or at least to demonstrate equal-regard,[8] but it does not view that imperative as overly demanding. It thus stands between, for example, ethical egoism, which fails to recognize *any* decisive reasons for performing other-regarding acts unless there is a self-regarding payoff, and strict consequentialism, which places no limits on how much we might be asked to contribute to the overall good. Commonsense morality identifies a number of minimally costly positive and negative duties whose performance is mandatory, as well as a category of actions that lie beyond, or are accomplished in addition to, those duties. That is, it is a view that recognizes *universal* norms of conduct and *supererogatory* deeds that transcend these norms.[9]

Today, in spite of the intuitive appeal of commonsense morality, in particular its recognition of moral options, the status of supererogatory acts remains heavily contested. Many continue to reject the existence, even the very possibility, of moral acts that go above and beyond duty. These "anti-supererogationists," as they have come to be known, believe that it is impossible to exceed moral duty, holding that any action for which we would receive moral praise is also one that we are required to perform.[10] Anti-supererogationists worry that by acknowledging the optionality of some morally good acts we will become complacent and accustomed to doing too little for others. Thus, such thinkers consider Urmson's modification of the traditional view to be an unacceptably lenient treatment of positive duty.[11]

At the other end of the spectrum lie those thinkers who, following Urmson, admit supererogation into the sphere of possible moral acts. Some of these thinkers, including certain feminists, appropriate the category of supererogation as a way of advancing their conviction that positive duty is not always what should be considered overriding in an agent's conduct. These thinkers favor a strong sense of self-regard and question whether the disposition to behave altruistically is as worthy as has generally been supposed.[12] They embrace Urmson's innovation, reasoning that the more the performance of demanding altruistic deeds is considered to be an optional matter, the more an agent remains relatively free to pursue the projects he or she desires throughout his or her life.

A good deal of the contemporary conversation about supererogation has evolved in tandem with the development of these two positions. Moral theorists tend either to be against recognizing the concept, and consequently opposed to the feature of commonsense morality that calls for the restriction of positive duty, or in favor of its recognition, and therefore in support of adopting a more relaxed standard of moral requirement. This is a dichotomy that for the most part remains unchallenged. While the question of whether supererogation is a good thing remains fiercely debated, both sides concur that the recognition of the concept would imply an acceptance of Urmson's arguments in favor of adopting an undemanding standard of positive duty. In other words, although antisupererogationists and supererogationists dispute both the range and moral status of acts located within the sphere of permissibility, they tend to agree about the function that the concept of supererogation *would* serve *if* it were recognized: it would serve as a conceptual device intended to free the moral agent from undue burdens. Because Urmson's *understanding* of the concept of supererogation does not seem to be in dispute in the ongoing debate, I will refer to it as the "standard" view. According to the standard view, one who goes above and beyond the call of duty is praiseworthy and always acts in an unconditionally optional manner. Since supererogation is irreducible to duty, it cannot ever be considered morally binding, even for the agent who is not inclined to regard especially demanding altruistic acts, such as "heroic" or "saintly" acts, as morally optional in the first place. The standard view assumes that the boundary that separates duty from supererogation is the same for everyone, determined irrespective of the ways in which particular agents perceive it.

David Heyd and the Concept of Supererogation

The thinker responsible for making the radical irreducibility of supererogatory acts fundamental to their meaning is David Heyd. Twenty-four years after the publication of "Saints and Heroes," Heyd assimilated Urmson's insights into the first comprehensive study of the problem of supererogation. He described his book *Supererogation: Its Status in Ethical Theory* as a reaction both to Urmson's essay and to the plethora of critical responses it incited in the decade following its appearance.[13] Heyd not only characterized duty as having certain universal limits, he tried to show what was desirable about this characterization. At the heart of Heyd's theory was the idea that individuals ought to be permitted not to devote themselves to the betterment of others' welfare. This belief led to what Heyd termed the "negative justification" of the category of supererogation, that our right to prioritize our own good over the overall good precludes our having to perform praiseworthy but morally demanding other-regarding actions.[14] Buttressing this conviction was Heyd's positive belief that spontaneous altruism was preferable to that procured under moral pressure. Following Urmson, Heyd argued that the spirit of altruism would decline if demanding acts of self-sacrifice came to be regarded as mandatory, concluding that some types of virtuous behavior could be realized only under wholly uncoercive circumstances.[15] Thus, beyond the function it served in limiting the scope of duty, the concept of supererogation was, in and of itself, morally good, for it was the optional nature of altruistic conduct that gave altruism its special quality.

However, Heyd's appropriation of the concept of supererogation could be interpreted less charitably. Notwithstanding the acknowledgment in his view of the mandatoriness of basic positive duties, critics could allege that like other theorists coming from a secular, neo-Enlightenment orientation, Heyd favored noninterference in individual pursuits and projects over the promotion of communal welfare. This charge was not far from the mark. A person who did not fall below the minimal standard of moral requirement, but who also routinely failed to do more than that standard, in Heyd's view, was considered to have the same moral standing as the agent who habitually exceeded his duty. While Heyd conceded that in this scenario the latter had more *virtue* than the former, he insisted that neither agent incurred any blame.[16] By Heyd's reckoning, people who lacked virtue could consistently refrain throughout their lives from doing anything more than what they were strictly required to do without its affecting our moral judgment of them. Not surprisingly, Heyd's opponents became concerned that the acknowledgment of a category of supererogation would have the effect of sanctioning the kind of lifestyle whereby agents could justifiably aspire to do only what was minimally required, without so much as contemplating the necessity of doing more. They worried that by labeling an act "supererogatory" we decrease the likelihood of its performance, especially among those who are not initially disposed to achieve more than mediocrity in their moral lives. Even an acknowledgment of the *concept* of supererogation induces moral laxity, according to this criticism.

Supererogationists do tend to be rigorous in their insistence that there are no circumstances under which we should reproach ourselves for failing to go above and beyond the call of duty.[17] For Urmson and Heyd, to say that we "ought" to go above and beyond the call of duty is to utter a contradiction. The very phrase "above and beyond" indicates a departure from the realm of moral compulsion. Supererogatory agents—for example, heroes and saints—are in every sense free not to do the things which they are known and praised for doing.[18] Urmson and Heyd maintain this to be so in spite of the feelings heroes and saints themselves may have to the contrary. As we will see, Urmson has a particular understanding of who heroes and saints are: noble but idiosyncratic, calm in their resolve to help others, yet inaccessible to us when we try to understand them. More importantly, according to Urmson's view, heroes and saints have an uncommonly robust sense of moral requirement, which, notwithstanding the special commitments Urmson acknowledges heroes and saints to have undertaken, is at the same time a false one. Heroes and saints thus should be highly esteemed, but not trusted as authorities for deciding what their respective situations morally require of them. When they assert that they have done nothing special, they are likely being morally modest. Consequently, we must interpret them with rhetorical sophistication. We must look at what they say in view of the extraordinary moral talents they possess. Most of all, according to Urmson and Heyd, we must not confuse a hero or saint's understanding of moral requirement with "duty" per se, lest we come to misunderstand the unique importance of the concept of a duty for ethics in general.

URMSON'S HEROES AND SAINTS: MORAL EXEMPLARS WITHOUT MORAL AUTHORITY

Defining "Duty" in the Standard View

Though groundbreaking in terms of its critique of traditional neo-Enlightenment modes of moral theorizing, "Saints and Heroes" is written to preserve the notion of "duty" as the fundamental concept in reference to which right action is determined. Urmson does not desire to overturn the model of duty-based morality, but to subject that model to internal reform. To see how this is so, it will be helpful to discuss briefly the idea of a duty, the view of it espoused by Urmson's Kantian and utilitarian contemporaries, and the Urmsonian modification of that view. This clarification is more than a formal exercise. Many moral theorists refer to "duty" as if there is only one appropriate way of using the term. They do this without realizing that they are incorporating their underlying philosophical and normative commitments into their understanding of the concept, even though these commitments are not intrinsic to the concept itself. In his own discussion of duty, Urmson betrays the extent to which he is informed by certain substantive convictions of a deontic nature.[19] He maintains, for example, that virtue is not constitutive of duty. According to Urmson, virtue is optional while duty is necessary. Duty does not vary. It binds agents in the same way and is presumed to subject them to the same level of burden.[20] These propositions are derived from premises introduced by Urmson himself; they do not follow from the idea of duty, as such. In order to be clear on what it means to exceed duty, and thereby to enter into a discussion about the nature of heroes and saints, it is important to be informed about what particular sense of duty is in use.[21]

To this end, it will be helpful to establish what, if anything, can be commonly extracted from the various representations of "duty."[22]

It seems to me that the concept of duty has two features that can be considered essential. The first is the idea of moral necessity. One *must* perform one's duty. A duty is a morally binding *requirement*. Duty does not admit of degrees. While one can act in a way that is "better" or "worse" with respect to the pursuit of some object of value, one can either fulfill or not fulfill one's duty.[23] If one does not fulfill one's duty, then one has not done what one ought to have done, and, as a result, one has morally failed. The second essential feature of duty is that we may *demand* those to whom it applies to accomplish it.[24] In other words, duty confers upon those who will be impacted by its performance the right to insist that it be carried out, even if such a claim is one made on oneself. The omission of a duty stands in violation of this right.[25]

These two features—moral necessity on the part of the agent, and expectation of fulfillment on the part of the recipient—apply to all senses of the meaning of "duty." They are part of its definition. However, these qualities alone do not take us very far toward answering significant questions about what it would mean to have a duty. For example, they do not tell us about the *scope* of duty. Does duty apply to everyone equally or to certain people under certain circumstances? In addition, we will want to know how a maxim that appears to be something which we should act upon can become, in a much stronger sense, necessarily binding. That is, by what authority does duty attain its compulsory *force?* Probing further still, we will want to determine what is eligible to be considered a duty. Urmson, for his part, asserts that a duty must be something that we can fulfill. However, this is surely not the only conceivable constraining feature of the notion. Thus, we will also want to ask: What, with respect to content, can be a duty? What is its *nature?* Questions pertaining to the *scope, force,* and *nature* of duty are fundamental to, but not exhaustive of, all possible lines of inquiry. While it is not my purpose here to present a comprehensive view of the ways in which these issues have been addressed throughout the history of ethics, it is at least important for me to discuss them in connection with the environment which forms the context for Urmson's essay.

Urmson identifies his intended audience at the outset of "Saints and Heroes." It consists of those secular moral philosophers, primarily Kantians and utilitarians, who fail to discriminate among more than three classes of moral actions: (1) the morally required and therefore morally praiseworthy; (2) the morally prohibited and therefore morally blameworthy; and (3) the morally neutral and therefore neither praiseworthy nor blameworthy.[26] This threefold typology, purported to complete the kinds of actions that can be recognized from the point of view of moral worth, historically corresponds to a specific view of duty whose origins lie in the tradition of the Enlightenment. It is a universalist view, in which duties are seen to be binding on all agents as such through a demand of reason (whether according to a principle of respect for persons or a principle of utility). Additionally, it is a view of morality that requires a very high standard of other-regard. Empirical assessments about agents' moral capabilities have no bearing on what can be considered morally required of them, for duty is justified for all agents by a prior demand of reason. By positing the existence of a category of nonrequired, praiseworthy acts, Urmson affirms the traditional understanding of duty as a universally applicable standard of moral requirement to which all agents qua agents are subject, while challenging both its sole basis in principles of reason and its presumption that considerations of cost to the agent ought not to constrain what can count as morally required. Duty, though still universal and binding, becomes for Urmson the result of a concrete, constructive process that results in the formation of obligatory conventions and social mores. With respect to the variables under discussion pertaining to moral requirement, one could say that Urmson's modifications to the traditional view apply to the *force* and *nature* of duty, but not to its *scope*. This is to say that for Urmson duty is still construed as something which *formally* specifies how all agents qua agents should act, but which is arrived at in an a posteriori, empirical fashion, and which, *substantively* speaking, makes fewer demands on the agent.

Urmson's fundamental move away from Enlightenment thinking is his emphasis on the need for duty to "work," by which Urmson means that it ought to be constructed to serve human needs.[27] Duty should not consist, for example, in the relentless pursuit of the good of the greatest number or in the enactment of maxims into universal law by a self-legislating will. According to Urmson, the problem with most utilitarians and Kantians is that they have erred by setting moral requirements too high. Instead of making unrealizable ideals obligatory, Urmson recommends a two-tiered framework of duty and love, wherein only the former carries the force of moral command.[28] He makes the contrast between the two explicit:

> It is important to give a special status of urgency ... [only] in those matters in which compliance with the demands of morality by all is indispensable. ... It would be silly for us to say to ourselves, our children and our fellow men, "This and that you and everyone else must do," if the acts in question are such that manifestly but few could bring themselves to

do them. . . . Admirers of the Sermon on the Mount do not in practice,
and could not, treat failure to turn the other cheek and to give one's
cloak also as being on all fours with breaches of the Ten Commandments, however earnestly they themselves try to live a Christian life.[29]

In this passage, Urmson gives a hint about what, for him, duty substantively entails. It consists not in the injunctions mentioned, for example, in
the Book of Matthew to forgive, to exhibit generosity toward one's aggressors, and to give charitably and magnanimously to those of lesser means.[30]
Rather, falling under the rubric of moral requirement are those negative
duties whose violation would impinge upon our most basic rights and liberties, and those positive duties that are needed to secure the minimal
conditions of cooperation and equity in society.[31] In Urmson's view there
are no real duties of charity, other than those that are absolutely necessary for society to function. Only those norms whose absence would mean
social anarchy can be considered obligatory. Urmson's view resembles that
of the contractarian heirs of the Hobbesian tradition of moral philosophy, according to which we have a moral obligation to assent by agreement to the norms of the commonwealth of any civil society.[32] According
to Hobbes, such norms are guaranteed by the authoritative "Leviathan"
who, in the common interest, brings order to society by creating a moral
code designed to prevent us from lapsing into an unrelenting power struggle that ultimately leads to our death. In Urmson's account, the "Leviathan" becomes the humanly constructed social contract comprised of
"rules" to which we all agree for our own safety.[33]

Urmson advocates a minimal standard of moral requirement, which
depends for its rationale on an empirical assumption about what level of
altruism we can plausibly hope for from the majority. For duty to remain
something that is considered universal, it must correspond to what lies
within the realm of what is possible for most people. To think of duty as
any more than this is to set ourselves up for failure and to risk losing
respect for the moral code that painstakingly has been established. Urmson deliberately sets the bar that separates duty from supererogation
where he does. His association of duty as lying *within* the range of the capacities of ordinary persons is constructed so as to allow for those agents
who possess only the ability to accomplish the moral minimum to be
included. In this way Urmson is able to see duty as something that applies
to everyone. Duty is perceived "objectively," while more demanding personal commitments to help others are perceived "deliberatively," as part of
one's "individual morality."[34] Only the former is impartial in the sense of
being cognitively accessible to and psychologically likely for all agents.

Secular and Religious Ethics Dichotomized

Thus, for Urmson duty is synonymous with what is *minimally morally required*. He manages to preserve the traditional notion of duty as being a universal "ought" at the expense of excluding certain altruistic deeds that are in all likelihood within the capacity only of *some* agents. In order to keep universality fundamental to the concept of a duty, one must draw a line "between what we can expect and demand from others and what we can merely hope for and receive with gratitude when we get it."[35] Urmson himself draws this line conservatively: what we can "expect and demand" is what we can expect and demand from everyone. In other words, certain relatively demanding altruistic deeds, which would be considered required if our aggregate capacity for other-regard were greater, acquire a supererogatory status by default. This minimal standard of moral obligation, which is imposed on all agents, is the consequence of introducing the criterion of fulfillability into the notion of duty while simultaneously attempting to preserve the criterion of universality. "Fulfillability," according to Urmson, pertains to what we are *likely* to be able to fulfill, not to what we possibly *can* fulfill, which is a higher standard. Thus, in order for an altruistic act potentially to qualify as morally required, its fulfillment cannot just be possible; it must be *probable* for all agents.

Urmson additionally insists that there can be only one "formulable" standard for determining *what* distinguishes the supererogatory from the morally required.[36] This standard, furthermore, remains fixed. It cannot be altered, even in the case of particular agents whose specific character traits equip them to be subjected to more demanding burdens. Wherever the line between moral requirement and supererogation is drawn, it is a line to which we will all become accustomed over time, and, as a result, one that we are justified in expecting not to change. This rigid way of determining duty resembles utilitarian and Kantian models for understanding what is morally required. However, in the case of Urmsonian morality such rigidity actually serves to release us from having to modify our conduct in the direction of moral stringency.

In *defining* obligatory conduct as conduct that most people will be likely to be able to achieve, Urmson describes morality in jurisprudential terms.[37] To be dutiful we need merely exhibit minimal decency. It is not part of the function of duty to make us stretch our other-regarding capacities. In fact, we can be dutiful while lacking virtue altogether. Virtue supplements but is not essential for the fulfillment of moral requirement. It is morally unnecessary yet can be maximally demanding. It aims at moral distinction, or at least high moral achievement. Duty, on the other hand, is morally necessary yet minimally demanding. It specifies what must be done to avoid moral wrongdoing.[38] Without virtue, Urmson continues, our interactions with one another would be impoverished, but without a moral code that it is our duty to uphold they would disintegrate into "rabble."[39] The only way to avoid the latter consequence is to keep duty and virtue conceptually separate. Urmson achieves this by not defining duty too ambitiously: duty has definite limits that do not encroach upon virtue's terrain. "It cannot be one's duty to go the second mile in the same basic sense that it is to go the first," he states; otherwise it could be argued that it is one's duty to go two miles, and then four miles, and by repetition "one could establish the need to go every time on an infinite journey."[40]

Urmson's rejection here of the injunction announced in Matthew 5:41 is not meant to be subtle, and it perhaps calls attention to a moment in the history of modern ethics when secular and religious norms stood farther apart from one another than during any other time. His characterization of duty befits a society such as ours in which moral constraints are understood as concessions to the pragmatic concerns of security, safety, and the protection of rights and liberties, and in which charity is presumed to originate appropriately within the smaller setting of family and community. In such a society, we ought not to expect benevolence from those whom we do not know personally, much less under circumstances when significant costs are involved. Traveling the second mile is an activity properly consigned to the religious domain.

In the present day, this partition between the secular and religious realms is generally affirmed, and not merely by advocates of the Urmsonian view who emerge from the secular side. Some recent Christian ethicists, for example, are attracted to the idea that moral perseverance and excellence is possible only through recourse to religious resources. Without God's assistance, contends the Calvinist John Hare, we are not equipped to meet the demands of an adequate moral existence. According to Hare, a virtuous life in which one fully participates in a morally ordered universe "is not something I can acquire by trying to acquire it"; rather, "it is something that some people seem to have and others seem to lack," depending on whether or not they choose to surrender to the notion that they ought to be "what they cannot by their natural capacities become."[41] Augustine's famous remark that "God bids us do what we cannot, that we may know what we ought to seek from him" may seem to refute the maxim "ought implies can," but the principle is in fact upheld, for what is not possible is not our attempting to *do* what God bids, but our attempting to do it *without his help*.[42] According to Hare and others, traditional maximalist moral frameworks, such as Kantianism and utilitarianism, are impractical due to their reliance on the motivating force of human reason alone. Except for very few exceptions, we cannot look to our own abilities to overcome selfishness and the human disposition to commit evil acts. Urmson and Hare both assign to the secular realm its proper scope: minimal morality. In this domain, moral requirement corresponds strictly to the proverbial first mile.

It is important to note in this case what Urmson, a secular theorist, and Hare, a Calvinist, share in common, namely, a belief in the fixity rather than the malleability of human nature. They contend that the constraints of human psychology are such that we are unlikely to change—to become *better*—of our own accord. For Urmson and those who defend the commonsense view, the religiously lived moral life remains an option, but only in exceptional cases for those who consent to take on the additional commitment living such a life entails. We may or may not appeal to religion to govern our moral sensibilities, but insofar as we are grouped as a plurality in society, we should not be bound by religion's additional moral demands and constraints. By contrast, according to Hare and other theological ethicists, the limitations for what can be morally required of us in secular society are precisely what *necessitates* the resort to higher, sectarian guidance. However, in both instances the secular and religious realms are dichotomized. In the first case, religious morality is cast as an option for the hearty and ambitious. In the second, religion represents the only viable alternative to an otherwise inadequate moral existence.[43] In neither view does religious ethics "spill over" into the secular realm.

Urmson's Heroes and Saints

A similar point could be made if instead of contrasting the secular and religious, we contrasted the ordinary on the one hand and the heroic or saintly on the other. According to the standard view, heroic or saintly morality and ordinary, secular morality are separate things and do not influence one another. Heroes and saints, to the extent that they are heroic or saintly, consent to assume extra moral burdens. According to Urmson, heroes and saints are made up of those who do go the proverbial second mile, but who regard that distance as required, at least in their own case. The difference between heroes and saints is that *heroes* act fearlessly and courageously, while *saints*, even more remarkably, act with total disregard for any form of inclination or self-interest. Both, however, do their duty in contexts in which most people would choose not to do it (Urmson refers to these as "minor" heroes and saints), or exceed the limits of duty altogether (these are heroes and saints, par excellence).[44] Urmson notes that heroes and saints may feel as though they ought to perform costly altruistic acts in just the same way that they feel they ought to do what is minimally morally required, which leads them to bind themselves to perform such acts and to subject themselves to self-reproach if they fail to do so.

But in committing themselves to a level of altruism beyond what is fulfill-able for the majority, heroes and saints come to possess a sense of "duty" that exceeds what is *really* required of them. Thus, in Urmson's view, a "heroic" or "saintly" understanding of moral requirement is an illusory one.

There is, furthermore, no limit to what heroes or saints may undertake. Urmson attempts to harness support for this claim through his allusion to St. Francis. He writes:

> It is recorded by Bonaventura that after Francis of Assisi had finished preaching to the birds on a celebrated occasion his companions gath-ered around him to praise and admire. But Francis himself was not pleased; he was full of self-reproach that he had hitherto failed in what he now considered to be his duty to preach to the feathered world. There is indeed no degree of saintliness that a suitable person may not come to consider it to be his duty to achieve. Yet there is a world of difference between this failure to have preached hitherto to the birds and a case of straightforward breach of duty. . . .[45]

In this passage we get the sense that St. Francis himself sees no real dis-tinction between the act of preaching to the birds and the act of fulfilling the most basic obligations. Urmson has similar things to say about the soldier who heroically falls on a grenade in order to save comrades, and about the doctor who leaves a thriving practice to travel to a plague-ridden city.[46] In all three of these cases, the obligatoriness of the supererogatory deed is portrayed as being on a par with truth-telling and promise-keeping from the perspective of heroes or saints themselves, in spite of the obvi-ous differences among the kinds of acts under consideration. Yet, wagers Urmson, if pressed to reflect honestly about their deeds, heroes and saints would have to acknowledge the supererogatory nature of what they do. Why are heroes and saints prone to delude themselves in this fashion? At one point Urmson implies that heroes and saints are excessively modest and thus tend to miss how fundamentally different they are from ordinary persons.[47] Later, he suggests that they are prone to confusing commit-ments that they personally undertake for morally compulsory duties.[48]

In making these speculative observations, Urmson purports to speak for heroes and saints. There is a process of interpretation that we must undergo when we encounter them, he informs us, and even though their actions are commendable, we cannot take them at their word when they contend in earnest to have done merely their duty. Rather, suggests Urm-son, heroes and saints utilize this phrase to express that at the time they perform their heroic and saintly deeds, such deeds *present themselves* as ones that are morally obligatory. However, upon due reflection heroes and

saints will come to attribute the proper status to their acts. He expresses
this conviction in the case of the heroic soldier, whom we are told is fully
aware of the inappropriateness of modeling a notion of duty based on his
personal view of moral requirement:

> [If] he were to survive the action only a modesty so excessive so as to
> appear false could make him say, "I only did my duty," for we know, *and
> he knows*, that he has done more than duty requires. Further, though he
> might say to himself that so to act was a duty, he could not say so even
> beforehand to anyone else, and no one else could ever say it. Subjectively,
> we may say, at the time of action, the deed presented itself as a duty, but
> it was not a duty.[49]

According to this characterization, there is a sense in which Urmson's soldier is at a loss to describe the nature of what he does. He remains unflinchingly committed to a course of action that he believes to be the only
right one, but which he also understands to be regarded as purely optional
from an objective standpoint. Just what is it, then, that leads him to bind
himself to do more than he must?

While we never get an explicit answer to this question, Urmson's observations pertaining to the soldier's self-awareness of the gap that can exist
between his duty, objectively construed, and his subjective perception of
moral obligation lead me to speculate that Urmson attributes the hero's
unique sense of moral requirement to the idiosyncratic traits of the hero
himself. On the positive side, such traits give the hero moral fortitude in
the form of courage, enabling him to sacrifice himself for the sake of others; however, on the negative side they diminish his capacity to characterize his actions in an impartial fashion.[50] The hero's psychological state
induces him to act *as if* what he does is required, even though he may realize at a deeper level that he is in fact going above and beyond his duty
when performing the heroic deed. If this account is correct, then the hero
binds himself to do more than he must as an expression of a commitment
to fulfill a *personal ideal*. Once fully embraced, the ideal transforms his
way of viewing moral obligation. He accepts a new moral code on the
faith of his convictions. This transformation compromises his capacity to
distinguish basic duty from more demanding altruistic deeds. In not
blaming others for failing to follow his lead, he reveals that he still recognizes the legitimacy of the impartial viewpoint from which he has veered.

Urmson's presumption of the existence of a universally applicable standard of moral requirement that puts limits on what agents must sacrifice
of themselves is a crucial component of his overall view. Only on such
a presumption is Urmson able to dismiss the perspective of heroes and

saints themselves as a reflection of what they *perceive* to be true. Heroes and saints do not really offer their understandings of moral requirement as "pieces of objective reporting."[51] On its face, this claim seems plausible. Supererogatory agents will frequently understate the meritoriousness and valiancy of their actions, not because they are prone to confusion, but because doing so is part of what it means to be a hero or a saint. Heroes and saints, in other words, are *served* by their heroic and saintly perceptions of what is required. Without them they would lack the requisite motivation to do more than their ordinary duty, and they would cease to warrant our esteem. One of the things we prize about saints and heroes, in fact, is their readiness to blame themselves when they fail to meet the commitments that we acknowledge them not to be obliged to undertake. In a sense, we esteem them for deluding themselves. It is this heroic and saintly quality, however, which, in Urmson's view, precludes them at the same time from being considered moral authorities. If heroes and saints *were* moral authorities, then *our* way of seeing things would be in need of correction. This practical consideration accounts for the appeal of Urmson's argument. By characterizing heroic soldiers, for example, as "extraordinary" moral agents whose inclination to deny the meritoriousness of their conduct is but a facet of their "heroic" aura, Urmson leaves intact assumptions about the legitimate level of moral burden which is *our* share.

The tendency to protect this impartial sense of duty is not the only explanation for Urmson's decision to describe his soldier as a moral exemplar who lacks moral authority. This characterization is also motivated by Urmson's belief that the hero *is*, in fact, fundamentally different from the rest of us and is consequently not a good model on which to base our conduct. "Human nature," which becomes so crucial to the way in which Urmson sets the limits of moral obligation, is at odds with the hero's "nature." Humans scarcely fulfill their duty, let alone exceed it. It is part of human nature, furthermore, not to expect too much of others, much less of ourselves, once we have settled into established patterns of other-regarding practices. Heroes are not subject to the same limitations. Unlike the rest of us, they possess the capacity to add to the minimal level of responsibility initially allotted to them. Urmson paints a picture of a mediocre majority, scarcely capable of engaging in real moral development, and a contrasting picture of a scattering of born heroes and saints, who, as a result of their unique place in the world, come to see themselves as beholden to a different set of expectations than the rest of us.[52]

This double standard is emphasized in considering the case of saints. Unlike heroes, saints are motivated by selflessness to the point of transcending all desire and self-interest. There is seemingly no end to what saints might interpret to be their responsibility in attending to the needs of others. Likewise, in the case of saints, there is no meaningful way to establish criteria for limiting moral duty. Anything could conceivably become required. This is the point behind Urmson's decision to refer to the example of St. Francis's preaching to the birds. The act in question already so far exceeds what could reasonably be considered morally required conduct that we may assume there are no limiting criteria at all. It may occur to us that if St. Francis had an even greater sense of responsibility for the suffering of the world, he might have decided to subject himself to self-reproach for failing to preach to the floral world, or to the wind. What saints consider to be required transcends the realm of universal duty, and obviously so. In some cases, we may even have concerns that what the saint proposes is immoral.[53] At least we have reasons to want to draw a sharp distinction between the saint's morality and ordinary morality, in which only the latter would be regarded as obligatory.[54]

Urmson thus argues that it is the nature of saints to perform acts that may appear excessive, if not ridiculous, to the rest of us, even though they may consider themselves bound to behave as they do. The question, however, is whether the saint is *morally* bound to perform saintly acts. To what extent are saints in a position to make *this* judgment of themselves? How do we classify, for example, the activity of preaching to the birds? Urmson specifies that saintly acts "cannot adequately be subsumed under the concept of duty," regardless of how saints themselves may choose to interpret them.[55] As he does with respect to his imaginary heroic soldier, Urmson gives us reason to doubt the testimony of the saint, who may decide to award any activity he or she chooses to pursue the same status as that of truth-telling and promise-keeping. As the case of St. Francis shows, the testimony of the saint may even be *more* suspect than that of the hero, for we can at least predict to some extent what the hero might come to regard as required.

In spite of Urmson's sympathetic depiction of heroes and saints with respect to the *value* that they place in their heroic and saintly acts, Urmson insists that heroes and saints err by taking this evaluative decision for a judgment about what morally *must* be done. Urmson denies that heroes or saints are justified in thinking themselves to be in a privileged position from which to view the world and their moral responsibility in it. Heroes and saints do supererogate, even if they do not acknowledge the concept of supererogation. They do warrant our commendation for their unexpected intervention in our lives, notwithstanding their failure to see themselves as extraordinary. Heroes and saints have special roles and commitments that occupy them in unique ways, but this does not imply that when they fulfill these roles they perform their moral duty. There is only one meaning of "duty," argues Urmson, and it is the same for everyone.

FROM URMSON TO HEYD: STANDARDIZING SUPEREROGATION

Unqualified Supererogation

In the two decades following "Saints and Heroes," Urmson's unprecedented appeal to moral options gave way to new innovations in duty-based ethics that explicitly made room for a category of supererogation. Correspondingly, Urmson's practical characterization of duty as being universal yet fulfillable by the average person came to supplant the traditional, rigorous view of duty as an unconditionally obligatory demand of reason intended for ideally rational people. Notable philosophers working in secular normative ethics, such as Thomas Nagel, R. M. Hare, W. D. Hudson, and John Rawls, were among the representatives of this paradigm shift.[56] They argued that the term "duty" was misused if not utilized by everyone in the same way, and that it no longer comprised the whole of the moral sphere. This is not to say that these thinkers did not acknowledge the existence of special duties of vocation, special relations, religious commitments, and the like. However, on their account, such special obligations acquired the status of duty for anyone so circumstanced. Parents had duties to their children, the clergy to their congregations, and rescue workers to their communities by virtue of the nature of the special relationship between giver and recipient. Due to their especially costly nature, heroic and saintly deeds could not similarly be re-envisioned. From these assumptions such thinkers concluded that there could be no sense of "ought" that could be used in connection with works of supererogation.

The major problem that confronted these reformers entailed keeping the new category of supererogation formally consistent with the old category of duty. There could not, for example, be some altruistic acts which were considered above and beyond for certain people and required for others, lest the whole of the universality of moral requirement fall under suspicion.[57] One possible way to keep the two consistent was to propose a theory of supererogation in which all supererogatory acts remained irreducible to duty. This would entail demonstrating that supererogatory acts were in every instance optional and that their omission could never cause an agent's moral censure or warrant reproach of any kind. In writing *Supererogation: Its Status in Ethical Theory*, it was David Heyd's purpose to undertake this task. In the volume, Heyd sought to carry Urmson's argument for the existence of praiseworthy non-obligatory actions to what he believed was its natural conclusion: a theory of "unqualified" supererogation.

According to Heyd, judgments about rightness and wrongness of conduct are determined independently of judgments about character, emotions, dispositions, and intentions. Thus, we find Heyd saying that an adequate account of supererogation implies "a rejection of theories which analyse [the concept] in terms of states of affairs that ought to exist,... or in terms of traits of character or virtues that a person ought to have."[58] Who we are—and who we might become—may have a bearing on what we do, but it is solely *what* we do that counts as the basis for judging our moral standing.

In Heyd's view, therefore, supererogation, as a concept, retains its coherence only when considered in reference to certain actions. Supererogation is something that describes an action that is *more* than what it is right to do and something that it is not wrong to refrain from doing. Supererogatory acts have the same kind of altruistic quality as duty, but are "more" in terms of their degree of altruism and in terms of their costliness. Heyd's presumption against the expectation of a morality beyond duty is explicit in his proposed definition of supererogation. According to Heyd:

An act is supererogatory if and only if
(1) It is neither obligatory nor forbidden.
(2) Its omission is not wrong, and does not deserve sanction or criticism—either formal or informal.
(3) It is morally good, both by virtue of its (intended) consequences and by virtue of its intrinsic value (being beyond duty).
(4) It is done voluntarily for the sake of someone else's good, and is thus meritorious.[59]

From these conditions, it can be inferred that supererogatory acts produce as much if not more goodness than do acts that fulfill duty, yet they are not required, as acts of duty are. In other words, while both duty and supererogation have positive moral value, only the latter is completely optional. The principle here advanced is that individuals ought to remain utterly free to refrain from doing morally good acts that exceed duty. The condition of permissibility, Heyd explains,

renders any theory which maintains the possibility of duties of supererogation incompatible with the definition. The self-contradictory term 'duty of supererogation' is often used by philosophers who are more interested in making a distinction between different kinds of duties (usually according to their stringency), than in offering a theory of supererogation.... The failure to justify the notion of a 'supererogatory duty' stems from the confusion of supererogation and imperfect duty. While the former can be applied to particular actions (as well as to classes of actions), the latter has meaning only as an attribute of classes of action. Furthermore, . . . the idea of imperfect duty implies a distinction between what is obligatory ('the minimum') and what is supererogatory ('beyond the minimum').[60]

Acts of supererogation are not the same as specific required acts of charity, "which each agent ought to do on some occasions."[61] Neither are they more rigorous acts of benevolence, which some agents (i.e., those filling a role duty) ought to do on some occasions. In the first case, there is a straightforward confusion of supererogatory conduct with duty; in the second, duty is denied its universal status. For Heyd, if it has been determined in the moral code that something is not required, then there is not even a residual sense in which we ought to do it. This is why he calls his theory of supererogation "unqualified." In making these distinctions, Heyd gives philosophical justification to the commonsense view of morality, according to which we are never morally on the hook for failing to go above and beyond.

Heyd contrasts his view with "qualified" supererogationism, in which the supererogatory is ultimately reducible to moral requirement on some level. In qualified supererogationism, while we are by definition not required to go above and beyond the call of duty, there is still a sense in which we should endeavor to do so nonetheless. Qualified supererogationism attempts to do more justice than unqualified supererogationism to our common belief in the value and praiseworthiness of supererogatory conduct by admitting that in some abstract or ideal sense all good actions carry some prima facie obligatory force, even though many lose their obligatory status when the costliness of their performance is taken into consideration.[62] Thus, qualified supererogation is *reductive*. It insists on accommodating supererogatory acts within the framework of duties and obligations. Were it not for considerations of risk, personal incapacity, difficult psychological circumstances, and so on, every moral action that produced good results would in principle be required.[63]

There are many varieties of qualified supererogationism. In one version, qualified supererogationists hold that acts of supererogation are technically not required but that their nonperformance can still cause offense.[64] In a second version, human weakness of will serves as the ground for relieving us of what we would otherwise be obligated to do.[65] In this case, as Heyd states, the "immunity from critical response . . . is granted more as a matter of excuse . . . than as a right derived from the optional character of the act itself."[66] Here, supererogatory acts are considered so by default: our inability to perform them as duty overrides the fact that we ought to do them nonetheless. In still a third version, there is a recognition of a double standard for agents whereby those intent on rising above the required moral minimum in their conduct, for vocational reasons or otherwise, are acknowledged to have certain duties that are considered supererogatory for everyone else.[67] These three versions all stand in marked contrast to Heyd's "unqualified" supererogation, which acknowledges no degrees in the level of moral requirement, and for which no sense of ought or blame attaches to supererogation. Heyd does recognize that there is wide disagreement about *where* to draw the line between duty and supererogation, especially in the case of a line that is to be drawn between charitable contributions and required giving of a more minimal sort.[68] However, he insists that the two are distinct and irreducible to one another. Supererogation, in other words, is designated by some constant that unconditionally indicates the exceeding of moral requirement. It sets duty apart from optional good actions.

Moderate and Minimalist Approaches in an Ethics of Duty

While Heyd does not provide us with the exact criteria for drawing the sharp distinction between duty and supererogation that his theory requires, he does give us some indication as to where duty ends and supererogation begins. To clarify his view, Heyd refers to Rawls's enumeration of "natural duties" in *A Theory of Justice*.[69] Rawls states that although the natural duties cannot adequately be categorized under one unified principle, they are in all instances universal, obtaining "between all as equal moral persons."[70] He mentions four conspicuous examples of these: the positive duty of "helping another when he is in need or jeopardy, provided that one can do so without excessive risk or loss to oneself"; the negative duty "not to harm or injure another"; the negative duty "not to cause unnecessary suffering" (in some more indirect manner); and the fundamental positive duty of mutual respect, which is shown in "our willingness to see the situation of others from their point of view, from the perspective of their conception of their good; and in our being prepared to give reasons for our actions whenever the interests of others are materially affected."[71] The overall purpose of the natural duties is to promote fairness among all individuals and to ensure the equal protection of our individual liberties. The natural duties enjoin us to attempt to understand others' aims and interests from their own standpoint. Additionally, they induce us to distribute equitably the benefits and burdens that derive from a shared common life.[72] The purpose of doing one's duty, according to Rawls, is to forgo any particular attachment to self, and to act instead from an impartial concern for all human beings. To the extent that duty is impartial, it has definite limits, for it is assumed that we are justified in allocating some disproportionate degree of attention to the things that motivate us the most, such as basic interests and special relations.[73]

On Rawls's account, it is excessive cost to the self that constrains what we are required to do for others. What qualifies as excessive cost to the self is determined by "reasonable self-interest," which, according to Rawls, outweighs an agent's generic natural duties to promote the good of others.[74] In other words, we should offer aid and assistance to others when the cost to ourselves is less than the benefit to the recipient, and even then only up until a point (e.g., we are not required to seriously injure ourselves to save the life of another). It is thus not our duty to do whatever is, overall, the *best* possible thing; it is not even our duty to do what is *better* than what we have become accustomed to doing, assuming we at least have been doing what is minimally required. There is in this view a kind of concession by impersonal morality to human motivation. In this concession, the demands of duty are relaxed so as to make duty more accessible to human beings with all of their preferences, flaws, and imperfections.[75] Nagel suggests something along these lines when he discusses the need to "strike a bargain between our higher and lower selves." In this bargain, the antecedent claims of impersonal morality are modified "to accommodate the normal limitations of human nature."[76] Millard Schumaker puts the point even more strongly:

> [W]e are morally required . . . only to be just and . . . it is therefore our right to do whatever is not unjust. In the realm of distributive and retributive justice [this] consists in fairness; hence, in this realm one is duty-bound only to be fair and therefore has a right to do whatever is not unfair.[77]

The domain of impersonal morality, in which we can properly be said to be "duty-bound," is finite in scope. In Schumaker's language, impersonal morality corresponds to "justice," which alone imposes obligations. In this account the supererogatory is proper to a morality of love, which lies beyond the impartial realm of universal standards and rules.[78] Rawls, Nagel, and Schumaker each contend that fairness is morally required, but that this does not entail the notion that we are duty-bound to do the best thing for all concerned.

There is a difference between Rawls and Nagel's way of framing the problem on the one hand, and Schumaker's on the other. In the former, the presumption is that the impersonal standpoint is the one most proper to morality and that out of empirical necessity a concession must be made to "human nature." According to Nagel, for example, we exist in the first instance under obligation to help others until they no longer need our help, but as part of the concession to human nature, our moral duty pertains only to promoting fairness. In Schumaker's view, by contrast, we do not exist in life already under obligation, and there is no posited moral ideal of which we will inevitably fall short. Rather, the impersonal perspective is constructed with our flawed human nature in mind. In Schumaker's account, duties thus arise for us once others' welfare and well-being are put into jeopardy. These two positions roughly resemble certain interpretations of the classical views of Locke and Hobbes, respectively. In the case of Locke, man is understood to be under a natural state of obligation. According to Hobbes, duties and rights are constructed as a means of preserving our mutual self-interest.

While Heyd appropriates the contrast Rawls draws between a morality of justice and duty and a morality of virtue and love, he, like Schumaker, maintains that the natural state of human beings is to be under no moral obligation. Duty is something whose only function is to serve us. Heyd makes this point explicitly:

> Morality, as a system of duties and obligations, puts *some* constraints on [the] basic freedom of the individual. Yet like social institutions and systems of rules, morality (in the form of duty and justice) should serve the individual in his search for self-realization rather than be served by the individual for its own sake. In this sense, rights precede duties. The autonomy of the individual means that he has a special reason to fulfill his own needs before getting involved in the fulfillment of other people's needs.[79]

Morality works against us as a collective of individuals rather than for us if we do not see ourselves in the first instance as free to pursue our own life plans and ideals.[80] Heyd invokes Bernard Williams's critique of utilitarianism to strengthen the point:

> [A]ccording to utilitarianism an agent should adopt "the general project of bringing about maximally desirable outcomes," but he can carry out that project only if (other people) have "lower-order projects" which he can help to realize. These projects are personal, and depend on individual inclinations, interests, capacities and preferences. But "unless there were first-order projects, the general utilitarian project would have nothing to work on, and would be vacuous." . . . Williams's argument is aimed at utilitarianism, but it is no less valid as a critique of extreme universal altruism or pure anti-supererogationism. For if everyone worked for the promotion of the *general* good, *whose* good would be promoted?[81]

For Heyd, like those theorists who focus exclusively on civil and individual liberties, "first-order" life plans and projects take priority over the "second-order," abstract ideal of promoting the good of everyone. The former are the starting point of human existence. By contrast, the morality of duty, as a system of requirements, is needed to ensure the free pursuit of everyone's plans and projects as well as the equitable distribution of their means of realization.[82] While moderates like Nagel make equal-regard primary and limit it on an exceptional basis, Heyd makes self-regard primary and limits it by negative and minimal positive duty only when it is necessary to do so for the sake of self-regard. Thus, writes Heyd, even if from the perspective of impartiality it is morally good or valuable to help someone else to achieve his goals, "it cannot be generally required, even if his goals are higher or more important than the agent's, . . . [for] the integrity of the individual consists exactly in the special weight he gives to his own ends."[83] It is for the sake of our "integrity" that our duty is limited and that supererogation becomes a necessary innovation. Heyd, who concurs with Nagel's duty-based approach to ethics, takes issue with Nagel's view that acts of supererogation are mere exemptions to what would otherwise be required if we were agents more capable of sustaining the inevitable loss or risk involved in engaging in such acts. To see supererogation in this way, according to Heyd, is to misunderstand the fundamental relationship that ought to exist between morality and the individual.

Heyd is explicit in his claim that we ought to be biased toward the promotion of our own welfare. Moral duty is "only a means of securing some minimal conditions of cooperation and justice," which cannot "exhaust the whole realm of moral value, and hence leaves room for acts beyond duty that are nevertheless morally good."[84] The needs of others, in and of themselves, do not confer upon us duties to offer our aid and assistance. "[W]e need no excuse for not acting beyond the call of duty," Heyd says, "and . . . even if we are capable of acting heroically (and it suits our character and inclinations), we are still free not to do so."[85]

In terms of its level of demandingness, Heyd and Schumaker's strong version of supererogation lends itself to moral minimalism, while that of Rawls and Nagel is conducive to a more demanding morality. However, in both the minimal and moderate versions of supererogationism, people who refrain consistently from doing more than they "ought" do not do any wrong and are therefore not considered morally blameworthy. In the moderate view, there is the lasting feeling that those who do merely their duty are morally lacking from a more idealistic standpoint. In this sense, the qualified supererogationism of Rawls and Nagel has one more line of defense against the antisupererogationist's charge of moral complacency. The compromise it proposes is in effect an admission that its "moderate" stance is in fact not "natural" at all but a default position that would be immediately nullified if human beings were different (i.e., better) sorts of people. Unqualified supererogationism, by contrast, makes no such concession. What the moderate and minimal views do share is their way of describing duty. In both instances, duty is understood in a deontic framework. It does not vary from agent to agent, and it remains the sole basis for evaluating the rightness or wrongness of an agent's actions.

Once again, we may note the disparity between certain secular and religious ways of characterizing moral requirement. The deontic understanding of duty described above, whether outlined in its moderate or minimal variety, can be contrasted with the non-deontic, religious one advocated, for example, by the prominent twentieth-century Christian theologian Paul Tillich. In supplanting the model of proportional justice with one of "creative" justice, Tillich argues for a conception of moral obligation that entails the maximal development of all of one's virtues.[86] Whereas Rawls and Heyd assume that what is "excessive" can be ascertained uniformly for all people at all times, for Tillich the predicate "excessive" varies depending on one's character development and one's corresponding other-regarding capabilities. According to Tillich, the moral act, or what Tillich calls the "essential human demand," ought not to be regarded as a restrictive yoke but as an expansive imperative which allows for the fulfillment of human potential.[87] Such an understanding of morality implies that justice ought to be extended beyond the notion of minimal justice. On this account justice is, in effect, a form of love, and the supererogatory becomes synonymous with what for the time being is truly in excess of that which falls within the range of an agent's existing moral capabilities. We may note that the "natural duties" that Rawls mentions—the negative duties not to harm others and not to cause them unnecessary suffering, and the positive duties to show others respect and to offer them help and assistance when doing so does not pose too high a cost to the self—do not require the maximal development of one's virtues. Their fulfillment, for example, does not entail that we exhibit kindness toward others, or that we be sympathetically motivated to improve others' situations. Rawlsian "natural duties" function only to preserve the balancing of everyone's interests, causing the realm of the supererogatory to encompass anything beyond "justice," narrowly conceived.

Compared to the view of duty expounded by Tillich and the Christian ethicists discussed in the introduction, the one embraced by Heyd, Rawls, and the other secular normative ethicists appears static. Yet secular and religious characterizations of moral requirement *need* not be contrasted so starkly, for it is conceivable that duty could be envisaged in a more elastic manner than it traditionally has been in the secular realm. In this case the establishment of duty's limits would give way to an emphasis on the development of virtue in understanding moral requirement. This would entail supplanting "unqualified supererogation" with "qualified supererogation," a possibility that I explore in the next chapter.

The Intrinsic Value of the Category of Supererogation

So far, I have discussed the justification for the category of supererogation in deontic ethics from the negative side only. I have said little about the intrinsic value of the concept, what David Heyd calls its "positive justification." I have explained the concept of supererogation as a necessity that accommodates human beings and their moral limitations. To leave the conversation at this point, however, would undersell the appeal of unqualified supererogation, for when we choose of our own accord to go above and beyond there is also a sense in which we do something unprecedented and wonderful. Hardly is there a case in which we more aptly assert ourselves afresh as vigorous moral beings as when we decide to give others an unexpected and nonrequired gift of love. Qualified supererogation, in which the supererogatory is reducible to the obligatory on some level, may be understood to preclude this kind of voluntary act. This failing can be taken to be a criticism of Tillich and the other theologians mentioned earlier. Can an understanding of moral requirement in which duty is cast as an ever-expanding concept truly allow for spontaneous, unexpected acts of gift-giving? The unqualified supererogationist doubts that such is possible since he or she also assumes that moral compulsion is incompatible with genuine altruistic behavior. This brings us to Heyd's characterization of the positive aspect of supererogation. Distinguishing between the negative and the positive aspects, Heyd writes:

> In negative terms, supererogation is justified by showing that some supererogatory acts must exist because society cannot require of the individual every act that would promote the general good, and because the individual has the right to satisfy his wants and to achieve his ends and ideals regardless of their social utility.... On the positive side, supererogation can be proved to have moral value by pointing out the freedom of the individual involved in purely optional choice, the social cohesion resulting from supererogatory behaviour, and the rationality of voluntary altruistic behaviour.[88]

Heyd elucidates three aspects of the positive justification for an unqualified theory of supererogation: its optionality; its conducivity to social interaction; and its "rational" accommodation to the human disposition against coercion. I consider these three in turn.

First, Heyd maintains that the purely optional status of supererogatory acts makes them especially valuable insofar as they "can be realized only under conditions of complete freedom and would be stifled under a more totalitarian concept of duty."[89] Heyd's view is that since the supererogatory act goes beyond what is required, if one acts altruistically, we are assured that one is doing it only because that is what one wants to do. In other words, one's act is not motivated by moral requirement but by genuine concern for the recipient of one's kindness. Here Heyd assumes that were the supererogatory act in question to become required, it would be impossible, or at least much more difficult, for the agent still to act out of this higher kind of motive.[90] The fact that what is rendered through works of supererogation is *not* required, argues Heyd, gives the potential giver the opportunity to share and to be spontaneously loving, and it enables the potential recipient to know that what has been received was the result of a desire on the part of a benefactor who has not been compelled by his or her adherence to a moral requirement. It is only the condition of optionality, claims Heyd, which guarantees the quality of a supererogatory gift. Not being universally required, "supererogatory action breaks out of the impersonal and egalitarian framework of the morality of duty—both by displaying individual preferences and virtues, and by allowing for some forms of favouritism, partial and unilateral treatment of someone to whom the agent wishes to show special concern."[91]

This observation is related to the second positive justification for unqualified supererogation, the "social cohesion" that results from voluntary altruistic behavior. There is something qualitatively distinct, Heyd thinks, about getting together in groups to raise money for charity, and like activities. That we *volunteer* in a communal setting to help with the Special Olympics, for example, and, while helping, encounter others similarly motivated, means that we also come to enjoy our act of giving more fully. The category of supererogation is not only something that we acknowledge by default, as a consequence of our need to limit moral duty because of considerations of costs and burdens to the agent. It is also a category that we would want to acknowledge in an ideal world, bereft of all selfishness and replete with resources. Because some altruistic acts are not required, we are able to *desire* the acts of giving and receiving. The idea that altruism based on free choice is of higher quality than that which is produced by the pressure of trying to fulfill a moral requirement is expressed by Millard Schumaker, who asks us to

> imagine a super-human ideal society, a world in which circumstances are such that no claims are ever laid upon anyone, ... in which there is no scarcity (or, alternatively, no needs) and no vulnerability and in

which therefore no possibility of rightful claim or meaningful threat. . . . [T]he concept of duty would become otiose and lose its use. Strictly speaking, in such a circumstance the concept of supererogation would also lose its use, since one can do more than his duty only if it makes sense to speak of his doing his duty. . . . Would such men engage in giving gifts? I suspect they would; for such seems to be consistent with the essential nature of man. Indeed, I fancy that even the angels themselves spontaneously give and receive gifts for no reason other than the sheer joy of sharing. In our ordinary world, too, men often give and receive gifts for no other reason than the sheer joy of sharing; and it is this, I suspect, which accounts for the continuing popularity of Christmas in a post-Christian world. We can conclude, then, that supererogation is not only valuable as a remedy for injustice; it is also a desirable end in itself. Good men would supererogate even if there was no need of any kind.[92]

Supererogation results not only in the immediate alleviation of injustice or others' suffering, but also in long-term friendships, as well as in the establishment of one's good character. That people are morally free not to be virtuous is what gives them the occasion to acquire virtue.[93] This is how the category of supererogation complements the category of obligation: the former supplements love of one's neighbors with the duty of respect that is owed to all persons. We have returned to Heyd's stark separation of duty and love, which mirrors the distinction Urmson makes between what is "indispensable" to morality and what is part of its "higher flights." Love fills in where duty's broad strokes fail to remedy the social ills that befall us. But there can be no "duty to love" that leaves untainted the love that would result from such a command.

Finally, Heyd emphasizes the moral value in the rationality of voluntaristic behavior. As human beings, it makes the most rational sense to base morality on how we actually are, and not on, as Urmson puts it, "fatuous ideals," to which we are unlikely ever to aspire. As finite beings, we have finite capacities. The category of supererogation conceptually allows us to reflect on the ways in which we can, from time to time, exceed these capacities with special daringness and displays of human spirit. Without the category of supererogation we would be left to dwell on our moral shortcomings, which would not be conducive to the overall point of morality.

Supererogation in Secular Society

Heyd's arguments support Urmson's general proposal for a double-tiered morality of duty and virtue, where duty is held to be universal and necessary, and virtue is held to be individually chosen and contingent.[94]

According to Urmson and Heyd, there is an unpredictability to acquiring virtue, the possession of which is a prerequisite for heroic or saintly conduct. If they are correct in this assessment, then there can be no duty to be virtuous. Rather, virtue should be left to the realm of the supererogatory in order to safeguard the conditions for true gift-giving. We commonly hold that heroes or saints are deserving of their high title because they are self-motivated to act as they do. Their deeds epitomize the "altruistic spirit," for they are voluntary in a much stronger sense than the kind of voluntarism that motivates the duty-fulfilling agent.[95]

This contention rings true at a practical and intuitive level. Even in traditions in which love is commanded, works of love are more welcomed by the recipient when the agent desires to perform them and does not merely perform them in response to decree. If these works are motivated by duty alone, then there is a lingering concern that they are somehow suspect. The recipient knows not if they were performed grudgingly. Kant's well-known objections to this observation notwithstanding, there is something to be said for the notion that the spirit with which a gift is given accounts for the value of the gift itself.

Still, one might be inclined to question whether the "spirit of altruism" needs to be as unrehearsed and beyond the reach of moral obligation as Urmson and Heyd characterize it to be. The question is whether we may dispose ourselves to become motivated to give to others in precisely the kind of spontaneous and magnanimous fashion that Urmson and Heyd describe. Urmson and Heyd worry that a moral system in which the supererogatory became reducible to the obligatory would devolve quickly into one that required us to devote ourselves ceaselessly to the welfare of others. In this case, morality would no longer "work for us." The question is whether or not this concern is warranted. What are the ramifications of thinking about a moral framework in which duty "spills over" into the realm of free choice, which in the standard view is also the realm in which virtue resides? According to Heyd's theory of unqualified supererogation, there are no grounds for thinking about duty and virtue in this manner. Heyd bases this conclusion on the premise that the vast realm of actions that contain moral value exceeds the limited role of the morality of duty in an individual's life.[96] Since the latter cannot exhaust the former, and since individuals are not tools for the promotion of the good, Heyd maintains that we have a right to moral relaxation. We should not always "take the *needs* of others as constituting a *claim* for help, even if such help could be lent at a reasonable price."[97] The implication is that virtue, especially virtue as it manifests itself in other-regarding action, cannot even weakly be compelled, lest we treat human beings as means and not ends and in so doing challenge the grounds for individual choice.

Here it is perhaps important to note that this resistance to seeing duty and virtue as other than irreducibly separate is a secular, neo-Enlightenment tendency. The individual is imagined in the first instance to be an autonomous agent who willingly chooses from among society's competing visions of the good. In a secular, neo-Enlightenment worldview, we do not presuppose one's connection to this or that vision of the good, but rather afford one the choice of affirming or denying all that has, as a matter of course, been inherited from one's tradition. The secularist does not deny that we are heavily influenced by the circumstances of our birth and upbringing, and that it is often our inherited culture and religious traditions that give our lives meaning. However, in a secular worldview, we are not bound by prior commitments to others. We find ourselves obligated to others only in instances in which we voluntarily choose to associate with a particular group. In the neo-Enlightenment view, we are self-sufficient and unencumbered. Heroes and saints *choose* to be heroic and saintly, just as other persons choose how they will conduct themselves. This view allows for the possibility that heroes and saints themselves may come to *regard* their heroic and saintly conduct as profoundly unchosen, morally required in the strictest sense. However, in the end, the normative model to which Urmson subscribes dictates that the perception of heroes and saints will likely oppose what is, in actuality, the fact of the matter, namely, that heroic and saintly acts are performed above and beyond the call of duty. Unqualified supererogation makes no exceptions in this regard.

A theory of supererogation in its "qualified" form accommodates the counterintuitive notion that heroic and saintly acts may legitimately be regarded as required in some cases. Defenders of the traditional view criticize qualified supererogationism on the grounds that it calls into question the supposition of the universality of moral requirement and, by implication, the foundation upon which duty-based ethics traditionally rests. Thus, if one is eventually to endorse qualified supererogationism, the first issue that must be addressed pertains to the tenability of the deontic approach to duty and supererogation assumed in the standard view. If the standard account, which already has the advantage of being intuitively appealing, withstands critical examination, then there will be no need to postulate an alternative hypothesis that rivals it.

NOTES

1. J. O. Urmson, "Saints and Heroes," *Essays in Moral Philosophy*. ed. A. I. Melden (Seattle: University of Washington Press, 1958), 198–216.
2. Ibid., 210.
3. Alasdair MacIntyre, *After Virtue*, 2d ed. (Notre Dame: University of Notre

Dame Press, 1982), 58; Charles Taylor, *Sources of the Self: The Making of the Modern Identity* (Cambridge: Harvard University Press, 1989), 34ff. While MacIntyre and Taylor are two of the most formidable critics of the Enlightenment project, their insights were actually preceded by, and to a degree form a response to, two earlier thinkers who attacked modern moral philosophy for remaining unnaturally divorced from human psychology, namely, Elizabeth Anscombe and Iris Murdoch. See G. E. M. Anscombe, "Modern Moral Philosophy," *Philosophy* 33 (1958), 1–2; and Iris Murdoch, *The Sovereignty of Good* (London: Routledge and Kegan Paul, 1970), 1.

4. MacIntyre, *After Virtue*, 66ff.

5. Ibid., 67.

6. In spite of all of the attention that has been given over the last couple of decades to the neo-Aristotelian alternative advocated by MacIntyre, Taylor, and other critics of the Enlightenment project, the dominant model for understanding what is morally required of us in society still remains based on a neo-Enlightenment approach to ethics. Indeed, our whole legal system reflects a morality of rules, proscriptions, and procedures. For more on this connection between rules in normative ethics and our construction of the law in society, see Frederick Carney's discussion of positive morality in "The Role of Rules in Law and Morality," *Southwestern Law Journal* 23 (1969): 438–53.

7. "Commonsense morality" is not Urmson's term, but one whose use became prevalent following the publication of "Saints and Heroes." The term itself predates the essay and was given its first explication by Henry Sidgwick. See Sidgwick, *The Methods of Ethics*, 7th ed. (Chicago: The University of Chicago Press, 1962), 214–15.

8. By "equal-regard" I mean, following Gene Outka, that concern for the neighbor is both independent of any forms of favoritism (i.e., equal-regard is concern for the neighbor *as such*, and not any particular neighbor) and unalterable (i.e., equal-regard is irreducibly valuable, present prior to the neighbor's doing anything in particular that makes him or her worthy). In this sense, the "other" is regarded generically; he or she is anyone and everyone impacted by an agent's actions. "Other-regard" is essentially equal-regard toward the other and does not include the self. See Gene Outka, *Agape: An Ethical Analysis* (New Haven: Yale University Press, 1972), 9–12.

9. It was not until Urmson's essay in 1958 that the term "supererogation" came to be widely discussed in other than theological contexts, and throughout I shall refer to the concept in its contemporary usage. The term actually dates back to the Vulgate, where it appears in the parable of the Good Samaritan (Luke 10:30–35). After compensating the innkeeper for the costs of bringing the robbed and wounded man to recovery, the Samaritan tells the innkeeper: "[T]ake care of him; and when I come back, I will repay thee whatsoever thou shalt spend over and above (*quodcumque supererogaveris*)." In the Middle Ages, works of supererogation commonly referred to "evangelical counsels," which, in contrast to religious commandments, were considered by the Catholic Church to be meritorious nonrequired acts. The church's system of indulgences was based on the notion of a "treasury of good works" built by saintly people whose supererogatory

deeds were thought to compensate for the wrongdoing of others. Reformers, notably Martin Luther and John Calvin, vociferously attacked the idea that salvation could be bought through the sale of indulgences, and furthermore asked how any human being could hope to do more than God required of him or her. For more on the Protestant critique of the church's abuse of indulgences and its relation to the concept of supererogation, as well as the Roman Catholic response to this critique, see David Heyd, *Supererogation* (Cambridge: Cambridge University Press, 1982), 16ff. For a more thorough discussion of the etymology and history of supererogation and of how the theological debate over the concept serves as a model for the parallel discussion in secular ethics, see Heyd, "Obligation and Supererogation," *Encyclopedia of Bioethics*, vol. 4 (New York: Macmillan, 1995), 1833–38; and Gregory Mellema, *Beyond the Call of Duty: Supererogation, Obligation, and Offence* (New York: State University of New York Press, 1991), 1–12.

10. For an involved discussion of the many versions of antisupererogationism, see Mellema, *Beyond the Call of Duty*, chapters 3 (on theistic objections to supererogation) and 4 (on Kantian and utilitarian objections to supererogation). In my discussion I assume that the term "antisupererogationists" characteristically refers to those who do not recognize morally good acts that are not also morally required. In denying the existence of *moral options*, they espouse a much more stringent view of moral duty than that assumed in the supererogationist view. A weaker version of antisupererogation recognizes the existence of permissible acts but insists that such acts can never be considered *praiseworthy*. It is conceivable that this version of antisupererogationism is *less* morally stringent than supererogationism, as it entails an expansion, rather than a contraction, of the realm of the permissible. I do not address this version of antisupererogationism in this book. Finally, according to a stronger version of antisupererogationism than the first one I mentioned, there are no permissible actions at all: every act, no matter how small, has some overall consequence which will be negative or positive, and we are required always to act in such a way as to bring about the most positive results. Since I believe that there are some trivial actions whose performance has no moral consequences, I am inclined to dismiss the stronger version of antisupererogationism as untenable. The interesting issue that surrounds the supererogation versus antisupererogation debate in any case centers on whether there can be morally good actions that are not at the same time morally required. For this reason, when I refer to antisupererogationism I am referring to the first version described above, which denies the existence of moral options.

11. The concept of supererogation allows for the permissibility of some harms (e.g., supererogatory forbearances) in addition to allowing for the failure to help. Because I am interested in the saintly and the heroic, I am led to emphasize the relationship between supererogation and positive duty. For an example of one who considers both instances of supererogation equally, see Roderick Chisholm, "Supererogation and Offence: A Conceptual Scheme for Ethics," *Ratio* 5 (1963): 1–14.

12. Susan Wolf, for example, argues in her well-known essay "Moral Saints" that we should not endeavor to live as altruistic a life as possible on the grounds that to do so would be humanly inappropriate. Wolf maintains that by disposing ourselves to act self-sacrificially, we tend to underestimate our own self-worth.

According to Wolf, the category of supererogation is thus necessary in order to give the self room to pursue its own interests more easily. See Susan Wolf, "Moral Saints," *Journal of Philosophy* 79, no. 8 (1982): 433, 439. At times Wolf even speaks as though "morality" itself (i.e., moral duty) is not always what should be considered overriding in determining one's conduct (426–27). Jean Hampton and William Galston also object to the notion that humans ought to prioritize selfless, supererogatory behavior, although for them such objections are explicitly justified on moral grounds. See Jean Hampton, "Selflessness and the Loss of Self," in *Altruism*, ed. Ellen Frankel Paul, Fred D. Miller, Jr., and Jeffrey Paul (Cambridge: Cambridge University Press, 1993), 135–65; and William A. Galston, "Cosmopolitan Altruism," in Paul, Miller, and Paul, eds., *Altruism*, 118–34.

13. Heyd, *Supererogation*, 11. While Heyd's is the only book devoted to Urmson's thesis, numerous articles appeared after Urmson published "Saints and Heroes." Millard Schumaker provides an excellent bibliography of these in his monograph *Supererogation: An Analysis and Bibliography* (Edmonton: St. Stephen's College, 1977), 45ff.

14. Heyd, *Supererogation*, 173. Heyd calls this right "autonomy," which is obviously a different sense of the term than that employed, for example, by Kant.

15. Ibid., 175–76.

16. According to Heyd, the presence or absence of virtue in a particular agent might affect our perception of how morally praiseworthy that agent is, but it does not affect that agent's *moral standing*, which depends only on the avoidance of wrongdoing. This means that the self-sacrificing agent who on occasion fails to do what is minimally morally required is more blameworthy than the person who never falls below the moral minimum, but never rises above it either.

17. Gregory Trianosky is one notable exception. Trianosky, who does acknowledge the category of supererogation, maintains that we are vice-ridden, and therefore may even be deficient in terms of our character, if we consistently refrain from performing supererogatory acts. See Trianosky, "Supererogation, Wrongdoing, and Vice: On the Autonomy of the Ethics of Virtue," *Journal of Philosophy* 83 (1986): 26–29. Gregory Mellema has produced three short articles that explore, though do not explicitly argue for, Trianosky's idea that there are grounds for morally blaming people who indifferently exempt themselves from having to perform nonrequired praiseworthy acts. See Mellema, "Must We Do the Best We Can?" *Philosophy Today* 36 (1992): 39–43; "Supererogation, Blame, and the Limits of Obligation," *Philosophia* 24 (1994): 171–82; and "Is It Bad to Omit an Act of Supererogation?" *Journal of Philosophical Research* 21 (1996): 405–16.

18. Heroes and saints, as Urmson tells us, are not the only examples of supererogatory agents; they are just the most conspicuous ones (Urmson, "Saints and Heroes," 205). Heyd devotes a full chapter of *Supererogation* to distinguishing among the paradigm cases of supererogation, which include saintliness and heroism, beneficence, favors, volunteering, supererogatory forbearances (from permissible harms), and forgiveness and mercy. These cases range in terms of costliness from very onerous to mildly taxing. Since I am most interested in the supererogationist's arguments for establishing the justifying grounds for the existence of supererogation and the optionality of supposed supererogatory acts,

I restrict my emphasis to the most extreme instances of supererogation, those which entail the greatest cost to the giver and the greatest benefit to the receiver. Thus, in this book I focus primarily on heroic and saintly conduct rather than on the other paradigmatic forms of supererogation. For a discussion of the other forms of supererogation, see chapter 7 of Heyd's book, in which the author presents his full taxonomy of the category.

19. I follow Linda Zagzebski in her characterization of deontic moral theories as ones that see right action as determined independently of goodness of character. They can be contrasted to "aretaic" moral theories, in which right action is determined in terms of moral character. In the former, a moral duty is defined as an imperative to follow universal rules of conduct (which does not presuppose an agent's virtuous character), while in the latter duty is what a person who is virtuous, and who possesses insight into a particular situation that a virtuous person would have, would feel morally compelled to do in like circumstances. See Linda Trinkaus Zagzebski, *Virtues of the Mind: An Inquiry into the Nature of Virtue and the Ethical Foundations of Knowledge* (Cambridge: Cambridge University Press, 1996), 233–35.

20. I do not mean to imply that according to Urmson duties strike agents in the same manner. Depending on particular agents' habits, proclivities, and weaknesses, basic moral requirements will be easier for some to follow than for others. Kleptomaniacs will have a particularly hard time obeying the duty not to steal. However, there is an assumption in the standard view that the level of moral demandingness to which we are subjected by moral requirements remains constant among agents insofar as such requirements are measured against an independent evaluation of the actions to which they correspond. Giving ten percent of one's income to charity is objectively less onerous than giving twenty percent. Refraining from harming another tends to be less onerous than standing in harm's way to help another. Depending on where one draws the line, duty may be thought to apply universally to the former, while the latter may be considered to be above and beyond.

21. Heyd makes the important point that supererogation and duty exist in a logical relation to one another. This relationship is characterized by the feature of "correlativity." Since duty and supererogation are correlative, acts of supererogation derive their special value from being more than duty requires (i.e., they are of the same kind of altruistic quality as duty, but are "more" in terms of degree and costliness). If it is true that acts of supererogation are conceptually dependent on the idea of moral obligation, then any serious attempt to characterize supererogation must be preceded by a discussion of duty. See Heyd, *Supererogation*, 5.

22. The notion of "duty" has a long history in moral philosophy. The most prevalent understanding of "duty" is probably still Kant's ideal of moral self-governance, which was a reaction to the previous conception of duty as obedience to an external law. In his volume, *The Invention of Autonomy*, J. B. Schneewind offers a comprehensive and historically grounded treatment of the evolution of the concept of duty as self-governance throughout Western intellectual thought. The volume is particularly useful insofar as it clarifies the relationship of Kant to his predecessors, many of whom receive unprecedented acknowledgment from the

author. Schneewind reminds us of the mistake in looking at "duty" in a mono-lithic, historically insensitive fashion. See Schneewind, *The Invention of Autonomy: A History of Modern Moral Philosophy* (Cambridge: Cambridge University Press, 1998), esp. 78ff. and 513ff.

23. On this particular distinction between "good" and "ought," see R. M. Hare, *Freedom and Reason* (Oxford: Oxford University Press, 1963), 153.

24. Schumaker, *Supererogation*, 12.

25. Thus, it is fair to say that supererogation exceeds what it is morally neces-sary to do and that the failure to perform works of supererogation does not result in the violation of others' rights. This much holds true for any view of supereroga-tion. However, it behooves us to notice what is *not* implied by this understand-ing: for example, that "supererogation" remains a constant that carries the same meaning from agent to agent and throughout a particular agent's life. Claims like this one are assumptions about the notion of supererogation, not features intrin-sic to the concept itself.

26. Urmson, "Saints and Heroes," 198.

27. Ibid., 210.

28. Rawls similarly contrasts a "morality of right and justice" to a "morality of the love of mankind" in which only the latter is supererogatory. John Rawls, *A Theory of Justice* (Cambridge: The Belknap Press of Harvard University Press, 1971), 478.

29. Urmson, "Saints and Heroes," 212.

30. See Matthew 5:39–44; 6:14; 25: 37–38.

31. Heyd, *Supererogation*, 174.

32. See especially David Gauthier, *Morals by Agreement* (Oxford: Oxford Uni-versity Press, 1986).

33. By focusing on rules, it can be said that Urmson restricts his attention to "positive morality," that is, morality as it actually functions in society, as opposed to a morality of ideals, or "private morality." Rules are proper to the former; they are universal guidelines to which we are all morally required to assent. This dis-tinction between positive and private morality is discussed and criticized by Car-ney in "The Role of Rules in Law and Morality," 438–53. Specifically, Carney takes Urmson (and moral and legal theorist H. L. A. Hart) to task for assuming that in order for a moral standard to qualify as a rule, it must be acknowledged by soci-ety as a whole, rather than by a group within a society, or only by an individual person (446). He then expands the concept of a moral rule to include, on case-specific occasions, the saintly and the heroic.

34. Urmson, "Saints and Heroes," 204.

35. Ibid., 213.

36. Ibid., 212.

37. See Schumaker, *Supererogation*, 13; and Loren E. Lomasky, "Justice to Char-ity," *Social Philosophy and Policy* 12, no. 2 (summer 1995): 32–33. As Lomasky explains, the "jurisprudential paradigm" is a morality modeled on law, "such that its subject matter is taken to be individuals' rights and duties," its declarations per-taining only to what must be done and what must not be done rather than how one ought to live one's life within the zone of permission (33).

38. Lomasky, "Justice to Charity," 43.

39. Urmson, "Saints and Heroes," 211.

40. Ibid., 205.

41. John E. Hare, *The Moral Gap: Kantian Ethics, Human Limits, and God's Assistance* (Oxford: Clarendon Press, 1996), 113.

42. Ibid., 113–14.

43. Stanley Hauerwas and John Yoder are two Christian thinkers who take this view even further. Both assert that the religious practitioner should remove him or herself, when possible, from the messiness of the real world in order to focus better on the kingdom beyond. See, for example, Stanley Hauerwas, *Character and the Christian Life* (San Antonio: Trinity University Press, 1975); Hauerwas, *Against the Nations: War and Survival in a Liberal Society* (Minneapolis: Winston Press, 1985); John Howard Yoder, *The Politics of Jesus* (Grand Rapids, Mich.: Eerdmans, 1972); and Yoder, *The Priestly Kingdom: Social Ethics as Gospel* (Notre Dame: University of Notre Dame Press, 1984).

44. Urmson, "Saints and Heroes," 200–201. In Urmson's analysis, both heroes and saints who merely fulfill their role duty when performing their heroic and saintly deeds *and* heroes and saints par excellence (who go beyond even their role duty) exceed what we reasonably could expect of anyone within the confines of ordinary morality. In this broader sense, both kinds of heroes and saints can be said to be supererogating. From this point forward when I refer to Urmson's understanding of heroes and saints, I will assume that they are portrayed as going above and beyond the call of duty.

Urmson also notes that heroes and saints exhibit their heroic and saintly traits in one of two ways, either through exercising abnormal self-control or effortlessly. This distinction subsequently has been raised by Susan Wolf in connection with saints. Wolf calls saints who self-sacrifice by virtue of self-control "rational saints" and saints who act effortlessly "loving saints." She claims that each possesses various kinds of character flaws. Rational saints act out a kind of "pathological fear of damnation," or extreme form of self-loathing that precludes them from enjoying life, while loving saints are missing that "piece of perceptual machinery" that renders them blind to all the pleasures the world has to offer (Wolf, "Moral Saints," 424). Both kinds of saints, Wolf claims, are "dull-witted or humorless or bland" (421). Wolf has been criticized for this characterization of saints. See especially Robert Adams, "Saints," *Journal of Philosophy* 81 (1984): 392–401.

45. Urmson, "Saints and Heroes," 203–4.

46. Ibid., 200–201.

47. Ibid., 203.

48. Ibid., 204.

49. Ibid., 203 (emphasis mine).

50. Gene Outka uses the term "agent stringency" to refer to the phenomenon in which the supererogatory agent goes the second mile with respect to acts done above and beyond the call of duty with the same urgency that he or she goes the first mile in respect to duties. See Outka, *Agape*, 293–94. While Urmson grants that heroes and saints can make self-imposed commitments and that these can become binding in the sense that a promise to oneself is, such commitments are binding only in a secondary way. The *content* of these presumably

costly commitments, Urmson would maintain, retains its supererogatory status, regardless of how heroes and saints come to regard it.

51. Urmson, "Saints and Heroes," 204.

52. David L. Norton, "Moral Minimalism and the Development of Moral Character," in *Midwest Studies in Philosophy, Volume XIII—Ethical Theory: Character and Virtue*, ed. Peter A. French, Theodore Uehling, Jr., and Howard K. Wettstein (Notre Dame: University of Notre Dame Press, 1988), 191.

53. Consider saints who neglect their family, friends, and community to go out into the world and "heal." We may wish to raise questions about their brazen dismissal of the importance of special relations to morality in general. Still another problem that arises is how to be sure that those who propose to follow a saintly course of action are reasonably likely to be successful in this endeavor, a judgment that becomes very important when we consider that their failing potentially entails risking or even costing them their own lives. This becomes an issue even with respect to proposed altruistic sacrifices that are merely heroic. Consider the example of the potential organ donor, who wishes to give her kidney to a recipient who would not die if he did not receive the transplant, and who, due to old age and failing health, might not even benefit from the operation. Or consider those who engage in low-probability rescue attempts. In both of these cases the supposed supererogatory agent arguably engages in foolish, perhaps morally prohibited behavior. For more on the distinction between supererogation and the foolhardy, see Curtis Barry, "The Supererogatory, the Foolish, and the Morally Required," *Journal of Value Inquiry* 15 (1981): 311–18. On the importance of cost-benefit analysis for determining whether an act ought to be considered required, supererogatory, or foolhardy, see David Little, "The Law of Supererogation," in *The Love Commandments: Essays in Christian Ethics and Moral Philosophy*, ed. Edmund N. Santurri and William Werpehowski (Washington, D.C.: Georgetown University Press, 1992), 157–81.

54. As I will discuss in the next chapter, A. I. Melden argues for an even stronger version of the "dichotomy" thesis in the case of saints. Saints, argues Melden, are saints of their respective traditions only by virtue of the extent to which they have been touched by God, which is exclusively a matter of grace. There is absolutely nothing *we* can do to try to be like them. According to Melden, it is *by definition* that saints have different obligations than the rest of us. It is as if they are described as the "angels" around whom Urmson warns us morality should not be built. See A. I. Melden, "Saints and Supererogation," *Philosophy and Life: Essays on John Wisdom*, ed. Ilham Dilman (The Hague: Martinus Nijhoff Publishers, 1984), 65–70.

55. Urmson, "Saints and Heroes," 204.

56. See Thomas Nagel, *The View from Nowhere* (Oxford: Oxford University Press, 1986), 202–4.; Hare, *Freedom and Reason*, 32; W. D. Hudson, *Modern Moral Philosophy* (Garden City, N.Y.: Doubleday & Co., 1970), 221; and Rawls, *A Theory of Justice*, 439.

57. We may consider what Nagel has to say on this point. He writes: "When we regard people objectively and think about how they should live, their motivational complexity is a consideration.... [A]t some threshold, hard to define, we will

conclude that it is unreasonable to expect people in general to sacrifice themselves and those to whom they have close personal ties to the general good. The hard question is whether this understanding—this condition of 'reasonableness'—will show itself in a modification of moral requirements, or merely in acceptance of the fact that most of us are miserable sinners, which is probably true in any case" (Nagel, *The View from Nowhere*, 202). Ought we to conform our behavior, notwithstanding our likely sinful nature, to the standards of moral requirement, or ought we to devise our standards of moral requirement according to how we naturally are? While we vary in terms of the degree to which we are sinful (or good), Nagel concludes, "impartial morality," wherever we set the bar for moral requirement, does not vary. Thus, rather than calling into question the impartial character of morality in an attempt to account for individual motives and values, which vary from agent to agent, "the moral standpoint should try to recognize and explain its own limits" (203).

58. Heyd, *Supererogation*, 115.

59. Ibid., 115.

60. Ibid., 121.

61. Ibid. Heyd illustrates the confusion he thinks many moral philosophers have between imperfect duties and works of supererogation in the following manner. He takes "imperfect duties" to be those morally required acts that can be fulfilled in a variety of ways, which, for the sake of argument, we may assume include all positive duties. The fulfillment of imperfect duties is just as *necessary* as that of perfect duties, but their *means* of fulfillment is flexible. The argument is that "while an imperfect duty to perform an act-type A implies that it is a perfect duty to do any act-token 'a' that would be tantamount to fulfilling A, a supererogatory act-type B does not mean that it is our duty to perform *any* act-token of B" (121–22). In other words, while imperfect duties *would be* perfect duties if there were not problems of agency (e.g., lack of opportunity, lack of at-present resources, lack of awareness) that precluded their immediate and definite fulfillment, under no circumstances could supererogatory actions be considered duties. Not all supererogationists agree with Heyd on this point. Millard Schumaker, for example, contends that the boundary between imperfect duty and supererogation is not so much a line as it is a common ground. He writes, "the discharge of some imperfect duties is virtually indistinguishable from the doing of some, usually minor, acts of supererogation" (Schumaker, *Supererogation*, 38).

62. Heyd, "Obligation and Supererogation," 1835.

63. Ibid.

64. Heyd discusses this version of "qualified supererogationism" on pages 125–28 of *Supererogation*. He focuses especially on Roderick Chisholm, who introduces the category of "offence"—or "permissive ill-doings"—in order to clarify the separation between value (goodness or badness) and deontic status (permissibility). See Chisholm, "Supererogation and Offence," 2–4. Chisholm contends that just as some positive acts are not required but praiseworthy, some harms are not prohibited although their performance is considered offensive. If this is so, then an act of supererogation could be construed as an agent's decision not to perform an offensive act. I. L. Humberstone attempts to make the further argument

that an act of offense, while not blameworthy in the deontic sense that its performance constitutes a violation of duty, is still blameworthy in some weaker
sense. See Humberstone, "Logic for Saints and Heroes," *Ratio* 16 (1974): 103–14.

65. Heyd, *Supererogation*, 29–130. For example, Nagel argues that "supererogatory virtue is adherence to the claims of impersonal morality prior to their
modification to accommodate the normal limitations of human nature. This
modification takes the form of a relaxation of these requirements through toler-
ance, as it were, rather than the discovery of new moral reasons that outweigh the
original impersonal ones." See Nagel, *The View from Nowhere*, 204.

66. Heyd, *Supererogation*, 130.

67. See ibid., 33–34, 48, 70, 74, 129–130. Heyd considers the positions of several
classical figures whom he considers to be "weak" (i.e., "qualified") supererogationists. While I do not attempt to scrutinize the historical accuracy of Heyd's
interpretation of these figures here, brief mention of a few of them is instructive.
For example, Heyd discusses the view of Thomas Aquinas, who argues that while
the commandments apply to everyone, the counsels are directed (and by being
directed are considered morally required) to the few people who have committed themselves to following a life of perfection. See Thomas Aquinas, *Summa Theologica*, I.II, Question 108; II.II, Question 184, trans. Jordan Aumann O.P. (New
York: MacGraw-Hill Book Co., 1947–48). Additionally, Heyd reads Henry Sidgwick as making a distinction between what a person ought to do if he wishes to
be a fully virtuous person, and what people are in all circumstances justified in
blaming him for not doing. See Sidgwick, *The Methods of Ethics*, 32ff. Finally, Heyd
construes Kant as a qualified supererogationist by focusing on his distinction
between external, "juridical," duties and internal duties of virtue that are concerned with general ends rather than specific actions. Kantian duties of virtue,
writes Heyd, "can be described as those that go beyond institutional or contractarian contexts (such as doing one's professional duty, or promise-keeping, truth-
telling, etc.)," and as such are morally compulsory for ordinary moral agents in
a weaker sense than "essential" duties of minimal moral requirement (Heyd,
Supererogation, 57).

68. Ibid., 143.

69. Ibid., 99–106.

70. Rawls, *A Theory of Justice*, 115, discussed by Heyd in *Supererogation*, 119.

71. Rawls, *A Theory of Justice*, 114ff., 337.

72. Ibid., 338.

73. Samuel Scheffler, *Human Morality* (Oxford: Oxford University Press, 1992),
122.

74. Rawls, *A Theory of Justice*, 439. See also Henry Sidgwick, who states that the
duty of beneficence is "the positive duty to render, when occasion offers, such
services as either require no sacrifice on our part or at least very much less in
importance than the service rendered" (Sidgwick, *The Methods of Ethics*, 253).
Rawls and Sidgwick still advocate a more demanding standard of moral requirement than that advocated by Heyd, who maintains that even small favors, which
entail some cost to the self, are supererogatory. For this reason, it would perhaps
be most accurate to call Rawls and Sidgwick's view *moderate* rather than *minimal*.

For a criticism of Sidgwick's method of distinguishing acts of duty from acts of supererogation, see Peter Singer, "Famine, Affluence, and Morality," in *World Hunger and Morality*, 2d ed., ed. William Aiken and Hugh LaFollette (Upper Saddle River, N.J.: Prentice Hall, 1996), 26–38. For a careful explication of the constraints upon what one can be required to sacrifice, see John P. Reeder, Jr., "Beneficence, Supererogation, and Role Duty," in *Beneficence and Health Care*, ed. Earl Shelp (Dordrecht, Holland: D. Reidel, 1982), 83–108. Like Rawls, Reeder acknowledges a "reasonable" cut-off point that sets duty apart from supererogation, but his standard for this cut-off point is higher than Rawls's. Reeder contends that we are required to sacrifice our welfare up to the point of, but not beyond, a loss equivalent to what we give (87). On this view we are required to help others up to the point of "no comparable cost" to ourselves (92–96). Reeder contends that we justifiably blame agents who withhold aid where the cost to the giver is outweighed by the gain of the recipient.

75. Scheffler, *Human Morality*, 125.

76. Ibid. Scheffler quotes Nagel, *The View from Nowhere*, 125.

77. Schumaker, *Supererogation*, 34.

78. "Care" ethicists such as Carol Gilligan follow Schumaker's way of separating love and justice, or at least talking about them as if they are distinct moral impulses. See Carol Gilligan, "Moral Orientation and Moral Development," in *Women and Moral Theory*, ed. Eva Feder Kittay and Diana T. Meyers (Savage, Md.: Rowman and Littlefield Publishers, 1987), 19–33.

79. Heyd, *Supererogation*, 173.

80. Contrary to those moral philosophers, such as Joseph Raz, who assume that an "agent has reason to maximize human welfare, assigning equal weight to the interests of every human being including himself," and pursuing his own interests as an exception to the rule, Heyd maintains that we have reason only to maximize our own welfare, which is an end that is itself to be sacrificed in exceptional cases. The statement is made by Raz, quoted by Heyd in *Supererogation*, 169. See Joseph Raz, "Permissions and Supererogation," *American Philosophical Quarterly* 12 (1975): 167.

81. Heyd, *Supererogation*, 173–74 (emphasis Heyd's). See J. J. C. Smart and Bernard Williams, *Utilitarianism: For and Against* (Cambridge: Cambridge University Press, 1973), 110.

82. Heyd, *Supererogation*, 174.

83. Ibid.

84. Ibid.

85. Ibid., 175.

86. Paul Tillich, quoted by Schumaker, *Supererogation*, 39. See Paul Tillich, *Love, Power, and Justice* (New York: Oxford University Press, 1960), 63–65.

87. Paul Tillich, *Morality and Beyond* (New York: Harper and Row, 1995), 21–23. Schumaker also alludes to these passages in his *Supererogation*, 39–40.

88. Heyd, *Supererogation*, 166.

89. Ibid., 175.

90. The philosopher Shelly Kagan argues that this assumption is contestable in his article criticizing Heyd. See Kagan, "Does Consequentialism Demand Too

Much? Recent Work on the Limits of Obligation," *Philosophy and Public Affairs* 13 (summer 1984): 244.

91. Heyd, *Supererogation*, 175.

92. Schumaker, *Supererogation*, 43.

93. Heyd, *Supererogation*, 177.

94. Judith Jarvis Thomson seems to echo this distinction in her famous article "A Defense of Abortion," in which she associates universal, minimal morality with "minimally decent samaritanship" and the non-universal morality of self-sacrifice with varying degrees of "good samaritanship." See Thomson, "A Defense of Abortion," in *The Problem of Abortion*, 2d ed., ed. Joel Feinberg (Belmont, Calif.: Wadsworth Publishing, 1984), 184.

95. Throughout *Supererogation*, Heyd speaks of altruism that is required by duty as if it is "coerced" by morality and is therefore not voluntary. This vocabulary is confusing because it implies that only acts of supererogation are motivated by an agent's desire and that, conversely, actions motivated by duty can never be chosen freely. Kant, for one, would strongly disagree: even though good works are required by the morality of duty, they can still be performed out of genuine concern for the neighbor. Additionally, Kant would say that those bound by duty are still in a very important sense free. We are free *because* of our self-legislating, autonomous nature. Heyd is nevertheless right to worry that if an altruistic deed is considered obligatory, the recipient has no way of knowing whether it is performed because it is required, or because it is what an agent would have wanted to do in any case.

96. Heyd, *Supererogation*, 174.

97. Ibid.

CHAPTER 2

The Standard View under Critical Scrutiny

I began this book by asking the basic question "How much should be morally expected of normal, ordinary persons, like ourselves?" The answer provided by the standard view is straightforward and intuitively appealing. We ought to act so as not to violate those basic rights and liberties without which, as Hobbes warned, society would become chaotic and uncivil. In terms of positive duty, we ought to do what is minimally required for society to provide for those basic goods that all need or would want to enjoy. For example, we ought to pay taxes in order to support an infrastructure that provides for key public services such as clean water and effective waste disposal. Beyond this level of burden, duty qua duty gives way to supererogation. We can *individually* bind ourselves to do more, as, for instance when we consent to assume specific role duties or make special promises to ourselves. Generally speaking, however, onerous self-sacrifice is morally praiseworthy but remains optional. The standard view is attractive because it mirrors our intuition that as mortals we have a limited capacity with which to transcend our selfish impulses. The existence of a category of supererogation beyond duty allows us to maintain a sense of righteousness that does not, at the same time, permit morality to intrude too severely into our lives. In the standard view, society compels us to act morally to the extent that it is already in our best interests to do so. The benefits we accrue by imposing minimal to modest constraints on self-interest outweigh the costs we would otherwise collectively incur by remaining free to act in an unrestrained fashion.

The standard view is also flexible enough to allow for the possibility that for some extraordinarily virtuous persons, cost-benefit analysis does not enter into the moral decision-making process at all. Heroes and saints, for example, do not stop to consider whether they are doing their duty or going above and beyond when performing their heroic and saintly deeds.

Quite simply, they see someone in need, and are moved to perform the appropriate loving deed. A heroic or saintly way of acting, though noble, is also one, it is supposed, of which the majority of people are not realistically capable. A major selling point of the standard view is its frank recognition of the contrast between heroes and saints on the one hand, and ordinary people on the other. By characterizing heroes and saints as extraordinarily courageous and selfless, rather than as predominantly self-interested, like the rest of us, Urmson constructs ethics in a fashion that aspires to be psychologically honest. Duty becomes the normative glue that holds society together rather than an idealistic construction imposed from the outside. Likewise, in forming a notion of other-regard that insists on options beyond duty, Heyd keeps morality a fundamentally human enterprise, intended to serve but not subsume the individual in his or her quest for fulfillment.

There are, nonetheless, issues to be raised with Urmson's characterization of heroes and saints and the strong version of supererogationism to which it corresponds. These all relate to the idea that there exist objective, universal criteria for determining the boundary that separates duty from supererogation. Such criticisms of the standard view lead us to speculate about the tenability of "qualified supererogationism," the idea that the supererogatory is ultimately reducible to the obligatory on some level. In this chapter, I take a close look at these criticisms, subsequently contrasting the view of moral obligation embraced in the standard view to a different one that can be discerned from within traditional Jewish and Christian sources.

Evaluating Urmson's Treatment of Heroes and Saints

My examination of Urmson's portrayal of heroes and saints centers around four key assumptions inherent in his approach: (1) *Universalism.* Urmson posits the existence of supposedly objective criteria for marking a permanent boundary between duty and supererogation, yet he sets this standard at an empirically arbitrary level, namely, one that is "fulfillable," a standard that would seem to vary among agents. (2) *Characterization of the hero or saint's "ought."* Urmson draws a stark contrast between the deontic sphere and the evaluative sphere, between what we *ought* to do and what we commit ourselves to doing because of what we *value.* In following this approach, he fails to appreciate the circumstances under which actions that are considered morally good or beneficial can become morally prescriptive for especially virtuous agents. (3) *Dismissal of the testimony of supererogatory agents themselves.* Urmson construes heroes and saints as persons who, owing to their heroic and saintly character, are prone to overestimate what they are morally required to do for their beneficiaries.

Specifically, he thinks that heroes and saints erroneously characterize their behavior as obligatory rather than supererogatory. As such, his view of heroes and saints does not conform with their own self-image. (4) *Portrayal of the supererogatory agent as the extraordinary "other."* Urmson describes heroes and saints in the abstract, philosophically, without any appreciation given to their concrete historical context. This leads him to dichotomize human beings into the unknowable, extraordinary "other" and the familiar, ordinary agent. This approach, which assumes the fixity of human nature, does not sufficiently take into account the humanity of heroes and saints; conversely, it does not allow for the potential for heroes and saints to serve as guides to the way we morally conduct ourselves.

1. *Universalism.* Urmson assumes that beyond the heterogeneous characteristics that distinguish everyone from one another, human beings are certain *kinds* of beings. We have a discernible, uniform human nature. It is human nature that determines what kinds of rules we ought to obey in society and human nature that excuses us from having to obey a would-be rule that is judged too onerous to be required of everyone. The purpose of morality is to make a unity out of difference, to assimilate the boundless variety of desires and preferences possessed by individuals into a *moral community.*[1] The moral community in this sense consists of moral subjects, or moral agents stripped of their differences. While there are various debates over what constitutes moral subjectivity, what is common to all potential conceptions, in the standard view, is their *thinness.*[2] A conception of moral subjectivity represents an abstraction of those features of personhood deemed to be significant to our human existence. Such features of personhood can be described as truths about human nature, stated as ideals of a metaphysical nature, or as the result of an inevitable, empirical, pragmatic consensus about what rules we ought uniformly to adopt for social life.[3] However various the justifications are for establishing the particular features of personhood, the features themselves, and the moral norms to which they correspond, are presumed to be stable, enduring, and present in all cultures and societies.

Urmson's conception of duty is thus universalist in a strong sense. Because of human nature, the duties to which human beings are subject are universally applicable (duties are owed to all by all) *and* universally justifiable (all agents, qua agents, are subject to such duties for the same reasons). Beyond these minimal norms of conduct for which everyone ought to be held equally responsible, Urmson also contends that no one is morally compelled to live up to a *more* demanding standard of other-regard. In other words, duty is bounded at two ends: there is both a universal standard that separates the permissible and morally neutral from the morally required *and* a universal standard that separates the morally required from the supererogatory. Much of the recent debate between universalism and particularism in the literature has centered on the issue of whether there can be said to be *any* universal norms of conduct.[4] Urmson's contention that there is an objective standard for determining where duty ends and supererogation begins assumes that a prior debate, which addresses the existence of universal minimal norms of conduct, has already been settled in favor of the universalists. The arguments in favor of and against the existence of these cross-cultural "moral minimums" abound. What I wish to point out here is that even if we do assume their existence, it does not necessarily follow that they are commensurate with "duty" as such, for it is possible that duty could *extend beyond* minimal moral requirement.

The problem with Urmson's approach to characterizing "duty" is thus not that it assumes that there exists a moral minimum below which we cannot fall, but that it also affirms that the line that separates duty from supererogation is a constant that does not vary from agent to agent.[5] Urmson claims that the territory of duty is not diverse in *any* respect. It is as if there is a formula applicable to all individuals that explains the conditions under which they are bound by moral compulsion and the conditions under which they are absolved from moral compulsion because of "undue burden."[6] According to Urmson, supererogation consists of anything that entails self-sacrifice at a level beyond the established limits of what the majority of persons are capable. But why should the criteria for deciding which altruistic actions can be considered morally required depend on what the majority is likely to be capable of? What we regard as "undue burden," which is the measure for what we assess to be "reasonably" required of us, is often inherited and can be deeply affected by the communities in which we find ourselves. Urmson offers an account of universal moral requirement that categorizes actions into "duty" and "beyond duty" without examining the particular moral communities in which people function. *How* groups of persons or communities come to acquire their respective levels of virtue is a secondary, independent issue that arises from the question of what duty is.

In place of Urmson's universalist approach to defining duty, Lawrence Blum argues for a "limited community relativism" according to which whole societies, due to the level of virtue that they collectively exhibit, experience their burdens—and thus perceive their duty—differently.[7] In limited community relativism, according to Blum, "we can stand outside two communities and say that one exhibits (in some important regard) a higher degree of virtue than another, and although this virtue is tied to what each takes to be something like a moral requirement, nevertheless we cannot say that one community has a more valid notion of what constitutes duty than the other."[8] This claim implies that there is an "irreducible relativism in assessments of duty and dutifulness absent in the case of virtue."[9] Blum's alternative to the Urmsonian minimalism allows for the cultivation of different standards for capping moral requirement among different societies, while also recognizing the possibility that there are certain minimal norms of conduct that must be observed by everyone. In determining right action independently of cultural context, Urmson speaks of "undue burden" as if it were a constant, thereby dismissing the views of duty and supererogation of those societies whose perception might vary from the presumed objective norm. Even more problematic in this approach is the disregard for the potential we possess to redefine for ourselves what our duty is. In maintaining that we need only *do* our duty, which is the same for everyone, Urmson trivializes the importance of asking ourselves whether we can—and therefore should—become more inclined to expand our existing sense of duty.

2. *Characterization of the supererogatory agent's "ought."* A second problem that arises in Urmson's portrayal of heroes and saints is that it does not adequately explain the force of the "ought" that prompts them to see themselves as strictly morally bound to pursue their heroic and saintly acts. Many ethicists maintain that there is a sense in which we ought to do things that are not strictly required, even though they specify that there is a difference between these "recommended" acts and acts that are properly considered part of duty. But in the case of heroes and saints, it may be that even *this* perceived distinction between senses of "ought"— between deeds that are good but only recommended and deeds that are obligatory—is missing. Urmson does not dispute that the heroes or saints may see their actions, without qualification, as no less than what is required of them regardless of the degree to which these actions are "inadequately subsumed under the concept of duty." However, by distinguishing the heroes' or saints' personal sense of responsibility from "duty," Urmson forces us to ask a question that does not receive adequate treatment in his own examination, namely, just what *is* the force of the "ought" that leads heroes or saints to make of their own case an exception? Urmson does not have a view of what this "ought" is other than to attribute it to the idiosyncratic set of motivational desires of heroes and saints. Heroes and saints "ought" to help others in the sense that those who want to become accomplished musicians ought to practice their instruments. That they "ought" to help others in this sense does not mean that they *must* help; the "ought" of heroes or saints is not *morally prescriptive*.[10] Heroes and saints who speak of their heroic and saintly deeds as moral duties, according to this way of interpreting Urmson's analysis, confuse a *hypothetical* imperative, which makes an allowance for the distinctiveness

of their own perspective, with a *categorical* one, which makes no such allowance.

By attributing heroic and saintly behavior to the personal idiosyncrasies of the hero and saint, Urmson indicates that the "ought" in question merely has the force of a personal ideal. In other words, Urmson understands the hero or saint to be doing what heroes and saints do, if they want to be a hero or a saint. But such an explanation begs the question, for we shall want to know what, if any, moral motivations lie behind this special character trait. *Why* would the hero or saint think that he or she ought—in the strictest sense—to perform an altruistic deed that exceeds his or her duty? Presumably, Urmson believes that the hero or saint is motivated by a passion to help those in distress, or something along this line. Yet he does not think that this passion bears on the moral status of the deed in question.

Urmson leaves us wondering how heroes and saints can appear to bind themselves so completely to what, by his own supposition, they themselves know to be no more than optional. On the one hand, Urmson characterizes heroic and saintly deeds as morally good. On the other, he relegates them to having the status of personal ideals. Urmson's admission that there is at least *something* to the special "ought" of the hero or saint seems to exist in tension with an approach to morality that determines right action exclusively in terms of universal moral principles and independently of considerations of motive, traits of character, or emotion. The problem is that according to this approach there is a distinction posited between actions that fall under the rubric of duty, which are *morally necessary*, and actions that we pursue because they are good, or *morally valuable*, while at the same time there is a sense in which the latter are still considered subjectively binding. This move prompts one to ask how such a subjective—what I have called evaluative—"ought" can fail to be prescriptive at the same time.[11]

Heyd, who calls this problem the "good-ought tie up," comes to Urmson's defense on just this point. Heyd suggests that there are actions that no one in particular is responsible for performing, such as saving lives in an area of the world geographically remote from the agent(s) in question, but that nonetheless would result in good if someone or some group of people attempted to do them. Heyd notes that heroic and saintly actions are perfect examples of these, for heroes and saints are heroic and saintly precisely because of their unexpected intervention in others' affairs. In other words, regardless of the hero or saint's own perception of what is to be done on a particular occasion, the likelihood of any valuable state of affairs in itself does not constitute a morally compelling reason to bind the hero or saint to act.[12] According to Heyd, what heroes and saints fail to realize in forming their perceptions of what a situation morally requires is that "good" does not entail a moral "ought" (although it may contain a hypothetical "ought"). Only a moral ought, argues Heyd, is an imperative that obtains from an identifiable and describable *relationship* between an agent and his or her potential beneficiary. Personal ideals, which are idiosyncratically adopted by heroes and saints, do not supply these needed "relationships." Heroes and saints have no more of a connection to their beneficiaries than anyone else, and thus if they were required to perform their heroic deeds, then so would anyone else similarly situated.

What Heyd misses in defending Urmson is that heroes and saints in fact *may* have a unique relationship with their beneficiaries, a relationship which is established as a direct result of their virtuous character and increased sense of moral responsibility for others. Heyd considers neither the capacity of heroes and saints to be in a special position to help potential beneficiaries simply *because* of their capacity for sympathy, nor that this capacity obliges them in a unique way. In other words, a critic might object, it is because heroes and saints *value* the good—and certainly deplore the suffering—of their potential beneficiaries more than others do that they have a greater *duty* to act on their behalf.

The notion that the evaluative and deontic spheres are connected would seem to explain how heroes and saints can appear to bind themselves so completely to what has been defined as optional, and would seem to give some insight into the reason why heroic and saintly actions are not mere instances of personal preference on the part of the agent performing them. Indeed, according to this objection, heroic and saintly actions *do* have moral value, as Urmson has insisted all along, but this value ultimately stems from their prescriptive component. In this way heroic and saintly actions can become morally obligatory for those few who come to adopt them as part of the practices that regulate their conduct.

3. *Dismissal of the testimony of heroes and saints.* The third problem with Urmson's treatment of heroes and saints lies in his reinterpretation of the view they express about their own actions. By drawing a distinction between what heroes and saints *perceive* to be required and what is *really* required, Urmson implies that heroes and saints are susceptible to deluding themselves into believing that certain supererogatory actions fall under the rubric of duty. It is interesting that while extolling heroes and saints for their selflessness and fearlessness, Urmson says that they should not be regarded as authorities on what is morally required. Although heroes and saints can be distinguished from the rest of us on the grounds that they have the moral fortitude to see unusually costly altruistic acts as non-optional, they themselves have to admit that such realizations are not "pieces of objective reporting" but imaginative falsifications that would be revealed as such if they were to be applied to ordinary people.

However, the critic might say that this is not at all what heroes and saints would admit to themselves. Indeed, if it is the case, as Urmson grants, that heroes or saints see themselves as responding in the only morally honest way they can to a given situation, then why should it not also be the case that heroes or saints are capable of interpreting that reality for what it truly is? Perhaps it is the hero or saint who is the better equipped to interpret our shared moral realities and we who are, at least to a certain extent, deluded. Urmson constructs a universal point of view from an amalgamation of the perspectives of ordinary people. Such an approach equates the majority with the enlightened. Yet history is replete with examples in which the keenest of moral insights come from those whose views are among the lone, minority voice. Just because common sense reflects what the majority believes on a given occasion, it does not follow that we should regard the commonsense view as the more credible one.

In light of this skepticism, it again makes sense to consider the more balanced position charted by Lawrence Blum, according to which there is more than one legitimate conception of duty that can be found across cultures, communities, and even individuals. In this view, heroes and saints would be no more correct in their construals of what is morally required than the majority, and vice versa. The advantage of Blum's approach, as opposed to Urmson's, becomes clear when it is applied to *communities* of heroes and saints. Urmson's example of the soldier who falls on a grenade to save comrades is constructed to contrast the actions of one person with those in the surrounding group. It would not be as easy to draw this distinction at the level of community. To say, for example, that an entire village of Huguenots deceived themselves into thinking that it was their duty to provide shelter for Jewish refugees in Hitler's occupied France—and to offer the attitudes of those in surrounding communities as proof of this judgment—seems arbitrary and unfounded. According to this objection, Urmson is not justified in dismissing the hero or saint's claim to having a *more* enlightened perspective than the majority. Indeed, the hero or saint, presumably at an advanced stage of moral development, is arguably *better* equipped than the majority to determine what his or her moral duty is. We may consider the example of Camus's Dr. Rieux, who refuses to leave Oran and join his wife while he still has the opportunity to do so, choosing instead to remain and fight the plague because he thinks that one's life derives its value by helping others in their time of need.[13] It seems plausible to suggest that Rieux, who perceptively evaluates himself as capable of making a difference in Oran, is also competent to judge whether or not he ought to stay. We certainly have no overriding reason to disbelieve Camus's narrator when he writes, "The essential thing was to save the greatest number of persons from dying and being doomed to unending separation, and to do this there was only one resource: to fight the plague. There was nothing admirable about this attitude; it was merely logical."[14] Here, Camus intends Rieux to speak as an authority on what is morally required of himself. Yet, if we are to be persuaded by Urmson, we must cast doubt on Rieux's reasoning.

Camus's portrayal of Rieux-as-hero as one with an accurate sense of his moral duty is corroborated by reports of Holocaust rescuers who insist that they are not deserving of any extra praise for the effort they expended to help the Jews survive the Nazis. When interviewed, rescuers state with remarkable consistency that they were only "doing their duty." Had they not done it, they would have judged themselves to be morally blameworthy and deserving of rebuke.[15] There is an argument for trusting rescuers' abilities to have identified their duty correctly that is rooted in the clarity and confidence with which they articulate what was, for others, often a matter of indecision and ambivalence.[16] When interviewed, rescuers tend to convey that they were *sure* of the necessity of what they did, as well as of the need to do it now rather than later. As one interviewed rescuer put it: "Look. Look. Who else would have taken care of them if we didn't? They needed our help, and they needed it *then*."[17] If we are to contest the testimony comprised of remarks like these, we need a basis for the challenge that does more than speculate on the nature of duty, as such. It must provide new insight into rescuers' states of mind and explain why they tended to interpret their own situation incorrectly. I see no reason why we should accept Urmson's voice as the authoritative one when he claims that heroes and saints are under a misapprehension about the nature of what they do. Just as it does not make sense to contest the report of one with exceptional sight who claims to have spotted a ship on the edge of the horizon, so should we be careful when questioning those with the most fully developed moral character about what their—and perhaps even our—moral duties are. They are perhaps in the best position to know.

4. *Portrayal of the hero or saint as the "other."* Finally, and perhaps most seriously, Urmson divides humanity into the extraordinary, or the heroic and saintly, and the ordinary, and members of each of these groups are thought to approach the world and their responsibility in it under radically different sets of assumptions. In the standard view, neither heroes nor saints share the same psychological handicaps as ordinary human beings. They have the capacity to overcome the drive to self-preservation and to substitute the interests of others for their own, respectively, either through remarkable self-discipline or effortlessly. We are not told, however, how heroes and saints acquire the capacity to do this. We are told

only that they are different than we are and that consequently their conduct has little normative relevance to the formulation of a moral code
intended for wider observance. Not only do ordinary human beings have
limitations that prevent them from following the hero and saint; from an
ordinary perspective we are hard-pressed even to *understand* what motivates heroes and saints. A. I. Melden makes this point emphatically. Speaking of the saint, he writes:

> [I]t is not simply a matter of what he, unlike others, is morally bound
> to do, a matter concerning which differences of opinion might arise, but
> one that pertains to what he takes to be his unique relation to others, a
> relation that colours the whole character of his life—his thoughts and
> feelings about himself and others—in ways that are radically different from
> these ordinary human beings. . . . To see the saint in this way is to see a
> being who is a radically different sort of man, one who not merely is
> endowed with unusual love for others or with an unusually high degree
> of benevolence or beneficence—*that* we can understand, for there *are*
> moments, rare as these are, in which we may be so disposed to a stranger
> in distress. Rather, it is to see a being whose whole life—in his thought,
> feeling and action—is coloured by the unshakable and ever present con-
> viction he has about his unique relation to other human beings.[18]

While Melden's comments are sensitive to the way saints might actually
describe themselves, in the sense that he gives credence to saints' self-
perceptions of their actions being morally required, the comments nonetheless reveal the extent to which saints are perceived as wholly other
beings with whom we share nothing in common. More than this, in
Melden's view saints are characterized as being self-consciously aware of
their special nature, which leads them to engage in activities which they
know are appropriate only for themselves or others like them.

The problem with this characterization is not only that it attributes
to saints a paternalism that they likely do not possess, but also that it
seems empirically flawed. Saints often regard themselves as among and
not above those upon whom they exert their influence. Many have
remarked upon this saintly trait. One notable example is Robert Adams.
Responding to Susan Wolf's charge that saints forgo special relations and
choose to live a solitary existence in order to seek the maximization of
others' good, Adams observes that saints actually see themselves as inti-
mately connected to other human beings. Saints are often perceptive,
charismatic, emotional, and, perhaps most tellingly, keenly sensitive to the
concerns of those around them.[19] Saintliness, understood in this way, is

not the equivalent of ascetic withdrawal or aloof perfectionism but the kind of goodness and kindness that is revealed in the saint's interaction with other people. While saints may live by an ideal of character, and indeed scarcely if ever acknowledge the category of supererogation with respect to their own conduct, they achieve their saintly status within and not apart from their respective communities.

This revised characterization of the saint conforms to the this-worldly orientation exhibited by Dorothy Day. To be a saint is to take a stand on controversial positions in society and to try to influence the outcome of important political and moral debates.[20] Additionally, the critic of the standard view may be apt to point out, the saint is humble and very much identifies with the place where the nonsaint currently stands. We may consider Dostoevsky's portrayal of Alyosha in *The Brothers Karamazov* to elucidate the point. Alyosha is the compassionate youngest brother who possesses a mixture of inner strength and outer expression that unexpectedly involves him in efforts to redeem his other siblings. Dostoevsky's initial description of the protagonist is characteristically poignant:

> As a child and a boy, Alyosha was rather reserved, one might even say uncommunicative. He was not distrustful, however, or shy and unsociable, just the opposite, in fact. His apparently distant behavior was due to a constant inner preoccupation with something strictly personal, something which had nothing to do with other people, but which was so supremely important to him that it made him forget the rest of the world. *But he certainly loved people: throughout his life he seemed to believe in people and trust them, and yet no one ever thought him simple-minded or naive. There was something in him (and it stayed with him all his life) that made other people realize that he refused to sit in judgment on others, that he felt he had no right to, and that, whatever happened, he would never condemn anyone. He gave the impression that he could witness anything without feeling in the least outraged, although he might be deeply saddened.*[21]

Alyosha is portrayed as embodying a pure goodness that emanates from within. Yet his goodness becomes apparent only by virtue of his honest and mutual relations with others, especially his despairing brothers. While Alyosha stands as his brothers' potential redeemer, Dostoevsky impresses upon the reader that Alyosha is and remains *one of them*. Urmson and Melden downplay the extent to which saints seek solidarity with their social world. Alyosha's virtues do not separate him from his brothers. They bring him closer to them.[22]

An additional problem with the Urmsonian dichotomization is that it makes no allowance for the possibility of character development. Urmson and Melden assume that for the most part we lack the resources to improve upon our already existing other-regarding capacities, which are highly limited. While ordinary morality can be transcended by a few people on some occasions, even these few cannot fundamentally change who they are. In Urmson and Melden's approach, we never learn how heroes and saints *become* heroes and saints. From our point of view this process remains a mystery, just as we remain in awe of them. Again, Melden's comments about saints suffice to clarify this:

> We recognize that the psychopath is a different sort of being and hence that punishment, moral approval or disapproval, praise or blame do not apply to him. It is high time that we recognize that the saint who, unlike the psychopath, does have moral virtues and fully grasps the moral concepts we employ, is a different sort of being, one to whose status, given the sorts of beings we are, *we* cannot aspire.[23]

Melden's view is somewhat defeatist; for by assuming that how virtuous we are is something predetermined by forces beyond our control, it fails to address an important question in ethics, namely, "How can we make ourselves better people than we currently are?"[24]

Urmson assumes that we ought not to try to set the conduct of ordinary persons in relation to an ideal because it would be futile to do so. There are limits to our ability to become other than we currently are. Ethics should operate within these limits. This is not an assumption that is shared by many religionists. The Jewish thinker Ahad Ha'am, for instance, writes that "all men, including the self, are under obligation to develop their lives and their faculties to the limit of their capacity and, at the same time, each is under an obligation to assist his neighbor's self-development so far as he can."[25] This sentiment is consistently echoed in the Christian tradition, and we are again reminded of Paul Tillich's model of "creative" justice, in which the fulfillment of moral requirement entails the maximal development of all of one's virtues. The views of Ahad Ha'am and Paul Tillich require us to *change* our character. They do not affirm the incorrigibility of human nature. They do not contain built-in clauses that establish limits to the general duty to expand our other-regarding capacities. Melden's view that "it is high time" that we recognize how inaccessible saintliness is precludes the possibility of self-transformation in light of self-knowledge. This is a possibility that is highlighted in the account advanced by Ahad Ha'am and Tillich. According to these two religious thinkers, we ought not to see ourselves as finished products, or indeed as morally incorrigible in any sense. We are better understood as malleable creatures, as works in progress.

Historical and Theological Approaches to Understanding Saints and Human Nature

Just as human nature does not preclude the possibility of a heroic or saintly existence, the lives of heroes and saints are firmly rooted in human experience. In Urmson's account, the "heroic" and "saintly" are conceptual categories. They are defined in opposition to "ordinary morality." Urmson's purely philosophical orientation to understanding heroic and saintly conduct blinds him to other, contextually "thick," perspectives from which to regard the practices and self-understandings of religious people. Historians and theologians who address the issue of saintly practice and self-perception, for example, often defend a sense in which human nature and saintly existence overlap.

One historian who comes to mind in this regard is Caroline Walker Bynum, whose seminal volume *Holy Feast and Holy Fast* highlights the tension between the extreme spirituality and mundane embodiment of medieval women saints.[26] Bynum's thesis is that women saints, in their attempt to imitate Christ suffering on the cross, tended to assert control over their lives not through the traditional saintly renunciations of poverty and chastity, but rather by engaging in different rituals concerning food, some of which were dangerous and involved fasting or eating harmful items. At the same time, her accounts of the eating practices of women saints reveal the highly social and functionalist aspects of religious devotion. Bynum seems to support Urmson's thesis when she announces explicitly in her introduction that saints ought not to be considered models for ordinary mortals, that like "Christ himself, they could not and should not be imitated in their full extravagance and power."[27] Yet, when she recounts the exceptional or extravagant deeds of some of these woman saints, she does so by explaining the motive of the particular act in question within the context of their religious and social worlds. This becomes clear in her discussion of Catherine of Siena and Catherine of Genoa, whom she counts among the greatest women writers and figures of medieval Italy. For both women, obsessive fasting and eucharistic piety (the substituting of the Eucharist for food) became "lived" miracles: both sought in their own hunger to call attention to the hungry and, by virtue of their own restraint, to emphasize the virtues of suffering and serving.[28] Suffering and serving, in turn, became virtues in which nearly everyone could participate if they so chose. Bynum's discussion of Catherine of Siena demonstrates the moral predicament the saint and nonsaint alike were presumed to share. Bynum remarks:

> In addition to the many eucharistic miracles and visions recounted by Catherine's hagiographers, we have Catherine's own descriptions of the centrality of the eucharist. She urges a number of her correspondents to frequent communion.... She says explicitly that God provides the eucharist as a substitute for "heavy physical bread," which excites gluttony and lust.... The visions that Catherine's biographers associated with turning points in her life all had as their central theme the redemption of humanity as physicality by the substitution of Christ's flesh for human fleshliness.... But she herself saw that flesh less as a substitute and protection than as blood and agony, shed for the sake of the world. Although Catherine abhorred her own flesh, condemning it as a "dung heap," she saw the fleshliness of Christ not as some sort of miraculous protection to save us from human vulnerability but as the "way" or "bridge" to lead us to salvation through suffering.... For Catherine, the hungering of ordinary Christians is service....[29]

For Catherine of Siena, the extreme practice of depriving oneself of gustative enjoyment became a vehicle through which Christians aspiring toward spiritual betterment could learn to empathize with and care for the suffering. Bynum thus characterizes Catherine's orientation as this-worldly. Regardless of whether Catherine's chosen methods of devotion were meant for imitation (Bynum has her doubts), the message to the lay population is clear. As Catherine writes in her own words: "Seat yourself at the table of the cross. There, all inebriated with the precious blood, take the food of souls, suffering pain, opprobrium, curses, villainy, hunger, thirst, and nudity.... You must suffer pain and be in shadow. My soul knows it, and it is hungry for your salvation."[30] Catherine's devotion is intended to surpass that of ordinary Christians in terms of degree but not quality: salvation of one is tied to relieving the suffering of others. In this endeavor we share a common purpose. Dorothy Day, for whom Catherine of Siena served as an important mentor, credits Catherine for the insight so central to her own writing, namely, that we are each, at every moment, cocreators with God, "divinized" to take the raw materials with which God provides us in order to produce for human needs.[31]

The church historian and classicist Peter Brown supports Bynum's emphasis on the inherent human connection between saints and non-saints. In *The Cult of the Saints*, Brown links the mundane and the "upper world," the earthly and the heavenly, in Christendom's witnessing of the rise of the cult of the saints in the western Mediterranean between the third and sixth centuries A.D.[32] In his volume, he casts aside David Hume's longstanding "two-tiered" model for explaining religious change. According to Hume's approach, a vulgar populace stands to gain insight into religious life only insofar as it has the wherewithal to rely on an elite, wise few to guide it properly. In contrast, Brown argues that we ought to see the rise of the cult of the saints as a sweeping development motivated by movements at work at all levels of society and religious life.[33] This informs the central thesis of his book:

> Rather than present the rise of the cult of the saints in terms of a dialogue between two parties, the few and the many, let us attempt to see it as part of a greater whole—the lurching forward of an increased proportion of late-antique society toward radically new forms of reverence, shown to new objects in new places, orchestrated by new leaders, and deriving its momentum from the need to play out the common preoccupation of all, the few and the "vulgar" alike, with new forms of the exercise of power, new bonds of human dependence, new, intimate, hopes for protection and justice in a changing world.[34]

Martyred saints of the early medieval world were not regarded by those who revered them as wholly "other," argues Brown. Rather, they were "invisible companions," sources of comfort in whom the devotee could see a "shared humanity."[35] Echoing Augustine's observations in book 10 of the *City of God*, Brown notes that the acknowledgment of saints provided a solution to the need in late fourth century Christian piety for "intimacy with a protector with whom one could identify as a fellow human being, ... [which] could be conceived in terms open to the nuances of known human relations between patron and client."[36] Understanding and empathy are in this sense cast as the counterparts to companionship.

In light of Bynum and Brown's historical analyses of saintly conduct and existence, Melden's claim that saints, like the psychopath, are best regarded as radically different beings from the rest of us rings false. Melden assumes that in making judgments about the radical separability of saints and ordinary mortals, saints are miraculously exempt from the kind of constraints that keep mortals tied to the earthly realm. However, if we are to trust the historical analyses of Bynum and Brown, then it is saints' intimate connection to humanity itself that counts among their most esteemed features.

The thesis propounded by Urmson and Melden is not merely refuted through reference to historical scholarship. One might also consult theological approaches to understanding the relationship between the extraordinary and the ordinary. As has been mentioned, Urmson's idea that some people are simply born heroes or saints, while the rest of us are born ordinary, incorrigibly lacking key traits of the extraordinary person, assumes a fixed notion of human nature. In the Urmsonian view, we remain as we are born. We are particularly unlikely to be able to overcome our propensity for selfishness. Yet this assumption contravenes recent theological insights pertaining to the potential for love to serve as moral norm. One Catholic theologian who stands for the malleability of the human condition is Stephen Pope. Pope's Thomistic view is that grace improves rather than opposes nature—that it is in our nature, in other words, to be open and respond to the other, whom we have been graced with the capacity to love.[37] Pope argues that human beings, even the most virtuous or spiritual among us, are not "transcendental spirits" but rather embodied, limited, social beings who nonetheless "share an evolved emotional constitution that under reasonably healthy conditions can motivate us, consciously or unconsciously, to love others for their own sakes."[38] This insight Pope offers as a "corrective" to traditional theological approaches to understanding the love of the neighbor, according to which the love commandment is imposed from the outside on a human nature that is otherwise resistant to it. Pope writes as a Catholic theologian with the stated purpose of reforming the way ethics is done in his own tradition. However, his overall point about the naturalness of considering love as a norm also applies to how we describe the nature of heroes and saints in relation to us. If it is natural for us to morally develop, then it is perhaps also likely that heroes and saints, disposed as they are to overcome the drives to self-preservation and selfishness, exemplify rather than transcend their humanity in performing their heroic and saintly deeds. The historical and theological perspectives on saints offered by Bynum, Brown, and Pope raise questions as to whether we are as irrevocably distant from heroes and saints as the standard view suggests.

Urmson is interested in especially virtuous moral agents, like heroes and saints, only to the extent that their existence offers a counterexample to the assumption made in certain maximalist normative frameworks, such as many versions of utilitarianism and Kantianism, that we ultimately ought to acknowledge no difference in the moral capacities of human agents. Thus, Urmson discusses heroes and saints as a phenomenologist would, fascinated by them because they cause problems for the tripartite division of actions into the morally required, the morally neutral, and the morally prohibited, as well as appreciative of their existence due to all of the moral goodness that they produce. However, according to Urmson, heroic or saintly conduct does not ever, even in a weak sense, constitute a normative ideal that we are required to pursue. Consequently, the question of whether we ought to acquire virtue and if so, how, lies outside Urmson's field of inquiry. In addition, Urmson maintains that to attempt systematically to pull back the boundaries that have been set by self-interest is to participate in the creation of a moral system that would no longer work for human beings. In concluding that morality can only operate in a framework in which it is not too demanding, Urmson assumes that the promotion of overall human welfare is in the final analysis incommensurable with ordinary psychological patterns of human motivation.

A Critical Appraisal of Unqualified Supererogationism

It is precisely this assumption, I think, which also constitutes the kernel of Heyd's thesis. Heyd claims that individuals must have the privilege to pursue their own ends, to satisfy their own wants, and to realize their personal ideals unfettered, so long as they do not fail to do what is minimally morally required, lest they be stripped of their right to seek these ends, wants, and ideals and end up enslaving themselves to an impersonal moral cause that would benefit no one in particular.[39] According to Heyd, we should focus on our own welfare, thinking of others only when minimal morality requires us to do so. This conclusion is warranted on practical grounds: any other construal of the relationship between the individual and moral duty would result in our serving morality, and not the reverse. Yet Heyd's idea that our autonomy should depend on this sort of moral minimalism, which condones the "right" for us to withhold aid and assistance from needier others in order to protect our own pursuits, is based on an argument that makes two assumptions. The first assumption is that it is equally to our advantage that we be accorded this right. The second is that for morality to "work" it must posit a threshold of moral requirement beyond which agents are utterly free to disregard the welfare and well-being of others if they so choose.

The idea that it is in everyone's interest to act on an initial presumption of withholding aid and assistance sees all persons in the abstract, as self-interested agents equally capable of promoting their own welfare and well-being. It fails to acknowledge the vast differences that exist among us in terms of class, social standing, and opportunity. Heyd writes that just as "individual persons should not be sacrificed for the promotion of overall happiness (as in the case of punishing an innocent man in order to save the lives of many others)," so too "considerations of justice make it unacceptable to require any individual to work ceaselessly for the welfare of others."[40] In claiming as much, he does not sufficiently take into account the enduring societal imbalance between those who happen to be fortunate and those who are not. Under these very real conditions of overwhelming disparity, the laissez-faire stance of unqualified supererogation in effect becomes a policy of consistently favoring those societal groups that need the least amount of help. We must wonder whether unqualified supererogation sanctions the indifference of those with means at the expense of weaker groups. Heyd insists that beyond our fulfillment of minimal moral requirement, which entails only the most modest principles of aid, we have the prerogative to stand idle in instances when our assistance would otherwise be solicited actively. Yet this is a prerogative which, when exercised, worsens rather than leaves unaffected the relative condition of the needy. Viewed pragmatically, we have cause to be concerned that unqualified supererogationism results in moral complacency. It is this concern that serves as the impetus for the familiar antisupererogationist critique. Is there a way of rescuing the concept of supererogation in normative ethics without remaining committed to moral minimalism? This is the question that the *qualified* supererogationist, who is sympathetic to the antisupererogationist's concerns about moral complacency, must address.

While this question will be dealt with in detail in chapter 5, it is worth briefly addressing here the perceived necessary link between moral minimalism and the concept of supererogation in the standard view. Heyd's advocacy of unqualified supererogation hangs on the sound Urmsonian observation that many of us are often not capable of exceeding the moral minimum, that some of us may never be capable of so doing, and that there consequently ought to be a presumption of the optionality of a good many altruistic deeds, due to their costly nature. This observation leads Heyd to posit an objective threshold for morally required actions.

Yet it is simply not the case that a *presumption* of optionality should be tantamount to *unconditional* optionality; for such a presumption, it seems, could be overridden for certain agents as they became morally capable. Perhaps the way morality will most effectively "work for us" is for it to demand different things from different people at different times. We are not human automatons, capable of marching toward the goal of betterment at a uniform pace; nor, as Susan Wolf and others have remarked, would we want to be.[41] By the same logic, we should not be uniformly subject to the same normative constraints. It is within the capacity of "working" morality to allow for moral development, according to which what is required of one person at one time would not be required of another, or of the same person on a previous occasion.

To say as much is not to fail to appreciate the category of supererogation for its positive aspects. Heyd, Schumaker, and others rightly contend that what makes supererogation valuable is its voluntary nature. Such an assumption speaks to our motivation for helping others: we self-sacrifice not because we are constrained by moral requirement, but because we want to do so. The concept of supererogation makes room for us to determine what we are capable of doing for others. Insofar as it does this, it optimally "allows for the exercise of individual traits of character and for the expression of one's personal values and standards of moral behaviour."[42] However, this reasoning serves only to refute the antisupererogationist, who wants to make all morally good acts morally required. Heyd determines that the category of supererogation would ultimately dissolve for the qualified supererogationist, according to whom there are *some* circumstances under which an act of supererogation can be reinterpreted to be a duty. Yet, for this qualified supererogationist, the conceptual distinctiveness of the category remains in use. While the precise relationship between duty and supererogation is ever-changing for a particular agent, the distinction between the two categories is consistently maintained.

My criticisms have led me to conclude, against the intuitions of commonsense morality, that the supposed limitations of what we can do for others are apparent rather than ultimate. What grounds, if any, are there for taking this preliminary conclusion seriously? To answer this question, I turn to sources that come from within the Jewish and Christian traditions.

A Duty to Go Beyond the Call of Duty?

Lifnim Mishurat Hadin *and the Second Love Commandment*

In a well-known passage from the Talmud, *Baba Meziá* 30b, a rabbi is reported to have commented that Jerusalem was destroyed because the Israelites were acting only according to strict biblical law (*din Torah*) and failed in their ordinary dealings to go beyond the requirements of the law (*lifnim mishurat hadin*).[43] What is particularly interesting about this passage is that even though the people of Israel are blamed and punished for falling below the standard expected of them, this standard is distinguished from the less demanding standard of Halakhically obligatory conduct. Apparently, the author of the passage thought it important to clarify that the issue was not that the Israelites had failed God by not fulfilling what was strictly required of them, but that they had failed God by either having too modest a sense of duty or by regarding duty to be their only moral compass. This interesting subtlety is considered by Louis Newman in his analysis of the commentary on the passage:

> The idea appears to be that the Torah ordains all acts of righteousness, including both fulfilling prescribed legal duties and exceeding these duties. This midrash then supports the view that *lifnim mishurat hadin* is obligatory in some sense. This, of course, does not necessarily imply that this is a duty which is actionable in a court of law. It may still be that one who fails to act *lifnim mishurat hadin* is liable to no punishment,

just as there may be none for failing to visit the sick or bury the dead. Rather, the point is that these are all righteous acts which, punishable or not, are part and parcel of what God expects of Israel.[44]

Notwithstanding the difficulties of interpretation with respect to matching up the concepts of law and morality with Halakhah, it is clear that in this passage there are two standards of conduct to which the rabbis refer, *din torah* and *lifnim mishurat hadin*, even though failure to meet the demands laid forth in the latter, higher standard apparently warranted dire consequences in terms of God's judgment of Israel. From this observation Newman draws the following conclusion:

> God expects people not only to uphold the law, but also to be merciful and compassionate where the law does not specifically require it. The point of the passage, then, is not that judging in accordance with the law is wrong and deserving of punishment, but rather that this, in itself, is not all that God expects of Israel.... *God expects, and all earthly courts should demand, that people act more mercifully than the letter of the law requires.*[45]

This is an odd conclusion indeed. Newman implies that what we learn from this set of commentaries is that the courts should legally demand more than what the law itself requires. The self-referential dilemma that arises from this understanding of the matter is interesting: the Israelites are required to do more than that which is identified as morally required. This seeming paradox could easily be resolved by expanding "strict legal requirement" to accommodate the referenced higher standard of moral conduct. It should strike us as highly significant that this route is not taken.

I think that we may reasonably conclude from Newman's discussion of *Baba Meziá* 30b that the rabbis regarded the distinctive identification of *din Torah*, or "strict law,"[46] as indispensable not only for its own sake, as a specification of what the Torah explicitly demands of the people of Israel, but also for the sake of having it stand as a point of contrast to a more demanding standard of moral conduct that reflects what ought to have comprised the Israelites' fuller moral ambitions. No matter where the line that delineates what is "strictly required" had been drawn, it apparently would have been insufficient, even though the very point of such a line is to serve as an indicator of morally sufficient conduct. What we learn from this passage, in other words, is that one's acknowledgment of a double standard is precisely what is necessary for determining what one is ultimately morally required to do. It is only by virtue of a double standard that one can act *lifnim mishurat hadin* and thereby demonstrate that one is righteous.[47]

This example has a parallel in the Christian tradition with respect to one prevalent interpretation of the Second Love Commandment, in which the mandate to treat one's neighbor as oneself is understood to require Christians to will themselves to cultivate the emotion of compassion, which is construed as a responsibility that surpasses the duty to show respect for all humans.[48] The point of the Second Love Commandment, according to this interpretation, is to require Christians to orient themselves in relation to an ideal that is more demanding than that for which they are already held accountable at a more basic level. It might be remarked that because compassion is an emotion, which by its nature a person cannot summon immediately, the Second Love Commandment is ineffective at motivating altruism when such an impulse does not arise naturally from within. Nevertheless, from this it does not follow that *agape* demands any less of us than of those few in whom compassion arises easily. While the nature of the Second Love Command is such that it cannot have the same obligatory *status* as, for example, the Ten Commandments, which can be followed by all regardless of their capacity to be compassionate, the more demanding standard of other-regard that the Second Love Commandment entails is ultimately what is required of the practicing Christian. Indeed, the Ten Commandments should *not* be expanded to include the higher but also ultimately required standard of moral conduct, for it is by virtue of compassion's special quality, including the fact that it is not immediately summonable by one seeking its influence, that one will be motivated to go through the painstaking but self-actualizing process of trying to acquire it.

In this example, as in the case of the Talmudic passage about the cause of Jerusalem's demise, ordinary people are instructed to regard a standard of conduct that exceeds what is specified by the moral minimum as no less than what is ultimately required of them. It seems that the idea that there is something morally significant about feeling compelled to do *more* than what is initially defined as required, then, is present in both the Jewish and Christian traditions. Can contemporary secular ethicists make use of this Western religious insight?

One major disadvantage to claiming that there is a sense in which we "ought" to look beyond the call of duty is that such a claim has the potential to frustrate us, especially if we honestly perceive ourselves as being able to do no more than what we are already doing. The question is whether such frustration will lead to defeatism. If we continuously set for ourselves higher standards, or try to ascend into the "higher flights of morality," as Urmson called them, will we simply be headed for disappointment and end up feeling negatively about morality in general? This is what the defender of the standard view fears will happen. By contrast, those who ultimately regard as morally compulsory conduct that is *lifnim mishurat hadin*, or the cultivation of compassion sufficient to act agapistically, wager that the resulting double standard serves to motivate rather than deter the attainment of a morally righteous character.

There are additional grounds for not interpreting the phrase "duty beyond duty" as a contradiction, grounds that are evident in the writings of some of the last century's most important theologians. Thus, I conclude this chapter by looking briefly at two prominent Catholic theologians from the twentieth century, Gérard Gilleman and Bernard Häring. Both Gilleman and Häring identify in the Christian concept of moral obligation the idea that obligation itself is an ever-expanding concept. Whereas the idea that we "ought" to do more than what is strictly morally required tends to be regarded as counterintuitive and even self-defeating by the majority of contemporary secular ethicists, theologians tend to be more comfortable with the notion. I examine the work of Gilleman and Häring to explore whether or not defenders of the standard secular view might benefit from those working in religious ethics whose model of moral requirement is based on assumptions that differ from their own.

The "Duty to Go Beyond the Call of Duty" in the Roman Catholic Theology of Gérard Gilleman and Bernard Häring

Gérard Gilleman and Bernard Häring, contemporaries of Urmson, advocate an understanding of moral duty that is determined in reference to moral goodness, especially goodness embodied in the virtue of charity.[49] Both Roman Catholic theologians heavily influenced by their moral tradition's long-standing reliance on Thomistic natural law, they maintain that we can be found morally blameworthy for failing to dispose ourselves to go out of our way to do more than the minimum requires. One way that they explain this sense of the duty to go beyond is by relating the concepts of "law" and "love." These two concepts are often kept deliberately separate in secular ethics, as they are in Heyd's theory of unqualified supererogation. In the moral theologies of Gilleman and Häring, by contrast, it is the nature of moral duty to extend beyond itself. Far from employing a contradictory understanding of the two terms, both theologians emphasize that the norms to which duty points in the present are stable yet revisable; we are not to rest content with what they require of us. Obligations to perform certain actions at any one time are specific and can be clearly defined. However, they are also simultaneously superseded by an overarching mandate to transform ourselves and surpass our limitations.

In *The Primacy of Charity in Moral Theology*, Gilleman conceives of duty as a correct ordering of priorities.[50] Insofar as the Christian strives to be in union with God, the highest priority, charity, serves as a final, overriding impetus for all moral acts.[51] Charity is an unrestrained love that manifests itself in the exertion of efforts directed at the betterment of others. Through God's grace, the Christian is given the capacity to love the neighbor as God loves him or her, and thereby to act charitably. The success of living a life in union with God, however, depends on one's will to develop this capacity to the best of one's ability.[52] In describing the moral act, Gilleman observes:

> Action is always heavy with an ontological weight since it is always an actuation; it causes us to exist more fully, making us pass from what we were to what we want to be. The grandeur of human action appears in that it is a step in our assimilation to God and an actual participation in the divine creative activity.[53]

The moral command—duty—is a command to will oneself to become more like God (by becoming more loving like God). In this way, the command (or God's law) and freedom are connected: "As soon as I perceive a moral object, I will my ultimate end; I cannot not will it, and I will it freely in the present act. Such is the meaning of duty."[54] Elsewhere, Gilleman connects "law" to "love" more explicitly. Consider the following passage, in which the contrast appears as a relation between the "duty-to-do" and the "duty-to-be." Writes Gilleman:

> Ours is an incarnate spirit; being spirit, it is invited to surpass the limitations of its carnal condition; our being is "bent" toward fuller being, toward infinity. It is urgently invited and even absolutely impelled to surpass its own being and, since being is love and communion, to communicate always more fully with God and with others without ever stopping at any particular determination. But insofar as it is incarnated, this same spirit is "bent" toward fixing its spiritual movement in determinations and stable norms.
>
> Therefore, this fundamental drive is exercised at the same time on two general levels or under two aspects—expanding interiority and limiting exteriority—but in the unity of one and the same total activity. We recognize at once in this ontological drive which is at work in our being the root of obligation. It is first, in its more general meaning, a duty-to-be before being channeled on the level of determined activities into a properly moral duty-to-do.[55]

The "duty-to-do" corresponds to strict obligation in the present and is limited by human, "carnal" capacity. However, as grace gives us the ability to surpass our condition, we are not only "urgently invited" but "absolutely impelled" to fulfill our "duty-to-be." This extends in the direction of infinity and, at junctures over the course of a lifetime, appropriately modifies the "duty-to-do." Taken to an extreme, the love-obligation is a duty to yield in one's entirety to the interior pole of spirit.[56] This obligation does not necessarily translate into a duty to be ceaselessly giving in every respect. However, it does compel one to maintain a sense of dissatisfaction with respect to one's current level of charity. According to Gilleman, we are always under obligation to "bend" toward a fuller being of spirit. Law and love are complements. They interact as correctives of one another, even as the latter subsumes the former.

Bernard Häring's *The Law of Christ*, written in 1963, just four years after Gilleman finished *The Primacy of Charity in Moral Theology*, not only parallels the latter's emphasis on bringing together the concepts of law and love, but also expresses a general disdain for those who would equate duty with the universalism of minimal moral requirement. A duty that does not grow is tantamount to shallow legalism. Häring insists:

> As love implies obedience, so it implies law, and love and law are essentially and mutually interchangeable. Obedience of love is surely more comprehensive than mere legal obedience, for mere observance of law is the lowest degree of obedience. Mere legal obedience is not yet in the shadow of love. External laws are no more than universal regulations and therefore basically only minimum requirements. Universal rules cannot in fact even prescribe what is highest and best, since the best is not universal and cannot be demanded from men universally.... How can one who does not fulfill the minimum requirements of the law progress toward that which is higher and better? Since the minimum requirements are basic for the fulfillment of the law of love, love may never violate or ignore the law. At the same time one who truly loves may not remain at the lowest level of obedience and be satisfied with the bare legal minimum.[57]

Although it was written almost twenty years before Heyd's *Supererogation*, this passage seems deliberately to refute the central thesis of unqualified supererogation, namely, that there are no circumstances under which charity beyond minimal moral requirement can legitimately be considered morally compulsory. According to Häring, the law is broader than its substantive definition otherwise indicates at any one moment. Since "by law (in its total meaning) we understand the directive toward ever loftier heights (laws directed to ends and ideals rather than merely to the prescription and prohibition of acts), ... love and only love fulfills the law entirely."[58] One who is motivated by sheer legalism seeks to avoid violation of the law. The motivation of giving charity, by contrast, "prompts one to ask humbly and modestly: In my own present situation, with the capacities now at my disposal (perhaps these are not very prepossessing), what is the better course for me, what is the most pleasing to God for me?"[59] The double standard that Häring advocates between lower and higher levels of obedience is reminiscent of discussions about *lifnim mishurat hadin* in the Talmud and traditional interpretations of the Second Love Commandment in the Christian tradition. The higher of the two standards serves to keep the moral subject morally bound, even once he or she has fulfilled duty in a strict sense. Häring implies that charity is not an option, at least at this further remove. Is this antisupererogationism?

Even though the agent is seen as doubly bound, we ought not to assume that Häring is opposed to the concept of supererogation. To the contrary, he is insistent that charity itself always be motivated by free personal decision. The very meaning of grace is that one acts from a loving impulse, not under duress. Hence, claims Häring, one "can fulfill the individual laws according to their profoundest significance, only if one obeys them in the spirit of love."[60] The concept of supererogation is valuable because it indicates what is *not* yet strictly required at the "lower level of obedience." The concept of supererogation opens the door for acts of charity. With the help of grace, it becomes possible to exceed the minimum. By contrast, a normative framework that does not make use of the category of supererogation refers to a single, perhaps unrealistically demanding, standard of expected obedience. Left out of such a framework is the possibility of the existence of a mechanism by which human beings become able to overcome their initially handicapped condition with respect to their other-regarding capacities, or what Gilleman would call their "exterior" limitations.

Gilleman and Häring consider the distinction between duty and supererogation to be important, but believe that this distinction is not always equivalent to that between the morally required and the purely optional. They maintain—as the rabbis do in considering what is morally compulsory about *lifnim mishurat hadin*—that there is something significant about the value in feeling morally compelled to do that which is defined as being more than minimally morally required. The theological understanding of "law" developed by Gilleman and Häring, in which duty is seen as an inherently expansive concept, stands in contrast to the Urmsonian secular, universalist characterization of duty as minimal moral requirement. For Gilleman and Häring, duty is tantamount to qualified supererogationism, the view according to which acts of supererogation are temporally optional and are ultimately reducible to the category of the morally obligatory. The qualified supererogationist acknowledges that there are acts that are at the same time morally good and beyond moral requirement. However, the qualified supererogationist also maintains that the consistent nonconsideration and nonperformance of supererogatory actions throughout one's life should be regarded as morally blameworthy.

The claim that we are not entirely free from moral blame if we consistently do not expand our sense of duty stands as a challenge to Urmson's insights pertaining to the hero and the saint as much as it does to Heyd's advocation of a theory of unqualified supererogationism. If the theological hypothesis about the expansive nature of duty (and the corresponding fleeting nature of the supererogatory) is correct, then perhaps there is another way of explaining heroes' and saints' sense of moral requirement than the one provided in the Urmsonian account. According to Urmson, heroes and saints are agents whose unusual courage or selflessness renders them capable of doing more for others than the rest of us could hope to do. But this description is itself not sufficient to explain how heroes and saints come to feel morally bound to do what they do. According to the "theological" alternative explored above, heroes and saints would be seen as persons who have extraordinary moral talent, but they would also be regarded as persons who have seriously contemplated the ongoing and expanding nature of their responsibility toward others. One of the problems with talking about agents in the abstract, as Urmson does, is that there is no account of what actually informs their conceptions of how they stand in relation to others, or how these attitudes bear on judgments about moral requirement. The theologies of Gilleman and Häring, and in particular their discussions of how grace and charity figure into the essential purpose of man, stand as one explanation for how a seemingly supererogatory act can come to be considered required by a particular person. The view of duty that Gilleman and Häring propose is elastic. Their discussions about the nature of the relationship between law and love, duty and charity, suggest a way of conceiving the term "ought" other than that offered by Urmson and Heyd. We may form a hypothesis that it is this elastic, expansive sense of "ought" that reflects most adequately what motivates heroic and saintly conduct.

In part II, I test this hypothesis by undertaking my own investigation into the nature of actual heroic and saintly figures. Thus, in the next two chapters, I take some modest steps toward unraveling some of the mystery that enshrouds heroes and saints. Underlying these investigations is an important, albeit basic, question: How relevant to the formation of a workable moral code intended for ordinary persons are the life choices and corresponding actions of heroes and saints? Urmson and Heyd maintain that heroes and saints respond to their own calling, which is what leads them to heed a code of conduct that transcends the universal standard. However, it is not insignificant that heroes and saints do reportedly see a connection that exists—and that ought to exist—between themselves and the rest of humanity. In chapter 3, I investigate this connection in the case of human heroes.

NOTES

1. David Heyd, "Moral Subjects, Freedom, and Idiosyncrasy," in *Human Agency: Language, Duty, and Value: Philosophical Essays in Honor of J. O. Urmson*, ed. Jonathan Dancy, J. M. E. Moravcsik, and C. C. W. Taylor (Stanford: Stanford University Press, 1988), 153–54.

2. Ibid., 154. On the contrast between "thick" and "thin," see Michael Walzer, *Thick and Thin: Moral Argument at Home and Abroad* (Notre Dame: University of Notre Dame Press, 1994), esp. ch. 1. Walzer contends that the dualism between thick and thin is an "internal" feature of every moral system in which a "thin" set of abstract, universal principles is "thickly" adapted to, or elaborated within, particular historical and cultural contexts.

3. Heyd, "Moral Subjects," 154.

4. The literature critiquing "universalism" is expansive. Three well-known critiques of the strong sense of universalism (i.e., universal truth *and* universal justification) present in what can broadly be labeled the "neo-Enlightenment" tradition can be found in Alasdair MacIntyre, *After Virtue*, 2d ed. (Notre Dame: Notre Dame University Press, 1982); Jeffrey Stout; *Ethics after Babel: The Language of Morals and Their Discontents* (Boston: Beacon Press, 1988); and Richard Rorty, *Contingency, Irony, and Solidarity* (Cambridge: Cambridge University Press, 1989). None of these thinkers recognizes universal justification as possible. Stout, and to a lesser extent MacIntyre, do allow for the possibility of universal moral truth. Stout, for example, argues that the statement "slavery is wrong" can hold for all times and all places even though the reasons for this vary across contexts and cultures. The implication is that we may speak of moral "truth" about which there can be widespread cross-cultural agreement, if only at the level of content but not at the level of justification. See John P. Reeder, Jr., "Foundations without Foundationalism," in *Prospects for a Common Morality*, ed. Gene Outka and John P. Reeder, Jr. (Princeton: Princeton University Press, 1993), 198.

5. It is important to stress that the existence of a universal moral minimum is not what is at issue here. Urmson's view raises concerns not because it posits the existence of a standard of minimal moral requirement, but rather because it does not allow for a type of duty that goes beyond this moral minimum. Even the staunchest human rights advocate could, without undermining his or her aims, accept a more fluid notion of duty that is bounded at one end only. Morally required actions would still be delineated from permissible and prohibited actions, but they would not be restricted to actions that were not deemed unusually burdensome from a supposed universalist perspective. On such an account, we would all still incur blame for violating others' rights or for not fulfilling basic duties, but not everyone would be entirely free from blame if they abided by the moral minimum alone.

6. Lawrence Blum, *Moral Perception and Particularity* (Cambridge: Cambridge University Press, 1994), 166.

7. Ibid., 159ff.

8. Ibid., 160.

9. Ibid.

10. R. M Hare discusses the distinctive senses of "ought" in *Moral Thinking: Its Levels, Methods, and Point* (Oxford: Clarendon Press, 1981), 54ff.

11. For a more thorough discussion of this criticism of Urmson, see Jonathan Dancy, "Supererogation and Moral Realism," in Dancy et al., eds., *Human Agency*, 180.

12. David Heyd, *Supererogation* (Cambridge: Cambridge University Press, 1982), 171.

13. Albert Camus, *The Plague*, trans. Stuart Gilbert (New York: Vintage Press, 1991), 163.

14. Ibid., 133. The way I read this passage is that Rieux does not simply do his duty as a doctor, but also as a human being. While he is not self-righteous and so does not condemn others who do not stay in Oran to help fight the plague, he has a firm sense of who he is and what is morally required of him. By his own declaration at the end of the novel, Rieux has taken the "victims' side," has shared with them their "love, exile and suffering," and so he can say in earnest that "there was not one of their anxieties in which he did not share, no predicament of theirs that was not his" (301–2).

15. There are a myriad of firsthand reports of rescuers claiming that they were ordinary people who merely fulfilled their duty. For example, see Kristen Renwick Monroe, Michael C. Barton, and Ute Klingemann, "Altruism and the Theory of Rational Action: Rescuers of Jews in Nazi Europe," *Ethics* 101 (1990): 109ff.; Kristen Renwick Monroe, *The Heart of Altruism: Perceptions of a Common Morality* (Princeton: Princeton University Press, 1996), 70ff., 104–5; Nechema Tec, *When Light Pierced the Darkness: Christian Rescue of Jews in Nazi-Occupied Poland* (Oxford: Oxford University Press, 1987), 153–54, 169, 188; Samuel Oliner and Pearl M. Oliner, *The Altruistic Personality: Rescuers of Jews in Nazi Europe* (New York: Free Press, 1988), 227–28, 239.

16. Oliner and Oliner, *The Altruistic Personality*, 238ff.

17. Phillip Hallie, *Lest Innocent Blood Be Shed: The Story of the Village of Le Chambon and How Goodness Happened There* (New York: Harper and Row, 1979), 127.

18. A. I. Melden, "Saints and Supererogation," *Philosophy and Life: Essays on John Wisdom*, ed. Ilham Dilman (The Hague: Martinus Nijhoff Publishers), 77.

19. Robert Adams, "Saints," *Journal of Philosophy* 81 (1984): 393.

20. Dorothy Day was well-known for her criticism of products purchased at the expense of exploited workers, especially with respect to trades as major as the tobacco, rubber, and railroad industries. Her book *On Pilgrimage* chronicles these efforts and discusses her long-standing support of unions. See Day, *On Pilgrimage* (Grand Rapids, Mich.: William B. Eerdmans Publishing Company, 1997), 247–56.

21. Fyodor Dostoevsky, *The Brothers Karamazov*, trans. Andrew H. MacAndrew (New York: Bantam Books, 1970), 21 (emphasis mine).

22. Like Melden, Susan Wolf is equally open to criticism for characterizing the

saint as "other," and, by implication, as anti-human. Wolf claims, for instance, that the moral virtues possessed by the saint are apt to "crowd out" those many interests and personal characteristics that comprise a "healthy, well-rounded, richly developed" human life. She suggests that "there comes a point in the listing of virtues that a moral saint is likely to have where one might naturally begin to wonder whether the moral saint isn't, after all, too good—if not too good for his own good, at least too good for his own well-being." See Wolf, "Moral Saints," *Journal of Philosophy* 79, no. 8 (1982): 421. Whereas Melden extols the saint's departure from conventional society, Wolf laments it.

23. Melden, "Saints and Supererogation," 79.

24. Iris Murdoch, *The Sovereignty of Good* (London: Routledge and Kegan Paul, 1970), 78.

25. Ahad Ha'am, *Essays, Letters, Memoirs—Ahad Ha'am*, trans. Leon Simon (Oxford: East and West Library), 129–30.

26. Caroline Walker Bynum, *Holy Feast and Holy Fast: The Religious Significance of Food to Medieval Women* (Berkeley: University of California Press, 1987).

27. Ibid., 7.

28. Ibid., 165ff.

29. Ibid., 174–75.

30. As quoted by Bynum in ibid., 176.

31. See, for example, Dorothy Day, *By Little and by Little: The Selected Writings of Dorothy Day*, ed. Robert Ellsberg (Maryknoll, N.Y.: Orbis Books, 1999), 310.

32. Peter Brown, *The Cult of the Saints: Its Rise and Function in Latin Christianity* (Chicago: University of Chicago Press, 1981).

33. Ibid., 17–22.

34. Ibid., 21–22.

35. Ibid., 62.

36. Ibid., 61.

37. Stephen J. Pope, *The Evolution of Altruism and the Ordering of Love* (Washington, D.C.: Georgetown University Press, 1994); see esp. 67–70. Pope's book is particularly important because of the explicit connection it draws between human altruism and behavioral biology, which the author uses to remedy deficiencies in recent Christian interpretations of love. Typical accounts insist that human nature is something to be overcome. Pope's observation, which he takes from Aquinas, is that sociobiology offers knowledge about both the natural limits and the enabling conditions of love of the other, the awareness of which will help us to order love properly in theological ethics. Pope is particularly useful, I think, as a critic of the cynical view posed by classical thinkers as various as Freud and Kant that aggression and selfishness, and not altruism, constitute the kernel of an unrestrained human nature. While I strongly endorse Pope's point that the impulse to altruism is perhaps at least as central to human nature as selfishness is traditionally thought to be, I do not necessarily agree with him that kin and friendship preference ought to supplant love of the stranger in terms of what is paradigmatically implied in the love commandment.

38. Ibid., 153.

39. Heyd, *Supererogation*, 172.

104 HEROES, SAINTS, AND SUPEREROGATION

40. Ibid., 174–75.

41. Wolf, "Moral Saints," 419.

42. Heyd, *Supererogation*, 175.

43. See Babylonian Talmud, tractate *Baba Meziá* 30b, reprinted in Louis Newman, "Law, Virtue, and Supererogation in the Halakhah: The Problem of *'Lifnim Mishurat Hadin'* Reconsidered," *Journal of Jewish Studies* 60, no. 1 (1989): 70–71. The word "Halakhah" is usually translated as "Jewish Law." It pertains to the legally binding portion of the Talmud and complements the "Aggadah," or stories and homilies in the Talmud that comprise the oral tradition.

44. Newman, "Law, Virtue, and Supererogation in the Halakhah," 70.

45. Ibid., 71 (emphasis mine).

46. Ibid.

47. Drawing on the work of Niklas Luhmann, the philosopher of contemporary Jewish thought Robert Gibbs calls the supererogatory an "overdraft on the normative" that constitutes a "surplus performance, which nobody can require, but which … generates claims" nonetheless. Thus, writes Gibbs, "the function of the supererogative appears to be that it *transforms conditions for emergence into conditions for persistence.*" See Gibbs, *Why Ethics?: Signs of Responsibilities* (Princeton: Princeton University Press, 2000), 147, note 5 (his emphasis). The supererogatory, in other words, represents a future standard by which to assess the obligatory. Gibbs's insight brings clarity to the seeming double standard advocated in *Baba Meziá* 30b.

48. For example, see Dana Radcliffe, "Compassion and Commanded Love," *Faith and Philosophy* 11, no. 1 (January 1994): 62. Radcliffe draws on Robert C. Roberts's work on the emotions in order to explore the idea that feelings, inclinations, and dispositions are not totally beyond our control, as some Kantians believe. See Roberts, "What an Emotion Is: A Sketch," *Philosophical Review* 97, no. 2 (April 1988): esp. 204–5. See also J. B. Schneewind's discussion of Grotius and his "law of a well-ordered love," in Schneewind, *The Invention of Autonomy* (Cambridge: Cambridge University Press, 1998), 78–80.

49. For a comprehensive contemporary account of the subtle ways in which "rightness" relates to "goodness" in the work of St. Thomas Aquinas, see James Keenan, *Goodness and Rightness in Thomas Aquinas's Summa Theologiae* (Washington, D.C.: Georgetown University Press, 1992). Keenan demonstrates that for Aquinas goodness is in large part antecedently a matter of striving to live and act rightly. There is thus a clear emphasis in Keenan's interpretation of Aquinas on *disposing* oneself to live rightly. Keenan clarifies that for Aquinas, "badness" is the equivalent of not striving to move in the direction of right living. "Rightness" is not static but is rather an ongoing expansive concept. It begins with right reasoning but ultimately depends on one making the effort both to overcome immoral impulses and to become as good as one can, primarily through participating in God's love and exhibiting charity. See Keenan, *Goodness and Rightness,* 15ff., 120ff.

50. Gérard Gilleman, *The Primacy of Charity in Moral Theology,* trans. William Ryan and André Vachon (London: The Newman Press, 1959).

51. Ibid., 5ff.

52. The manner in which grace acts on the Christian subject is, to be fair, considerably subtler than this, and Gilleman adopts the Thomistic distinction between "infused" and "acquired" virtue in his explanation of how love is transformed into charity (see ibid., 162ff.). In the case of infused virtue, charity is a reflection of God acting through man in which the naturally limited capacities of man are divinely expanded so as to allow for the possibility of one becoming devoted to the spiritual and material betterment of others. With acquired virtue, by contrast, moral progress is primarily attributable to the will and to character development. Gilleman suggests that the way we become charitable over time is a result of both of these processes. I read him as saying that while we are already teleologically oriented toward becoming charitable, it is due to grace that we are given a push in the right direction. The tendency to charity and the knowledge that one, in fact, ought to act in a charitable manner are not enough themselves to produce charitable living. Also required is for one to habituate oneself to the virtuous life. For a succinct discussion of the difference between infused and acquired virtue, as well as discussion of a possible mediating view, which Gene Outka calls "elicitation," see Outka, *Agape: An Ethical Analysis* (New Haven: Yale University Press, 1972), 150–51.

53. Gilleman, *The Primacy of Charity in Moral Theology*, 6–7.

54. Ibid., 11.

55. Ibid., 254.

56. Gilleman, like Joseph Kotva, favors a "non-brittle," or "teleological," perfectionism. He writes: "Perfection ... consists in the total giving of self out of charity; here then there is a question of a love-obligation extending to the perfect gift, that is, not primarily a duty to carry out determined obligation, but to liberate the total force of charity and to yield to the full spirit of charity" (ibid., 256).

57. Bernard Häring, *The Law of Christ*, vol. 2, trans. Edwin G. Kaiser (Westminster, Md.: Paulist Press, 1963), 94.

58. Ibid., 94.

59. Ibid., 95.

60. Ibid.

PART II

Morally Extraordinary Persons

To leave the mean is to abandon humanity.
—Pascal, *Pensées,* number 378

In those times, one climbed to the summit of humanity
by simply remaining human.
—Elie Wiesel, *The Courage to Care*

Whatever is possible for me is possible even for a child.
—Mahatma Gandhi, *An Autobiography:*
The Story of My Experiments with Truth

CHAPTER 3

Ordinary Human Heroes

THE "HERO" AS A TYPE

One of the reasons that Urmson's "Saints and Heroes" is such an important essay is that for the first time in contemporary ethical theory it raised the possibility that terms of positive moral evaluation (e.g., "praiseworthiness") do not apply strictly to what we *have* to do. Before the essay was written there was little recognition of morally good actions that were not at the same time considered morally required. The innovation of the concept of supererogation, Urmson noted, was the result of an effort to arrive at a classification of moral actions that was no longer "inadequate to the facts of morality."[1] Heroic and saintly actions, and by extension heroes and saints, could no longer be ignored by theorists who wished to provide a full and credible account of the concept of moral obligation. This chapter, and the one that follows, can be regarded as a furtherance of this aim. Just as Urmson sought to reconcile the empirical fact of the existence of exceptional moral agents, such as heroes and saints, with conventional models for understanding moral duty, I aim to revise Urmson's innovative "fourth category" in order to reflect more accurately what heroes and saints are really like. In this chapter, I place my emphasis on revising the conventional characterization of moral heroes.

According to Urmson, heroes are those moral agents who characteristically go beyond duty, in contexts in which terror, fear, or the drive to self-preservation would prevent most people from doing so. They distinguish themselves by their courage, which is the trait that enables them to perform the costly altruistic deeds by which they come to be known. In spite of their claims to the contrary, Urmson insists that heroes are morally *praiseworthy*. Heroes who insist on the obligatory nature of their heroic conduct do not offer this judgment as a "piece of objective reporting,"[2] but as a commitment to an ideal that they individually pursue. Thus, their way of perceiving what is morally required in a situation calling for altruistic conduct is not a reliable guide for us. Urmson concludes that heroic actions may be considered obligatory in a personal, *evaluative* sense, but not in a prescriptive, *morally binding* sense.

In the last chapter I discussed a serious difficulty with this characterization, namely, that it extols heroes for their moral fortitude while undermining their credibility as moral authorities. In this, it assumes that the moral perception of heroes is irreducible to that of ordinary persons. But what if heroes *are* exemplars of good human living? In some obvious respects, heroes are no different from the rest of us. Like us, they are mortal. As mortals, they are surely aware of the vulnerability and precariousness that comes with being human. Moreover, there is no reason to think that heroes do not *feel* vulnerable and precarious from time to time, as we do. It is just that their feelings of fear and doubt are not *overriding* like they are for the rest of us. As mortals, heroes are limited by the instincts to survive and to protect themselves. But, unlike us, they have resources to overcome these limitations for the sake of a greater human good.

These reflections lead us to wonder whether heroes are best described as figures who transcend humanity or as humans who excel at it. The tendency in the standard view to dichotomize humans into the heroic and the incorrigibly less-than-heroic is problematic because it gives the impression that heroes have little in common with ordinary persons.[3] A revision to the standard view characterizes heroes as persons who ascend to lofty heights but who do not fully climb out of the human situation. According to such a revision, heroes would best be characterized as extraordinary *and* ordinary persons who distinguish themselves within rather than apart from their social contexts. Heroes would be seen as eminently among us, charismatically inspiring us to become more like them by appealing to those aspects of our humanity that we already have in common. In the revised characterization, heroes are thus oriented toward the communal. They see themselves as connected to and responsible for those around them. They likely do this because they remember what it was like to be merely ordinary, for they were not *born* heroic but became so gradually, over time. For these reasons, an investigation into the nature of heroes ought not to begin by attempting to locate an essential "heroic" core from the outset, but by examining the circumstances that surround heroes' historical background and rearing. This is an empirical inquiry. It proceeds by attempting to place heroes contextually.

In their recent work on heroism in the tradition of Christianity, Brian S. Hook and R. R. Reno emphasize the importance of imitation in the development of heroic traits. According to them, the very term "hero" becomes an empty, "honorific" title, useless for purposes of writing about the good life, if not linked to concrete patterns of recognition:

Heroism is not an abstract quality; it is not an innate property that shimmers, like gold, simply by virtue of its mere essence, without exercise or enactment. Nor is heroism a solipsistic conceit, a forceful way of expressing our likes and dislikes. Quite to the contrary, heroism is deeply communal. It demands and evokes acknowledgment. We can become heroes in our own minds, or we can imagine that a parent or a friend is heroic, but only as others laud and magnify deeds and character, only as the hero is recognized, does a heroic gestalt emerge.[4]

The idea of the heroic entails the development of heroic traits that beckon acknowledgment and active participation among the nonheroic. The implication of this observation is to recover the role of *excellence* in daily life.[5] In terms of Christian ethics, with which Hook and Reno are primarily concerned, the hero-as-exemplar becomes a focus for the religious practitioner in training. That is, the hero is a *resource*, a model for the nonspectacular agent trying merely to live decently and happily. Hook and Reno argue that the call of Jesus is not a "call to self-denial," but "part of a menu of therapies for sick souls" desiring to feel better about the ways they live their lives.[6] In this account, the Christian act of surrendering oneself to Jesus, self-abandonment, becomes an instance of humility rather than one of transcendence.[7] The heroic does not signal an exclusive sanctity. It connotes solidarity and fellowship.

Hook and Reno's insights about the usefulness of the category of the "heroic" for guiding the ordinary Christian practitioner in pursuit of the good life can be applied more broadly to the ordinary person striving to live decently in secular society. Let us, then, extrapolate and entertain the following hypothesis: what separates heroes from ordinary persons is not *exemption* from their own mortality but rather their *exemplification* of it. In being able to perceive "humanity"—and the duties that are ingredient in this enlightened perception—more clearly than the rest of us, heroes become especially equipped to intervene in their communities on humanity's behalf. What *we*, from afar, might be inclined to interpret as "courage," that virtue of bold willingness to put aside the desire for self-preservation for the sake of a beneficiary, is according to my proposal what heroes themselves would see as a basic expression of their worthiness as human beings. Accordingly, "courage" is moral maturity as much as it is sheer talent. It is, as Iris Murdoch puts it, an "operation of wisdom and love" that results in "seeing the order of the world in the light of the Good and revisiting the true, or more true, conceptions of that which we formerly misconceived."[8] In this sense, heroes' courage represents the conquering of complacency. It enables them to modify their level of accountability for others to a standard higher than the one to which they are

already accustomed, and to challenge the received set of mortal limitations that others are inclined to accept as a given.

When we put heroes too high on the pedestal, we risk transforming
them into the impenetrable "other" about whom we know (and prefer
to know) little, save the distorted and often aggrandized version of them
that we ourselves create. One good example of this can be seen in how
many people have come to regard those who risked and in many cases lost
their lives rushing into the north and south towers of the World Trade
Center on September 11, 2001.[9] In fact, the firefighters and rescue workers
who became the heroes of September 11 were regular people, with rou-
tines and families. The efforts they exerted facing a danger of unprecedented magnitude, knowing as little about that danger as they knew, were
for them the stuff of a day's work: unglamorous, methodical, and in keeping with the standards and expectations of the profession they had chosen. In this sense, they were both special and not special. We remember
those who died with the fondness that we do, not only because they did
what we likely would not have had the courage to do ourselves, but also
because we can identify with their human plight. Like us, they were merely
mortal. Their values reflected ours. They cared deeply about their families, just as we care deeply about our own. It is therefore worthwhile to
try to discover how their heroism might have manifested itself in those
last moments through their own eyes: as spouses, parents, employees
at work, and human beings reaching out to help other human beings in
distress.

David Halberstam's *Firehouse*, which tells the somber tale of the fate
of thirteen firefighters from Engine 40 and Ladder 35 (twelve of whom lost
their lives), is one of the better books to have appeared since the tragedy
of September 11 because it reminds us of the subjective side of human
agency.[10] *Firehouse* conveys a sense of community experienced by coworkers who came to love each other in all their imperfect, diverse particularity. Many of the firefighters, Halberstam writes,

> were not necessarily angels or saintly—far from it, in fact—and they
> were not, in the traditional sense, necessarily very religious. But there
> was a certain spiritual redemption to what they did. They could be on
> occasion rowdy and combative and they had their allotted share of
> human flaws, of which they themselves were all too often aware. But
> whatever they had done wrong the night before, the next morning when
> they were at the firehouse, they were able to take extra meaning from
> their lives, and to find some form of redemption because of the nature
> of the job, because of the risks they take for complete strangers.[11]

This "meaning" derives from a particular tradition in which firefighters are reared. In the firehouse there is a code of unspoken rules and expectations. Halberstam conveys the importance of these through his description of the "chauffeur" of Engine 40, Jimmy Giberson. The job of a chauffeur was typically to find the most efficient route to a fire and to set the rigs so the men could best work the fire. It was also the chauffeur who informally would provide directional guidance to the younger firefighters and instill in them their own commitment to the job and to their fellow workers. Halberstam explains that the sense of inner obligation to the other firefighters was particularly strong with Giberson:

> [He] expected that same sense of duty in others. If you were screwing up, he would simply give you a look, and there was no doubt what it meant—that you were cheating on the others, and therefore pulling the house down. Things were to be done right ... and no one was to get even a little sloppy.[12]

This code was acquired in the same way that wisdom is passed down from generation to generation—through the formation of bonds of trust between mentors and novices, all insiders to "a vast extended family" that enforced among its members the value of saving a human life to the exclusion of any competing consideration.[13] Halberstam's depiction of the firefighters as human beings acting in unison from specific reasons and emotions affirms the success of adopting an empirical approach to understanding the nature of heroes. Who are heroes? From where do they derive their heroic traits? What makes a rescuer rescue?

Three hundred and forty-three firefighters lost their lives on September 11, 2001. One of the most striking impressions with which Halberstam leaves the reader of *Firehouse* pertains to the contingency of the tragedy that took the lives of twelve men. These firefighters who placed themselves in harm's way were not destined to become "heroes" any more than they knew that when they entered the south tower of the World Trade Center it would be the last day of their lives.[14] Such is the nature of heroes, who seem to lack any self-awareness of their heroism, much less accept such a characterization when it is issued on their behalf by others. A plausible reason for this denial is that heroic deeds, when performed, occur in response to unpredictable situations to which the hero simply reacts, bereft of the self-conscious objective of playing the hero. He or she reacts as he or she thinks anyone would react, though in such a way that importantly reflects advance preparation. In a sense, the hero does what he or she has been trained to do.

The purpose of training is to acquire a preparedness that can be used as a resource in a crisis situation. Training contains technical, and in the case of heroes, moral components. It requires the right skills and the right attitude. Once acquired, these traits make it possible for the "heroic" in the potential hero to surface. Admittedly, we must not lose sight of the fact that the firefighters who rushed into the burning towers were trained in a particular profession. It was their *job* to rush into the towers, and so it is not simply heroic courage, but also their occupational competencies, that led them to perform the "heroic" acts they did. At the same time, the actions of the firefighters demonstrate more generally the value of training and preparedness in morally exemplary action. The firefighters distinguished themselves because they were prepared to do their job when they were most needed. Heroes who are heroic in contexts in which they are not merely fulfilling a role display a similar preparedness. People diverge in terms of how they respond to others in need during a crisis. This divergence, while wide, is not accidental. Heroes act heroically because they are prepared in a way nonheroes are not. They have traits that nonheroes lack. The purpose of this chapter is to explore both the nature of this preparedness and of those traits to which it gives rise.

My observations draw from two general areas, the "hero" from literature and the "hero" in history. These treatments prepare me to develop my own view of the "hero" as a type in moral theory. My examination of the nature of literary heroes is exploratory. I examine four classical protagonists, each of whom contributes to a composite picture of the hero who is at once both "ordinary and extraordinary." The characters are Homer's Odysseus; Sidney Carton from Dickens's *A Tale of Two Cities*; Joseph Conrad's Lord Jim, from the work with the same title; and Dr. Rieux, the determined physician in Camus's *The Plague*. The courage of all these fictional characters presupposes their sense of human finitude. Through reference to them, we can imagine a construction of the hero other than the one presented in the standard view, in which their classification as exceptional, duty-exceeding agents is taken for granted.

The analyses of these heroes pave the way for the central focus in this chapter, the case of real-life rescuers of victims of genocide. I examine Holocaust rescuers, known as "righteous gentiles," considering briefly also the related case of a hotel owner who rescued Tutsis fleeing Hutus in the Rwandan genocide of 1994. Like heroes in the realm of literature, rescuers consider themselves ordinary, mortal humans, deserving no special praise for having sheltered their victims from almost sure death. Studies reveal that, almost invariably, such persons understood their rescue activities to fall under the rubric of duty. Rescuers challenge in their own voice Urmson's central claim that moral heroes who insist on the obligatory nature of their acts are not in a position to offer this declaration as the "objective fact of the matter." Contemporary sociologists and historians have, in the last two decades, started to listen. The result has been a wealth of literature that accounts for the motivations of rescuing and avoids minimizing the perspective of the rescuers themselves.[15] Such accounts do not merely describe the acts of righteous gentiles. They also attempt to explain the righteous gentile phenomenon and discuss what impact, if any, our consideration of this historical event ought to have on the way we determine our own normative standards.

In my analysis, I make use of Lawrence Blum's characterization of heroes, such as rescuers, as "noteworthily virtuous moral agents" who see the world differently from those around them, owing both to their individual character development and to the influence of the communities in which they live.[16] As a result of the virtue that they possess, I argue, heroes have a more enhanced capacity than the rest of us to perceive the moral necessity of helping others in need. On this hypothesis, what is morally distinctive about heroes is not the specific "heroic" traits with which they are born, but their highly developed virtuous character. This is what gives them an advantage over the rest of us in being able both to determine what, in the strictest sense, they morally "ought" to do in a given situation, and to follow through on this insight by actually doing what they ought. Moral heroes are not "falsely modest" in assuming a greater burden of responsibility for others than the rest of us do;[17] nor, due to personal idiosyncrasies, are they prone to fail to acknowledge a supposed objective cut-off point that separates acts of duty from acts of supererogation.[18] These verdicts about heroes are inconsistent both with the way heroes from fiction see themselves and with the self-images of actual heroes, such as rescuers. Contra Urmson and Heyd, the defender of the revised view maintains that heroes ought *not* to be seen as supererogatory agents. They do not in their actions exceed their moral duty. Rather, they are agents who have an expanded, and continually expanding, sense of duty relative to ordinary persons. Their level of altruism, while significantly higher than others, is not excessive.

HEROIC REPRESENTATIONS

The heroes in whom we take an interest and with whom we identify in the stories we read tend to find themselves in jeopardy at critical junctures in the narrative. Being mortal, they are familiar with the discouragement that accompanies defeat, the pain involved in losing a loved one, and the risk undertaken when daring death. In short, the heroes of good storytelling *struggle*. They typically embark on dangerous ventures that are at the outset unlikely to be met with success. At the same time, their willingness to try to stretch beyond human limitations compels us to care about their plight. If heroes were permitted to pursue their endeavors without resistance, and to meet with success rather easily, they would surpass their humanity altogether and thereby cease to retain their appeal. In this sense, heroic successes are measured against human limitations, without which heroic virtues as diverse as courage, temperance, and justice would lose their point.[19] Notwithstanding their abundant possession of these traits, heroes impress us to the extent that they continue to remain mortal and, to an extent, flawed. We rally behind their cause and root for them because their lives are characterized more by painful toil than by stable contentment, because of their "anthropomorphic imperfection."[20] The fictional characters considered below force us to reflect about what it means to be a hero within the human context. In distinctive ways, they each provide a counterexample to the Urmsonian interpretation of the hero who transcends human limitation. Specifically, they offer us three significant traits: (1) the hero's solidarity with and embeddedness in his or her community, as seen in Odysseus; (2) the hero's originally less than heroic nature and subsequent transformation *into* a hero by means of character improvement, in the cases of Sydney Carton and Lord Jim; and finally, (3) the hero's ability to make an informed judgment about the nature of his or her responsibilities to others, as in Camus's Dr. Rieux. All three of these heroic traits lend support to the idea that the hero is both ordinary and extraordinary.

The Hero as Mortal and Exemplary:
The Case of Odysseus

In a famous passage from *The Odyssey* that represents the protagonist's defining moment, Odysseus rejects Calypso's offer to spend the rest of eternity with her, a beautiful goddess, on an island that is a veritable paradise.[21] Odysseus's decision is at the same time perplexing and the one that is most eligible for him to choose. On the one hand, he denies himself an endless life of pleasure and youth, one that is equally enticing to us due to its universal appeal. He elects instead to continue subjecting himself to the fatigue, sorrow, defeat, and death that comprise the heart of the mortal experience. On the other hand, Odysseus, to our relief, is unable to conceive of a life for himself that *is* other than the human life.

Odysseus is aware of the tension caused by these two equally appealing yet jointly contradictory reactions to Calypso's offer. Responding to the goddess who was his lover and warder for seven years, Odysseus remarks with due respect:

I know my wise Penelope, when a man looks at her, is far beneath you in form and stature. . . . Yet, notwithstanding, my desire and longing day by day is still to reach my own home and to see the day of my return. And if this or that divinity should shatter my craft on the wine-dark ocean, I will bear it and keep a bold heart within me. Often enough before this time have war and wave oppressed and plagued me; let the new tribulations join the old.[22]

Odysseus is aware that Calypso is superior to Penelope in terms of appearance and ability. He knows that he is forgoing an unsurpassably pleasurable alternative existence for the sake of an imperfect woman whom he may never live to see again. However, what he gains are the manifold possibilities of excelling as a human being, possibilities that are available to him only if he remains human. Odysseus predicts correctly the troubles that await him once he resumes his journey homeward. No sooner does Calypso assent to Odysseus's request to return to his wife, dress him in sweet smelling garments, and "summon up for him a fair wind that [is] warm and kindly" for his journey, than does Poseidon proceed to remind the hero of the cost of retaining his mortality. Still angered by Odysseus's blinding of his son, the Cyclops Polyphemus, Poseidon places him in peril once he is no longer under Calypso's protection. With purpose, Poseidon

massed the clouds, clutched his trident and churned the ocean up; he roused all the blasts of all the winds and swathed the earth and sea alike in cloud; down from the sky rushed the dark. East and south wind clashed together, the stormy west and the sky-born billow-driving north. Then Odysseus felt his knees and his spirit quail; in desperation he spoke to his own heroic heart: 'Alas for me! What will become of me in the end? I fear the goddess spoke all too truly when she prophesied of trouble on trouble to bear at sea before I reached my own land.'[23]

True to form, the hero faces the consequences of his choice. He has risked all for his loyal commitment to a life that is distinctively human. Yet, while Odysseus's decision is one about which, on the face of it, both he and we are ambivalent, it is at the same time the decision that we would have him make. As Martha Nussbaum observes:

We don't quite know what it would be for this hero, known for his courage, craft, resourcefulness, and loyal love to enter into a life in which courage would atrophy, in which cunning and resourcefulness would have little point, since the risks with which they grapple would be removed, and in which love, insofar as it appears at all, would be very different in shape from the love that connects man to wife and child in the human world of poem. The very possibility makes one uneasy: for where, and who, in such a life, would our hero actually be?[24]

To live well is not to transcend life but to live it with all of its adventure, danger, and uncertainty. What sets Odysseus apart from more ordinary mortals is not his exhibition of superhuman capabilities, but his excellence in the human ones.

In principle the heroic life is accessible to all, even if lived only by a few. Nussbaum connects this insight to the Aristotelian conception of virtue. She writes:

> [A]lthough I do not believe that human beings are originally evil or sinful, it is all too plain that most people are much of the time lazy, inattentive, unreflective, shallow in feeling; in short, that most human action falls well short of the fully human target of complete virtue set up by Aristotle's view [of ethics]. Aristotle holds, on the one hand, that the completely virtuous life is "common to many: for it is open to anyone who is not by nature maimed with respect to excellence." But he holds, as well, that acting virtuously requires not only going through the motions of correct action, but doing so with the appropriate thoughts, motives, and reactive feelings. And he holds that this is a very difficult business, requiring much experience and practice, much flexibility and refinement of thought and feeling.[25]

The Aristotelian hero does not escape his or her humanity but "descends into it," harnessing his or her human faculties.[26] Aristotelian striving takes the form of pushing against the boundaries that restrict human life. An athlete who breaks a world record is attracted to that event in part because of the foreknowledge that there is a level of accomplishment beyond which success is impossible for a human being to achieve. Without their respective ultimate limits, any and all such activities would not be worthwhile. By the same logic, while we require our heroes to struggle against and even temporarily to defy their mortality, we never wish for them total success in this struggle. The athlete's ambition becomes a paradox: it is a "struggle for victory in which *complete* 'victory' would be disaster and emptiness—or, at any rate, a life so different from our own that we could no longer find ourselves and our valued activities in it."[27] Similarly, the hero is caught between the imperative always to be improving—"transcending internally"[28]—and the prohibition against transcending the human point of view entirely. What is therefore recommended is a fragile balancing act between "the claims of excellence, which lead us to push outward, and the necessity of the human context, which pushes us back in."[29] *The Odyssey* can be read as a repudiation of the tempting prospect of choosing the divine life over a human one. Odysseus, for all the times he prevails against the obstacles with which the gods burden him, strives in an appropriately human way. He does not have *hubris*. This is not to say that Odysseus does not have moments when he pushes the constraints of his humanity to their limit and even flirts with the prospect of the divine. One good example of this is when he ties himself to the mast of his ship rather than putting wax in his ears, as he does for his men, so that he may enjoy, albeit in tortured fashion, the "honey-sweet" song of the Sirens.[30] However, even then, his action is one of being tempted by the divine, not of attempting to imitate it.

The Homeric hero is not the "other" who overcomes mortality but a kinsman whose virtue is recognizable by everyone in the heroic society.[31] We have expectations for how Odysseus is going to act even before he is put into jeopardy by the gods or placed in a situation that tests his honor, wisdom, or courage because, like all of the other characters in *The Odyssey*, he observes the rules which give his life purpose and enable him to stand out within the context of a larger framework. He warrants our esteem because he follows these rules better than anyone else, not because he makes an exception with respect to them in his own case. The hero's "heroic" particularity is thus the counterpart to his accountability to the standards of conduct that are common to his society as a whole.

The example of Odysseus is helpful for reflecting on the question of how we ought to situate the hero in relation to others. Throughout *The Odyssey* the hero's expressed goal remains constant: it is to arrive home to his family and to reestablish himself in his society. Odysseus is an insider. In his choice to refuse immortality, he reveals the strong link that he sees between himself and the people of Ithaca. Through his example, we in turn discover the value of aspiring beyond our current limitations, while simultaneously learning why we ought to reject the aim of living a "godlike transcendent life," which is an inappropriate if not incoherent aim for a human being to pursue.[32] Odysseus's noble character is revealed to the extent that he exhibits the shared values of his society. It is because of the existence of this shared standard that he is able to shine. His cleverness and sheer athletic ability, for example, are traits that bring him closer to us the more he distinguishes himself through exhibiting them. By looking at this example from classic Greek literature, we are able to appreciate the significant role that communal solidarity, a criterion overlooked in the Urmsonian characterization, plays in the identification of the hero.

The Hero and Moral Development: Sydney Carton and Lord Jim

The theme of hero as both ordinary and extraordinary is brought into clearer focus in the case of our next two characters, Sydney Carton and Lord Jim.[33] We may consider a couple of contrasts between these two and the case of Odysseus. First, in these characters we as readers get to witness common, indeed flawed, human beings developing *into* heroes. By the end of their narratives, Sydney Carton and Lord Jim come to reflect on whether they are living worthwhile human lives, both finally holding themselves accountable for improving the overall quality of their character. The heroic decisions that Sydney Carton and Lord Jim make near the conclusions of *A Tale of Two Cities* and *Lord Jim* are a direct result of this self-critical introspection. Second, the heroism of Sydney Carton and Lord Jim is reflected in the performance of self-sacrificial, other-regarding acts. In this sense, they are *moral* heroes.[34] Odysseus is a moral hero only in the weak sense that in his sustained attempt to return to Penelope and the people of Ithaca he exhibits the virtues of Homeric society, and thereby fulfills the duties proper to his particular role. Sydney Carton and Lord Jim, by contrast, meet their death by sacrificing themselves for the sake of others with whom they come into contact late in their lives. By the close of their narratives, both characters exhibit a firm and righteous resolve that contrasts with their former cowardice. They distinguish themselves through their sacrifice, yet their actions remain fully within our grasp, for, like Odysseus, their heroism represents an affirmation rather than an overcoming of their human attributes.

Sydney Carton's decision to trade his life for Charles Darnay's is an act of profound moral courage that at the same time represents the culmination of the deliberate attempt on Carton's part to break away from his otherwise empty and slovenly existence. Dickens is forthcoming about Carton's flaws, at one point calling him the "idlest and most unpromising of men."[35] Carton is, to be sure, a man of remarkable intelligence and acumen; however, he is also a classic underachiever who has never made much of his life. The underling of Mr. Stryver, his unappreciative, pompous law partner and former classmate, Carton nonchalantly devotes himself to the betterment of his senior's career, spending the rest of his time either drunk or aimlessly wasting his time with other distractions. When he encounters Lucie Manette, Carton is inspired by her beauty and purity of character, causing him for a moment to envision a "mirage of honorable ambitions, self-denial and perseverance."[36] Through a number of twists of fate, coupled with his own ingenuity and resolve, Carton finds himself in the unique position of being able to help Charles Darnay, whom Lucie has married. His decision to save Darnay is simultaneously an act of extreme altruism and self-salvation, equally motivated by the unselfish prospect of saving a family from its sure demise and by the desire to give a wasted life some meaning.[37] It is not Carton's remarkable ability to *overlook* his self-preservation that enables him to act heroically. To the contrary, nothing short of his assumption of Darnay's place at the guillotine will rescue him from a life of debauchery and boredom. In dying for Darnay, Carton achieves stature and self-respect, and he regains his humanity. In this sense, his self-sacrificial act is also an act of self-affirmation. Ultimately, his courage stands as the reflection of the way he has transformed himself late in his life.

The motif of the "human hero," and in particular the developmental aspects of the hero's transformation from merely ordinary to ordinary and extraordinary, is made perhaps even more clear in Joseph Conrad's *Lord Jim*. Like Dickens, Conrad introduces the reader to his hero through an act that reveals the protagonist's shortcomings. We first meet Jim as a young officer on the *Patna*, a ship carrying eight hundred Muslim pilgrims. Within the first fifty pages he falls from grace. The bulkhead of the *Patna* is apparently falling apart at the same time that a severe storm is approaching, prompting Jim, in a panic, to leap to safety into one of the few available lifeboats and to abandon his duties to those who remain stranded. This act of cowardice is subsequently discovered when the *Patna* is tugged to port with its passengers still alive. Overcome with guilt and shame, Jim is consigned to live out his days in exile. The rest of the novel details Jim's attempt to achieve redemption. Over time Jim finds himself living a constructive life in the forest of Patusan, where he reacquires a measure of self-respect and gains the confidence of the natives, who affectionately refer to him as "Tuan" (Lord) Jim. At the end of the novel, Jim confronts his second crisis when a group of English seamen whom he has befriended, led by the evil Brown, massacre a party of natives including Jim's best friend, Dain Waris, also son of the old chief, Doramin. Still haunted by his disgrace from the *Patna* affair, Jim ignores the pleas of Jewel, the native girl whom he loves, and gives himself up to Doramin to be killed in order to make amends for the crimes committed by Brown and his men.[38]

Like that of Sydney Carton, Lord Jim's heroism develops against the backdrop of imperfection. Marlow, who narrates the story and serves as Jim's advocate to the men witnessing Jim's trial over the *Patna* affair, observes at several junctures that Jim is "one of us."[39] In all likelihood, remarks Marlow, we would not have had the fortitude to act differently from Jim were we officers aboard the *Patna*. Jim's brave, suicidal decision to appear before Doramin is characterized as a rational if bold act, and one committed in solidarity with those in Patusan who had trusted him to "answer with his life for any harm that should come to them" from the "white men with beards."[40] This act of heroism is a display of Jim's friendship for Dain Waris and Dain's close comrade, Stein. It is also a demonstration of his integrity. The sacrifice is not purely an act of selfless, superhuman courage. Marlow relates early on in the novel that Jim's virtue consists of another sort of courage:

> [Jim] stood there for all the parentage of his kind, for men and women by no means clever or amusing, but whose very existence is based upon a kind of honest faith, and upon the instinct of courage. I don't mean military courage, or civil courage, or any special kind of courage, I mean just that inborn ability to look temptations straight in the face—a readiness unintellectual enough, goodness knows, but without pose—a power of resistance, don't you see, ungracious if you like, but priceless—an unthinking and blessed stiffness before the outward and inward terrors, before the might of nature, and the seductive corruption of men— backed by a faith invulnerable to the strength of facts, to the contagion of example, to the solicitation of ideas.[41]

There is a distinctive humanity to this sort of courage, which resembles Iris Murdoch's description of the trait: a courage more akin to a "particular operation of wisdom and love" than "a sort of specialized daring of the spirit."[42] Jim's is a courage begotten from an earlier cowardice, his struggle to achieve success as a human being made possible by his failures. His decision to submit himself to native justice can be interpreted as the culmination of this struggle.

Sydney Carton and Lord Jim were not born heroes. They became so through extended reflection and a despair that is ultimately alleviated only by answering their own shortcomings. One cannot see their virtue without seeing the precariousness of their situation. Sydney Carton stands out among the cast of characters in *A Tale of Two Cities*, for he is the only major character who is real. He is not portrayed as perfect, as Lucie Manette, Charles Darnay, or even Lucie's loyal governess, Miss Pross, are; nor is he motivated by purely bad intentions, as is the wicked and vengeful Madame Defarge. Carton is more nuanced than any of these characters, who in comparison seem like caricatures or idealized types. He has flaws that he perceives to be insurmountable, yet the whole thrust of his character development centers around his endeavor to overcome them. He is the only character in the novel that undergoes any real change.

Likewise, Lord Jim remains committed to the task of improving himself, long after he finds solace among the people of Patusan. He tells Marlow late in the story: "I've been only two years here, and now, upon my word, I can't conceive of being able to live anywhere else. The very thought of the world outside is enough to give me a fright ... because I have not forgotten why I came here. Not yet!"[43] Given new life and having gained the respect of the inhabitants of his new world, Jim knows inwardly that he is no better than anyone else, and is in fact capable of worse. The enduring memory of the *Patna* affair serves constantly to remind him of this. When Brown and his men arrive and prove almost immediately to be a destructive force in Patusan, Jim is simultaneously repulsed by and strangely attracted to Brown's evil. Jim's heroism does not make him innately different from Brown. On the contrary, it is the effort that Jim exerts at the end of the novel *not* to be like Brown, whose example he might also have followed, that represents the substance of Jim's heroism. Both Sydney Carton and Lord Jim emerge heroic from origins in a commonplace, cowardly existence. Like Odysseus, with whom we identify more when he is tempted by the Sirens than during any other point in the epic, Sydney Carton and Lord Jim appeal to us through their initial weaknesses and fallibility. Their heroic achievements ought not to be considered apart from the cowardice and self-doubt that motivated them.

The Hero as Moral Authority: Dr. Rieux and The Plague

A third attribute to consider in this cluster of heroic traits is the one of moral credibility. Are heroes qualified to serve as reliable arbiters of what is morally required in a given human context, in particular one characterized by a crisis? To help answer this question, we may examine Camus's Dr. Rieux, who strongly resembles the rescuers with whom I deal later in this chapter. Rieux is the first to see the situation brought about by the arrival of the plague for what it is, and the first to assume some responsibility for defending the people of Oran against it. Urmson likely has Rieux in mind when he begins to characterize the moral hero, for his description is of a doctor who volunteers to join depleted medical forces in a plague-ridden city. On closer examination, however, the comparison appears to be no more than a superficial resemblance, for while Urmson concludes that the doctor's decision to stay behind and help the afflicted is supererogatory, Rieux denies that his deeds earn him any praise. He sees himself as one man among many. His is the plight of everyone in the stricken town of Oran. He interprets the plague as an absurd "given" of life with which humanity now has to contend in the everyday realm. Here Rieux implies that he has a clear view of the moral situation at hand and that his interpretation of it may be accepted as authoritative. Camus portrays Rieux as a doctor who is sensible and down to earth. He is neither characterized as mistaken about his moral responsibility, nor as excessively modest in his ambition to fulfill it.

Camus humanizes Rieux by having him narrate the story, which he does in a detached, objective fashion. He handles the adversity that comes with the plague by using common sense and by acting when action is called for. Throughout the narrative, Rieux is a doctor responding to an emergency. Early on, for example, it is Rieux who insists that the victims of the unidentified fever should be quarantined, while the other doctors fail to draw any conclusions.[44] Such leadership foreshadows his methodical approach to treating those who will later be afflicted. When it becomes clear that the plague is a real force with which the people of Oran will have to contend, Rieux becomes the person upon whom others depend to mount a strategy of defense. The leadership role Rieux assumes is not easy, and we identify with the frustrations he experiences as he confronts the plague: first, his orders to isolate the infected are not initially carried out because of an ineffective bureaucracy; then, when the plague is finally acknowledged by the Prefect, Rieux is directed not to attract attention in his handling of the crisis and must contend with a doctor who, at the Prefect's behest, explains away the plague in technical vagaries; and, finally, the plague itself confounds Rieux, who initially has a hard time coming to terms with the fact that there is no possible logical explanation for the singling out of Oran for such a tragedy.[45] We can empathize with Rieux, who feels rather small next to the plague, and who has a hard time getting through to the incompetent city officials charged with organizing a response to the crisis. Rieux nevertheless does what he can, continually reminding himself and the reader: "The thing was to do your job as it should be done."[46] He is afraid of what the plague might do, but he does not shy away from the battle. We constantly witness him searching for more hospital beds, requisitioning public buildings to quarantine patients, trying to procure sufficient serum, and helping victims, including some who thrust themselves at him in agony.[47] While doing these things, Rieux reflects on how no one is above the horror of the plague, which erases all social distinctions and traps the people of Oran together and isolates them from the rest of the world. Like the heroes from the other literary works examined above, Rieux sees himself as fundamentally connected to those around him.

It is this feeling of connectedness that leads Rieux to deny that he and others who fight the plague are doing anything "heroic," or more than human. In the thick of the crisis, his days proceed "as usual." He engages in a struggle "against creation as he found it."[48] When pressed by his friend, Tarrou, to account for how he is able to keep fighting in a seemingly godless world, Rieux replies:

> Yes, you're thinking it calls for pride to feel that way. But I assure you
> I've no more than the pride that's needed to keep me going. I have no

idea what's awaiting me, or what will happen when all this ends. For the moment I know this; there are sick people and they need curing. Later on, perhaps, they'll think things over, and so shall I. But what's wanted now is to make them well. I defend them as best I can, that's all.[49]

Rieux's struggle with all that is bad—disease, suffering, death—is the most and least he can do. Of Tarrou's commitment to organize a group of civilian "plague-fighters," Rieux remarks that it would be a mischaracterization to describe the endeavor as a "heroic" one, for helping in an emergency situation is as elementary as "two and two making four."[50] To help is one's duty, and to see things otherwise is to lack clear-sightedness. Rieux's attitude is rare in comparison to that of others, yet he considers it representative of the norm. That it is one's *duty* to fight the plague, he feels, needs no explanation.

Rieux's faith is borne out with the conversion of the journalist Rambert. Rieux and Tarrou appeal to Rambert to join one of the sanitary squads commissioned to fight the plague. After thinking over the request for a few days, Rambert, who initially wants to escape the quarantine issued in Oran in order to be with his wife, eventually agrees to help them in their struggle. Rambert's misgivings about doing so center around the notion that he does not want to die for an ideal, like a "hero" would. However, Rieux induces him to see the situation differently, as is demonstrated in the following exchange:

> "You're right Rambert, quite right, and for nothing in the world would I try to dissuade you from what you're going to do; it seems to me absolutely right and proper. However, there's one thing I must tell you: there's no question of heroism in all this. It's a matter of common decency. That's an idea which may make some people smile, but the only means of fighting a plague is—common decency."
>
> "What do you mean by 'common decency'?" Rambert's tone was grave.
>
> "I don't know what it means for other people. But in my case I know it consists in doing my job."[51]

Is Rieux doing his job or is he doing more than his job? While it is true that Rieux is a doctor who would seem to have special responsibilities in battling a medical epidemic, there are several places in the novel where he indicates that he is doing "merely his duty" in a more generic sense, that is, as a concerned resident of Oran. While it is true that "common decency" consists of doing one's job, fighting the plague is at the same time something to which everyone should contribute, as they can. The ambivalence of the text on this point is made apparent in an exchange between Rambert and Rieux late in the novel, in which Rambert reflects upon the extent to which fighting the plague is part of the duty of a journalist like himself. Rieux's attitude that one cannot simply choose to exempt oneself from the crisis is compelling and contagious. Rambert acknowledges this explicitly when he finally has the opportunity to leave Oran and join his wife in Paris but instead remarks: "Until now, I always felt a stranger in this town, and that I'd no concern with you people. But now I've seen what I have seen, I know that I belong here whether I want it or not. *This business is everybody's business.*"[52] Rambert's decision, which Rieux influences, is based on insight rather than fleeting emotion. It is a decision that Camus tells us is "on the side of truth."[53] Camus's point is not that we should go out of our way to achieve glory or esteem; rather, we should aspire simply to be responsible as human beings, an imperative that in and of itself can be a task of a lifetime.[54] Even upon the departure of the plague, which claims Tarrou as its final victim, Rieux reveals himself to be no more than a human being who has done the best he could under the circumstances. While watching his friend die, Rieux is again reminded of how frustrating it can be to battle absurdity, and we are told that the tears that blinded Rieux's eyes "were tears of impotence." Rieux's reflections continue:

> Tarrou had "lost the match," as he put it. But what had he, Rieux, won? No more than the experience of having known plague and remembering it, of having known friendship and remembering it, of knowing affection and being destined one day to remember it. So all a man could win in the conflict between plague and life was knowledge and memories.[55]

Man is never larger than the great force of the plague, which, when it finally does leave Oran, leaves of its own accord. Rieux is no exception. Upon confessing that he is the narrator of the story, Rieux explains that "he has deliberately taken the victims' side and tried to share with his fellow citizens the only certitudes they had in common—love, exile, and suffering. Thus he can truly say there was not one of their anxieties in which he did not share, no predicament of theirs that was not his."[56]

Urmson's indictment of the authoritative credibility of the hero is premised on the assumption that the hero does not share the common moral viewpoint. This assumption is called into question in the case of Rieux, who has more in common with the ordinary victim than with, for example, Urmson's self-sacrificing soldier. We are led to ask ourselves what the legitimate basis is for Urmson's dismissal of Rieux's understanding of what is morally required of him upon the arrival of the plague. In *The*

Plague, Rieux is portrayed as heroic *because* he is able to decide the best, truest course of action, whereas other characters are confused or ambivalent about what to do. Camus explains this capacity as part of the protagonist's *virtue*. It involves both the capacity to recognize human suffering when it arrives and the capacity to "bear witness [to such suffering] in favor of all those plague-stricken people."[57] In other words, Rieux is heroic in part because of how perceptive he is. He *is* a credible witness and, at least in the context of a crisis like the plague, it seems he should therefore be considered a legitimate moral authority.

The characters of Odysseus, Sydney Carton, Lord Jim, and Dr. Rieux are heroic not in spite of, but because of, their humanity. I have examined them together here because they call to our attention certain features of the hero that according to Urmson's characterization are not only not highlighted, but also in some instances explicitly denied. According to Urmson, heroes transcend their status as human beings. They practically lack imperfection. By contrast, as we have seen, Odysseus is heroic because he chooses mortality; Sydney Carton and Lord Jim because they finally succeed at their respective endeavors of self-realization—which are not ones of self-transcendence; and Rieux because he sees clearly what the appropriate and decent "human" response is in the face of a calamity that threatens humanity as a whole. All four characters are virtuous as well as charismatic. In the case of Rieux, the hero's virtuous character rubs off on those around him. Finally, it is significant that the heroic identity of these heroes emerges through their life struggles. They are not born heroes. Their heroism is a product of the development of their character through life's trials and tribulations. Admittedly, Odysseus can be said to be a moral hero only in the weak sense that he is fulfilling a role duty; the morality of the heroism of Sydney Carton and Lord Jim is primarily derived from a particular event that occurs at the end of their lives. Only Dr. Rieux can properly be depicted as a hero whose other-regarding efforts are sustained throughout the novel. Yet, in each case, the hero's heroic identity is derived from his humanity; his virtue is the manifestation of good human living. In light of these four examples, it seems that there is a tenable alternative to the construal of the hero advanced in the standard view. What remains to be seen is whether this alternative reflects more or less accurately what actual heroes are really like.

Human Heroes

Testing Urmson's Characterization of Heroes: Heroic Rescuers

Can a compelling case be made for the refutation of the Urmsonian characterization of the moral hero from nonfictional sources? To what extent are actual heroes, in the words of Conrad's narrator Marlow, "one of us?" The case study I employ is that of rescuers, particularly in the form of "righteous gentiles," who are Christians who rescued Jews from Hitler during the Holocaust. I choose this case because these rescuers engaged in the clearest example of heroism as it is conventionally construed: their actions were altruistic in intent, highly laden with risk, and followed through fearlessly and without concern for self-preservation. In these respects, rescuers epitomize the Urmsonian hero. Courage and the willingness to act without regard to one's welfare constitute the very criteria built into Urmson's definition of the heroic. The question is whether or not Urmson's conclusions about heroes—that they follow a separate code, appropriate for themselves only, which leads them to act in a manner best described as supererogatory—follow from these premises. Can one accept the premise of courageousness and still challenge the conclusion to which this premise is thought, in the standard view, to lead, namely, that heroes function at the margins of society, putting them in a poor position to comment on what ought to be morally required of ordinary agents? The answer depends largely on one's view of courage, whether it is thought to be a virtue that can be acquired, or an innate accidental talent. In other words, we have to determine whether it is heroes' possession of courage that is distinctive or their ability to possess courage in the first place. If the former, then the hero could turn out be a reliable source for determining how we ought to live our lives; for the hero, on this hypothesis, acts in ways we should all aspire to act and, with effort, can act.

The Case of Righteous Gentiles

Yad Vashem's definitive chronicle of the various testimonies of Holocaust rescuers appears in the volume *Sheltering the Jews*, written by Mordecai Paldiel, who served as director of Yad Vashem's "Commission for the Designation of the Righteous" for fifteen years.[58] Among the seven lessons to be learned from the acts of righteous gentiles that Paldiel lists, numbers four through six together comprise a hypothesis about the nature of moral heroes.

4. The Righteous were not saints, but ordinary people doing their bit, when everyone else either crowded under for fear of retribution, placed blinders on their eyes, or hailed the perpetrators or joined them. Herein lies the significance of their deeds.

5. The Righteous phenomenon is ample proof that it was indeed possible to help. Fear has a paralyzing effect but need not bring us to a complete standstill. When society fails, the individual can assert humanity's

undying moral principles, even under the most trying circumstances, as thousands have demonstrated. True heroism is of the spirit, not of crude matter. The human being is (or at least can be) a responsible being. Caring for the helpless other represents a most elevated form of self-fulfillment.

6. The rescuers saved Jews not necessarily because of their love of Jews, but because they felt that every human being, whatever his or her worth and merit, has a right to life and a minimum decent existence; that this most precious gift ought not be arbitrarily trampled upon. They believed ... that when confronted with the challenge to save, they had no choice but to help. There is a bottom line that no one dare trespass, or else life loses its ultimate meaning and becomes indeed what the Nazis professed it to be—a brutal struggle for the survival of the fittest.[59]

The reflections of Paldiel do not square, at all, with Urmson's claims. First, Urmson does not regard heroes as "ordinary people doing their bit," but as moral agents who (either effortlessly or through self-control) overcome their fear and their drive to self-preservation. Secondly, Urmson does not see the assumption of responsibility for others in need as a "form of self-fulfillment" for the majority of people. To the contrary, Urmson expends a great deal of effort explaining the importance of delineating the limits to the sacrifices that morality can require of us. For Urmson, and especially for Heyd who follows him, such limits override all other considerations for determining moral duty. "Caring for the helpless" at most represents only a private ideal in an Urmsonian framework. Finally, and perhaps most controversially, Urmson maintains, as Paldiel does not, that heroes are susceptible to deluding themselves about the nature of their duty toward others. This is not consistent with Paldiel's conclusion that rescuing was an example of the "most elevated form of self-fulfillment" and that rescuers were indeed able to judge correctly what gives life its "ultimate meaning." Paldiel implies that what makes heroes heroic is not their "larger than life" view of what they might be able to contribute in a crisis situation, but their frank and even commonplace assessment of what a fully human life demands in the face of a great horror such as the Holocaust.

What evidence is there to support Paldiel's position? The case of rescuing Jews from Hitler is an interesting one, particularly because the benefits and costs of the action are so high. On the one hand, rescuers had a legitimate incentive not to render aid, for doing so invariably meant risking their own lives and those of their families.[60] On the other hand, no less a good than the survival of innocent victims lay in the balance. Thus, while there is little doubt that Holocaust rescuing was altruistic and good, there is debate over whether to classify the *act* of rescuing as morally required or supererogatory. The conviction that "there is a bottom line that no one dare trespass" needs to be examined carefully when it is rendered in testimony connected with an activity with benefits and costs as great as those that prevail in the case of Holocaust rescuing.

There are a number of issues to distinguish from one another in examining such testimony. First, how do righteous gentiles perceive and describe their own actions? Do they see themselves as rescuing for the sake of fulfilling a personal ideal, or do they see their actions as morally required in the same sense that they would see other basic duties as morally required of them? If the latter, what set of values gave them this impression? Whence do they derive their moral convictions? Secondly, there is the question of how righteous gentiles perceive and describe the actions (and inaction) of others. If the righteous truly *do* believe that they do their duty when rescuing, then does this mean that they hold those who fail to rescue blameworthy, or does it mean that they hold themselves accountable to a different standard than the one to which they hold others? That is, how do rescuers view bystanders? These are all essentially questions of description and do not yet involve the difficulty of characterizing the act of rescuing itself.

The descriptive enterprise of examining righteous gentiles' views of their rescue activities gives way to another set of questions, which comprise the *explanatory* task of articulating the significance of the righteous gentile phenomenon.[61] One set of questions that are not descriptive in nature pertains to the relationship between the "duty" to rescue, of which righteous gentiles speak, and moral duty, as such. What relative weight should we give to the testimony of righteous gentiles in light of commonsense societal assumptions about how demanding we can consider moral duty to be?[62] Does the existence of rescuers lead us to challenge these assumptions? Sociologists working on the righteous gentile phenomenon, such as Samuel and Pearl Oliner and Kristen Monroe, have taken on this "second-order" explanatory task by attempting to account for all possible motivational explanations for rescuers' conduct and by subsequently weighing the plausibility of these various accounts in light of rescuers' own testimony. As we will see, their work on the righteous gentile phenomenon suggests that there are compelling reasons for regarding the same act—Holocaust rescuing—as morally required in some instances and above and beyond in others, depending on the one making the judgment. If this conclusion is correct, then we ought to accept the rescuers' claim that they did merely what was required of them. However, in saying this we are confronted head-on with the problem of interpreting Paldiel's strong statement that "every human being, whatever his or her own worth and merit, has a right to life and minimum decent existence," and that as a result, when we encounter the Hitlers of the world, we have "no choice but to help." This reflection raises the important question of whether or not *all* bystanders were in the wrong. If rescuers are shown to be mere ordinary people and yet able to engage in rescue efforts, then it would also seem that the majority who stood by and watched Hitler carry out his genocidal campaign did less than they could—and therefore should—have done. Indeed, if rescuers did not exceed the bounds of human expectation in their actions, then there are grounds for arguing, against the commonsense view, that we should not merely admire rescuers, but also emulate them, and that their achievements potentially represent our own. All of these questions need to be worked out carefully. Thus, it is time to examine those persons who, in thinking of themselves as no more than ordinary, issue a challenge to the standard interpretation of their own "heroic" conduct.

How Rescuers See Themselves and Others: The Chambonnais and Other Righteous Gentiles

It is no accident of history that Camus wrote the majority of *The Plague* during 1942 in the little Protestant town on the Lignon River in southeastern France called Le Chambon. In *The Plague*, Camus's hero, Dr. Rieux, clearly perceives the threat posed to the town of Oran by the plague and, through his cool and organized persistence, serves as an example of how it is possible for human beings to counter its drastic effects. In the village of Le Chambon we encounter a community of individuals who rise to the occasion of resisting a moral evil just as overwhelming and absurd as the natural evil with which Rieux has to contend. The rescue activities of the Chambonnais are captured in their entirety by Philip Hallie in the inspirational book *Lest Innocent Blood Be Shed*.[63] Relying largely on the testimony of the Chambonnais themselves, Hallie relates the unlikely scenario of a poor town coming to focus on a single good purpose to the exclusion of all other activities: the sheltering of hunted innocents. The Chambonnais, who ironically made up one of the poorest communities in Europe, gave refuge to a total of five thousand Jews, slightly more than the number of residents who lived in the town.[64] They did so, furthermore, in protest of the policies of the Vichy government, without being intimidated by the watchful eye of a nearby division of the Nazi SS. However, what was perhaps most remarkable about the Chambonnais was the simplicity of their altruism. While their methods for hiding and caring for Jews required a great deal of creativity and planning, they were carried out unglamorously and as a matter of routine. Jews disappeared into the forests and basements of the village as methodically as garments were hung on clotheslines to dry. The harboring of refugees was not a topic of conversation among the villagers. It is simply what happened at Le Chambon, as a part of villagers' daily routine. In the words of some of the villagers, the harboring of refugees was a "kitchen struggle," contributed to by women and children as much as by men, by the grassroots community as much as by its leadership.[65]

This is not to say that the leader of the Chambonnais, pastor André Trocmé, did not play an indispensable role in mobilizing the rest of the villagers to resist the Nazis. One of the refugees, Daniel Isaac, compared Trocmé's presence to "a glorious performance of Beethoven's *Eroica*: it lifted you, excited you, warmed you. It made you rise to your own highest level of joy and vitality. And it did this not by command but by contagion."[66] The resolve and righteous nature of Trocmé uplifted others in his proximity and inspired them to follow his lead. There was no need for explanation among the Chambonnais. They knew inwardly what sacrifices needed to be made. They did not await directions for how to conduct themselves, as, for example, when the village was subject to surprise raids by the Vichy police. Like Trocmé, the people of Le Chambon understood both the complexity of their situation and what they were morally required to do. This is because the convictions shared among the villagers, like Trocmé's, were based on a Huguenot upbringing in which centuries of persecution and the religious value of demonstrating fellowship in a time of trial figured prominently. Hallie relates: "Being a minority had helped make them clear-cut in their thinking and firm in their convictions. Having been tested by adversity, they had kept themselves alive by remaining lucid and unshakable. The Psalmist in Psalm 26 had said to God: 'Prove me, O Lord, and try me, test my heart and my mind.' History had done this for the Huguenots."[67] What Hallie here explains—that the Chambonnais were prepared to rescue because of their training in a specific religious way of life—is of critical importance for understanding what motivates moral heroes. Heroes do not exist in a vacuum. They have a history, a story, and their heroism is a product of this story. The virtue they display is not a random phenomenon. It is the result of a deliberately experienced way of life. In order to grasp the reasons why the Chambonnais helped Jewish refugees, we must take a closer look at their particular story.

The Chambonnais-as-Huguenots: Religion and the Bonds of Community

To understand the Chambonnais is to understand their religious upbringing. Their Christianity is what motivated them to supply food and shelter to desperate strangers. Having given strangers refuge, as compassionate Christians, it became unimaginable to release them from their care, as this would be tantamount to sending them to sure death.[68] In addition to the religious duty the Chambonnais felt they owed to strangers in need, the empathy the Chambonnais felt for fleeing Jews was in part inspired by their own historical memory. Four hundred years earlier, they themselves stood as the objects of religious persecution. This phenomenon of a shared and "remembered" experience of religious persecution facilitated the identification of the Huguenots with a suffering people.[69]

The term "Huguenots" pertains to the minority population of French Protestants who were members of the "Reformed Church" established by John Calvin in the sixteenth century and hunted as heretics by the Roman Catholic Church over the next two hundred years. On January 29, 1536, a general edict was issued in France that promoted their extermination. Twenty-six years later, on March 1, 1562, twelve hundred Huguenots were murdered in Vassey, France. This led to rebel Protestant uprisings, and eventually to the religious wars that would tear France apart for the next thirty-five years, as well as periodically over the next two and a half centuries.[70] These three hundred years or so entailed a long period of repression for French Protestants known among Protestants as *Le Desért* (the Wasteland). Over this period, Protestants were regularly enslaved, imprisoned, or killed for their beliefs; Protestant temples were destroyed and pastors frequently executed for their spiritual leadership in Protestant communities.[71]

One of the most conspicuous examples of the ongoing persecution occurred on August 24, 1572, St. Bartholomew's Day, when ordinary Frenchmen killed over three thousand other ordinary Frenchmen en masse because of their religious beliefs.[72] This massacre began as a political desire to rid France of its Huguenot leadership by the ruling Guisards (who believed that the long-term security of France required the preservation of the Roman Catholic faith). It then extended to an exercise in ethnic cleansing similar in kind to the program of Nazi extermination that would take place on the European continent four hundred years later. Huguenots were pulled from their beds unaware in their own houses.[73] They endured the frenzied wrath of an unchecked mob. At the end of the day, a campaign that had begun with the limited political aim of purging the Huguenots of their leadership became a bloodbath carried out by the masses in which thousands lost their lives.[74]

Following St. Bartholomew's Day, the Huguenots formed in scattered, underground communities of resistance. Survival became for them a way of life. They risked their lives to smuggle in Bibles, Psalters, and the religious literature that nurtured their faith.[75] The text that perhaps made the most difference was the book of Psalms, which served as a vehicle through which the Huguenots could express both their anguish and their faith in the bond that they believed to have been established as a result of a special trial set forth by God.[76] The historian Barbara Diefendorf explains that French Protestants attached three levels of significance to the Psalms:

They understood them first within the Old Testament context of David's own sufferings and his eventual triumph over his enemies; second, as prophetic of the sufferings and the triumph of Christ; and third, as prophetic of the sufferings and triumph of the church. These three levels of meaning may have been traditional in Biblical exegesis, but the Huguenots' appropriation of the third level of meaning to refer to their actual sufferings and anticipated triumph—the suffering and triumph of the true church—was unusually direct and immediate ... help[ing] to teach [them] to view persecution as a trial imposed by God and a special mark of his covenant. In a variety of forms, the message of treatises written by Huguenot pastors during the war years is the message of Psalm 119:71: "It is good for me that I have been afflicted; that I might learn thy statutes." ... This is not the anxious introspective religion frequently associated with later generations of Calvinists, preoccupied with seeking out each mark or sign of election; it is rather a confident, outgoing, even joyous faith. . . .[77]

The Psalms gave Huguenots under assault the confidence to appeal to a higher authority, to look past the apparent decimation of their communities, and to extend as far as possible their capacity to suffer what they regarded as a divinely imposed trial. In the Psalms, they found direct encouragement to withstand the strain of persecution. To use Calvin's paraphrase of Psalm 57, they took refuge in "the shadow of the wings of God."[78] No political authority could supersede this exhortation. Their faith in a justice beyond earthly justice lifted them from fear and the impulse to preserve themselves in the face of condemnation and death.

Such a faith was further strengthened within the bonds of a close-knit community. Huguenots resisted persecution by forming clandestine, underground pockets bound up by ties of kinship and mutual service. They were characteristically stubborn in their resistance to governmentally imposed bans on Protestant literature, and many cut across traditional class and social boundaries to conspire to smuggle in forbidden texts.[79] What this all amounted to was an affirmation distinct from the kind they received when consulting religious literature. In many cases, the courage to resist sprung from watching how others in the same predicament conducted themselves. Through years of religious wars, resistance for the Huguenots became a way of life. While they did show ambivalence about whether or not the resort to violent resistance was warranted in order to defend their faith,[80] the conviction with which they knew that their faith had to be defended never waned. The values and way of life they upheld over the ages survived communally in a way they could not have on an individual basis. As a result, the crucial sense of right and wrong that dissipated among many bystanders of the Nazi era due to societal pressure—what we may call "conscience"—remained noticeably intact among them. Indeed, the same communal strength from which Huguenots derived their will not to succumb to those trying to rid France of them in the sixteenth and seventeenth centuries would later serve them in their resistance on behalf of other persecuted groups.[81]

This sense of communal strength, coupled with a heritage of suffering that had been etched into the "gestalt" of the Huguenot mind-set, disposed the residents of Le Chambon to help out non-Huguenots facing a trial similar to the one their ancestors had to endure a few centuries earlier. The Chambonnais had a long history of sheltering needy refugees, and they identified with the Jews in particular as a suffering minority in a homogeneous society. The Christian theologian David Gushee notes that perhaps this is one reason why the Chambonnais "consistently chose not to take advantage of the Jewish plight by proselytizing their charges."[82] The Huguenots' acute memory of having been attacked by a government-sponsored populace gave them the resources to repudiate the legitimacy of a persecution aimed at the renunciation of an entire faith and to act instead according to their own conscience. The Chambonnais knew, for instance, that at times they would have to lie to the police, forge official documents, and break the law in other ways in order to help:

> The people of Le Chambon knew about the false identity cards; they knew that sheltering foreign refugees and not registering them under their true names was in violation of the laws of France. But they also knew that sometimes—and this was one of those times—obeying the law meant doing evil, doing harm. It all lay in that one little French word *mal*: evil was harm, nothing more, nothing less.[83]

On the occasions when the Chambonnais did come into contact with the Vichy police, or the Nazi SS, they did so with poise and cunning. Hallie recounts one instance in which representatives of Vichy leader Henri Philippe Pétain were conducting a random inspection and Magda Trocmé, André's wife, welcomed them into her home and offered them biscuits while villagers hid the Jews.[84] In several of the interviews, the light-hearted nature of the Chambonnais comes across, their unassuming, at times humorous, attitude around governmental authorities serving to quell potentially perilous situations. Clearly, the Chambonnais inwardly knew what had to be prioritized if they were to be successful in their rescue efforts.[85]

A second resource that the Huguenots brought to bear in their efforts to rescue Jews pertained to their memory of the intervention of others who stood by them when Protestants were being rounded up and ex-terminated in the religious wars of the sixteenth and seventeenth cen-turies. Some of the Huguenots who did not die during those onslaughts survived because of Catholics who resisted the tide and came to their defense. Through the generations the Huguenots as a people did not forget this gesture. The Catholics who helped them presumably recognized the incompatibility between the injunction to love the neighbor and the reli-gious persecution of any minority. It is here where religion furnishes its own means to combat genocide. Sympathy for the one in need grows not only out of a shared experience, but also out of an acknowledgment of and respect for the preciousness of every human life. In the case of Le Chambon, this commitment was displayed by the *responsables*, the inner circle of thirteen that made up the Chambonnais spiritual leadership. In organizational meetings with André Trocmé, the *responsables* recalled the Psalms and various other biblical readings on compassion and love for their congregations to inspire the resistance among the Chambonnais. Hallie writes:

> [I]t was they who became the backbone as far as sheltering and hiding refugees was concerned.... In those meetings they all discovered what the Good Samaritan passage meant (who the neighbor was whom we were being told to love and to help) and they discovered the meaning of the Sermon on the Mount—not in terms of some abstract, pious the-ory, or even in terms of a long-term plan, but in terms of day-to-day decisions appropriate to the circumstances of Le Chambon. Here is the way Trocmé summarizes the work of the *responsables* in his notes: "It was there, not elsewhere, that we received from God solutions to com-plex problems, problems we had to solve in order to shelter and to hide the Jews.... Nonviolence was not a theory superimposed upon reality; it was an itinerary that we explored day after day in communal prayer and in obedience to the commands of the Spirit."[86]

The activity of rescuing correlated with the Chambonnais' perception of themselves as worthy Christians, whose commitment to the value of sav-ing lives was grounded in a long-standing tradition held together by the transmission of values within a community. The "heroes" of Le Chambon were not isolated anomalies. They were the purveyors of the tenets of faith that were reflective of a religious tradition. At the same time, the Cham-bonnais exhibited a complex moral identity. Having once been the humil-iated group themselves, they were able to empathize with the pain of another group who had been denied equal status in society. They did not see the Jews as an "out-group" on whom to take pity, but as fellow creatures of God with whose plight they could readily identify.

The history and shared consciousness of the Chambonnais—their minority status, religious conviction, and demonstrated endurance through a trial in which their very identity lay at stake—all furnished them with the traits of character that would enable their participation in the rescue of Jewish refugees fleeing the arm of Hitler. These features of their identity, furthermore, gave them plausible reasons to regard their participation as morally obligatory. From both a historical and a theological perspective, the Chambonnais were neither deluded about the nature of their moral duty, nor committed, in their decision to shelter, to a personal ideal that justified each particular villager's "heroic" gesture. They acted together, as a community acts. In this sense, the Chambonnais were not heroes in the abstract, nor was their heroism inevitable. They were ordinary people whose life lessons had collectively prepared them to respond with goodness in the face of a crisis that happened to occur in their midst. If there were those within the community whose resolve temporarily weakened, they had the benefit of the encouragement of others who could remind them of the rationale behind the cause for which they together fought.

This is not to say that sheltering the Jews was easy or that it didn't take its toll. Rescuing was exceedingly demanding and afforded the Chambonnais few respites. Hallie introduces the French noun *surmenage*, translated in English as "overwork," to describe the mental fatigue that ceaselessly taxed the townspeople, especially Magda Trocmé, who complemented her husband's spiritual and organizational role in Le Chambon by undertaking the material tasks of feeding, hiding, and caring for refugees. Magda was always on call to respond to anyone who asked for her help. Her concern for others consistently outweighed her own welfare. Characterizing the extent of her sacrifice, Hallie writes:

> Interminably involved with refugees and their special, often terrible problems, she also managed the big house, her energetic children, and her ever-inventive husband, although "managing" him would have been a full time job in itself in a normal woman's life.... Many a day she would not feel like eating because she was so *surmenée* (tired and strained). And so she lost much weight and aged terribly. Sometimes all she could feel was weary disgust over the endlessness of the work.[87]

As with Rieux, Magda Trocmé exhibits what one could call an "emergency room" ethic. She exists "on call," always in wait for the next crisis. The doctor who works in the emergency room accepts as a given that there will always be more patients than can be accommodated by the staff in attendance. One can only do one's best, committing oneself as earnestly as one can to each new victim that walks through the hospital doors. Magda was this kind of person: empathetic, boundlessly giving, and pragmatic. She cared "for others on their own terms, not in order to parade her own virtues, but in order to keep them well. In the many years to follow, [André] would see how poignantly Magda felt the cold in the bodies of others, and how she would spend much of their lives covering or uncovering children. At the moment, all he could see was that she quite simply cared for others, cared both emotionally and in action."[88]

While there were limits to what Magda was in fact capable of giving, she did not consider her actions to be optional. She consistently conveyed in her testimony the notion that helping was the only morally available choice, and that it did not merit special praise. Hallie notes the explicitness in Magda's denial of praiseworthiness:

> [Magda] is . . . reluctant to use words like *good* and *saintly*. She does not believe that there is such a thing as a moral nobility that sets off some people—the saints—from others—the common, decent people. . . . There are only people who accept responsibly, and those who do not. For her, as for them, a person either opens the door or closes it in the face of a victim.[89]

Magda was among the large majority of the Chambonnais who dismissed the attribution of moral praise to actions performed on behalf of Jewish refugees. "In almost every interview I had with a Chambonnais or a Chambonnaise," recounts Hallie, "there came a moment when he or she pulled back from me but looked firmly into my eyes and said, 'How can you call us good? We were doing what had to be done. Who else could help them? And what has all this to do with goodness? . . . You must understand that it was the most natural thing in the world to help these people.'"[90] Helping the needy, with its attendant risks and hardships, counted, in the final analysis, as a basic moral obligation. It was no more optional than the Huguenot history and set of convictions that the Chambonnais inherited from past generations.

Righteous Gentiles

Hallie's conclusions about the moral exigency of rescuing are corroborated by extensive studies conducted by social scientists and historians who work on the righteous gentile phenomenon.[91] Testimonies offered by rescuers reveal an abundance of statements like the following:

I don't think I did anything that special. I think what I did is what every-body normally should be doing. . . . It is common sense and common caring for people.

Oh, I don't know if I'm the world's most desirable citizen. Let's not get too focused on me. We live on one world. We are one people. Working together, basically we are all the same.

I did nothing unusual; anyone would have done the same thing in my place.

As little as we could accept the title of "traitor," so little can we accept the title of "hero" for things we did to help the Jewish people. We just helped people who were in need.

It's pretty near impossible not to help.[92]

Not only do we see in these reports the rescuers' explicit denials that they did anything deserving of special commendation; we also witness their belief that they truly did nothing out of the ordinary. *Anyone,* they are inclined to assert, would surely see this. That rescuers feel as though they are no different from anyone else, however, is a bit puzzling, for clearly most people did not act as these rescuers did, and rescuers themselves knew that they were an extremely small minority.[93] How, then, do rescuers account for the infrequency of Holocaust rescuing among the population generally, while insisting at the same time that they were motivated by the most minimal standard of decency?

One plausible answer to this question calls attention to the attribution of a certain lack of insight among nonrescuers. When rescuers assert the moral "impossibility" of not helping, while knowing that in actuality so many people refused to lend aid, they implicitly state that those who did not help acted contrary to how they otherwise would have acted if they had been more informed about the nature of their inherent connection to those that needed their help.[94] This perception of bystanders on the part of rescuers is raised in an exchange between the sociologist Kristen Monroe and one of her interviewees. In response to the question of why he felt that only some people were able to perceive and act upon what should have been morally obvious, the interviewee replied that a major reason was a "lack of exposure." He continued:

I hear people talking about homeless people, saying, "Well, they're all a bunch of drunks. They admit they don't want to work." They don't real-ize that there are many homeless people who are simply mothers without husbands who cannot get transportation, cannot get their wardrobe or their hair done sufficiently to get a job, and who consequently are totally trapped in homelessness. Yet here people lump them together and say, "None of these people really wants to work, and they're all a bunch of drunks, and that's it."

If they spent one afternoon in downtown L.A. or even in the park in Santa Monica and looked and learned to see through their eyes, *they could not give that same answer*. But most people look away.[95]

In other words, people are complacent, and their complacency causes them to fail to gather the evidence that would convince them of what they ought to do (e.g., by exposing themselves to what is going on around them). Moreover, it causes them to fail to inculcate the virtue that would enable them actually to do it (e.g., by becoming more courageous). The implication of this particular rescuer is that *if* bystanders had these fundamental human traits, then they would have felt that they had to act as the interviewee himself did. Assuming that Monroe and others are correct that this response is indicative of how other rescuers account for the inaction of bystanders,[96] we may conclude that the frequently heard statement "Anyone in my shoes would have done the same thing" really means that the right course of action ought to have been obvious, even if it was not obvious to some. Any *informed* decision would "have to" be a decision to rescue given that one had the opportunity to do so.

We can now see how the historical particularity and theologically shaped identity of the French Huguenots of Le Chambon becomes relevant to an analysis of rescuers' views of themselves and others, for it is precisely their history and religious faith that *has* informed them of their responsibility to intervene on behalf of other human beings and additionally has disposed them to act according to this responsibility. In this sense, I suggest that the Chambonnais belong to a morally advantaged community. They have had not only the fortune of their own historical experience, but also, to their credit, a long-standing moral tradition based on the values of solidarity and fellow-feeling that this history has produced. In this moral tradition, the right kinds of dispositions and other-regarding impulses toward strangers were formed. This is why rescuing became the most natural thing in the world for the Chambonnais.

Rescuers were able to see plainly, where the majority could not, what truly *was* a matter of "common sense"—hence the appropriateness of their referring to their conduct as no more than ordinary. If rescuers' descriptions of themselves and their actions are correct, then in claiming that their behavior is ordinary, rescuers are not making a sociological point about the *frequency* of their conduct in society, but a cognitive point about its moral status. They did what anyone sufficiently informed would feel that they ought to do (even if, at present, they lacked the requisite courage). In this sense, rescuers can be characterized as "people before their time," or visionaries, who saw what was right more quickly than those around them.[97]

The Case of a Rescuer in the Rwandan Genocide

Pinning down rescuers' view of nonrescuers is important because it gives us an indication of how normative we ought to deem the activity of rescuing to be. Are bystanders morally blameworthy for not rescuing victims of genocide? In some cases, rescuers who arrived at a view of bystanders that explained away bystander inaction (or that at least did not *blame* bystanders for their passivity) formed this impression in retrospect, after learning from their interviewers that their moral instincts were not shared by nonrescuers who were presumably equally positioned to aid refugees. Upon learning, to their surprise, of their exceptionality, these rescuers would come to proffer their own theories about why bystanders chose not to get involved, and even displayed an understanding of their perspective.[98] They understood that nonrescuers did not share their worldview. Failing to see the interconnectedness of humanity, nonrescuers could not be expected to respond to the crisis in their humanitarian manner.

Other rescuers, for whom the activity of sheltering also came naturally, were similarly shocked and dismayed when they learned that nonrescuers did not act as they themselves did, but for these rescuers such impressions remained with them. In the end, they could not accept any rationale for bystander inaction. A good example of this occurs in the account of one rescuer, discussed by Philip Gourevitch in his compelling account of the Rwandan genocide in the mid-1990s, *We Wish to Inform You That Tomorrow We Will Be Killed with Our Families*.[99] Gourevitch explains how, in April 1994, the government of Rwanda announced over radio and television that everyone in the Hutu majority ought to murder their Tutsi neighbors— leading, over the next three months, to the brutal slaughter of close to a million Tutsis.[100] A manager of a hotel, Paul Rusesabagina, used his rooms to give shelter to the Tutsi people and devoted his telephone lines to focusing international attention on the plight of his guests. In one anecdote, Gourevitch recounts the story of a religious leader, Father Wenceslas, who, to his moral discredit, had provided Hutus with lists of Tutsi refugees (almost all of whom were slaughtered upon their discovery by the Hutu government). Shortly afterward, Father Wenceslas came to Rusesabagina for help in providing a safe harbor for his mother, who was also a Tutsi. Rusesabagina, who was a good man and stood committed to helping all whose lives were in danger, accepted Wenceslas' mother. He nonetheless could not help but notice the hypocrisy, which was not uncommon among other Rwandans:

In fact, a number of men affiliated with the Hutu Power regime had in-
stalled their Tutsi wives at the Mille Collines [Rusesabagina's hotel], and
while their presence there surely contributed to the hotel's overall safety,
Paul felt it reflected shamefully on the men. "Wenceslas knew himself
that he wasn't even able to protect his mother," Paul said. "And he was
so arrogant that when he brought her, he told me, 'Paul, I bring you my
cockroach.' Do you understand? He was talking about his mother. She
was a Tutsi." ... Lots of people behaved as badly or worse than Wenceslas.[101]

Rusesabagina saw the Tutsis as human beings while many of his contemporaries, including a supposed spiritual leader, did not. Noticing this
engendered disgust in Rusesabagina, yet *he* was in the minority. This particularly captures Gourevitch's attention:

> I wasn't interested in what made Wenceslas weak; I wanted to know what
> had made Paul strong—and he couldn't tell me. "I wasn't really strong,"
> he said. "I wasn't. But maybe I used different means that other people
> didn't want to use." Only later—when people were talking about that time—
> did it occur to him that he had been exceptional. "During the genocide,
> I didn't know," he told me. "I thought so many people did as I did,
> because I know that if they'd wanted they could have done so. . . ."[102]

In this passage, in which a rescuer expresses his disappointment to learn
that others did not act as he did, Gourevitch draws a perfectly clear contrast between the vice-ridden and the virtuous moral agent. Father
Wenceslas and Paul Rusesabagina knew each other and traveled in the
same circles. They were on friendly terms. Yet they responded oppositely
to the same humanitarian crisis. One recognized the evil in what was hap-
pening and did what he could within his means to counter its effects. The
other condoned and even contributed to that evil. We, as observers of
Gourevitch's account, must somehow account for the different reactions.
    For his own part, Paul Rusesabagina had trouble making sense of why
others did not act as he had. Father Wenceslas's comments and behavior,
typical among others who had come to Rusesabagina at the hotel, vexed
him and even altered the way he would continue to look at his peers.
Gourevitch explains:

> The riddle to Paul was that so many of his countrymen had chosen to
> embrace inhumanity. "It was more than a surprise," he told me. "It was
> a disappointment. I was disappointed by most of my friends, who
> immediately changed with that genocide. I used to see them just as gen-
> tlemen, and when I saw them with the killers I was disappointed. I still

have some friends that I trust. But the genocide changed so many things—within myself, my own behavior. I used to go out, feel free. I could go and have a drink with anyone. I could trust. But now I tend not to do so." So Paul had a rare conscience, and knew the loneliness that came with it, but there was nothing false about his modesty regarding his efforts on behalf of the refugees at the Mille Collines.[103]

When Rusesabagina learned the truth about his friends and associates, that they failed to show any sympathy for the hunted Tutsis, he displayed surprise but made no attempt to apologize for them. On the contrary, his recognition of his own exceptionality led to disillusionment with people whom he had formerly trusted. Disillusionment, in turn, gave way to a feeling of isolation, the only option that he felt allowed him to maintain his integrity. Rusesabagina simply could not continue to interact with friends and associates who had countenanced the killings without being overcome by feelings of contempt for them for the role they had indirectly played in the deaths of so many innocents.

The example of Paul Rusesabagina complements the self-understandings of the rescuers who offer a justification for the inaction of bystanders in one important respect: namely, as a contrast to the depiction of heroes offered in the Urmsonian account. Whether rescuers maintain that they acted no differently than nonrescuers would have acted if they were better informed and more virtuously disposed, or claim that nonrescuers—no excuses—in fact *should* have acted differently, as Rusesabagina believed, in both cases rescuers have little doubt that they did the morally right thing and that nonrescuers did not. In the former instance, mitigating reasons are provided to explain away nonrescuing; however, in both cases the idea that rescuing is what *should* have occurred is affirmed. In neither set of self-descriptions do we notice that rescuers rescued because of some special commitment they had voluntarily made to themselves. Rescuing in each instance is understood to be morally compulsory in the strictest sense.

The case of this particular rescuer, acting in the context of the Rwandan genocide, helps to confirm some initial conclusions we may wish to draw about the self-descriptions of righteous gentiles. Rescuers' descriptions of themselves and their actions do not conform to Urmson's characterization of moral heroes as virtually superhuman self-sacrificers who are motivated by their desire to fulfill a personal ideal. Prior to our examination of rescuers, we might have been inclined to accept without argument the commonsense observation that heroes' claims to ordinariness are instances either of false modesty or of mistaken self-understanding. The foregoing examination of the actual testimony of rescuers at least makes us pause before adopting this judgment. It cannot escape our notice that rescuers believed in the correctness of an insight they possessed, even when learning that they alone possessed it. Even when rationalizations could be offered to explain why nonrescuers "naturally" saw things differently than they did, rescuers still supposed that if bystanders were less complacent and more informed, then they surely would have seen the situation in a more morally appropriate manner and would have disposed themselves to act accordingly. We at least ought to be convinced that in arguing in this fashion, rescuers give us a good reason not to *dismiss* their claim that they responded "ordinarily" to an extraordinary humanitarian crisis.

What relative weight, then, ought we to give to the testimony of rescuers as we go about the task of interpreting rescuers' actions in light of how they see themselves? Should we locate the acts of righteous gentiles within the scope of moral requirement or identify them as acts of supererogation? To ask these questions is to move beyond the task of mere description and try to explain why rescuers acted as they did in a manner that plausibly assimilates, but does not uncritically accept, rescuers' own testimony.

Understanding and Explaining the Righteous Gentile Phenomenon

Kristen Monroe, Michael C. Barton, and Ute Klingemann account for the enhanced moral perception of rescuers by attributing to them a special perspective in which they see themselves as part of a common humanity.[104] These authors refer to the rescuers as John Donne's people and invoke a famous passage:

> No man is an island, Intire of itself:
> every man is a piece of the Continent. A part of the Maine; . . .
> Any man's death diminishes me because I am involved in Mankinde;
> and therefore never send to know for whom the bell tolls;
> it tolls for thee.[105]

The proposal advanced here is meant to supplant the model dominant in the social sciences, most commonly known as "rational actor theory," according to which all human behavior, including altruism, "can be viewed as involving participants who maximize their utility from a stable set of preferences. . . ."[106] In rational actor theory, the maximization of self-regarding preferences is primarily what guides agents' choices. In terms of rescue activities, rational actor theory might interpret the decision to act altruistically as one motivated, for example, by the desire to alleviate guilt by living up to a morally demanding ideal, or alternatively by the desire to show group or tribal preference.[107] The example of rescuers, argue Monroe and her colleagues, undercuts the plausibility of rational actor theory because of the sense of "connectedness" rescuers felt for Jews in spite of the ways they were stigmatized as foreigners in Hitler's Europe. It is a particularly inadequate model in light of the fact that people who rescued Jews knew that if they were caught, their family members would likely be killed.[108] While this consequence may have initially entered into the deliberative reflections of rescuers, it was overridden by the good they perceived to be at stake in helping. With the lives of so many innocents at stake, it was as if rescuers became blind to costs they and their loved ones might incur. As Monroe reports:

> When I focused on the constancy of [rescuers'] perspective and asked how susceptible it is to external appeals to group identities and empathy, the results were . . . surprising. While both familiarity and empathy with the person in need explain . . . philanthropists' altruism, neither factor accounts for acts of rescuers. . . . For rescuers, there is indeed a bond established between the altruist and the person helped, but the bond is universal, available to everyone merely by virtue of their existence. This is not the more particularistic empathetic connection traditionally said to occur through entering into the other's place, although it does bear a superficial resemblance.[109]

Dismissing particularistic empathetic connection as a dominant factor in rescuers' deliberations, Monroe proceeds to attribute to rescuers a distinctive way of looking at humanity, which she calls the "altruistic perspective."[110] Having this perspective, she argues, rescuers were able to bypass the process of considering the costs and benefits of rescuing as part of their deliberation process (other than in regard to the prudential success of their efforts). Their decision to render aid was a simple one, requiring no careful consideration. Rescuing formed such a central core of their identity, in other words, that it left them no choice in their behavior toward others.[111] Rescuers were heroic not so much because they overcame their fear and their drive to self-preservation—although this may be how *we* interpret their heroism—but because they had the wisdom to perceive correctly the responsibility that life had unexpectedly thrust upon them, and the courage actually to meet the demands of such responsibility. What distinguished rescuers from others was therefore not their lack of concern with themselves, but rather, as Samuel and Pearl Oliner put it, "their ability to develop a strong and extensive sense of attachment to others and their feeling of responsibility to those outside their immediate familiar or communal circles."[112] Monroe and the Oliners suggest that the trait of being able to overcome fear and the drive to self-preservation, which, according to Urmson, is what distinguishes the hero, does not by itself sufficiently account for rescuers' distinctiveness. An explanation through appeal to this trait alone does not yet begin to address the virtuous *insight* by which rescuers were able to see the nature of their moral responsibility for those who needed their help. If this account of rescuers' motivations is correct, then rescuing might plausibly be interpreted as an act of self-fulfillment inasmuch as it is an act of self-sacrifice; for rescuers, through exhibiting wisdom and courage, were able to flourish fully as human beings.[113]

The value of Monroe's work on the righteous gentile phenomenon is that it points to the indispensability of calling attention to rescuers' special way of determining what is morally required of them as a means of subsequently understanding their heroic nature. Her observations that rescuers are in possession of a special "altruistic perspective" by which they form their views about their relationship to others in society suggest that rescuers are also *especially attuned* to suffering, and therefore *especially competent* in terms of forming a humanly appropriate attitude in response to it. Moreover, as we saw in the case of the Chambonnais, Monroe's theory about the "altruistic perspective" of rescuers is consistent with the historical and cultural context within which rescuers form their views about the moral necessity of rescuing. It would be an overstatement to contend flatly that rescuers are right and that bystanders are wrong in characterizing the activity of rescuing as morally required. However, if we are willing to grant that the "altruistic perspective" constitutes a legitimate mode of perception for particular moral agents, then it would be just as rash to make the opposite claim that rescuers perceived the nature of their duty incorrectly. This means that while we may not yet be ready to accept that what rescuers say about their duty to rescue is true, we must at least grant that, not knowing what they know, we can neither assume that what they say is false nor interpret what they say as excessive modesty.

The observations of Hallie, Gourevitch, Monroe, and others working on the phenomenon of sheltering refugees from the threat of genocide help us to determine how we ought to characterize the actions of rescuers insofar as they call into question the standard assumption in ethical theory that there is a universal algorithm for distinguishing acts of duty from acts of supererogation. The standard approach, we recall, categorizes altruistic actions as either "obligatory" or "optional" by making a determination about what actions are always too costly to require of an agent. In this approach, "undue burden" is considered to be a constant for all moral agents. But while for most of us, giving to others *does* entail requisite

deliberations about where the line between the obligatory and the supererogatory ought to be drawn (due to considerations of cost), rescuers,
because of their special way of looking at the world, made no such appeal
to this kind of deliberative process. They simply responded to the victims
whom they saw needed their help. Given their espousal of what Monroe
calls the "altruistic perspective," not to have acted in this manner could
only be regarded by them as a breach of duty. It seems, then, that the same
act, rescuing, cannot *simply* be characterized as an act of duty or as an
act of supererogation. How rescuing is assigned moral status will depend
on the character, and in turn the judgment, of the particular agent who
contemplates performing the act. Yet this conclusion will have to be examined further; for how are we in earnest to accept heroes' claims to ordinariness if especially altruistic acts, like rescuing, are *only* considered
obligatory when heroes themselves perform them? If the altruistic perspective corresponds to a worldview that is shared only by a few, then how
can we meaningfully decide what, precisely, ought to be required of one
who finds him- or herself in the position of being a potential rescuer?

Part of the problem rests with the idea of perception itself. Rescuers are
propelled by their distinctive way of looking at the world. They perceive
vividly, while others perceive palely, or not at all, their responsibility to a
common humanity.[114] Thus, their conviction that they are no different
from anyone else, and the corresponding notion that "anybody in their
shoes would have done the same thing," is ironically one that is particular to them alone. In a very important sense, they are "heroic" because of
the degree to which they view themselves as ordinary. Others, with a less
robust sense of moral responsibility, see the hero's actions as praiseworthy, and certainly as noteworthy. But from the hero's perspective, such a
judgment is the result of an understandable, though limited and arguably
morally complacent, moral outlook. This conclusion is supported by the
response of rescuers who were asked to account for the limitations of others who had the opportunity to contribute to the rescue efforts, but chose
not to because they were unable to reach out across the boundaries of
ethnicity and nationality. According to rescuers, such bystanders lacked
the capacity to give a human face to misery; they did not "see" others
as human subjects but rather objectified them.[115] Not "seeing" in this
respect—not being able to keep the picture of the human victim fresh in
their mind—made them cognitively deficient, precluding them from acting as rescuers did. Hence, by the maxim that "ought implies can," they
did not have the same moral duties as rescuers.[116] Rescuers' capacity to see
the victims—filthy, emaciated, and exhausted from fleeing their aggressors—
as human beings enabled them both to appreciate the imperative to offer

their assistance and to cultivate the courage necessary to carry out the moral task at hand. Rescuers were *heroic*, and thus could be distinguished from nonheroes, because they possessed this capacity in abundance.

The characterization of heroes as fearless stalwarts who exceed the bounds of moral duty in contexts in which fear and the drive to self-preservation would lead ordinary persons not to do so stands in need of revision. Heroes do not necessarily go beyond the call of duty when performing their heroic acts. They have different duties from the rest of us, which exist for them because of their especially virtuous character. This does not mean that *we* are not justified in thinking certain morally demanding acts of altruism to be supererogatory from *our own* perspective. Rather, the characterization of moral heroes under consideration here assumes a flexible view of moral agency in which heroes *become* heroes by coming to acquire an expanding—and therefore *changing*—sense of duty over time.

CHARACTERIZING HEROES WITHIN A MORAL FRAMEWORK

Maximalism and Minimalism

To insist that there is one standard of duty for all moral agents is either to hold the majority of nonheroes accountable for falling short of a standard of conduct beyond their capability, or to deny the explicit testimony of rescuers who claim that what they did was what was required of them. Lawrence Blum refers to these alternatives, both of which assume one standard of duty for all agents, as the "maximalist" and "minimalist" positions, respectively. He attempts to demonstrate the incompleteness of both by explicating their failure to capture the way in which duty and virtue interrelate.

According to the maximalist view, those who are not inclined to let notions of cost and "undue burden" deter them from behaving altruistically, like Holocaust rescuers, are correct about what their duty is, while the rest of us, who claim that potential costs to the benefactor ought to set limits on how much we can give to the recipient, are mistaken.[117] According to maximalism, the conduct of heroes becomes what is morally expected of everyone. In the case of Le Chambon, "the maximalist claim would be that the Chambonnais are entirely correct to regard themselves as having the degree of moral compulsion they do—which entails risking their freedom and possibly their lives to try to save the refugees—and that others who might admire these actions but do not feel a moral compulsion to perform them (or not a strong moral compulsion) would be incorrect in their view that there was no such moral ... requirement."[118] The maximalist position would make it a duty to undertake even extremely risky activities when doing so would promote a good as valuable as, for example, saving lives.

The maximalist view implies that considerations such as a person's own capabilities of contributing to the overall good are given little priority when compared to what lies at stake in performing an altruistic deed with potentially significant benefits. Herein lies the problem with the maximalist position: it overlooks the central role that moral ability plays as an enabling factor in the performance of altruistic deeds. In neglecting to account for the different capabilities of moral agents, it fails to speak to those who are presently unable to live up to what they perceive as an overly demanding standard of other-regard. The maximalist position does not sufficiently acknowledge the maxim that "ought implies can," where "can" is understood to mean that it is possible for the agent to desire the performance of such altruistic deeds enough to be motivated to do them.[119]

One of the things that becomes clear in examining the decision making of rescuers is that they were—already—"noteworthily virtuous people."[120] They perceived the *importance* of rendering aid to refugees and knew that they *could*, in fact, make a difference by helping them to survive the campaigns launched by their aggressors. Thus, for them the activity of rescuing could come to be considered morally required without violating the maxim "ought implies can." Nonetheless, while we may claim that, *ceteris paribus*, persons or communities that adhere to elevated levels of moral demandingness are preferable to those that do not, this does not necessarily imply that those whose level of virtue limits them to a lower standard are under a misapprehension about what their duty is.[121] Some people are not only incapable of certain kinds of altruism, they also fail to perceive the overriding importance of acting altruistically in a particular situation to begin with, regardless of the good their potential beneficiaries stand to gain. As indicated earlier, some rescuers seem to have appreciated this facet of human nature, which explains the nonreproachful attitude they display toward bystanders. Indeed, it is arguably heroes' awareness of this fact of human nature—that at any moment in time we are each capable in varying degrees of acting in an altruistic manner—that accounts for their seeming modesty and lack of self-righteousness in characterizing their own actions. Thus, it is significant that, in a sense, heroes create their own norms rather than asserting that others around them fall below a standard one. The possession of virtue among moral agents is not a constant that we each have regardless of our stage of moral development, as our rock-bottom, minimal duties arguably are (including a minimal duty to offer assistance if it comes at relatively little cost to the self). What makes heroes heroic, what makes them distinctive, *is* precisely their possession of virtue. To follow the maximalist line of thought to its logical conclusion would be to undermine the importance of the gradual nature of the acquisition of virtue, as well as to call into question the relation of virtue to moral obligation. In fact, it is hard to imagine how heroes would be understood at all according to the maximalist view. Either there would *be* no heroes, or heroes would be defined strictly as those persons who managed not to shirk their duty toward others (while everyone else fell short).

Like the maximalist position, the minimalist one adheres to a rigid standard of duty that confers legitimacy on only one perspective of moral agency and accountability. However, the minimalist position defines virtuous behavior, like rescuing, as supererogatory from the outset. It assumes that there is one, minimal, standard of moral requirement for everyone. The hero, according to minimalism, is by definition an agent who supererogates. Whereas in the maximalist view noteworthily virtuous agents can at most be understood as those who do what is required in any case, according to minimalism, agents need only do more than their ordinary duty to distinguish themselves. So characterized, we may associate the minimalist position with the perspective of the standard view, which Urmson shares.

The problem with minimalism is the converse of that of maximalism: it is now not ordinary persons, but the noteworthily virtuous agents who are mistaken in their perception of what they are morally required to do. The Chambonnais report with abundant clarity that they did what they were required to do. They would have regarded themselves as committing an act of substantial wrongdoing if they had not behaved as they did. While it is perhaps true that the Chambonnais saw their actions as voluntary, in the sense that they fully desired to act as they did and did not require legal or social pressure to compel them to behave altruistically, they still felt a moral compulsion to rescue.[122] Thus, it would be a mistake to characterize their actions as morally optional. They responded in a required manner to a given moral reality, one held by an entire community of villagers who shared the same sense of right and wrong. It should again be noted that this "common morality" shared by the Chambonnais does not *necessarily* imply that they thought that the ethic that formed the basis of their own actions was appropriate for everyone. It "is perfectly consistent to say—and seems in accordance of the portrayal of [them] ... — that the Chambonnais affirmed neither the universality nor the exclusivity ... of their ethic."[123] Their way of interpreting their moral reality, in other words, was neither ubiquitous (all-inclusive) nor unique (completely exclusive). It was instead affected by the norms embodied by the community, norms that had and still have the potential to be adopted by other communities as well.

Limited Community Relativism and the Relationship between Duty and Virtue

The maximalist and minimalist frameworks that we have just considered have been found wanting, respectively, on the grounds that they fail altogether to distinguish heroes from nonheroes or that in characterizing agents of noteworthy virtue they fail to conform to the agents' own descriptions of the perceived obligatoriness of their deeds.[124] In lieu of these alternatives, we may again consider Lawrence Blum's alternative of "limited community relativism," which was discussed in the last chapter. According to this view, it is possible to make judgments about which communities are more virtuous than others, while simultaneously accepting the notion that all persons, regardless of the communities from which they come, have valid notions of what encompasses their "duty" given their particular moral perception.[125] Limited community relativism assumes that virtue and duty are directly proportional to one another. Certain duties cannot be perceived, much less acted upon, without the requisite amount of virtue. According to this approach, the line that separates the morally obligatory from the morally optional varies depending on the level of virtue exhibited by a particular community of agents. Some communities will have a more extensive sense of duty than others because they are more objectively virtuous, but each community's *particular* standard of moral requirement will remain legitimate given that it accurately corresponds to that community's level of virtue.[126]

The advantage of this approach over the others is that it explains how different agents can have different accounts of what is morally expected of them without either dismissing the authenticity of their particular testimonies *or* precluding comparison among them through judging how virtuous they are relative to one another. Limited community relativism grants—in fact, insists—that some communities are more virtuous than others; yet it sees this disparity as a factor which challenges the minimalist claim that undue burden is a constant for all agents. To be sure, the acknowledgment of "noteworthily virtuous" communities alongside less virtuous communities puts pressure on the latter to reexamine themselves rather than condone their moral complacency.[127] For example, limited community relativism makes room for the possibility that French citizens who lived on the outskirts of Le Chambon in Vichy France could be inspired by their French Huguenot neighbors to alter their own assumptions about moral responsibility. This would be interpreted as a case of one community's norms influencing those of a less virtuous one. Where limited community relativism becomes *relativistic* is in its rejection of a universal sense of moral requirement beyond the moral minimum. While certain basic norms may be required of all agents everywhere, the outer limit of what may be considered morally required changes from community to community and within a particular community over time.

Blum's discussion of limited community relativism is instructive for thinking about how to characterize individual heroes, for central to the model is its accommodation of the idea of an *expanding* sense of duty over time. According to Urmson, the hero, or at least the hero par excellence, supererogates. Going above and beyond the call of duty is the hero's identifying mark. Urmson's characterization requires the hero to overcome fear and the drive to self-preservation, both of which are assumed to be inborn traits, either effortlessly or through self-discipline. The hero's heroic act, in other words, is made possible by a special trait that cannot be deliberately acquired, which allows the hero to circumvent the conditions that naturally constrain the rest of us. The counter-suggestion being offered here is that heroes do not supererogate, but instead have an expanded sense of duty, owing to their uncommonly virtuous nature. In this alternative construction, heroes are likely not to possess abnormal traits that exempt them from the supposed "natural" or "human" constraints that burden the rest of us. The difference is rather one of character, which is in part shaped by the community in which they acquire and develop their values. According to both the Urmsonian and the revised characterization, heroes achieve moral excellence. However, only in the latter is excellence understood to be a function of character development. Thus, in the revised characterization, heroes are not born heroes; they *become* them. They do so while retaining a modest sense of their roots, and while living routine lives among others in their communities. This judgment accords well with the Oliners' conclusions about righteous gentiles:

> They were and are "ordinary" people. They were farmers and teachers, entrepreneurs and factory workers, rich and poor, parents and single people, Protestants and Catholics.... Most were marked neither by exceptional leadership qualities nor by unconventional behavior. They were not heroes cast in larger-than-life molds. What most distinguished them were their connections with others in relationships of commitment and care. It is out of such relationships that they became aware of what was occurring around them and mustered their human and material resources to relieve pain. Their involvements with the Jews grew out of the ways in which they ordinarily related to other people—their characteristic ways of feeling; their perceptions of who should be obeyed; the rules and examples of conduct they learned from parents, friends, and religious and political associates; and their routine ways of deciding

what was wrong and right. They inform us that it is out of the quality of such routine human activities that the human spirit evolves and moral courage is born.[128]

There is no monopoly on the hero's courage. Rather, it is a product of community and connectedness to other human beings. Like Odysseus, Sydney Carton, Lord Jim, and Dr. Rieux, rescuers were heroes not because they transcended their humanity, but because they aspired to be more human.

Interpreting the hero's characteristic altruism as a function of his or her expanded sense of duty, rather than as a result of the presence of certain preexisting heroic traits, lends credence to the suggestion offered in the last chapter that the force lying behind the hero's "ought" is a legitimately *moral* one. Urmson makes a distinction between the hero's personal sense of obligation and "duty" as such, in which only the former has a morally optional status. In Urmson's view, heroes act heroically because they are idiosyncratic. That is, they *deliberately* choose to act heroically, even though they are not morally compelled to act as they do. They *consent* to assuming especially costly burdens for the sake of others. They do this by choice. For this reason, Urmson understands the heroes' decisions to accept great costs to themselves as evaluative ones: they have *morally good consequences*, but they are not, strictly speaking, *morally necessary*. This characterization of heroes strikes Urmson as the only plausible way of accounting for their unusual sense of responsibility for others. Without making the distinction between personal ideals and moral duties, he implies, we could not identify heroes as heroic. Notice, at this point, how incongruous Urmson's characterization of heroes is with rescuers' own self-descriptions, especially their repeated claims that "they simply *had* to do what they did" and that rescuing was not a "matter of choice."

Characterizing Moral Heroes

By allowing that the hero is one among the group of ordinary people with whom he or she interacts—even though the hero has an enhanced level of virtue, which also makes him or her extraordinary—we can properly identify the hero as heroic while at the same time acknowledging the "nonpreferential," moral sense in which the hero sees him- or herself as bound to perform the heroic act. In the revised characterization, the force of the hero's "ought" would no longer be one that is not morally binding, the equivalent of merely a personal ideal, as it is in Urmson's approach.

The definition of "heroes" that I shall now propose builds off of Urmson's initial characterization of them as fear-resistant altruists, though it does not attribute to heroes the feature of acting supererogatorily. I define "heroes" through reference to specific criteria. These are not meant to be the necessary and sufficient conditions for heroism. They are the basis for a stipulative definition. Since the line that separates heroes from non-heroes is neither sharply defined nor constant over time, the following criteria are flexible, not exhaustive. They are constructed to accommodate the special qualities possessed by heroes, seen from the perspective of the nonheroic, ordinary agent, in such a way that does not ignore heroes' own accounts of their conduct. Thus, I offer five criteria for moral heroism. Heroes are distinctive moral agents in that:

(1) They are, as Lawrence Blum calls them, *"noteworthily virtuous"*— and especially noteworthily benevolent—moral agents. Heroes have an exceptional moral character which disposes them to feel, desire, and act altruistically, and which enables them to involve themselves in the lives of others, particularly strangers, to a far greater extent than most people.

(2) They have an *expanded, and continually expanding, sense of duty* as a result of their noteworthily virtuous character. Heroes come to perceive the world differently from nonheroes; they see vividly, where others see palely, or not at all, what their responsibility for others truly entails. The fulfillment of this responsibility is, furthermore, not supererogatory, but rather morally required of them.

(3) They perform *considerable altruistic actions*, owing to their expanded sense of duty and to their willingness to obey it. Heroes promote the welfare and, in some cases, even save the lives of those needy others who are their beneficiaries.

(4) They perform these actions at great *cost* to themselves and to those near to them. Heroes, as Urmson rightly notes, have the ability to conquer both their fear and their drive to self-preservation to a far greater extent than most people. Heroic acts tend invariably to entail some major risk or cost to the hero's welfare and well-being.

(5) They are, in spite of their heroic traits, *among, and not apart from,* those who are their beneficiaries. Heroes, while noteworthily virtuous, are also *ordinary*. They affirm rather than transcend their humanity when performing their heroic actions.

This definition, while adopting from the standard view the idea that heroes perform considerable altruistic actions at great cost, departs significantly from it in claiming both that heroes have an expanded sense of duty and that they are extraordinary *and* ordinary. With respect to the first criterion, the hero's noteworthily virtuous character, it may be said that the characterization in the standard view is not necessarily incompatible with the one just offered, although it should be noted that here the hero is identified by his or her virtuous *character* rather than through the deeds he or she performs.

Furthermore, according to this definition, the moral hero is not the extreme altruist, who devotes him- or herself ceaselessly to promoting the good of others. The hero does not *completely* transcend his or her desire for self-preservation. As discussed above, Hallie tells of the few occasions when the Chambonnais were limited with respect to how much they could intervene on the Jews' behalf. On these occasions, they withheld aid not so much because they self-consciously placed a limit on the amount they could give of themselves, but rather because they were *human*: they had a finite amount of resources at their disposal and had to channel their efforts sensibly if they were going to make a difference. Heroes have a healthy sense of themselves, their families, and their own projects. Even though they risk these goods when they engage in acts of heroism, they do not lose sight of their value. Heroes are not emotionless or purely rational consequentialists. Their sense of right and wrong is motivated by compassion and decency. This point is of particular importance when one considers Urmson's challenge to moral theories to accommodate human beings as they actually are by not requiring them to perform actions that are unreasonably demanding. The revised characterization of heroes respects this Urmsonian insight. While it maintains that heroes feel as though they have no choice but to perform their highly costly acts of altruism, and that they are likely correct in their view about what is morally required of them, the view is flexible enough to allow that the moral expectations thereby placed upon heroes remain reasonable. To be sure, the revised characterization of moral heroes provides an account of the psychology of moral excellence, and in so doing picks up Urmson's concern about the shortcomings of an "idealistic" morality.

From this determination one can come to a further conclusion about the relationship between heroes and the rest of us: moral heroes are to be universally admired, and emulated as well, though in varying degrees. While heroes are to be praised both for their virtue and for the expanded sense of duty in which this virtue results, the revised characterization of them accepts that heroism is not within the realm of what can be achieved by many of us, regardless of how earnestly we try to improve our character (as we should).[129] Because of the sheer nature and scope of the demands placed by moral excellence on the resources of the self, heroism is something accessible to very few people. At the same time, the revised approach affirms that we do not know what we are ultimately capable of doing, and it is likely that we can *approximate* moral heroism to a far greater degree than we might expect. This is to say, we each have the capacity to become more virtuous. Moral heroism is relevant to ordinary morality.

These reflections become particularly important when one assesses Susan Wolf's seminal argument regarding moral exemplars. Wolf claims that, in striving to maximize the good and to achieve moral perfection, moral exemplars lose their humanity by not attending to their own projects as thoroughly as they ought to, and by denigrating the pursuits of others who choose not to devote themselves to such maximally demanding ends.[130] According to Wolf, the moral exemplar is both austere, in the sense of being self-denying, and self-righteous. These two vices, she argues, preclude us even from admiring, much less emulating him or her. Furthermore, the possession of these traits by the moral exemplar reveals how unrealistic his or her goals will prove to be within the context of a lived human life. The exemplar's morality does not "work for us," or so Wolf argues.

However, if the characterization of heroes just offered is correct, then moral exemplars are neither austere nor self-righteous, for they strive neither to maximize the good nor to achieve moral perfection; rather, they strive to be morally excellent, though not in a way that is unrealistic for them.[131] The point throughout this chapter has been to show that moral heroes, notwithstanding their heroism, fall within the range of ordinary persons, both with respect to what they are capable of morally achieving and with respect to what they can expect themselves to achieve. They *do* embody a moral code that "works" for them, as well as one that potentially works for others who, in rightly coming to admire them, endeavor in more limited ways to emulate them as well. But while it is true that their moral code is feasible rather than idealistic, heroes do not necessarily think less of others who manage only to live up to lower standards. In fact, "moral exemplars are no more likely, and may even be less likely, to think of their own standards and commitments as setting a standard for, or assessing, others."[132] We may conclude, then, that heroes neither adopt an ethic that is overly excessive, nor place unreasonable expectations upon others to follow them in their heroism. While heroes tend to hold themselves accountable to a higher standard of conduct than others, they are accurate in judging themselves to be morally bound in this respect.

If even heroes are correct in thinking of themselves as duty-bound when performing their acts of heroism, then we may wish to inquire whether there are circumstances under which agents can be so self-sacrificing as to exceed the bounds of moral requirement altogether? In analyzing this question it is necessary to shift our focus to moral saints, who, like heroes, have come to acquire an expanded sense of duty due to their character development and their correspondingly highly virtuous nature. Saints, however, exceed even this more demanding moral requirement in their routine interaction with others. Just how ordinary heroes are, in fact, will become apparent when we compare them with saints.

NOTES

1. J. O. Urmson, "Saints and Heroes," in *Essays in Moral Philosophy*, ed. A. I. Melden (Seattle: University of Washington Press, 1958), 199.

2. Ibid., 204.

3. A good example of a thinker who endorses the conventional, romantic notion of "hero-as-transcender" is Joseph Campbell. According to Campbell, the hero typically experiences a "mystical journey," in which the hero "ventures forth from the world of the common day into a region of supernatural wonder" wherein "fabulous forces are there encountered and a decisive victory is won," after which the hero "comes back from this mysterious adventure with the power to bestow boons on his fellow men." See Campbell, *The Hero with a Thousand Faces* (New York: Pantheon Books, 1949), 30.

4. Brian S. Hook and R. R. Reno, *Heroism and the Christian Life: Reclaiming Excellence* (Louisville: Westminster John Knox Press, 2000), 7.

5. Ibid., 10.

6. Ibid., 205.

7. Hook and Reno discuss parallel applications of this thesis to Christian heroes as various as John Paul II, Dietrich Bonhoeffer, Saint Augustine, and the Virgin Mary, in *Heroism and the Christian Life*, 175–80, 206ff.

8. Iris Murdoch, *The Sovereignty of Good* (London: Routledge and Kegan Paul, 1970), 95.

9. Tellingly, the firefighters and rescue workers of September 11 are graphically portrayed as larger-than-life, powerful, and morally righteous figures approximating superhero status in two recent, high-selling tributes, published by Marvel Comics and DC Comics. See *Heroes: The World's Greatest Superheroes Honor the World's Greatest Heroes* (New York: Marvel Comics, Dec. 2001); and *9-11*, volumes 1 and 2 (New York: DC Comics, 2001–2002).

10. David Halberstam, *Firehouse* (New York: Hyperion Books, 2002).

11. Ibid., 9.

12. Ibid., 50.

13. Ibid., 8.

14. It is believed that the firefighters from Engine 35 Ladder 40 entered the south tower ten minutes before its collapse. A video, which Halberstam discusses, corroborates this estimation. See ibid., 182ff.

15. I have consulted over thirty volumes and articles that probe into the righteous gentile phenomenon. Here I take the opportunity to list the most influential of these. For an overview of the activities of rescuers generally, see Kristen

Renwick Monroe, *The Heart of Altruism: Perceptions of a Common Morality* (Princeton: Princeton University Press, 1996), esp. chs. 5 and 10; Samuel and Pearl Oliner, *The Altruistic Personality: Rescuers of Jews in Nazi Europe* (New York: Free Press, 1988); and Eva Fogelman, *Conscience and Courage: Rescuers of Jews During the Holocaust* (New York: Anchor Books, 1994). Philip Hallie chronicles the rescue efforts of villagers from the southeastern French town of Le Chambon in occupied Vichy France in *Lest Innocent Blood Be Shed: The Story of the Village of Le Chambon and How Goodness Happened There* (New York: Harper and Row, 1979). Nechema Tec confronts the phenomenon of righteous gentiles in Poland in *When Light Pierced the Darkness: Christian Rescue of Jews in Nazi-Occupied Poland* (Oxford: Oxford University Press, 1986). Finally, Philip Friedman's *Their Brothers' Keepers* (New York: Holocaust Library, 1978) and Mordecai Paldiel's *Sheltering the Jews: Stories of Holocaust Rescuers* (Minneapolis: Fortress Press, 1996) present notable rescue stories from various European communities.

16. Lawrence Blum, *Moral Perception and Particularity* (Cambridge: Cambridge University Press, 1994), 167–69.

17. David Heyd, *Supererogation* (Cambridge: Cambridge University Press, 1982), 138.

18. Urmson, "Saints and Heroes," 204.

19. Martha Nussbaum, *Love's Knowledge: Essays on Philosophy and Literature* (Oxford: Oxford University Press, 1990), 374.

20. Ibid., 371.

21. See Nussbaum's treatment of this passage in ibid., 365–67.

22. Homer, *The Odyssey*, trans. W. Shrewing (Oxford: Oxford University Press, 1980), V. 215–224. This passage is cited by Nussbaum in *Love's Knowledge*, 365.

23. Homer, *The Odyssey*, V. 291–300.

24. Nussbaum, *Love's Knowledge*, 366. Nussbaum makes a similar argument for the Aristotelian conception of the human being, which lies between that of the gods and that of the beasts, in Martha Nussbaum, "Aristotle on Human Nature and the Foundations of Ethics," in *World, Mind, and Ethics: Essays on the Ethical Philosophy of Bernard Williams*, ed. J. E. Altham and Ross Harrison (Cambridge: Cambridge University Press, 1995), 86–131. The Homeric stories, Nussbaum remarks, "lead us to grasp the extent to which limits make us who we are, and to see the importance of the practices and values constituted by these limits in making a life that we can call our own" (96).

25. Nussbaum, *Love's Knowledge*, 378. Nussbaum is quoting Aristotle, *The Nicomachean Ethics* (1099b18–19). See also Martha Nussbaum, *The Fragility of Goodness: Luck and Ethics in Greek Tragedy and Philosophy* (Cambridge: Cambridge University Press, 1986), ch. 11.

26. Nussbaum, *Love's Knowledge*, 379.

27. Ibid., 381.

28. Ibid., 379.

29. Ibid., 381.

30. Homer, *The Odyssey*, XII. 194–202.

31. Alasdair MacIntyre, *After Virtue*, 2d ed. (Notre Dame: University of Notre Dame Press, 1982), 124–25.

32. Nussbaum, *Love's Knowledge*, 368.

33. Citations below are from Charles Dickens, *Works of Charles Dickens: A Tale of Two Cities and Sketches by Boz* (New York: The Kelmscott Society, 1904); and Joseph Conrad, *Lord Jim* (New York: Doubleday, 1922).

34. Characterizing the moral hero is not an easy task, and I shall offer my own definition by the close of this chapter. At this point, suffice it to say that altruism and willingness to perform costly acts in service of altruistic purposes comprise but two of the criteria for moral heroism. For definitions of moral heroism other than Urmson's, see especially Tom L. Beauchamp and James F. Childress, *Principles of Bioethics*, 4th ed. (Oxford: Oxford University Press, 1994), 494ff.; Blum, *Moral Perception and Particularity*, 68–75; and Monroe, *The Heart of Altruism*, ch. 4. Monroe actually distinguishes the moral hero from the rescuer, the latter representing for her an especially altruistic instance of the former. Monroe notes three respects in which rescuers exceed heroes: (1) the duration of their altruistic acts extends over long periods, whereas the acts of heroes can involve a much shorter time commitment; (2) rescuers engage in their altruistic activities at the expense rather than in the service of promoting their reputation in society (rescuers of Jews in Nazi Europe not only could expect social ostracism, but severe punishment by the civil authorities if their deeds were discovered); and (3) rescuers, unlike most heroes, put not only themselves but also their families at risk in performing their altruistic deeds. See Monroe, *The Heart of Altruism*, 17–18. Since I define the hero differently from Monroe (e.g., on my account, the altruism of the hero does typically involve a long time commitment and can, but need not, evoke praise from the immediate society), the distinction Monroe draws between heroes and rescuers is not of crucial importance to me. Samuel and Pearl Oliner, unlike Monroe, equate rescuing with moral heroism; see Oliner and Oliner, *The Altruistic Personality*, 49ff.

35. Dickens, *A Tale of Two Cities*, 88.

36. Ibid., 92.

37. The presence of both of these motives in Carton's thinking is confirmed by the famous words that conclude *A Tale of Two Cities*: "It is a far, far better thing that I do, than I have ever done; it is a far, far better rest that I go to, than I have ever known" (400).

38. We may wonder why someone has to be killed in order to make amends for other people, and much has been made of Lord Jim's heroism within the context of the Christian parable. For an exploration of the idea that Jim is a Christ figure, see Edwin Moseley, "Christ as Tragic Hero: Conrad's *Lord Jim*," in *Religion and Modern Literature: Essays in Theory and Criticism*, ed. G. B. Tennyson and Edward E. Ericson, Jr. (Grand Rapids, Mich.: William B. Eerdmans Publishing Company, 1975), 220–32; Robert Wilson, *Conrad's Mythology* (Troy, N.Y.: The Whitston Publishing Company, 1987), 48ff.; and John Batchelor, *Lord Jim* (London: Unwin Hyman, 1988), 146ff.

39. Conrad, *Lord Jim*, 43, 381.

40. Ibid., 392.

41. Ibid., 43.

42. Murdoch, *The Sovereignty of Good*, 95.

43. Conrad, *Lord Jim*, 305.

44. Albert Camus, *The Plague*, trans. Stuart Gilbert (New York: Vintage Press, 1991), 48–49.

45. Ibid., 58–59; 62–63.

46. Ibid., 41.

47. Ibid., 51, 61.

48. Ibid., 122, 127.

49. Ibid., 127.

50. Ibid., 132.

51. Ibid., 163.

52. Ibid., 209–10. (emphasis mine).

53. Ibid., 113.

54. In *Heroism and the Christian Life*, Hook and Reno acknowledge and positively value Camus's commitment to resistance to evil in this life, while disdaining his rejection of the category of the holy, which concerns itself with the next life. They proceed to argue that Dr. Rieux is not a hero but an "antihero," whose subjectivity is linked up with the collective of humanity. "Our task," write Hook and Reno, "as Camus develops his story of resistance, is to remain with each other, sharing a common fate. This task requires courage and endurance, to be sure, but Camus insists that our resistance to evil must not become elevated, unique, and distinctive. . . . We should resist evil, but also resist the temptation to aspire to the heroic" (ibid., 177–78). Based on my discussion, such a characterization would make Rieux the hero par excellence. However, according to Hook and Reno, Rieux's this-worldly focus precludes his consideration for heroism. On the other hand, Father Paneloux's zealous anticipation of martyrdom in the face of the plague makes him, in their view, an ideal candidate.

Insofar as Hook and Reno draw a contrast between aspirations for human solidarity and aspirations for heroism, they endorse the notion of the heroic used in the standard view, according to which the hero self-consciously transcends rather than affirms his human roots. Reno and Hook's Christian hero self-transcends through a life lived in and through Christ: "Not I, but Christ in me" (ibid., 202). They maintain that those who repudiate heroism, as does Rieux, cannot themselves be heroic. As I will argue, this conclusion fails to account for the scores of rescuers who do repudiate their heroism, men and women who insist stubbornly on living a human and not supra-human life during inhuman times. One advantage of adopting a view of the heroic as ordinary *and* extraordinary is that it accommodates a notion of heroic resistance according to which the hero remains profoundly committed to improving the conditions in this life on behalf of, and in solidarity with, those common and ordinary souls the hero would otherwise leave behind.

55. Camus, *The Plague*, 289, 291.

56. Ibid., 301–2.

57. Ibid., 308.

58. Since 1962, Yad Vashem's "Commission for the Designation of the Righteous" has honored the actions of those who risked their lives to save the Jews from Hitler. The commission has studied applications for the title of "Righteous

Gentile," taking into consideration the following seven factors in their evaluation: (1) context of contact made between rescuers and rescued; (2) nature (both quality and quantity) of aid extended; (3) amount of material compensation paid in return for this aid, if any; (4) dangers and risks faced by rescuers; (5) rescuers' motivations (insofar as this is discernible); (6) available evidence from the side of the rescued persons; and (7) any other relevant data which could shed light on the authenticity of the story. See Paldiel, *Sheltering the Jews*, 203–4. To date, approximately thirteen thousand people have been recognized as "Righteous Gentiles." This is significantly lower than the total number of those who were put forward as candidates.

59. Ibid., 201.

60. The dangers rescuers and their families faced is abundantly documented. See especially Paldiel, *Sheltering the Jews*, 159–85; Monroe, *The Heart of Altruism*, 84–90, 157–58; and Oliner and Oliner, *The Altruistic Personality*, 123–27.

61. The distinction I am making here can be found in Wayne Proudfoot's *Religious Experience*. In that book, Proudfoot argues that the scholar of religious studies presented with testimony from a religious practitioner who makes, for example, cosmological or metaphysical claims about the world, is faced with two separate tasks in trying to understand such testimony: (1) attempting to identify and describe these claims (whether they are religious beliefs or practices) in terms that the practitioners themselves would find acceptable; and (2) interpreting the significance of these claims, once they have been identified and described, in terms of a second-order, explanatory framework of understanding. Now, while Proudfoot focuses on this distinction in reference to the scholar's handling of testimony pertaining to *religious* beliefs and practices, I think the distinction is also very useful in terms of the discussion I have set out above. Rescuers are not in all cases religious practitioners, but they do qualify as "insiders" of another sort, namely, practitioners of virtue, who, like the religious insiders with whom Proudfoot is explicitly concerned, claim to have some added insight about the situation they are describing. See Wayne Proudfoot, *Religious Experience* (Berkeley: University of California Press, 1985), esp. 69–74.

62. Urmson, for his part, jumps to this level of inquiry almost immediately in "Saints and Heroes," asserting that the insider's own understanding of specific altruistic acts is irrelevant to our characterization of those acts, if the acts are sufficiently costly in terms of the sacrifice they require of the agent performing them.

63. Hallie's title is an allusion to Deuteronomy 19:10: "Therefore I command you, you shall set apart three cities ... then you shall add three other cities to these three, lest innocent blood be shed in your land which the Lord your God gives you as an inheritance, and so the guilt of bloodshed be on you." Hallie explains that in the Bible "it is people guilty of what we now call involuntary manslaughter who are protected in the cities of refuge until they can be brought to a fair trial. But the Jews were being persecuted not because of any crime, voluntary or involuntary, but only because they were Jews. [The Chambonnais] must have felt that these modern Jews were all the more deserving of refuge because of their utter innocence of any crime or even any charge" (Hallie, *Lest Innocent Blood*

162   MORALLY EXTRAORDINARY PERSONS

Be Shed, 109). Le Chambon, as Hallie explains, became an authentic "city of refuge," known by Jews and non-Jews alike as the safest place for Jews in Europe (125, 153).

64. Pierre Sauvage, *Weapons of Spirit* (documentary film) (Los Angeles: Friends of Le Chambon, 1989).

65. Hallie, *Lest Innocent Blood Be Shed,* 91.

66. Ibid., 159.

67. Ibid., 132–33.

68. Laurence Thomas, *Vessels of Evil: American Slavery and the Holocaust* (Philadelphia: Temple University Press, 1993), 66ff.

69. David P. Gushee, *The Righteous Gentiles of the Holocaust: A Christian Interpretation* (Minneapolis: Fortress Press, 1994), 125–26.

70. For a detailed discussion of the history of the Huguenots, their persecution, and the religious wars their persecution brought about, see Barbara B. Diefendorf, *Beneath the Cross: Catholics and Huguenots in Sixteenth-Century Paris* (Oxford: Oxford University Press, 1991), esp. ch. 8. Other sources on which my analysis of the Huguenots relies, in varying degrees, include: J. H. M. Salmon, *Society in Crisis: France in the Sixteenth Century* (New York: St. Martin's Press, 1975); Philip Benedict, *The Huguenot Population of France, 1600–1685: The Demographic Fate and Customs of a Religious Minority* (Philadelphia: Transactions of the American Philosophical Society, vol. 81, part 5, 1991); N. M. Sutherland, *The Huguenot Struggle for Recognition* (New Haven: Yale University Press, 1980); G. Elmore Reaman, *The Trial of the Huguenots in Europe, the United States, South Africa, and Canada* (Baltimore: Genealogical Publishing Co., 1972); and Philippe Erlanger, *St. Bartholomew's Night: The Massacre of Saint Bartholomew,* trans. Patrick O'Brian (Westport, Conn.: Greenwood Press, 1960).

71. Gushee, *The Righteous Gentiles of the Holocaust,* 126.

72. The circumstances leading up to the massacre of St. Bartholomew's Day were not only the result of religious conflict, but were also related to international politics and concerns about stable leadership in France. The massacre itself, in fact, happened in stages, beginning with the assassination of Admiral Gaspard de Coligny, the leader of the Huguenots who had already made several attempts to establish colonies for French Protestants in America, and culminating in the outright butchery of innocents. For a rich historical account of the days leading up to and after August 24, see Sutherland, *The Huguenot Struggle for Recognition,* 206ff.

73. Diefendorf, *Beneath the Cross,* 141.

74. Salmon, *Society in Crisis,* 186.

75. Diefendorf, *Beneath the Cross,* 127.

76. Ibid., 137–38.

77. Ibid., 138–41.

78. Ibid., 138.

79. Ibid., 134.

80. Ibid., 139.

81. By the time the Chambonnais sheltered Jews during World War II, a precedent for Huguenots coming to the aid of persecuted minorities had been firmly

established. For example, in the first decade of the 1900s the Chambonnais invited sick, exploited working-class children into their village and cared for them. Thirty years later, they gave shelter to refugees from the Spanish Civil War and were known generally for receiving refugees of all types during World War I and at the dawn of World War II. See Gushee, *The Righteous Gentiles of the Holocaust*, 126.

82. Ibid., 127.

83. Hallie, *Lest Innocent Blood Be Shed*, 22.

84. Hallie discusses the difficulty that the Chambonnais, and Magda Trocmé in particular, had in coming to terms with the fact that some of their values would have to be compromised if they were to render aid to the Jews. This issue is exemplified by the case of lying and making false identification cards. Hallie writes:

> To this day, Magda remembers her reaction to hearing about the making of the first counterfeit card. During the first winter of the Occupation, Theis came into the presbytery and said to her, "I have just made a false card for Monsieur Lévy. It is the only way to save his life." She remembers the horror she felt at that moment: duplicity, for any purpose, was simply wrong. She and the other leaders knew that the ration cards were as important as identity cards—the Chambonnais were so poor that they could not share their food with refugees and hope to survive themselves. Nonetheless, none of those leaders became reconciled to making counterfeit cards, though they made many of them in the course of the Occupation. Even now, Magda finds her integrity diminished when she thinks of those cards. She is still sad over what she calls "our lost candor." (ibid., 126)

85. Gushee explains that during religious services the Chambonnais leaders emphasized Romans 13, which argues that Christian obedience to the state has always to be tempered by the commandment to love the neighbor (Gushee, *The Righteous Gentiles of the Holocaust*, 127). Chambonnais theology, notes Gushee, contrasts sharply with a theology promoting uncritical obedience to the state, which served merely to condone if not encourage Nazi attempts to thwart rescue efforts across Europe.

86. Hallie, *Lest Innocent Blood Be Shed*, 173.

87. Ibid., 149.

88. Ibid., 64–65.

89. Ibid., 154; see also ibid., 20, 110, and 148–49, for similar Chambonnais denials of attributions of supererogatory conduct.

90. Ibid., 20–21.

91. Cf. note 15 above.

92. See, respectively, Monroe, *Heart of Altruism*, 104, 105; Oliner and Oliner, *The Altruistic Personality*, 113, 228; and Kristen R. Monroe, Michael C. Barton, and Ute Klingemann, "Altruism and the Theory of Rational Action: Rescuers of Jews in Nazi Europe," *Ethics* 101 (1990): 103.

93. Oliner and Oliner, *The Altruistic Personality*, 118.

94. According to this solution, rescuers would say that bystanders acted in "bad faith" in the Sartrean sense. That is, they acted against the wisdom of their "truer" selves because it was easier to do so. The core assumption of bad faith is that

164   MORALLY EXTRAORDINARY PERSONS

human beings remain aware, no matter how dim that awareness may be, of their
freedom in their various situations to act for the betterment of humanity. See
Lewis Gordon, *Bad Faith and Antiblack Racism* (Atlantic Highlands, N.J.: Humanities Press, 1995). According to this view, the claim that bystanders "simply couldn't
help" does not hold up under critical scrutiny, for it denies a freedom to act
that bystanders surely possessed. This issue will be addressed in more detail in
chapter 5.

95. Monroe, *The Heart of Altruism*, 101 (emphasis mine).
96. Ibid., 115–18.
97. Monroe explains rescuers' unique way of perceiving the world in terms of
their distinctive "canonical expectations," or their expectations about what *should*
occur (i.e., what is "right" or "proper") in the normal course of human behavior. While everybody has canonical expectations, these vary cross-culturally and
among people with different capacities for altruism. For especially altruistic individuals or groups, certain altruistic acts will not seem out of the ordinary. Monroe writes:

> The expectation about what is ordinary and right and proper translates into the
> idea that such behavior requires no explanation. When quizzed about it by ana-
> lysts, people are often puzzled; when pressed further, they often explain it
> through a quantifier ("Everybody does it") or through reference to a deontic
> model ("That's what you're supposed to do"). I found precisely this kind of
> response when I spoke with people who had rescued Jews from the Nazis. When
> I asked what made them risk their lives for strangers, they usually looked at me
> with some surprise and replied, "But what else could I do?" Their behavior was
> ordinary to them, although it seemed exceptional to me and was certainly excep-
> tional statistically during the war.
> Canonical expectations thus have a normative quality: it is "good" when the
> world operates in the expected way. To understand altruism, then, we must ask
> what the altruist expects will and should occur under ordinary circumstances.
> These expectations should differ in significant ways from those of nonaltruists.
> (Monroe, *The Heart of Altruism*, 11)

In explicating the concept of canonical expectations, Monroe is able to explain
why heroes regard their heroic deeds as nonheroic, a phenomenon Urmson
accounts for by raising the possibility of false modesty and the heroic propensity
to confuse personal ideals with moral obligations.

98. Ibid., 101ff.
99. Philip Gourevitch, *We Wish to Inform You That Tomorrow We Will Be Killed
with Our Families: Stories from Rwanda* (New York: Picador USA, 1998).
100. Most historians agree that what took place in 1994 in Rwanda was not
war but genocide. It was a campaign perpetrated by the Hutus against the Tutsis,
in which Hutus, traditionally thought to be "people of the soil" descended from
the Bantu of central Africa (supposedly giving them a more legitimate claim to
being the true natives of Rwanda), rose up in resentment, following Rwandan
independence, against the Tutsi royalty that previously had been supported by

Germans and Belgians during colonial rule. Civil discord and periodic violent clashes between the two groups devolved into genocide after Juvenal Habyarimana, the Hutu president of Rwanda, was killed in a plane crash, an act for which the Tutsis were popularly blamed. Massacres ensued. Busloads of Hutu soldiers raided schools, churches, and homes to murder as many Tutsis as they could. The killings were indiscriminate, evidenced by the thousands of Tutsi corpses—including women, children, and the elderly—which floated downriver to Tanzania and Uganda during the summer and early autumn of 1994. See Tony Waters, *Bureaucratizing the Good Samaritan: The Limits to Humanitarian Relief Operations* (Boulder, Colo.: Westview Press, 2001), 84ff.; and Jonathan Glover, *Humanity: A Moral History of the Twentieth Century* (New Haven: Yale University Press, 1999), 119–22.

The Rwandan genocide is often attributed to tribal hostility in which one group rose up with the intent to eliminate the other. The two groups had distinguishing characteristics. The Hutus were traditionally characterized as being short and stocky, and the Tutsis as tall and long-limbed; the Hutus tended to the land, while the Tutsis owned cattle and held positions of power. Yet this tribal picture is considerably more complex. Both the Hutus and the Tutsis spoke the same language, lived in the same districts, and frequently married one another. Very few Rwandans descended exclusively from one tribe or the other. This suggests that the genocide was not merely a spontaneous outbreak of tribal hatred, but also the result of a planned campaign launched by prominent Hutu propagandists who wanted to seize and keep power. According to one report, the Radio Television Libre des Milles Collines, a Hutu station with strong ties to the government, repeatedly advertised that the Tutsis were dishonest and that they should be shunned in business and education. The station announced one day: "The grave is only half full. Who will help us to fill it?"; as well as, "By 5 May, the country must be completely cleansed of Tutsis ... The children must be killed too" (Glover, *Humanity*, 121–22). The influential role the government played in perpetrating these crimes against humanity, primarily for the sake of retaining power, makes the Rwandan genocide as much a result of a corrupt and manipulative government as the result of a grassroots ethnic conflict.

101. Gourevitch, *We Wish to Inform You*, 140–41.

102. Ibid., 142.

103. Ibid., 142–43.

104. Monroe, Barton, and Klingemann, "Altruism and the Theory of Rational Action," 118. See also Kristen Renwick Monroe, "John Donne's People: Explaining Differences between Rational Actors and Altruists through Cognitive Frameworks," *Journal of Politics* 53, no. 2 (May 1991): 394–433.

105. John Donne, *Devotions upon Emergent Occasions*, XVII, ed. Anthony Raspa (Montreal: McGill-Queens University Press, 1975), 86–87.

106. Gary Becker, *The Economic Approach to Human Behavior* (Chicago: University of Chicago Press, 1976), 14, quoted by Monroe, Barton, and Klingemann, "Altruism and the Theory of Rational Action," 120. Monroe and her coauthors list a number of references from which they formulate their general picture of "rational actor theory." Among the ones I found the most helpful were R. Withrobe, "It Pays to Do Good, but Not More Good Than It Pays," *Journal of Economic*

Behavior and Organization 2 (1981): 201–13; Howard Margolis, *Selfishness, Altruism, and Rationality* (New York: Cambridge University Press, 1981); and S. C. Kolm, "Altruism and Efficiency," *Ethics* 94 (1983), 18–65. For the full list of references, see Monroe, Barton, and Klingemann, "Altruism and the Theory of Rational Action," 107–8, note 18.

107. Monroe, Barton, and Klingemann, "Altruism and the Theory of Rational Action," 117–18. In *The Heart of Altruism*, Monroe considers four traditional explanations for the phenomenon of altruism before advancing her own position that there is an "altruistic" perspective that is irreducible to models based on the maximization of self-regarding preferences. These alternatives are: (1) socio-cultural models; (2) economic models; (3) biological models; and (4) psychological models (see ibid., chs. 6–9). According to socio-cultural explanatory models, altruism tends to be motivated by demographic factors such as religious affiliation, residence, family background, occupation, education, and so forth. According to economic models, upon which rational actor theory is primarily based, other-regarding actions are in almost every case prompted by the prospect of reward, honor, or praise of some sort; produce some psychic good (such as alleviation of guilt); or are performed with an expectation of reciprocity. Cost-benefit analysis is central to utility calculations in economic models. Explanations for altruism from evolutionary biology focus on kin selection (wherein the process of natural selection works genetically) or group selection (wherein the process of natural selection works through the group of which the individual organism is a part). Both of these evolutionary explanations attempt to explain altruism within the Darwinian paradigm of individual selection. Finally, psychological explanations (both social and developmental) of altruism interpret the phenomenon of other-regard as but one more subtle manifestation of egoism more broadly construed. While Monroe grants that each of these theories prove somewhat plausible in the case of explaining the behavior of lesser altruists, such as entrepreneurs or philanthropists, they become increasingly inadequate in the case of rescuers. Her findings are supported by careful methodology in her interviews. For example, in organizing her demographic data, as part of the process of interpreting testimony, she checked out the stories of rescuers who claimed that they had rebuffed all attempts to honor them for rescuing, in order to establish that they were telling the truth about not caring at all about being rewarded for their heroic efforts. See Monroe, *The Heart of Altruism*, 121, 151–60, 178, and 194.

108. See, for example, Oliner and Oliner, *The Altruistic Personality*, 125–27.

109. Monroe, *The Heart of Altruism*, 234–35.

110. Ibid., 197ff.

111. Monroe, Barton, and Klingemann, "Altruism and the Theory of Rational Action," 119.

112. Oliner and Oliner, *The Altruistic Personality*, 249.

113. Monroe, who wants to insist on the purely other-regarding nature of rescuing, might take issue with this characterization. In my view, such an objection would fail to appreciate fully the potential for an other-regarding virtue, like benevolence, to serve as a profound key to self-development. This is a possibility that Monroe may not want to rule out, given the major points of her own theory.

Indeed, if she can distinguish between the general concept of flourishing and all versions of rational actor theory, as I think she can, then it may actually benefit her to take note of the potential coincidence between altruism and self-fulfillment. If anything, this would serve to buttress her endorsement of rescuers' claims that they had no choice but to rescue given their view of themselves and their responsibilities to others.

114. The difference between "pale" and "vivid" beliefs, notes Shelly Kagan, is that in the latter the agent sees cause to act in accordance with what may be prescribed by such beliefs, whereas in the former, the agent does not sufficiently grasp their importance to be motivated to action. Paleness and vividness do not bear on the *authenticity* of the beliefs in question, in the sense of their being "true" or "valid" beliefs. It is perfectly consistent for a pale set of beliefs to consist of propositions that are entirely true: for instance, propositions pertaining to damage that occurs to the environment as a result of littering. It is just that an agent has no overriding motives to meet the demands such beliefs may entail, especially when they conflict with self-interest. We may say that in this respect the agent lacks *conviction*. Kagan notes that we are most likely to perceive authentic beliefs about the suffering of others in a vivid fashion when they are close to us, either geographically (e.g., someone is starving in our midst) or emotionally (e.g., people who share our ethnic background are undergoing massive persecution in their homeland). Once we realize that pale beliefs are still true beliefs, then we can begin to realize that our not acting on them is *our own* failing, rather than a failing of the veridical strength of the beliefs themselves. One way of explaining heroes' heroism is in terms of their ability to make important but pale beliefs vivid ones. As pale beliefs become vivid, the urgency with which we dispose ourselves to become more benevolent expands. In other words, while beliefs in and of themselves might not be enough to induce the motivation to act according to duty, once one views a moral truth "vividly," one is in a position to habituate oneself to acting accordingly. This occurs through proper training, i.e., through practicing the virtues one comes to know that one ought to exhibit. See Kagan, *The Limits of Morality* (Oxford: Oxford University Press, 1989), 283–91, 299–300, 304–7.

115. Monroe, *The Heart of Altruism*, 215–16. While the literature on the moral praiseworthiness of rescuers or the moral blameworthiness of Nazis and their sympathizers is voluminous, surprisingly little attention has been given so far to the question of the failed responsibility (or, alternatively, the justified inaction) of bystanders. Perhaps one reason for this is that the extent to which bystanders were in the wrong is not entirely clear. Whereas in the case of rescuers and Nazis the interesting scholarly questions pertain to their motivations for acting as they did, rather than to our evaluations of their actions, in the case of bystanders—who constituted the majority of Europeans during Hitler's regime—we *do*, for the most part, understand why they did nothing rather than risk their lives by engaging in rescue activities. But we are puzzled when it comes to evaluating their conduct. What constitutes a justified reason for failing to help? To what extent are bystanders morally blameworthy? One ethicist who has recently taken up these questions is David Jones, who distinguishes between bystanders who had valid reasons for not helping and bystanders who were fully blameworthy. See David

Jones, *Moral Responsibility in the Holocaust: A Study in the Ethics of Character* (Lanham, Md.: Rowman and Littlefield, 1999). Jones considers three criteria from the "benefit" side for determining whether or not rescuing constituted a moral duty: "(1) the relative value of the benefit to the victim, (2) the value of the help or rescue as an act of resistance to Nazi oppression and values, and (3) the ability and opportunity of the actor to perform the act" (ibid., 207). While the presence of any of these criteria leads one in the direction of concluding that rescuing is morally required, Jones argues, if the costs are significant enough, then that is a sufficiently mitigating circumstance to release bystanders from moral blame. Missing from this cost-benefit calculus is any discussion of whether condition (1) on the "benefits" side ever ought to be considered overriding, as rescuers themselves perceived it to be. Jones's argument ultimately suffers from an Urmson-like assumption that there are clear, universal criteria for deciding whether the *act* of rescuing can be considered required. Upon posing the question "What guidelines should have been used to make decisions about whether or not to perform some act [of rescue] in a particular situation, as a matter of actual duty?," Jones seems naive in his reply: "Fortunately, there are good grounds for making these guidelines fairly simple and practical to use" (ibid., 207). Such guidelines, Jones proceeds to claim, are equally applicable to all moral agents. Although his analysis is sometimes simplistic, Jones's work is helpful if for no other reason than that it alerts us to the importance of the phenomenon of bystanders (see esp. ibid., ch. 9).

116. The claim that some bystanders, because they lack rescuers' virtuous vision, ought not to be held accountable for failing to perform particularly costly actions is not tantamount to releasing them from the obligation of *disposing* themselves to become the kind of people who will come to possess this capacity over time. In other words, the "is/ought" argument only works toward exonerating bystanders during snapshots in time rather than over long periods.

117. Blum, *Moral Perception and Moral Particularity*, 161.

118. Ibid.

119. A good representative of the maximalist position in contemporary circles is Shelly Kagan, who is a consequentialist. In *The Limits of Morality*, Kagan argues for a general requirement to promote the overall good, the central burden of which relies on his bringing to light the falsity of the assumption that if the promotion of the overall good *were* morally required it would be impossible, or at least unreasonably difficult, to become motivated to act according to this higher kind of motive of reason. Because we can influence our current set of motivational beliefs based on what we rationally accept to be morally correct (e.g., by transforming them from a "pale" to a "vivid" set of beliefs), insists Kagan, the claim that there are moral imperatives that lie outside of the scope of normal human capabilities is overdrawn. The critic can agree with Kagan that at least this much is true; however, he or she might take issue with Kagan's extreme assumption that there are, in fact, no overriding reasons that can contravene the *pro tanto* reason to promote the overall good. (See Kagan, *Limits of Morality*, 17.) Such an assumption is problematic, for it ignores the fact that different people (and communities) have different handicaps at different stages of their moral development. Some people *are* for one reason or another temporarily precluded

from transforming (or desiring to transform) their pale beliefs into vivid ones. Kagan is simply too optimistic about the ability of those who currently lack the requisite kinds of moral motivations to come to possess them by means of making an appeal to reason, or so claims the critic of maximalism.

120. Blum, *Moral Perception and Moral Particularity*, 148–49.

121. Ibid., 162.

122. Ibid., 163.

123. Ibid., 168.

124. Blum also considers a third, "personal calling," approach to explain the actions of noteworthily virtuous agents, which he distinguishes from maximalism and minimalism. In this case, duty is not considered to be universal. Rather, there is an assumption of two standards of moral requirement, one that is applicable to ordinary persons and one that is applicable only to the noteworthily virtuous agent. The noteworthily virtuous agent is on this account self-consciously aware that he or she is morally different from others, and therefore subject to a different standard of moral demandingness. As Blum points out, the "personal calling" approach has the advantage of validating the noteworthily virtuous person's own perception of his or her moral reality, which the minimalist approach fails to do (ibid., 167). Nonetheless, the case of the Chambonnais again serves to call into question the adequacy of this approach as a theory that explains the moral psychology of the extreme altruist, for the Chambonnais did not see themselves as *permanently* morally distinct from ordinary persons. On the contrary, they regarded rescuing to be among the most obvious responses to a given evil, and one that would become apparent to everyone were they to become sufficiently virtuous. A good representative of the "personal calling" approach is A. I. Melden. See Melden, "Saints and Supererogation," in *Philosophy and Life: Essays on John Wisdom*, ed. Ilham Dilman (The Hague: Martinus Nijhoff, 1984), 61–82.

125. Blum, *Moral Perception and Moral Particularity*, 160.

126. It is no doubt difficult to determine what counts as criteria for making a community virtuous, let alone to measure one community's level of virtue against that of another. I would expect that one who wished to make such a determination would have to do some empirical work on comparing the laws, customs, and social mores upheld by particular communities, as well as establish a means by which we could read "virtue" into these various institutions. Blum ignores this pragmatic difficulty in his largely theoretical treatment of noteworthily virtuous agents. The omission of this treatment is in any case not essential to my discussion here, since my main purpose is to point out simply that duty and virtue are related, that levels of virtue may vary from community to community, and finally that as the level of virtue shifts from one community to the next, so will that community's—valid—understanding of its moral requirement.

127. Some communities are, to be sure, not just morally complacent but vicious—and vicious by virtue of the acts of *ordinary* men and women. In terms of the Holocaust, the "goodness" of Le Chambon could easily be contrasted with the "viciousness" of places like the German town of Würzburg where people not particularly bent on or prepared for mass murder facilitated genocide by routinely tipping off the Gestapo to breaches in anti-Semitic policy. See Robert

Gellately, "'A Monstrous Uneasiness': Citizen Participation and Persecution of the Jews in Nazi Germany," in *Lessons and Legacies: The Meaning of the Holocaust in a Changing World*, ed. Peter Hayes (Evanston: Northwestern University Press, 1991), 178–95. See also Christopher Browning's dreadful account of the German reserve policemen who executed, one by one, fifteen hundred women, children, and elderly citizens of the Polish village of Jozefow in July 1942, in Browning, *Ordinary Men* (New York: Harper Collins, 1992). Gellately and Browning argue for the "ordinariness" of citizens who condoned and sometimes participated in murder. They argue that such citizens typically acted not out of desperation, political opportunism, or interest in protecting themselves and their families, but rather out of a desire to act in conformity with promulgated social norms. The portrayal offered by Gellately and Browning is that these citizens acted blindly and automatically, with an uncritical acceptance of the Nazi ideal of *Gemeinschaft* (community), which divided the residents of Germany into "good citizens" and Jews (Gellately, "'A Monstrous Uneasiness,'" 194). See also Glover, *Humanity: A Moral History of the Twentieth Century*. Glover's volume consists of a comprehensive, highly empirical, and ultimately hopeful effort to construct an ethical framework that realistically takes into account how we are psychologically disposed to conduct ourselves in light of the depths to which we, as human beings, are from time to time capable of sinking. As part of this effort, Glover explores the phenomenon of evil perpetrated by ordinary individuals in what Nietzsche terms a "festival of cruelty," which Glover implies is familiar and repeated cross-culturally in various contexts. In his chronicle, he records the atrocities witnessed by the world in the twentieth century, the most brutal century ever recorded. Glover's book is to be recommended alone for the lucidity and brazenness with which he addresses recent atrocities as wide-ranging as the Holocaust, Hiroshima, the Gulag, Cambodia, My Lai, the Balkans, Rwanda, and others.

   In light of these reports, my critic may object that I have, in this chapter, presented a somewhat rosy picture of the communal, and have furthermore implied that virtue characteristically arises and is passed on within the context of communities. Such a thesis would contrast sharply with that offered by no less significant a theologian than the Christian realist Reinhold Niebuhr, in his aptly titled *Moral Man and Immoral Society* (New York: Scribner and Sons, 1932). Niebuhr is suspicious of the communal and in particular is suspicious of its propensity to give rise to the mob mentality that emerges as political states vie for power among one another. My response to this is not to deny Niebuhr's thesis as a whole but rather to take issue with its strong claim that the communal *inevitably* brings out the worst in the individual. Niebuhr's more general assertion that societies devolve into competing entities whose members act out of self-interest can be used in support of my argument that there are better and worse communities, each made up of ordinary people. The former, though rare, may serve as an example for the latter, precisely because of the ordinariness of their constituent members.

   128. Oliner and Oliner, *The Altruistic Personality*, 259–60.

   129. While it is not necessarily beyond the capacity of the majority of us to achieve moral excellence in varying degrees, it is in all likelihood beyond the majority to be so consistently morally excellent as to rise to the level of moral

heroism. As Blum notes, "while one can *try* to adopt ideals, one cannot ensure success in doing so; sincerely *professing* ideals is not equivalent to adopting them. Moreover (a different point) even if one succeeds in genuinely adopting ideals, one cannot ensure that one comes fully to *live* by them, in the way required for moral excellence. Finally, one surely cannot by effort alone, or in any other way, simply bring it about that those ideals become deeply rooted in one's character in the way required for true moral excellence" (Blum, *Moral Perception and Particularity*, 95).

130. Susan Wolf, "Moral Saints," *Journal of Philosophy* 79, no. 8 (1982): 419–39.

131. Blum distinguishes between moral perfection and moral excellence in *Moral Perception and Particularity*, 91.

132. Ibid., 93. Many thinkers, as Blum notes, have argued persuasively that holding oneself accountable to a moral standard does not conceptually bind others to it, although such norms, while not *universal* (e.g., like "rock-bottom" duties), could in one sense still be considered *universalizable* and therefore binding for anyone comparably virtuous. For other authors who have made similar arguments, see especially the following: Michael Pritchard, "Self-Regard and the Supererogatory," *Tulane Studies in Philosophy* 31 (1982): 139–51; Thomas Hill, Jr., "Self-Respect Reconsidered," *Tulane Studies in Philosophy* 31 (1982): 132ff.; and Melden, "Saints and Supererogation," 61ff.

CHAPTER 4

Suffering Saints

ECCENTRICS OR EXEMPLARS?

ECCENTRICS OR EXEMPLARS?

Heroes are not merely moral paragons, but exemplars, demonstrations of human beings living the best kind of moral life. They are not pictures of perfection. While they stand out among us, the life to which they have habituated themselves is in principle accessible to anyone who becomes sufficiently virtuous. Thus, they stand worthy of our admiration *and* our emulation. They are distinctive moral agents in that they have routinized what, from our perspective, appears to be extraordinary altruistic conduct. Yet their noteworthily virtuous character does not preclude them from claiming that they are, in a very important sense, *ordinary*. They have non-heroic roots. They possess flaws. They live in, rather than outside, the social world of their beneficiaries. Finally, they are not necessarily morally praiseworthy; for, since heroes are more virtuous than we are, we have no reason not to trust them when they claim that they act in the most expected manner. Indeed, *we* may be morally blameworthy when we do not act as they do, even if there are mitigating circumstances that might temporarily excuse bystander inaction. Our exposure to heroes is instructive. It teaches us that in the long run the standard of moral ambition to which we normally subscribe is insufficiently ambitious. Heroes distinguish themselves by excelling, but we *can* excel. In this sense, heroes represent the best of humanity within the domain of mortal limitation. They are—already—how we should become.

This conclusion challenges the conventional view that an outstanding few are "born heroes," to whom one standard of moral appraisal applies, while the rest of us are subject to what can be identified by default as "ordinary" morality. Such a dichotomization assumes that we remain static over time, unlikely to be able to add to our resume of morally noteworthy character traits. A revision to the conventional assumption entertains the possibility that it is within our capacity to develop morally. In terms of the example considered in the last chapter, this means that we should regard with some skepticism the argument given by many bystanders during the Holocaust that they simply lacked the material resources and the emotional wherewithal to involve themselves in alleviating the plight of Hitler's victims. If the simple and impoverished villagers of Le Chambon could render aid and provide shelter to Jewish refugees, then arguably anyone could do the same. Heroic conduct is not *necessarily* excessive for nonheroes, although it may correspond to a level of altruism currently beyond the reach of those aspiring to achieve it. Courage, which in the standard view represents the inborn trait for distinguishing heroes from ordinary persons, is in the revised account a virtue that heroes acquire along with the virtuous insight that informs their expanded sense of moral obligation.

However, showing that heroes are exemplary rather than "other" does not in itself defeat Urmson's larger point that there are certain agents—however we choose to designate them—who perceive the world so differently from everyone else, and who retain such a peculiar perception of themselves in relation to others, that we would be hard-pressed to deny the sense in which they are subject to rules of conduct designed to apply only to themselves. Some—for example, the person who regards in earnest a self-mandate to preach to the birds—acknowledge no limits to what might be required of them. Such people tend to be known for making a vocation of sacrificing themselves for the sake of others whom they encounter. Should we see *these* people as ordinary? Do we describe their self-sacrificial acts of altruism as morally obligatory or as optional? Should we distinguish between their self-imposed responsibilities, which tend to be maximally demanding and never-ending, and, for example, the duty of the Holocaust rescuer to save Jews from Hitler, which arguably can come to have the same obligatory status as universal, "rock-bottom" duty? One who presents a revised picture of the moral hero is naturally confronted with the question of how to characterize the actions of this second kind of self-sacrificing agent—those of the *saint*.

The goal of this chapter is to test Urmson's claim—that self-sacrificing altruists invariably go above and beyond the call of duty despite how they themselves may be inclined to characterize their actions—by examining its most plausible case, namely, the case of those agents least inclined to recognize the existence of limits to what is morally required of them. Urmson's critics are faced with a particularly difficult problem in trying to accept the testimony of saints at face value. If we posit that saints qualify as moral authorities, must we then trust that whatever they come to define as their duty *is*, indeed, their duty? On the one hand, we do not want to extol the moral fortitude of noteworthily virtuous agents while

simultaneously raising questions about their credibility as moral authorities, thereby making Urmson's mistake. According to many traditions,
saints are pioneers with respect to the virtuous traits they display. They
forge new ground in their embodiment of compassion and piety, "exper-
imenting," as Gandhi put it, by accepting and living according to maxims
now deemed extreme, but which could quite possibly turn out to be true
even if they are not yet disclosed as true. As prophets of this sort, saints
see ahead of us. We should therefore not make the assumption that they
are deluded, or even unreasonably modest, in characterizing the status of
their own actions. Like heroes, their level of virtue informs their sense of
duty. Lacking their virtue, we are not in a position to claim categorically,
as Urmson does, that they supererogate or even that their seemingly
extreme, other-regarding convictions are altogether irrelevant to ordinary
morality.

On the other hand, we do not want to allow self-sacrificing agents who
stray radically from the norm to make any outlandish claim about what
duty entails, for this could call into question the very model by which we
understand what constitutes moral requirement in the first place. We are
here reminded of Caroline Bynum's warning, prompted by her study of
holy medieval women piously driven to starving themselves, that "saints
are not even primarily 'models' for ordinary mortals; the saints are far too
dangerous for that."[1] We should be wary of trying too hard to live like
saints, many of whom are too zealous or bizarre to imitate; instead, we
want to absorb and be guided by saintly light without blinding ourselves.
This raises some practical questions for the student and scholar of religious ethics. How imitable are saints, and what ought we to make of
saintly testimony on those occasions in which saints exhort nonsaints to
"go and do likewise"?

This is in part a hermeneutical matter, for saints can be read rhetorically, as promulgating an ideal that in actuality has limited practical relevance, or literally, as providing a blueprint for new ways of living. In the
last chapter, I argued that heroic testimony ought to be taken literally, and,
as a result, that we should endeavor to pattern our lives after a heroic one.
But can we also regard saints in kind? The matter is not so clear-cut, for
saints, unlike heroes, are extraordinary and patently not ordinary. In their
ability to devote themselves so interminably to what is beyond the self,
saints exempt themselves from the rules that normally constrain our
interactions with others. For example, consider the way in which saints
deal with the category of supererogation. So thoroughly do saints substitute the interests of others for their own that they fail to acknowledge even
the possibility that they will have to bear costs. As a result, the supererogatory, a concept that depends on the prior acknowledgment of a sacrifice

made, vanishes completely for them. In this respect, saints differ from us, and they even differ from heroes, who do see the costs of sacrifice but whose courage enables them to bear those costs. Thus, it stands to reason that we should not be as rapidly moved to action by the example of saints as we are by that of heroes. Since saints have less in common with us than heroes do, saintly influence is not as morally urgent; in fact, it may even be morally dangerous. While we potentially share heroes' way of looking at things, saints live according to an alternative worldview that they have specially adopted. Consequently, saints are often given to extremes. They possess strange, sometimes contradictory traits, and they possess them in abundance. They do not conduct balanced lives, in the Aristotelian sense. They are passionate and at times over-passionate.

These reflections conform to Urmson's discussion of the difference between heroes and saints. In terms of characterizing them within a moral framework, "saints," according to Urmson, are essentially "heroes" at a further remove. The primary difference between the two is that while heroes are able to conquer their fear and their drive to self-preservation, saints are recognized by their ability to overcome self-interest altogether. Thus, saints are self-sacrificing agents, par excellence. Their ability to transcend the pull of their own ego constitutes their primary defining feature. But Urmson's point is not simply that saints embody the highest level of moral goodness. He contends that they are different sorts of human beings than the rest of us. Their ability to transcend self-interest is uncanny and can hardly be expected of ordinary persons. The reader of "Saints and Heroes" gets the impression that the saint is truly "other," someone about whom we may read and come to admire, but at the same time someone whose life is essentially irrelevant to our own in terms of moral guidance.

Urmson's point is well taken. Saints often do not acknowledge limits once they have committed themselves to a particular course of action, and they tend not to regard their behavior as ordinary in the way that heroes do. It is alleged that many saints from the world's religious traditions are eccentric, obsessive, or both. There is a vast literature on the eccentricities of saints and, in particular, on the manifestation of these eccentricities in saintly asceticism. For example, in the case of St. Francis, Hester Gelber has written on the conflict between the saintly virtue of nurturing others and the practice of ascetic self-denial, two values that inherently contradict one another, but both of which St. Francis nevertheless struggled to inculcate following his conversion.[2] St. Francis's quirky, often extreme personality made his ambition to reconcile these two values especially difficult. Gelber recounts a well-known episode in which St. Francis arranged to have himself dragged naked through the streets for eating a portion of meat and stew while ailing, prompting St. Bonaventure to observe:

> The onlookers were amazed at the extraordinary spectacle and . . . deeply moved, but they made no secret of the fact that they thought his humility was rather to be admired than imitated. His action certainly seems to have been intended, rather as an omen reminiscent of the prophet Isaiah than as an example.[3]

Although we may be fascinated by him, St. Francis should not be regarded as exemplary, in the sense that he is an appropriate person after whom to pattern good living. In her autobiography, St. Teresa of Ávila similarly dwells on the turmoil and emotional imbalance she had to live through during her most pious moments. Warning that encounters with the divine are not for the casual-minded, she recalls: "When I took the habit the Lord immediately showed me how He favours those who do violence to themselves in order to serve Him. No one saw what I endured, or thought that I acted out of anything but pure desire."[4] Saintly union with God apparently comes at the price of no less than one's physical well-being. Saint Teresa's conversion is characterized with equal ambivalence in a passage taken from *The Lives of Saints*, which quotes directly from her autobiography:

> It was at this time, she tells us, that her most singular experience took place, her mystical marriage to Christ, and the piercing of her heart. Of the latter she writes: "I saw an angel very near me, towards my left side, in bodily form, which is not usual with me; for though angels are often represented to me, it is only in my mental vision. This angel appeared rather small than large, and very beautiful. His face was so shining that he seemed to be one of those highest angels called seraphs, who look as if all on fire with divine love. He had in his hands a long golden dart; at the end of the point methought there was a little fire. And I felt it thrust several times through my heart in such a way that it passed through my very bowels. And when he drew it out, methought it pulled them out with it and left me wholly on fire with great love of God." The pain in her soul spread to her body, but it was accompanied by great delight too; she was like one transported, caring neither to see nor to speak, but only to be consumed with the mingled pain and happiness.[5]

Saint Teresa of Ávila does not depict saintly existence in a healthy light. Divine love is described as "piercing" as hot fire, and yet it is the fire, along with the pleasure of divine encounter, to which Saint Teresa is attracted. Even William James, in spite of his overall positive treatment of saints, criticizes the saintly virtues of asceticism and purity, which in his view are virtues that inherently induce those who possess them in any substantial degree to exhibit an unhealthy intemperance. Among those whose behavior he scrutinizes is St. Louis of Gonzaga, who banished even his own mother from his presence in order to uphold his commitment to himself not to be led astray by feminine influence.[6] As many hagiographers have observed, saints are susceptible to suffering dysfunctions related to sex, their body, and material goods. In addition, it is commonly reported that saints have a penchant for self-reproach, one consequence of which is their failure ever to reach any level of satisfaction in relation to others and to society.

It is true that there is no saintly mold and that not all saints are eccentric. St. Thomas Aquinas was a systematic thinker and, by all accounts well-adjusted, rooted firmly in the world, and reputed to be a man of such high moral character that those coming into his presence seemed to be affected as if by a "fresh, cool breeze."[7] Other examples might include St. Ignatius of Loyola, St. Bonaventure, and Sir Thomas More, each of whom was well-adjusted and morally virtuous. Yet there is something about saints, Aquinas and the others included, that we cannot reach. The examples enumerated above show that we might be skeptical about the claim that saints do, as a group, serve as models for ordinary moral life. We are led to ask whether saints might be of more use to us in some other higher aesthetic or religious regard. In what, if any, sense should we pattern our lives after those of saints? Such a query leads us to recall John Stratton Hawley's well-known distinction between two senses of "exemplar" in reference to saints:

According to the word's first meaning, the saintly example instantiates and thus clarifies general principles of morality and qualities of character that can be articulated as meaningful and understood as possible for all participants in a society or community of faith. When one speaks of one's saintly mother, one is probably pointing in the direction of such perfection in the living out of ordinary morality. In its second sense, by contrast, the saintly exemplar does not always accord so easily with the moral standards that articulate a culture's highest sense of itself. Often saints do not just heighten ordinary morality. They implicitly question it by seeming to embody a strange, higher standard that does not quite fit with the moral system that governs ordinary propriety and often cannot be articulated in normal discourse.[8]

The characterization of "heroes" offered in the last chapter is reminiscent of Hawley's first sense of "exemplar." Heroes possess the most fully developed human characteristics and thus live the best kind of human life. They regularly act on impulses that we but faintly sense; however, it is not hard for us to comprehend what motivates them. This sense of exemplar is captured well in the cognate for the term "saint" in the Jewish tradition, *tzaddik*, which pertains to the most spiritually and morally righteous member of the community.[9] In his elucidation of saints, Owen Flanagan notes of the *tzaddik*:

> He tries always, as best he can, to do what is right. The *tzaddik* is better than most. But he serves as an ideal to which all can realistically aspire. Normally, to be designated a *tzaddik*, one needs to live the whole or better part of one's life in an ethically exemplary manner.... [T]he *tzaddik* is not thought to represent some unattainable ideal. He or she exemplifies an excellence, a set of excellences, or a worthy personality type that lies within the possibility space of ordinary persons.[10]

Flanagan suggests that it is the role of saints to lead the way but that the rest of us have the resources to follow. The commonsense theorist might object that this construal of the relationship between saints and nonsaints leads to the futile expectation of moral demands too high for the ordinary person to meet. However, Flanagan replies that we ought to distinguish between moral perfection in its purest form and the human endeavor to conform to that picture. It may be, in other words, that idealized goals, when they turn out to be impossible, are what most effectively induce us to stretch to the limit what is within the realm of possibility. Flanagan clarifies this with a helpful metaphor: although the greyhound runs after a rabbit it can never catch, it would not be able to run so fast were it not for the rabbit.[11]

Hawley's first sense of exemplar has the advantage of accommodating the notion that saints are imitable in degrees. Moreover, it allows that when they turn out not to be imitable, *trying* to imitate them still has benefits. Thus, saintly morality should not to be dismissed as either foreign or excessive, but rather as existing on the very high end of the spectrum that encompasses our appropriate range of moral objectives. At the same time, this sense of "exemplar" neglects to take into account important differences between saints and heroes: in particular, the fact that our connection to saints is far less tangible than our connection to heroes. Unlike heroes, saints experience an awakening to a new reality, one that they believe acts through them and through which they are led not only to erase the distinction between neighbor and stranger, but also to seek the material and spiritual betterment of both.[12] They are converts to unconventional ways of living, their faith in which prompts them to dispense with their former assumptions about the nature of their responsibility to others, and to assume a new calling as a reliever of pain and sorrow among the world's suffering. This leads us to consider whether Hawley's second sense of exemplar (which is in fact the one he advocates)[13] is the more appropriate way of referring to saints. Unlike the first sense, it has the advantage of fully respecting the danger ordinary mortals might face in trying to live a saintly life. However, in claiming that saints embody a "higher standard that does not quite fit with the moral system that governs ordinary propriety," Hawley brings us back to Urmson's stark dichotomization of people into saints and nonsaints, problematic for all of the same reasons that the standard view is problematic. In the end, the second sense of exemplar is inadequate because it implies that saints not only transcend, but also defy, ordinary standards of morality.

What sense of "exemplar" we *do* ascribe to saints is important for determining how relevant saintly conduct and the lives of saints are for our own lives. A middle view, held by some theologians and philosophers of religion, including William James, maintains that saintly morality is above, not against, ordinary morality. It is exemplary in the sense that it motivates us from afar, as a future ideal that impinges on us in the present. It is the goal of this chapter to spell out this *via media* more thoroughly.

Identifying Saints

The term "saints" has been given its dominant meaning by the Roman Catholic tradition and historically refers to publicly venerated figures of the church believed to have martyred themselves for Christ.[14] According to this definition, persons become saints by a formal process of canonization[15] and through the establishment of cults.[16] In my discussion I depart from this definition and present a formula for "saints" that can be more widely accepted. What is important about saints, according to the modified understanding, is their complete and uncompromising devotion to promoting the welfare of others. So construed, the term "saints" refers primarily to charismatic, moral, and spiritual paragons. This emphasis is not without precedent in philosophical and even theological literature.[17] Urmson himself gave the term "saint" a new, "contemporary" meaning by interpreting it as a word of "moral evaluation."[18] Since his essay "Saints and Heroes" appeared in 1958, the term has been used in that way by various scholars to identify exceptionally altruistic persons. Likewise, I shall understand "saint" to refer to someone of boundless compassion and generosity, or, in Lawrence Cunningham's words, a conveyer of "transparent goodness, deep holiness, and a broad and encompassing charity."[19]

By the same token, we must be careful not to speak of saints as if they are rootless. Saints, like heroes, have histories. They are the products of the traditions within which they first come to be recognized, and their hagiographic narratives reveal the extent to which religion does furnish them with the resources to develop their moral convictions. Throughout her life, Mother Teresa was consistent in her insistence that good works consisted in no more than "accepting, with a smile, what Jesus sends us."[20] Still, according to this working understanding of saints, Mother Teresa *is* a saint because of her life's work helping the poor, not because of her religious motivation for doing so. This is not to say that morality, per se, is the *object* of the saint's passionate devotion. The understanding of saints as persons of boundless compassion, generosity, and goodness is perfectly consistent, for example, with Robert Merrihew Adams's claim that saints are "people in whom the holy or divine can be seen," and who offer themselves, in faith, "to God, not only loving Him but also letting His love possess them, so that it works through them and shines through them to other people."[21] It is also consistent with James's observation that the saint "is grasped by a religious vision."[22] In other words, religion or religious experience may be the distinguishing motivating factor lying behind saints' compassion and generosity, but it is saints' attitudes and conduct toward others that gains them recognition. Whereas the conceptions of the divine in which saints place their faith vary according to the particular tradition in question, saints themselves are known and approved universally by their fruits.[23] They are in every case, as James notes, "authors, *auctores*, increasers, of goodness."[24]

In defining saints according to their boundless compassion and generosity, and not necessarily their spiritual piety, one more qualification must be made—a qualification provoked by Susan Wolf's famous characterization of the "moral saint" as a person "whose every action is as morally good as possible."[25] According to the characterization I will defend, saints are not, in fact, "moral fanatics"[26] or passionless do-gooders, who, like perfect utilitarians, commit themselves in machine-like fashion to the equitable distribution of material resources among the world's needy and desperate.[27] They do not worry about the maximization of the good, nor, for that matter, invest in any impersonal calculations of this sort. Rather, they exist in the grip of the "Other," literally obsessed by the immediate, all-encompassing demands placed on them by those in need. According to this characterization, a thoroughgoing utilitarian could not be considered a saint because the self would be included in the utilitarian's calculus of what the overall good required. Thus, saints are not model practitioners of a preferred moral theory. To the contrary, saints act out of a "first-order" desire to alleviate others' suffering. This desire motivates saintly practices prior to reflection about whether such actions are "good" or "right." Saints exist always already at the disposal of their beneficiaries. The saintly penchant to act altruistically is in this sense "primordial." It is an impulse not thought of as a moral demand before it is acted upon, perfectly natural for the saint, and not at odds with the saint's "human nature," as some have argued.[28]

A Postmodern View of Saints

As is true of any contemporary scholarship discussing notions of sainthood, I have entered a conversation in the middle. The view of "saints" being advanced here is significantly influenced by Edith Wyschogrod's depiction and positive appraisal of "hagiographic narrative," expounded and developed in her book *Saints and Postmodernism*, itself informed by the ethical philosophy of the French Judaic thinker Emmanuel Levinas.[29] According to Wyschogrod, the altruistic deeds that constitute "saintly practice" are cast not as life-choices but as "narrative factuality."[30] In other words, saints are compelled to be benevolent right at the point of contact with other persons in a social context, prior to any cognitive disposition they may have to help them.[31] Saintly practice is based on an avowal of saints' availability. This avowal is the mechanism by which saints become empowered to divest themselves totally of their own interests and receive the Other in utter passivity. It is expressed in the phrase "Here I am," which Wyschogrod identifies as "the hagiographic indicative."[32] This phrase is taken from the writing of Levinas, who quite strikingly uses it not in reference to distinctive moral figures such as saints, but as a means to convey our *universal* human ethical obligation.[33] According to Levinas, the unconditional responsibility for the Other is applicable to everyone, not just to those remarkable few ("saints") capable of meeting its demands. He maintains that we are each subject to the same "saintly" imperative of emptying ourselves in order to respond to the Other. Those of us who successfully follow this command live up to our original, human purpose without exceeding it.

In this judgment Levinas stands at the opposite end of the spectrum from Urmson, who concludes at the end of "Saints and Heroes" that "there is something horrifying" in the thought of pressuring ordinary persons to perform acts of a heroic or saintly nature.[34] Any posited command to self-sacrifice that exceeds a minimal level is to Urmson undesirable and inefficacious. While he grants that "no doubt from the agent's point of view it is imperative that he should endeavor to live up to the highest ideals of behavior that he can think of," these ideals do not carry the same obligatory force as duty, even for saints who do not distinguish between duty and supererogation.[35] Levinas, by contrast, does not distinguish between moral ideals and our duty to the Other, because he maintains that drawing distinctions between "required" and "above and beyond" is tantamount to avoiding responsibility. Nothing short of the self's yielding to its infinite devotion to the Other is morally acceptable. Thus, whereas in Urmson's analysis "saintly" conduct should not be seen as exemplary, in a Levinasian framework there is no such thing as saintly conduct to stand as an example. Rather, we are all potentially "saints," and the only question before us is whether or not we will choose to acknowledge our saintly humanity by acting "responsibly."[36] In this sense, Urmson and Levinas represent good examples of Blum's minimalist and maximalist, respectively. In contrast to both Urmson and Levinas, Wyschogrod acknowledges the existence of saints as distinctive from the rest of us in a de facto sense while still insisting on the relevance of hagiographic narrative to good human living. Her compromise attempts to negotiate its way through a too-easy minimalism and an unrealistic maximalism.

Wyschogrod maintains that saintly conduct is worth heeding because it motivates us to act altruistically where moral theory cannot.[37] According to her, moral judgments and beliefs are bound up with "epistemological" discourse: while they convince us that we *ought* to be less self-interested, they frequently fail to induce moral acts.[38] Hagiographic narratives offer a constructive alternative to conventional incentives for overcoming self-interest, either rational or contractual,[39] in that they inspire the reader to make the movement toward being the truly good person. According to Wyschogrod, this movement is inspired by a passion that induces action prior to cognition.[40] She acknowledges that very few people will actually be able to make this movement. However, even when "the effort to relieve suffering that is *constitutive* of saintly existence ... does not entirely succeed, saintly power can still be *effective* and its results can go deeper: saintly effort, even when it misfires, can morally transfigure other lives."[41]

Hagiographic narrative has moral relevance deriving from its inspirational value. It makes a demand on the lives of its addressees, a demand which must be either accepted or rejected.[42] The saint's response to the Other evokes a reaction from the listener, who then has no choice but to feel the impact of the saintly devotion to alleviating pain and sorrow. The listener can either affirm the commitment to saintly existence by searching for a similar impulse within him- or herself, or he or she can choose to remain what Wyschogrod calls a "cynic," someone "falsely enlightened," who has deliberately become numbed to human suffering.[43] While there are definite risks to opening oneself up to saintly narrative, including the obvious risk of exploitation, choosing to avoid the story's imperative introduces an even graver risk, namely, the risk of "moral inertness that belongs to the nonhuman or to things."[44] Well aware of the trouble with regarding saints as imitable, Wyschogrod devotes considerable energy to articulating the risk of saintliness. She suggests that it is our choice whether or not to accept a radically asymmetric conception of altruism that "begins with the Other."[45] By the same token, her contention that we are "swept up" by the imperative force of hagiography implicates her as an endorser as much as a phenomenologist of the saint's "ethics of excess."[46]

While as a rhetorical strategy, the gauntlet that Wyschogrod throws down is attractive, it is perhaps too strong a claim to suggest that saintliness is a skill we should all try to cultivate. If saintliness is primarily a function of character development and the habituation of virtue within the moral agent, then we might question the veracity of claims to an already existing, unconditional, "human" ability to privilege the Other. Such a claim conflates the possible with the necessary and thereby understates the gradual nature of character transformation. On the other hand, Wyschogrod's observation that saints force us to look inward and decide what kind of stance toward others we will adopt is constructive. Through our exposure to saints, we learn to dispense with the platitude that we should only be required to give of ourselves up to a pre-specified point. We also come to realize existentially our true potential for aiding others.

A great deal remains to be said about saints and saintly identity. Saints fall under a different category from heroes, and this difference will emerge throughout this chapter. In the next section, the characterization of saints so far developed, and the proposal for ethics patterned on saintly narrative, are tested through reference to two important modern figures from the Christian tradition: Martin Luther King, Jr. and Dorothy Day. I choose King and Day because their distinctiveness as moral paragons, combined with their lifelong commitment to suffering for the sake of others, sheds light on the complex nature of the "exemplar" status of the saint.[47] Somewhat contradictorily, saints draw nonsaints into their field of influence through their desire to alleviate pain and sorrow while they distance themselves from nonsaints by displaying an uncommon and intense altruistic impulse. The cases of King and Day are particularly interesting because they expected their audiences to follow in their footsteps. Both believed that they led humanly fulfilling lives, and thus ones that were desirable for others to pursue.

At the same time, the excessiveness to which King and Day were prone made them incurably anxious, barring them from ever considering their work completed, and, in turn, rendering them ineligible for living comfortably in any social environment not dominated by the recurring human crises that so fiercely occupied their attention. Through the course of this chapter, we will see that King and Day were saints, and not merely heroes, because they did not lead ordinary lives. Their altruism is not to be understood as a *reaction* to a situation in which they found themselves. Helping others was for them a *vocation*, a vocation which came to occupy the whole of their lives. King and Day were not merely responsive to the problem of evil when they encountered it in their midst—as were, for example, Holocaust rescuers (who were villagers-turned-rescuers), or Camus's Rieux (who was doctor in one context and then in another, more dire one). They actively sought out human beings in need, and defined themselves by their efforts to eradicate human suffering and sorrow, everywhere it existed.

Because of who saints are and how they perceive reality, they are incapable of acknowledging limits to their responsibilities. But under the circumstances of a limitless morality the concepts of duty and supererogation lose their decisive meaning. Consequently, ordinary morality, which does depend on formulable norms, is stripped of its potential to become compatible with saintly morality. Does this mean that the saintly conduct loses its moral relevance? Not necessarily, for it may be that the true nature of our responsibility for others *is* such that it should not be restricted to what can be codified, and that only saints can show us this. If so, then "ordinary morality" is in fact insufficient by itself for ordinary persons, and we would, after all, need saints to supplement us with the guidance to live a fuller, moral existence. King and Day arguably saw themselves in this role. Non-ascetic in orientation, both held a keen awareness of the times in which they were living and the ways in which their world might benefit from their presence in it.

FOLLOWING IN THE FOOTSTEPS OF MARTIN LUTHER KING, JR. AND DOROTHY DAY: THE CASE OF TWO MODERN SAINTS

Martin Luther King, Jr. and "Redemptive Suffering"

At the Bishop Charles Mason Temple in Memphis, Tennessee, on April 3, 1968, the eve of his assassination, Martin Luther King, Jr. was preparing to deliver a powerful but haunting speech to over 17,000 African Americans about suffering, death, and the costs associated with being a voice of righteousness in an age of injustice. The speech was in many respects a summary of the cause to which King had dedicated his life. That night he explained what it meant to "walk the Jericho road": to be a ready, responsible human presence during an era of historical darkness.[48] By this time, King himself had been stabbed and shot at, and he had endured nineteen arrests over the course of a lifetime of protest. He was contending with many threats on his life, roughly fifty of which were under FBI investigation, in addition to others made against his family.[49] According to those who knew him best, he was both exhausted from engaging in a lifetime of nonviolent resistance and despondent over the increasing jeopardy in which he placed himself and those close to him.[50] On a recent visit to his parents in Atlanta, King warned them "that someone is going to try to kill me, and it could happen without any warning at all." Nonetheless, he felt he had no choice but to respect "God's will" and to carry on with his work.[51] His parents were concerned, and rightly so, for the stakes were getting much higher in their son's sustained involvement in these struggles for two key reasons. First, the percentage of African Americans who had turned to violence to procure social change was growing, a shift which many of the country's prominent political leaders associated critically with King's freedom marches.[52] Second, King's firm stance against the war in Vietnam angered many of his previous supporters, and King, already having infuriated Lyndon Johnson in February with his outspoken criticism of the war, was being called an "unpatriotic Communist," and in some cases accused of being a traitor.[53] While outwardly confident and optimistic, King, according to one of his staff members, was waging his own battle with despair, caused by the enormous strain of both his direct involvement in the tumultuous political climate of the late 1960s and the unfavorable perception many were coming to have of him as a result of his involvement.[54] It was under these circumstances that King set out to deliver his most portentous sermon to date.

After briefly acknowledging the momentousness of the present day and the difficulty of the days to follow, King emphasized that if he were nonetheless

> standing at the beginning of time, with the possibility of a general and panoramic view of the whole human history up to now, and the Almighty said to me, "Martin Luther King, which age would you like to live in?" I would take my mental flight by Egypt through, or rather across the Red Sea, through the wilderness on toward the promised land. And in spite of its magnificence, I wouldn't stop there.[55]

Nor, despite his admiration for the great minds assembled in ancient Greece, such as Plato, Aristotle, Socrates, Euripides, and Aristophanes, would he have chosen to remain in that age if given the opportunity. Indeed, he would have passed over "the great heyday of the Roman Empire," the rebirth of human spirit and culture witnessed in the Renaissance, Martin Luther as he "tacked his ninety-five theses on the door at the church in Wittenberg," not stopping even to "watch a vacillating president by the name of Abraham Lincoln finally come to the conclusion that he had to sign the Emancipation Proclamation." Rather, King said,

> I would turn to the Almighty and say, "If you allow me to live just a few years in the second half of the twentieth century, I will be happy." Now

that's a strange statement to make, because the world is all messed up. The nation is sick. Trouble is in the land. Confusion all around. That's a strange, strange statement. But I know, somehow, that only when it is dark enough, can you see the stars.[56]

King would not live in a time of glory but would actively choose a time of suffering, a time that signaled the struggle for glory, or, rather, for him the "glory" derived from the struggle. He concluded his speech by telling his audience that he had "been to the mountaintop," where God allowed him to look over and "see the promised land." King informed them that a new world order was at hand, even if he may not be there to walk into the land himself.[57]

It was King's *desire* to become involved in humanity's shameful moments rather than its proud ones. His time was shaped by oppressors and victims. Like Moses, who was never permitted to enter the promised land of Canaan, King led his people—which became synonymous with all people, everywhere—into an era less marred by injustice, violence, and racial disharmony than the one to which he himself was inescapably bound. King was distinctive as a political and moral leader not only because he saw his own destiny bound up with that of all others in the "world community," but also because his life of struggle was the only one he would have chosen for himself.

The Endlessness of Saintliness

One of the features of King that we cannot help but notice is that every one of his achievements, especially those made possible through sacrifice, occurred against a backdrop of human suffering. Human suffering serves as the condition for the emergence of saintliness because it is suffering that necessitates the saintly work of relief. The more penetrating such suffering is at the societal level, the greater the need there is for saints. Saints see their relief work as a job to be carried out every day, habitually. They are not discouraged with the seemingly insurmountable conditions that afflict those whom they are trying to help. On the contrary, saints accelerate their service to humanity just at the point when most others would succumb to despair. For them, "human suffering" pertains to the suffering of all people, everywhere. In his "Christmas Sermon on Peace," delivered on Christmas Eve, 1967, King reiterated a message he had been sounding for over five years: "[A]s nations and individuals, we are interdependent ... all caught up in an inescapable network of mutuality, tied into a single garment of human destiny."[58] In this speech, King implored Americans to feel connected to starving Indians on the streets of Bombay and Calcutta. All Americans, he said, had a duty not to stand by while "the wrinkled stomachs" increased in number in Asia, Africa, Latin America, and even in our own nation. He charged that "our loyalties must transcend our race, our tribe, our class, our nation," even to include the "little Brown children of Vietnam."[59] King would not rest until the plight of all these victims had been relieved. He would continue to stress the interdependence of all human beings. In practice, this would entail more marches for freedom, more public challenges to the legitimacy of unjust laws, and increasingly provocative protests against the war, none of which would be politically expedient or popular.[60] The negative consequences did not deter King, who told his staff: "[T]he cross is something that you bear and that you ultimately die on."[61] All of King's struggles—from his bid to take up the cause of Rosa Parks and segregation in Montgomery, to the freedom marches that led to his prison sentencings, to his efforts to register blacks to vote in Selma, Alabama, to his unpopular campaigns against the war in Vietnam—were undertaken at great cost. His life was marked by the perpetual recurrence of the struggles in which he involved himself. Because he defined his responsibility as a duty to alleviate suffering wherever it could be found, his work would *never* end.

King stressed repeatedly that he was not naive about the Sisyphean nature of his labor. If racial harmony were achieved in America, injustice and oppression in need of remedy could always be found elsewhere. Attending to these concerns would have to be considered just as urgent. There would always be more suffering in the world than could be eliminated through the efforts of one man. While heroes have a more demanding conception of their moral duty than nonheroes, it is still, in principle, attainable. The saint, by contrast, commits him- or herself to a sense of responsibility that is by definition impossible to discharge completely. King's was an infinitely demanding sense of moral responsibility, justified by his faith in God and his commitment to love agapistically.

The entirety of the ethics of King, in fact, rests on the notion of *agape*, which he describes as a "love in action" that manifests itself in one's "willingness to go to any length to restore a community."[62] Such a love cannot accommodate a concept of supererogation that goes beyond duty. It "doesn't stop at the first mile, but it goes the second mile to restore community. It is a willingness to forgive, not seven times, but seventy times seven. . . ."[63] King was able to make the ideal of *agape* a reality in his own code of conduct by postulating the interconnectedness of all people. He wrote:

In the final analysis, *agape* means a recognition of the fact that all life is interrelated. All humanity is involved in a single process, and all men are brothers. To the degree that I harm my brother, no matter what he is doing to me, to that extent I am harming myself. For example, white

men often refuse federal aid to education in order to avoid giving the
Negro his rights: but because all men are brothers they cannot deny Negro
children without harming their own. They end, all efforts to the contrary, by hurting themselves. Why is this? Because all men are brothers.[64]

For King, *agape*, love for the sake of the other, is understood in terms of
its opposition to *eros*, love for the sake of the self, and its distinction from
philia, love for the sake of the mutual relationship between other and self,
in that it is a love directed away from the self. *Agape* is not only love for
the sake of the other, but also a love that requires one's maximal devotion
to the other. However, King's interpretation of *agape* ought not to be
understood as a love which is "self-denying" in the strict sense that it
entails the *subordination* of self-interest; rather, the practitioners of *agape*
literally desire the other's betterment. For them, the interests of the other
become, in a real sense, those of the self. They regard their own and everyone else's welfare as being bound up together.

Such an interpretation is consistent with King's understanding of the
Good Samaritan parable. Rather than asking ourselves what will happen
to us if we put ourselves in harm's way, he argues, we ought to ask ourselves what great good we stand to lose if we are presented with an opportunity to help others and decide to do nothing.[65] King posits this thesis
as a metaphysical axiom in which self-actualization is inexorably tied to
other-regard. "I can never be what I ought to be," writes King, "until you
are what you ought to be. You can never be what you ought to be until I
am what I ought to be. This is the way the world is made. I didn't make
it that way, but this is the interrelated structure of reality."[66] Of course,
King could never have made such a statement without his prior belief in
agape as the fundamental governing principle for human ethics. In this
regard, King bears the imprint of his particular religious background.
However, notwithstanding the requisite context of a particular religious
tradition—Christianity—for this statement's *formulation*, King intended
the statement itself to be applied broadly, as a truism about the human
condition and our shared human predicament. We cannot love ourselves,
or live authentic lives, if we do not help others first. In this case, the nor-
mativity of saintly conduct is advanced in a negative fashion. We are made
aware of the grave price we will pay if we have occasion to help those in
need and yet fail to act.

This global imperative to offer aid is matched elsewhere in King's writings, where he insists that we may be required to bear tremendous costs
to our physical well-being as part of our commitment to reforming the
minds and hearts of others. King, for example, instructed African Americans living in Southern states to stand up before Klansmen and say:

We shall match your capacity to inflict suffering by our capacity to endure suffering. We will meet your physical force with our soul force. Do to us what you will and we will still love you. . . . Bomb our homes and threaten our children, and, as difficult as it is, we will still love you. Send your hooded perpetrators of violence into our communities at the midnight hour and drag us out on some wayside road and leave us half dead as you beat us, and we will still love you. But be assured that we'll wear you down by our capacity to suffer, and one day we will win our freedom. We will not only win freedom for ourselves; we will so appeal to your heart and conscience that we will win you in the process, and our victory will be a double victory.[67]

In this passage King rejects traditional self-defense arguments in favor of the norm of interdependence, in which the interests of the other are substituted for those of the self. Such advice is counterintuitive to those who do not share the saint's perspective, and may even seem potentially exploitative. The idea is to end suffering by enduring suffering, to release oneself from the grip of the enemy by reforming the enemy. Our judgment about whether or not such advice is successful in the real world depends on the number of people to whom it is ultimately persuasive.

King's strategy was, of course, not always tantamount to the prudential aspect of the victory he imagined, as for example, when Hosea Williams, an activist in King's inner circle, led 650 people from Selma to Montgomery on a peace mission, only to see his followers beaten, sprayed with gas, and trampled on by a fifty-foot blue line of Alabama's state troopers.[68] Yet King maintained that those who died in this and other confrontations had something to say to us in their deaths. On September 15, 1963, King delivered a well-known eulogy for two African-American girls who were killed by a bomb as they attended Sunday school at the Sixteenth Street Baptist Church in Birmingham, Alabama. Here he proclaimed that these children were "the martyred heroines of a holy crusade for freedom and human dignity," and he embraced such unmerited suffering as "redemptive."[69] It seems clear, at least in this eulogy, that King was not talking merely of his own commitment, or of the sacrifices exclusively made by those who govern their conduct according to their faith in Christ. His very idea of justice for a whole people—as a means for redress and reparation in the present day—is defined in light of the commandment to love the enemy. He exhorts, even admonishes, and does not merely articulate a faith or personal conviction, when later on in the eulogy he enjoins the congregants of the Sixteenth Street Baptist Church not to become bitter or harbor the desire to retaliate, but rather to rejoice in the ameliorative force of the deaths of the children that "would bring light to this dark city," indeed which would "cause the whole citizenry of Birmingham to transform the negative extremes of a dark past into the positive extremes of a bright future."[70] For King, the power of nonviolence was real, if counterintuitive: nonviolence on the part of the victim disarms the oppressor, while violence suffered by the victim is empowering. Whether or not we, in the end, accept this tactical advice, we must grant the full scope of its intended audience. Gandhi, from whom King acquired his method, admittedly called *satyagraha* "experimental," in spite of his own faith in its redemptive, transformative effect. Yet King knew, as did Gandhi, that the only way the experiment would have a chance of working was if it were employed by the masses. Hence Gandhi's endorsement of the Dandi salt march in 1930, which, for the obvious good it did when publicized, had the immediate effect of provoking the arrest of thousands of Indians, as well as the brutality of the British, who methodically clubbed the Indians as they attempted, row by row, to enter the salt works.

This consideration again leads us to reflect on the difference between heroes and saints. While heroes take risks in performing their heroic acts, such risks are side-consequences of the moral task at hand. By contrast, a saintly life *is* constitutively a life of risk. This does not mean that saints engage in heedless other-regard, for even saints instrumentally need to attend to their own welfare in order to continue their work of replenishing. However, saints, unlike heroes, make it a point to live in such a way that their welfare will always be in jeopardy. Their altruism is proactive, and not merely reactive. They regard it as their purpose in this world to suffer the oppressor's violence, wherever the oppressor may be found. They embrace the Nazis, if only to redeem them. Because they see the interdependence of all things, they bear the responsibility to alleviate victims' agony and to account for enemies' sins. Hence, King exhorted African Americans to win a "double victory": to save the Klansmen persecuting them as well as to save themselves.

King was *attracted* to human hardship. He did not react to suffering by simply rising to the occasion when he came across it. He sought it out.[71] This is why he claimed that he would choose to live during no other time in history than during the second half of the twentieth century, when, as he put it, the world was "all messed up." King was a saint because of the consistent way in which he chose to expose himself to suffering. This was no truer than during the final years of his life. Gradually, the country came to accept the legitimacy of the civil rights movement. This was recognized both by King's receipt of the Nobel Peace Prize in the summer of 1964 and by Lyndon Johnson's signing of the Voting Rights Bill the following year. However, rather than pausing to take some satisfaction in what he had accomplished, King spoke restlessly of the "work still left to be done" and turned his attention to the war in Vietnam. Had King lived to see the end of this war, there can be little doubt that he would have then focused his efforts still elsewhere, attending to new concerns with the same anxiousness that characterized his former projects. By 1967 his goal had moved beyond the former objective of "saving the soul of America" to include redeeming "the whole of mankind."[72] There could be no goal more worthy and yet less eligible for accomplishment. Accepting his honor in 1964, King asked his hosts why such an award had been given to a movement so "beleaguered" by compromise and one "which has not won the very peace and brotherhood which is the essence of the Nobel Prize."[73] These words are neither disrespectful nor surprising for one whose sense of moral responsibility embraced the infinite, and who expected others to attempt to adopt this same sense of responsibility. The question is whether this sense of responsibility can be characterized as something that is practically attainable. How would ordinary persons go about accepting this level of responsibility? What strategies might they adopt? Helpfully, we may turn to the life and thought of another modern saint for guidance.

Dorothy Day, Voluntary Poverty, and St. Thérèse's "Little Way"

Like Martin Luther King, Jr., Dorothy Day devoted her life, at significant cost to herself, to causes pursued on behalf of the suffering and disenfranchised; and like King, she embraced a non-watered-down version of the love commandment in which *agape* became the sole guiding principle for any endorsed course of action. While King addressed broad social issues facing a nation, Day's focus remained on improving the conditions of the common, impoverished soul. Writing for the *Catholic Worker* in December 1948, she proclaimed: "Love of brother means voluntary poverty, stripping oneself of one's possessions. . . . It also means nonparticipation in those comforts and luxuries which have been manufactured by the exploitation of others. . . . If our jobs do not contribute to the common good, we pray to God for the grace to give them up."[74] This sentiment does not exactly reflect the "American way," whose emphasis on success and private space precludes the all-encompassing, anti-opportunistic mission entailed in such a thoroughgoing socialism as that advocated by the Catholic Workers. Yet in this passage we see articulated not merely an endorsement that is individually binding for those who are up to the spiritual challenge—in this case, that living simply and among the poor is a good thing for the would-be model Catholic to do because Jesus himself did so. Day is also referring to our unconditional moral responsibility to help others in need. She suggests that it is incumbent upon us, as a society, to together become poor in order to empathize sufficiently with the needy, the primary requirement for solving the problem of poverty. What makes Day so compelling a figure is her lifelong insistence that she was potentially no different from anyone else. In this light, her frequent repudiation of "saintly" as a term of description for her own conduct could be seen as an intent to place not just herself, but all of us, on the hook, morally speaking.[75] Aware of the massive reforms and modification of habit entailed in such self-transformation, Day set out to provide her readers, listeners, and those otherwise exposed to the Catholic Worker movement with a practical strategy for making the transition possible.

Day's claim that she is no different from anyone else, like similar testimony presented by rescuers, needs to be recognized. We should not negate her self-understanding by assuming that the duties she perceives are not really duties. At the same time, Day is a saint, which makes her morally extraordinary. As such, she is able to act altruistically in ways that most of us are not now, and may never be, able to act. In reading Day, it is therefore necessary to interpret her in such a way that appreciates her contention about the possibility of emulating her, without, at the same time, making psychologically naive assumptions about the feasibility of ordinary people coming to live a saintly life, which is even less imitable than a heroic life is.

"We cannot even see our brothers in need without first stripping ourselves," Day exhorts. That these were not just words for her is evident in the costs she herself incurred when pointing the finger at those within her own religious setting, many of whom were inclined to dismiss her exhortations as instances of hopeful idealism, if not counterproductive muckraking. Even before she met Peter Maurin, with whom she would later found the Catholic Worker movement in 1933, Day's judgmental temperament extended to no less a recipient than the church itself. In the few short years following her conversion to Catholicism in 1927, Day became an outspoken critic of the church's unresponsiveness to poverty, unemployment, and the exploitation of the working class. She began to question her allegiance to a Catholic faith that she perceived to be increasingly lacking in leadership, particularly during a time—the Great Depression— when, Day believed, the church ought to have made its presence felt. Day uttered the following sentiment to the biographer Robert Coles in one version or another on at least fifteen separate occasions:

> I remember those days, before I met Peter Maurin: I was on the brink of losing my faith, having just become a Catholic. I was very upset by what I saw—the church's apparent indifference to so much suffering. In [the early years of the Depression] people walked the streets, hundreds and hundreds of them, looked dazed and bewildered. They had no work.

They had no places to go. Some groups tried to help them, but neither the state nor the church seemed as alarmed as my 'radical' friends.[76]

Elsewhere, her criticism of church leadership and its tendency to force Catholics into falsely choosing between being patriotic capitalists or disloyal communists became more explicit.[77] Writing in her autobiography, *The Long Loneliness*, Day singled out Pope Pius XI's pessimistic remark that "[t]he workers of the world are lost to the Church" as evidence that the Catholic leadership, threatened by the formation of leftist unions such as the "Unemployed Councils" and "the Workers Alliance," had abdicated its special responsibility to the destitute and the downtrodden, the victims of the Great Depression.[78] At times, Day's criticisms resembled a nostalgic longing for the "church militant" and a corresponding cry to hold in check a "church triumphant" that had run amuck:

I remember . . . walking past certain Catholic churches and cringing; I didn't know whether I should start crying or scream with all my might, and I'll say it, start picketing. The sight of all that wealth—the buildings and the residences where bishops or priests lived. . . . The cardinals here, so many of them, thought of themselves as God's favorites—as princes not of that humble, humble Jesus, but that big company of theirs. I had a Marxist friend who called the Catholic church a 'great, big, successful corporation, an international corporation,' and I never cringed when I heard him speak like that. I didn't like his bias, but I knew he was speaking the truth—a partial truth, but an important truth. . . . Oh, who was *I* to criticize those people? Who was *I* to try to tell them what they should do! But I couldn't stop myself. I got angrier and angrier at what I saw. I wanted the churches to open their doors, to let the poor and the hungry and the homeless come inside, to feed them, to give them shelter.[79]

Comments like these, typical of others of hers that appeared in the *Catholic Worker*, provoked the criticism of mainstream Catholics, to say nothing of the bishops, priests, and cardinals, some of whom Day identified by name.[80] Clearly, to follow Day meant to risk journeying into exile, one that led Day herself to a solitary place: "a practicing Catholic who had no Catholic activist friends."[81] Although she never encouraged others to denounce the church, Day is on record for advocating a "permanent revolution"[82] for every Christian intent on "completing the sufferings of Christ," as well as for every brother, sister, and "fellow worker."[83] Voluntarily stripping oneself of one's possessions, speaking out against perpetrators of inequity—these are not the things in which merely the "exalted" are supposed to participate. To give of oneself does not require talent so much as it requires hard work. Love, she asserts, is a "matter of the will": difficult, impractical even, but possible for those who try and continue to try even as they fail.[84]

For Day, the imperative to love entails a neighbor-love so strong that "[w]hatever we have beyond our own needs belongs to the poor."[85] This is a strong claim, which assumes that such a love can be willed, and then sustained, by the nonsaint. Every "victim of poverty," Day writes in *Loaves and Fishes*, requires a "champion of poverty," that is, a *love* of poverty or "what St. Francis calls 'Lady Poverty.'"[86] Interestingly, for all the times Day herself tried to play "Lady Poverty," the role never came easily:

> Sometimes, as in St. Francis' case, freedom from fastidiousness and detachment from worldly things can be attained in only one step. We would like to think this is often so. And yet the older I get the more I see that life is made of many steps, and they are very small ones, not giant strides. I have "kissed a leper" not once but twice—consciously—yet I cannot say I am much better for it.[87]

Clearly, Day did not see herself as a successful "revolutionary." Yet, in Day's view of other-regard, to love is not necessarily to see oneself as loving, nor is it to see immediately the results of one's loving deeds. It is, quite simply, to require oneself, in good faith, to give.

The problem with such an approach is primarily psychological. *Seeing* the results of one's efforts is often what is tantamount to productivity. People are naturally motivated by the prospect of witnessing the changes that they help to effect. Achievements measured in small steps sometimes give off the impression that one has not achieved all that one has intended. At the same time, Day's assertion about the volitional nature of love depends on her understanding of love as consisting in steady, little efforts instead of grandiose, life-altering sacrifices. Understood as but one step in a long string of steps, an act of love, no matter how small, becomes something that is possible for the novice as well as the expert, for the ordinary person alongside the saint. In terms of voluntary poverty, this means that we relinquish our possessions and share with others slowly, as we are able.

Day's belief in the accessibility of voluntary poverty betrays her indebtedness to a strategy that traces back to her favorite saint, the late-nineteenth-century mystic and Carmelite nun Thérèse of Lisieux. This strategy, which Thérèse called the "little way," refers to the ordinary routine shared by twenty sisters, similarly circumstanced, pursuing a scrupulous and deeply religious way of life. At first glance, the "little way" seems counterintuitive, for it is a method that prescribes that which is contained within a mundane, daily schedule as a means to affecting the individual goals of self-transformation and spiritual communion. In her book devoted to this nineteenth-century saint, Day informs us that her reaction to Thérèse was initially negative: "What kind of saint was this who felt that she had to practice heroic charity in eating what was put in front of her, in taking medicine, enduring cold and heat, restraint, [and] enduring the society of mediocre souls...."[88] As she became increasingly acquainted with Thérèse, however, Day came to gain an appreciation for the nonspectacular regularity with which Thérèse worked steadily toward her objectives:

[I]t was the "worker," the common man, who first spread her fame by word of mouth. It was the masses who first claimed her a saint. It was the "people." What was there about her to make such an appeal? Perhaps because she was so much like the rest of us in her ordinariness. In her lifetime there are no miracles recounted: she was just good, good as the bread which the Normans bake in huge loaves.[89]

Day became fascinated with the effectiveness of Thérèse's approach, which emphasized persistence and repetition, eventually adopting it as the method of choice for the Catholic Worker movement.[90] She commented frequently about how naturally Thérèse's method fit into the contemporary agenda beset by the Great Depression, where, Day felt, the key to amelioration was to become *familiar* with the unpleasantness of a life bereft of luxury. And indeed, she thought such familiarity was possible, as when she wrote: "One gets used to ugliness so quickly. What we avert our eyes from one day is easily borne the next when we have learned a little more about love. Nurses know this, as do mothers."[91] This is voluntary poverty constituted as commonplace practice. Through familiarization and repetition, the praiseworthy and exceptional status of a saint's deed, "little by little," becomes transformed into a broad social norm. The transformation does not always occur as smoothly as possible, and Day was well aware of the distractions that could serve to thwart the practitioner's best intentions:

[D]aily, hourly, to give up our own possessions and especially to subordinate our own impulses and wishes to others—these are hard, hard things; and I don't think they ever get any easier. You can strip yourself, you can be stripped, but you will still reach out like an octopus to seek your own comfort, your untroubled time, your ease, your refreshment.[92]

It is difficult to become poor and it is even more difficult to remain poor voluntarily when, time and time again, luxuries of which we have the option of availing ourselves catch our eye. At the same time, it is the slow, deliberate, and nonspectacular nature of "ordinary" giving that makes the "little way," as opposed to other possible methods, accessible to the non-saint and gives it the aura of familiarity that makes it effective.

Given the frequency with which Day rebuked terms like "saintly" as an adequate description of her own conduct, and given the great lengths she went to clarify precisely how such a demanding standard of other-regard could be possible for the nonsaint, we may conclude that Day intended for her words to be interpreted literally, not rhetorically. Indeed, as much as Day's writings as a whole serve as a testament to the intrinsically valuable role of voluntary poverty in the lives of saints, they can also collectively be read as a manual of mundane tactics for the aspiring, nonsaint to follow.

In September 1983, three years after her death, the Claretian Fathers of Chicago, a missionary organization devoted to lay spirituality, waged a nationwide campaign to push Dorothy Day's candidacy for canonization as a "saint for our times."[93] The response from those who knew Day best was far from ambivalent. Maggie Hennesy, one of Day's grandchildren, wrote: "Take all your monies and energies that are being put into her canonization and give it to the poor. That is how you would show your love and respect to her." A fellow Catholic Worker invoked Day's own words to support a similar reply:

> It has often been recounted to me that Dorothy Day herself, in commenting on someone's mention of her sanctity, said, "Don't dismiss me so easily!" I find it ironic, then, that persons should be engaged in working for the elevation to sainthood of a woman who insisted on being taken seriously as a peer. As long as Day is one of us, we are challenged to be as much as she, but if she is [a] saint, we can remain passive in our sinner-hood.

In still a third letter, Father Daniel Berrigan, S.J., pleaded to the Claretians that we have here "a saint whose soul ought not be stolen from her people—the wretched of the earth."[94] Remarks like these could arguably be taken to mean that since Day was "one of us," and therefore not sufficiently distinguishable for canonization, we should retain the traditional notion that saints are not imitable. However, given that those quoted go out of their way to hold Day in esteem precisely *for* muddying the line between sainthood and the laity, I think they are more plausibly interpreted as implying a criticism about the process of canonization itself.[95] According to Father Berrigan's framing of the issue, canonization was costly, bombastic, intrusive, "overly juridical," and finally unnecessary; for the way saints are truly acknowledged is by following their example.[96]

What is important about sainthood is not what technically or formally makes one a saint, but whether the saint is able to express the voice of "the people."[97] In saying this, Father Berrigan calls attention to a school of thought (even within the Catholic tradition) that is receptive to a conceptualization of sainthood in which sanctity depends more on the capacity to lead a revolution in thought and lifestyle than on the performance of miracles.

This is a rather nonconservative view of sainthood where saints become symbols for reviving a consciousness of truths of which we are already dimly aware, and which deepen for us the more our exposure to saints persists.[98] As Robert Inchausti suggests of the legendary founder of the order of Missionaries of Charity: "Mother Teresa's life is the stuff of such symbolism, connecting us to truths, spiritual sensibilities, and a sense of sacred obligation *that already exist inside us* but are not yet fully realized."[99] We are about back to Hawley's first sense of "exemplar," but not quite. Saints are in principle imitable, but they are also revolutionaries. The lifestyle changes with which they induce us to experiment are life-altering. Their actions are conducted in excess of any "normal" standard. Any proposal about saints that hopes to make sainthood relevant within the context of ordinary morality must not shy away from these observations. If we wish to take the profoundly nonascetic stances of Martin Luther King, Jr. and Dorothy Day as sources of credible moral guidance, we do not have the luxury of excising the more extreme elements of their message.

Martin Luther King, Jr. and Dorothy Day as "World" Saints?

The qualified conclusion to which I seem to be coming—that saints, in spite of the altruistic excesses to which they are prone, are, after all, moral exemplars worthy of being heeded (as revolutionaries whose time has not yet caught up with them)—raises the very important issue about just who a saintly audience legitimately is. By invoking classical and contemporary philosophers of religion like James and Flanagan, or even the twentieth-century Catholic leader Father Daniel Berrigan, each of whom imply, in varying degrees, that saints are not only imitable but also accessible within a secular society, I risk understating the role that particular faith traditions play in the process by which saints gain and retain an appeal to their followers.

Can King speak of the value of "redemptive suffering" to those for whom the concept of martyrdom, understood in the context of the struggle of the early church, has no purchase? Can we really read Day's insistence on "voluntary poverty" without making reference to the very long historical tradition, which, encouraged by the recommendations of Jesus

and reinforced by Pauline theology, held in the highest regard the virtues
of charity and poverty? This is all to ask: Should we consider the various
urgings of the saints examined here, and the matter of their relevance to
us, both exemplary and *performative* (i.e., as requiring also the living out
of a particular faith tradition)? And if emulating saints is in part a performative praxis, is it not a mistake to think of saintly exhortations as
applying to anyone who does not assume some doctrine of grace, or an
imperative to commit to the ideal of nonpossession as it was practiced
by the early monastics, or some other maxim that gains its authoritative
force from within the tradition in which it originates? Finally, can we ever
speak of saints generically, as moving beyond their specific church traditions to "the world community" (King's phrase)?[100] William James, who
cared most about individual religiosity, thought we could. The saints, he
stressed, are prophets in a universal sense, each offering contributions for
all of mankind out of the spiritual resources to which their traditions
made them distinctively privy. Was James right? Is it the nature of saints
to move beyond the communities that made them saints? Will they be successful in appealing to nonsaints who are not a part of that community?
In attempting to answer these questions, a distinction needs to be made
between the role particular church traditions play in initially enabling
saints to carry out their vocation and the role they play, and continue to play,
once saints gain exposure to a wider public. While the communal as such
is an indispensable element in the formation of the saintly mission, the question of whether saints can move beyond the particular faith communities
that make them depends, I think, on which saint we are talking about.

James, who was primarily interested in *personal* religious experience, is
susceptible to criticism for missing the link that exists between formal
spiritual practice and the refinement of our spiritual and moral intuitions.[101] His discussion of saints, for instance, ignores the communities
within which saints are reared and instead focuses on the spiritual connection that has the potential to occur between any individual saint and
the addressee that finds his or her message compelling. In fact, the values
by which saints define their mission and the sources from which they
derive the strength to carry it out bear the mark of the faith traditions
within which they are first formed. Like the Chambonnais, who depended
on one another, and whose town flourished as a haven for victims fleeing
death because of the religious values and historical memory reinforced
by the villagers who lived there, King and Day spoke as representatives of
living traditions. They were not lone prophets who walked the earth, but
leaders with a base. In her recollections about the early days of the
Catholic Worker movement, described in *Loaves and Fishes*, Day dwells on
the support she received from "this Peter [Maurin] of ours," who, with

the other editors, organized a "community of the poor" by constructing a rigid schedule for them to follow. Its daily activities included mass, work in the field, and lectures and theological discussions, many of which, on the topic of the works of mercy, revolved around the Pauline kenotic decree to become "a spectacle to the world."[102] Likewise, King's prophetic emphasis on a destiny of brotherhood, his "American dream," was but a stone's throw from the Book of Exodus, which describes the Lord's promise to deliver an enslaved people from exile. Clearly, Day and King spoke as Christians and appealed to biblical concepts to articulate their views.

Yet King just as often saw himself in the tradition of Gandhi, and Day would speak of the great affection she had for the Jewish writers who inspired her awareness of the constructive value in suffering as a people. Day wrote of one friend, the Jewish author Mike Gold, that he was able to "understand my misery" and taught "[me] that there had to be a price to pay, sometimes a heartbreaking price, in following one's vocation."[103] As much as they invoked the word of Jesus as the impetus for their commitment to the suffering and wretched of the earth, Day and King continuously contended that they were but representatives of a linked human race. King, near the end of his life, was explicit in this regard: "We have inherited a large house, a great 'world house' in which we have to live together—black and white, Easterner and Westerner, Gentile and Jew, Catholic and Protestant, Moslem and Hindu—a family unduly separated in ideas, culture and interest, who because we can never again live apart, must somehow learn to live with each other in peace."[104] The struggle for racial equality for King was always understood to be a microcosm of the larger mission of universal brotherhood and respect for difference. In his worldview, communities overlap and subsume one another. Those who suffer share the same characteristics regardless of where they come from. Likewise, our obligation to attend to the suffering is equally urgent for us, regardless of where we come from, although our means of acquiring the motivation to provide relief may vary from one culture to another. In this regard, we may characterize King and Day as "world" saints because their message is not confined to the environment in which it originates.

Does this, then, mean that the saints of the earth do surpass their faith communities and that the nonsaints whom they embrace as part of their widening audience do not have to be part of such communities or to have accepted the tenets of faith that define them? The answers to these questions ultimately depend on which saints we read and how we interpret them. We would be hard-pressed, for example, to attribute Mother Teresa's understanding of the duty to alleviate poverty in the world as resulting from anything other than the instruction of Jesus. On the subject of poverty, Mother Teresa consistently alludes to the four gospels as providing the motivational basis for any taken action. According to her, the duty of charity and compassion derives from a "desire to share Christ's own poverty," which is "our dowry." She further specifies:

> With regard to God, our poverty is our humble recognition and accept-
> ance of our sinfulness, helplessness, and utter nothingness, and the
> acknowledgement of our neediness before him, which expresses itself as
> hope in him, as openness to receive all things from him as from our
> Father. Our poverty should be true Gospel poverty....[105]

In this passage, Mother Teresa unambiguously expresses the triangular nature of love of the other, in which altruism is cast as the crowning byproduct of a prior faith commitment. There is nothing generic about this saintliness. The intended audience consists of fellow readers of the gospels. By contrast, King and Day, whose messages at times explicitly bear the mark of Christianity, often also insist on the translatability of their message into other languages. They speak compellingly, where Mother Teresa does not, of a *human condition*. When they do, they can be considered saints whose notion of other-regard compels even their non-Christian admirers to not rest content as spectators and to make more of an altruistic investment in humanity than they currently do.

Such a reading of King and Day, however, raises a new problem for the interpreter: namely, how such an ambition could ever become feasible for those altruists in training who lack the spiritual resources available to members of a specific faith tradition. How does saintliness become a possibility in society at large? In *Saints and Postmodernism*, Edith Wyschogrod sets out to determine whether a saintly "ethics of excess" could ever be adopted by nonsaints for whom excess is, on its face, unnatural. Wyschogrod argues that saints are saintly by virtue of their ability to respond to an essential, human demand originally placed on all of us. In this light, exposure to the hagiographic narratives of "saintly excess" becomes our own best chance of acting morally responsibly in a postmodern world characterized by mass catastrophe and endless needs, a world where the encounter with the helpless, destitute Other becomes the primary ethical moment. The extent to which this claim is ultimately convincing is the subject of the next section.

SAINTS AND THE "ETHICS OF EXCESS"

The "Other" as a Departure for Ethics

A postmodern view of morality is distinctive in that, in contrast with the views it is meant to supplant, it begins neither with the fully virtuous person nor with the ordinary person, but with the Other.[106] In noting this, Wyschogrod suggests that the other person becomes both the point of departure and the venue for ethical discourse. The Other, as the "touch-stone of moral existence, is not a conceptual anchorage but a living force."[107] In other words, the Other of postmodern ethics is not the imper-sonal other referred to in moral theory but the concrete stranger, the suffering person across the world who is not known personally, has unique needs, and confronts us in unpredictable ways. Given Wyscho-grod's claim that we are in fact living in a postmodern age, it follows that she *advocates* this postmodern view of morality.[108] Wyschogrod does not maintain that a postmodern ethics is appropriate only for saints. According to her proposal, the Other signifies the point of departure for contemporary human moral existence. Hagiography is of interest to Wyschogrod because it is in the narratives of saints that we discover that the Other is given primacy. In making this claim so early in *Saints and Postmodernism*, Wyschogrod reveals that she is interested in doing more than merely describing saintly narrative. Her objective is also to speak to the reader normatively: saints, in putting the Other first, see something that the rest of us ought to see: namely, that in a world beset by hardship and suffering, the Other is inevitably neglected unless made the primary focus. A postmodern ethic should not be treated as an exclusively "saintly" one, even though saints are the ones who are exemplary in their response to the Other's command.

According to Wyschogrod, then, the saintly desire to immerse oneself in the lives of the needy and oppressed in order to effect some transfor-mation in their material condition constitutes the most humane kind of moral response in light of the last century, which has witnessed "within ever more compressed time frames," death, disease, oppression, famine, and calamity.[109] Wyschogrod describes the "Other" by using referents like the "wretched of the earth," the embodiment of "sheer absence," and the outsider who has been "banished"; she adopts Dostoevsky's characteriza-tion of the saint as the "wholly good man" depicted against a backdrop of moral decay.[110] This kind of complementary dichotomy allows Wyscho-grod to focus on the inherently moral nature of the two categories. The Other is not just a person we discover in the world but one who prompts us to act in certain ways. Saints, upon encountering the Other, act in the *right* sorts of ways. Furthermore, saints appear in the world under circum-stances characterized by a surplus of need, beckoned by the Other's lack. Theories based on principles and rules work fine as resources during times in which a community is not beset by the overwhelming presence of destitute persons. But during times of special hardship, when we are least inclined to forgo the claims of self-interest, these theories increasingly fail to motivate moral action. Worse, they have built-in assumptions that release those in a position of relatively little need from having to over-extend themselves for others less fortunate. At such times—and the post-modern era is the height of those times—it becomes necessary to regard "saintly" intervention as a regulative moral practice rather than a desper-ate or extreme measure. Under such dire conditions, argues Wyschogrod, it is *only* by virtue of seeing one's responsibility toward the Other as in-finite that the needs of the Other will be attended to *at all.* Thus, "respon-sibility" becomes an all-or-nothing proposition in the postmodern era, and the saint, who willingly accepts the burden of responsibility, becomes the Other's only hope.

Wyschogrod contrasts the ethical appeal to the saint to two other kinds of more traditional ethical appeals, those that are reason-based and those that are emotion-based. She argues that both of these alternatives make determinations about the needs of the Other in terms of projections of self-interest. Her principal opponents who endorse reason-based ethical approaches are John Rawls and Alan Gewirth. Both Rawls and Gewirth understand the primary ethical task to lie in the equal distribution of lib-erty and material goods in society. In this, they presume a symmetry between the self and the Other, making their concern for the Other ulti-mately an expression of self-love rather than other-regard.[111] The prob-lem with this move, Wyschogrod alleges, is that it reasserts rather than overcomes the human predisposition toward self-interest. We may ini-tially assent to the rationality of acting from Rawls's "original position," or agree with Gewirth that to violate the "Principle of Generic Consis-tency" is to act in a way that contradicts one's own purposive agency. But in conceptually making these concessions, there is no guarantee that we will not forsake the underlying reason for them when the needs of the least well-off put too much of a strain on our self-interest. We will be tempted to abandon the theories of Rawls and Gewirth because they do not in the first instance proceed from genuinely moral premises, but shift from rational (Rawls) or prudential (Gewirth) premises to moral ones. Wyschogrod spells out this criticism more precisely in the case of Gewirth:

> Gewirth's view presupposes the symmetry of self and Other so that fea-tures of the self relevant to a given moral context are also features attrib-uted to an analogous Other. . . . The freedom and well-being granted to another are ceded to a reposited self, numerically distinct from, but otherwise identical to, oneself. Unless the distinction between self and Other is radically drawn, the difference between prudential and moral judgments is blurred. Because in law multiple persons and interests must

be concerned, the parity of self and Other is a necessary fiction. When moral rather than juridical relations are considered, the term Other loses its force unless there is an incommensurability, an asymmetry, between self and Other.[112]

Wyschogrod makes two important points in this passage. The first has to do with the separateness of persons, specifically that self and alter are distinct; the second is that the Other must take *priority* over the self, lest the Other be seen as an extension of the self. If altruism is dependent on the conditions of agency alone, then it is bound to be restricted in scope and motivationally insufficient. The problem with conventional altruism is that it is structured to fail to put the Other first precisely under those circumstances in which the Other's needs are greatest.

Wyschogrod justifies the first claim, that self and other are conceptually distinct, on the grounds that a symmetric view of agency assumes that we can predict the Other's needs before any encounter. In an ethics based on reciprocity, we remain equipped to express our concern for the Other only in the same way and to the same degree that we have become accustomed to expressing concern for ourselves. An altruism that begins with the Other takes the self wherever the Other's needs dictate. This is why Levinas, from whom Wyschogrod appropriates her conception of the Other, speaks of alterity as *radically* Other, as a phenomenon that surprises—in fact shocks—the self out of its former complacency.[113] According to Wyschogrod, Otherness must be understood as something that is brand new, a phenomenon *sui generis*. The "Other" has unique needs that govern his or her unique demands, neither of which can be anticipated before encountering him or her.[114]

Second, Wyschogrod argues that a morality that begins with the self, in which the needs of the Other are derivative rather than constitutive, does not have the motivational force to endure the strong claims of self-interest under especially strenuous conditions. The risk is that during such times the "bodily" pull of self-interest will outweigh the appeal of an altruism based on rational criteria. Interestingly, Wyschogrod emphasizes the category of the bodily, calling it the "unit of significance" in saintly life.[115] As opposed to the agent acting from reason, whose allegiance to reason remains intact only insofar as it is not overridden by his or her immediate bodily needs, the saint, in responding to the Other, undergoes a "self-emptying."[116] Due to the saint's overpowering desire to replenish the Other, he or she is not susceptible to succumbing to needs emanating from his or her physical pain or material lack, as opposed to the agent acting strictly from reason. It is in this sense that the saint self-empties: the saint exists at the Other's disposal, eager to invest everything in the Other, including his or her own corporeal well-being. Wyschogrod argues that only an ethics that proceeds from the premise of alterity can ensure that this desire remains a genuine, "first-order" desire. Such a desire, Wyschogrod further suggests, translates into "saintly labor," which "gives altruism its moral character."[117] Labor takes the form of "dedication to the Other" and is what "authorizes the everyday work needed for altruistic accomplishment," the alleviation of pain and suffering.[118] It is the "psychological, social, and corporeal investment of the self's total resources," in which the saint does "all he can do" with "the time that is left."[119] The sort of urgency with which Wyschogrod associates the labor-intensive accomplishments of the saint is simply not present in an altruism motivated by reason-based criteria. The inherent desire in the altruist's psychological and bodily investment in the Other is needed to generate such urgency.

In addition to her criticism of reason-based justifications for other-regard, Wyschogrod also disputes the efficacy of conventional attempts to ground the altruistic impulse in moral sentiments. She critiques the work of Nicholas Rescher, who, in the tradition of Hume, attributes one's ability to harness the disposition to selflessness to benevolent feelings such as pity and compassion. In Rescher's view, sympathy lies at the root of the love that we have for the Other.[120] It is what makes the desire to be happy for the Other for the Other's sake real. The problem is that such an affectation is really self-interest at one further remove. Wyschogrod explains:

> Rescher correlates the vicarious affects with the degree of the relationship to those toward whom these affects are directed. The "closeness or distance of social and psychic linkage that exists between [persons]," including persons in future generations, will determine the sort of affect that is to be directed toward them. One will, for example, delight in one's child's joy but be only mildly pleased upon hearing of a stranger's happiness. Rescher points to the destruction of impartiality as the price that is paid for such affective discrimination.[121]

Just as an altruism based on rational or prudential grounds gives way to self-interest when the perceived burden becomes too high, an altruism that relies on the condition of special relations is from the start limited in scope and is therefore expectedly finite when taking into account the needs of the stranger. Wyschogrod commends Rescher's convictions about the authenticity of a morality that takes into account the passions, as well as his corresponding critique of a morality based on prudence, wherein the truly prudent person would simply engage in a cost-benefit analysis and act morally only when it is convenient.[122] She grants, furthermore, that Rescher's acknowledgment that sympathy can be extended across groups distinguished by race, class, and ethnic background makes his overall approach broadly applicable, certainly beyond its prima facie person-discriminating limitations. Yet the result of Rescher's strong reliance on the commonsense intuition of "preference based on kinship" is a conception of an Other about whom much is already known, and therefore one less likely to be the victim of abandonment or even disadvantage. Thus, Wyschogrod concludes that Rescher's defense of commonsense altruism insufficiently acknowledges the centrality of the Other's destitution as that feature which commands the desire to give aid. Rescher's archetypal "Other" is mistakenly construed as one who already stands in the right kinds of "morally appropriate sorts of relationships,"[123] or relationships most likely to produce feelings of sympathy on the basis of kin preference or special relations.

By contrast, Wyschogrod depicts the Other as one who is least familiar to the self, whom Levinas calls the "orphan" or "widow," the color of whose eyes is not yet known.[124] Saints complement the Other, consisting of those for whom the Other's destitution becomes a "vortex, a centripetal force, as it were, into which saintly desire on the Other's behalf is drawn."[125] For saints, sympathy toward the Other is inversely proportional to how familiar the Other is. "The more fissured the life of the Other, the greater the other's lack, the weightier its claim upon the saintly self."[126] Characterizing the Other in this way then creates an all-or-nothing rejoinder that represents Wyschogrod's repudiation of altruism based on moral theory. The rejoinder assumes a negative character. If we fail to regard those in need in terms of their naked, fissured, and socially disembedded selves, and instead rely on reconstructions of them from reason or sentiment, then we will inevitably fail to meet their needs precisely at those moments when their lack becomes most acute.

In the long run, according to Wyschogrod, the impetus to act altruistically can be sustained under conditions of widespread suffering and hardship only insofar as it is based on saintly desire. To be altruistic when it counts the most is, in effect, to act infinitely for the sake of the Other. This is for Wyschogrod both a motivational and a phenomenological point. Saintly desire is the only altruistic impulse effective enough to alleviate the suffering of the Other. Additionally, however, altruism is *intrinsically* infinite. Limiting it would contaminate its quality.

The Ethics of Excess and the Thought of Emmanuel Levinas

Thus, in addition to presenting the saintly construal of the Other as an alternative to conventional ways of theorizing the impulse to behave altruistically, Wyschogrod proposes the saint's "ethics of excess" as a normative recommendation for society in general. This constructive enterprise, which is the crux of *Saints and Postmodernism*, is not surprisingly the feature of the text that represents the hardest sell to the reader. This is because the subscriber to the "ethics of excess" is morally required to respond to the imperative force of the Other's cry for help before attending to his or her own welfare. If this Other is truly "Other"—naked, destitute, and vulnerable—then this is a cry that shall never cease, and the subscriber shall remain eternally bound. Altruism, usually an ordering that prioritizes the needs of alter, becomes for the "excessivist" a neverending project the very moment it is thought of. As Wyschogrod emphasizes: "*The saint is an extreme sumptuary, a subject that spends more than she/he has to the point of spending her/his own substance.*"[127] What Wyschogrod *likes* about "saintly" altruism, as opposed to other more conventional varieties, is that it reflects phenomenologically how human beings are constituted from the beginning of their corporeal and psychological existence. Against commonsense thinking, she wagers that the constraining of other-regard by self-love typical of moral theory represents a betrayal of human nature, not a manifestation of it. Duty is a concept best construed in terms of our *responsibility* to the Other. As such, it is best seen as not having limits.

In the ethics of alterity, just as the imperative force of the self's encounter with the Other commands an altruistic response, so does it create an insatiable desire in the self to *keep* responding to the Other in this manner. How is such altruism generated? Whence do infinite responsibility and indebtedness arise? It is at this juncture in her argument that Wyschogrod draws on the thinking of Emmanuel Levinas. In particular, she relies on his no doubt religious appeal to the transcendent "trace" of God, which is revealed in the face of the Other, and which gives the Other primacy over the self. Levinas's view is the antithesis of Hobbes's picture of the "state of nature," according to which morality becomes merely a socially constructed byproduct of our mutual desire to avoid the otherwise inevitable outcome of the "war of all against all." According to Levinas, the moral project is about *realizing* rather than *overcoming* who we are. As selves constituted by the Other, we are, in our essence, *good*. Given this assumption, our moral task is coming to know ourselves as good. This we do by accepting our inherited responsibility. Levinasian morality can be characterized as a rising to the occasion, one that marks the recognition of our humanity. Levinas posits that from the very beginning of human existence we are afflicted with "sensibility," an exposure to alterity.[128] We are *afflicted* because the transcendent trace, through the medium of the Other, "persecutes" and "accuses" us, even before we seek our own shelter. Immobilized in complete "passivity," we are laid bare to the Other's approach without having any possibility of escaping. In defiance of the Heideggerian starting point of a *Dasein* which exists for itself unto its own death, Levinas describes the approach of the Other as "proximity," the incarnate "exposure to wounding and to enjoyment, and exposure to wounding in enjoyment, which enables the wound to reach the subjectivity of the subject complacent in itself and positing itself for itself."[129] It is the Other, and not our being-unto-death, which is "primordial," older "than every past present."[130] And it is in this initial condition that we find ourselves existing *for* others, in the most literal sense possible.[131]

This picture of human nature, even the defender of Levinas would have to grant, assumes a specific view about the nature of human existence. While Levinas is perfectly within his rights as a religious, Judaic thinker to claim we have an a priori human responsibility to respond to the Other in whom we recognize a trace of the transcendent (i.e., God),[132] the strength of his claim as a *moral* command, intended to be unconditionally binding and to have universal applicability, depends more on the broadness of its appeal than on the conviction with which it is articulated. At the same time, there is no reason to regard the idea that the self exists, in its essential state, as a "one for the Other," as any less credible than the Hobbesian idea at the other extreme, which takes as its starting-point the primacy of self-interest. How are we to judge whether or not Levinas makes a plausible claim when he states that we are, at base, altruistic beings, ineluctably tied to the suffering Other?[133] In spite of her philosophical debt to Levinas, Wyschogrod's answer to this fundamental query is ambivalent. On the one hand, she embraces the Levinasian contention that the Other impinges upon the self as excess, declaring that the face of the Other commands by concentrating itself in "the totality of human suffering."[134] On the other hand, by calling those moral exemplars who live by the Levinasian creed "saints," which has the effect of distinguishing *these* persons from the rest of us, Wyschogrod reveals that she has doubts about presupposing the universality of the capacity for altruism. At one point, Wyschogrod raises this issue explicitly. If the "face of the Other is posited as a universal condition of social existence," she writes, "the rarity of altruism requires explanation."[135] The explanation she offers for the most part supports Levinas's position. All human beings, she affirms, are constituted by the Other, but there are only some persons, namely, saints, who in fact recognize their humanity:

[A] rudimentary sensitivity to others exists, but not everyone yields to the pressure of this primordial encounter. Uncontrolled desire and violence may be expressed by laying claim to the Other, by seeking to secure oneself against throwness and ultimate nonbeing in all its forms, social, psychological and symbolic. Saints, to the contrary, like gifted composers or musicians are exceptional individuals, virtuosi of the moral life. Almost everyone can reproduce a simple melodic line upon hearing it, but not all are able to perform a Bach cello suite, improvise a jazz harmony, or sing lieder.[136]

Wyschogrod likens saintliness to a talent latent in everyone, not an inborn gift, which some "naturally" possess, but a practice that is constituted retrospectively. Not everyone has the capacity to "yield" to this talent because of the tendency for human beings to escape their human potential by slipping into complacency. Interpreted in this way, saints are to be understood as those human beings who are most experienced or most skilled at being human. One is "responsible" to the extent that one realizes one's human potential.

At the same time, Wyschogrod further stipulates that no one can be completely responsible. The "saintly" capacity for self-emptying, precisely because it is a talent that can always be harnessed further, is never fully realized.[137] Those who *do* live up to this saintly ideal do so only in spurts and for the most part cannot sustain their saintly efforts over an extended period. This judgment is consistent with Wyschogrod's view that the needs of others are insatiable, their sheer overwhelming presence precluding saints from eliminating sorrow and suffering from the world.[138] This does not mean that saintly efforts are ultimately made in vain; for, Wyschogrod concludes, saints become inspired, not discouraged, the more they find themselves needed by the Other. While saints' acts are not a powerful enough force to *solve* the problem of evil, a saintly "excessive" orientation to evil and suffering represents the most effective kind of altruism there is. In this way Wyschogrod answers the objection leveled against Levinas on the grounds of the apparent disparity between our universal infinite obligation to the Other and the de facto observation that in reality there are very few altruists. Saints, as the "virtuosi" of moral life, awaken the rest of us to the true nature of the human condition and to our corresponding responsibility to the Other. By construing the "ethics of excess" as one that only saints adhere to in actuality, Wyschogrod does not deny the universality of the responsibility to the Other. However, she does raise questions about the ability for everybody to act responsibly. Indeed, by understanding saintly sensitivity to others as a "practice" that is constituted retrospectively, rather than as the a priori given of Levinas, she is able to insist that the "primordial encounter" with the Other is something that is universal, while simultaneously acknowledging that there are various degrees to which we yield to it. In other words, by construing altruism as a skill, or "practice," Wyschogrod shows some understanding of the empirical reality that our capacities to become other-regarding vary.

There is another aspect of Wyschogrod's treatment of Levinas that rescues the ethics of alterity from the charge that it is irrelevant to ordinary moral agents. This pertains to the rhetorical value of Levinas's radical approach to conceiving of other-regard. Wyschogrod asserts in several places that saintly extremism compels attention.[139] For example, in the wake of a tragedy, say an earthquake, seeing firsthand the saint divest him- or herself of his or her concerns in order to attend entirely to the victims' welfare puts *me* in a position where I must ask myself what I am prepared do. My capacity for altruism thereby becomes tested in a way that exceeds my expectations. Before actually encountering the Other, and witnessing saints who respond to the Other, I cannot fully know what level of altruism I am prepared to display. This is the central benefit that Wyschogrod sees in choosing narrative over theory. Whereas theory conceptually specifies for an agent what has to be done in order to be morally right, narrative makes a unique appeal to each individual addressee. As Wyschogrod notes, "narrative does not issue in a didactic conclusion in the form of either moral laws or prudential maxims," but rather offers "rules of thumb to the lived life itself."[140] We learn how to act toward the Other by actually encountering him or her, as well as by witnessing the conduct of those more perceptively attuned to the needs of the Other than we ourselves are. Saints implore us existentially to consider our fundamental relation to those in need. In so doing, they awaken us more fully to our humanity. Saints are therefore charismatic. They furnish us with a fertile source of inspiration to become more compassionate. Their stories clarify for us, in a way that is existentially compelling, what our moral requirements to the Other truly are.

Saints and Postmodernism under Critical Scrutiny

A judicious assessment of Wyschogrod's overall platform reveals that her view of the saintly "ethics of excess" is not meant to be advocated *only* for its rhetorical or inspirational benefits. Her general call in ethics is to supplant rather than supplement moral theory with hagiography. *Saints and Postmodernism* is speckled throughout with reminders that theory is simply inadequate to the altogether human task of helping the destitute and the oppressed, either as an accurate guide for elucidating what duty entails or as a motivational resource for fulfilling it. Wyschogrod revises the Levinasian contention that the imperative to respond to the appeal of the Other's face is a given, which would have the logical consequence of committing all moral agents to living up to their true, "saintly" nature, even if they do not realize they are saints. On the other hand, she follows Levinas insofar as he makes strong *substantive* claims about the level of other-regard that we ought to adopt in the postmodern age. In other words, the saintly devotion to the Other may be excessive, but nothing short of an excessive orientation can do justice to the Other's concerns. Given the overwhelmingly abject state of the Other who is suffering, only by adopting such an excessive, "wild"[141] attitude can we begin to address the enormity of the lack before us. To fail to be excessive is inevitably to undershoot the minimum of what we are required to do for the Other. In an age marked by the "death event," there is no minimally acceptable standard of other-regard that does not begin with alterity.[142] Thus, in Wyschogrod's view, failing to help the Other is tantamount to *harming* the Other. Either we respond to the command of the face by opening ourselves to the way of the saints, or we risk acting irresponsibly.

Wyschogrod thinks this either/or scenario is a plausible representation of our moral options. We are required to begin ethics with the Other if we wish to avoid neglecting the Other's concerns. Wyschogrod's argument pivots on the assumption that in the present, postmodern era, crises occur at an unprecedented rate, making the surplus of the Other's needs an interminable constant. Furthermore, Wyschogrod gives the impression that the moral life itself is more about responding to these crises than it is about interacting with special relations or establishing institutions of justice, activities wherein the ideals of mutuality and reciprocity figure importantly. Both presuppositions are susceptible to criticism, especially from feminists who will immediately object to the subordination of special relations as the focus of ethical concern.[143] But even if we overlook these objections, assuming, as Wyschogrod does, that radical altruism is the cornerstone of moral experience, we can still challenge her claim that it is the *only* kind of valid moral experience. Wyschogrod calls for a morality that transcends not only self-interest but also the individual self as the focal point of moral and political questions.[144] Implicit in Wyschogrod's morality, then, is the rejection of the category of supererogation, a category that in essence recognizes a domain of morality that releases us from the requirement to stay with the Other. This is where the critic might have the most reservations concerning Wyschogrod's approach. A morality that advocates a move beyond not only self-interest, but also selfhood, does not have the resources to make an appeal to the full variety of moral agents. Specifically, it does not sufficiently recognize that we are not all able to approximate, let alone live up to, an asymptotic saintly standard over the same duration of time. To Wyschogrod's credit, she acknowledges that saintliness is an ideal that even saints themselves often cannot fulfill—hence the rationale for the phrase "ethics of excess." However, in the same breath she contends that we *ought* to aspire to be excessive. It is in this normative jump that Wyschogrod's idealism betrays an insensitivity to the difficulties faced by agents at lower stages of moral development. Wyschogrod goes some distance toward alleviating this concern by distinguishing her approach from Levinas's, constituting radical altruism as a "talent" rather than as an a priori feature of the human condition, and further granting that no one, including saints themselves, can ever fully perfect this talent due to the all-encompassing nature of the Other's lack. Still, she essentializes the relationship between the self and the Other and thereby loses sight of the variations among different "selves." The dissolution of the category of supererogation from the ethics of excess brings this problem to the fore, for the concept of a class of actions done above and beyond is one that would otherwise measure the varying distances that exist between ordinary persons and saints. Such an omission begs a reconsideration of Urmson's warning that morality should not become a fatuous ideal that fails to take into account "man as he is and can be expected to become."[145] What we need is a way of adopting Wyschogrod's central insight, that altruism must give primacy to the Other, without endorsing an unrealistic view of morality.

In the next section, I develop the foregoing criticism of the "ethics of excess" by proposing a relationship between saints and ordinary moral agents that attempts to reach this compromise. Without either endorsing Urmson's pessimistic attitude toward the other-regarding capacities of nonsaints or claiming, with Wyschogrod and Levinas, that an infinite response to the Other is the only appropriate way of affirming an inherited responsibility, the view proposed below maintains that the lives of saints are continuous—though unlikely capable of overlapping—with our own lives. As John Hick once famously noted, saints are not "a different sort of being, traveling a different road, but are simply persons who are farther ahead of us on the same road."[146] We cannot walk as far as they, but we do have a limited capacity to follow them. Saints, like heroes, are exemplars in that they are noteworthily virtuous agents who have a remarkably expanded sense of duty; but unlike heroes, they also transcend their "exemplar" status and come to embody a higher law at precisely the point when their enhanced ability to see the Other commits them to the all-encompassing altruistic response that is commanded by the Other's face. While heroes, such as rescuers, rightly make us question our own sense of moral requirement *now* when they perform their acts of altruism, saints are more likely to speak for themselves when they refuse to admit of *any* sense of self-interest which could be said to compromise their other-regarding aims. The sense in which saints *do* impact the way we bind ourselves to the plight of the Other, in the present, is the question to which I now turn.

Saints and Supererogation

Saints as "Different Sorts of Beings"

In his essay "Saints and Supererogation," A. I. Melden disputes the widespread belief, introduced by Urmson, that saints typically perform works of supererogation.[147] Melden notes that Urmson's characterization stems from an underlying pragmatic consideration that it would be foolish and idealistic for any ethical code to require those who did not share saints' personal convictions to act like saints do, since it is on the basis of these convictions alone that saints leave the world of ordinary morality—and universal duty—behind. However, Melden insists that such reasoning is flawed, for it misses

> what is of central importance to an understanding of what it is that distinguishes the saint from the rest of us, namely, that what he takes to be his distinctive moral status is not simply a matter of what he, unlike others, is morally bound to do, a matter concerning which differences of opinion might arise, but one that pertains to what he takes to be his unique relation to others, a relation that colours the whole character of his life—his thoughts and feelings about himself and others—in ways that are radically different from those of ordinary human beings.... To see the saint in this way is to see a being who is a radically different sort of man.[148]

Melden suggests that saints, as *different sorts of beings*, naturally work from a different set of assumptions than do the rest of us—assumptions which inform the nature of their responsibility toward others. Echoing a similar sentiment, John Coleman writes: "[S]ainthood is primarily not about ethics," and is rarely "generated in a search for virtue, heroic deeds, or ethical goodness." Rather, it is "more frequently an aspect of a thrust toward union with God, and virtue ... flashes forth from that union."[149] Coleman suggests that saints possess an "other-worldly" orientation. They serve as intercessors in this life and stand in a hierarchical relation to the rest of us, presenting us with a utopian, unattainable ideal that is nonetheless appropriate for them.[150] According to both Melden and Coleman, it is misleading to talk about saints going beyond duty, since in transcending the limitations that normally help define humanity, saints go beyond the morality *of* duty altogether. To put it otherwise, saints have duties that only the saints themselves know.

This consideration leads to what might be called a "separability thesis" that governs the relationship between saintly and ordinary ethics, according to which the two codes of conduct, notwithstanding their appropriateness for saints and ordinary persons, respectively, are presumed, in the end, to be incompatible and even dangerous if conflated. If the separability thesis is true, then we may not both take saints at their word when they exhort nonsaints to act as they do (regardless of their tendency to refer to their own conduct as nonsaintly) and simultaneously regard their message as normative for the societies that they inhabit. Thus, according to the separability thesis, saints are either naive about the nature of ethics in the real world or, knowing that they are "radically different sorts of persons," intend their message in a way that does not conform to its literal implication. This takes us back to the issue of trusting testimony and the disjunction that we should like to avoid—that we might praise saints for having the moral fortitude to act as they do without recognizing them as credible moral authorities. What we want is an alternative way of interpreting saintly testimony that preserves the criterion of literalness but does not, at the same time, dismiss such testimony as irrelevant to ordinary morality.

A Jamesian Proposal

In contrast to the thesis that saints and ordinary persons are radically separable, William James contends that saints awaken us to our undeveloped altruistic capacities. He characterizes saints as "impregnators of the world, vivifiers and animators of potentialities of goodness which but for them would lie forever dormant."[151] Saints vitally pave the way for our own good-doing, by, for example, making a habit out of giving charity when there is no precedent, or by employing the method of non-resistance as a means to ending violence. James observes that "if things are ever to move upward, someone must be ready to take the first step, and assume the risk of it."[152] James's point is that sometimes saintly methods do succeed when implemented in a broader program of social action. Indeed, it has been the hope of many a political saint—Martin Luther King, Jr. and Dorothy Day, for example—that they not merely be revered but followed, however tentatively, by others daring enough to trade in worldly prudence for something more. The hope expressed is that what perhaps begins as an experiment becomes with time and familiarity a new standard. Such an ambition would, on Melden or Coleman's account, be considered an exercise in futility. According to Wyschogrod, by contrast, the scenario just discussed represents not just a live option, but also the only apt one in terms of its effectiveness. Wyschogrod insists that the addressee of hagiography is *forced* to decide whether he or she will attempt to bring saintly practices into his or her own life. The prevalence of the suffering Other in the contemporary world, which is marked by the "death event," makes this decision even more pressing. James's way of understanding the relationship between saints and ordinary persons, unlike Melden or Coleman's on the one hand, or Wyschogrod's on the other, neither sets arbitrary limits on the potential for humans to become human saints, nor overestimates the degree to which that potential can be actualized by the majority of us. According to James, the value of saints lies in their influence as much as it does in their actions. The proximity of their lives to ours will likely influence us in different ways. But whenever we encounter them, we will be inspired to reexamine ourselves and our responsibilities to others.

The implication of James's approach for how we are to understand saints in relation to the concept of supererogation is less clear. Is Urmson correct in his claim that because saints are unconditionally willing to sacrifice themselves for the sake of others they cannot be said to be doing merely their duty, regardless of how they themselves describe their actions? How should we interpret the testimony of saints when it opposes our commonsense intuitions? James himself raises these questions:

> "Resist not evil," "Love your enemies," these are saintly maxims of which men of this world find it hard to speak without impatience. Are the men of this world right, or are the saints in possession of the deeper range of truth? No simple answer is possible. Here, if anywhere, one feels the complexity of the moral life, and the mysteriousness of the way in which facts and ideals are interwoven.[153]

James notes that although there is no objective perspective from which to deny the testimony of saints who speak of their duty to "resist not evil," or their duty to exercise charity and show sympathy for all sentient beings, neither is there one from which to confirm such testimony, especially given that we live in an environment where saints are so scarce. The difficulty in trusting saintly testimony is compounded by the consideration that saints, worse than conflating duty with supererogation, may in their excessive zeal even require themselves to follow a course of action that is the wrong one. As James warns:

> The best intention will fail if it either works by false means or addresses itself to the wrong recipient. Thus no critic or estimator of the value of conduct can confine himself to the actor's animus alone, apart from the other elements of the performance. As there is no worse lie than a truth misunderstood by those who hear it, so reasonable arguments, challenges to magnanimity, and appeals to sympathy or justice, are folly when we are dealing with human crocodiles and boa-constrictors. The saint may simply give the universe into the hands of the enemy by his trustfulness. He may by non-resistance cut off his own survival.[154]

The pragmatic kernel of this judgment is apparent enough. Even if saints speak the truth and we are deceived about the maxim to "turn the other cheek," such a truth may become transformed into a falsehood when it happens to fall on deaf ears. Yet, James further specifies, no one can judge whether saints' perception of what is morally required remains correct over time. The reason for this is that on innumerable occasions saints have shown themselves to be prophetic in believing wholeheartedly in the universal applicability of their convictions. Indeed:

> Treating those whom they met, in spite of the past, in spite of all appearances, as worthy, they have stimulated them to *be* worthy, miraculously transformed them by their radiant example and by the challenge of their expectation.... The potentialities of development in human souls are unfathomable. So many who seemed irretrievably hardened have in point of fact been softened, converted, regenerated, in ways that amazed the subjects even more than they surprised the spectators, that we never can be sure in advance of any man that his salvation by the way of love is hopeless. We have no right to speak of boa-constrictors as fixedly incurable beings. We know not the complexities of personality, the smouldering of emotional fires, the other facets of the character polyhedron, the resources of the subliminal region.... The saints, with their extravagance of human tenderness, are the great torch-bearers of this belief, the tip of the wedge, the clearers of the darkness.[155]

Saints may be dupes in the present, but, as the "world is not yet with them,"[156] we lack the perspective to decide whether or not they are right in the long run.

In judiciously presenting arguments for both sides, James makes a compelling case for "bracketing" the question of truth. Although talk of "saintly duties" may seem preposterous to us, not knowing the future, we have no way of telling. In the final analysis, the matter is inscrutable. Not only does James suggest that we do not know how effective saintly acts themselves will ultimately prove to be, but he also implies, more strongly, that the standard of other-regard appropriate for the saints now may be one that is possible for us in the future. We cannot simply dismiss a saintly way of life as foreign or irrelevant to our own. By contrast, Urmson, Melden, Coleman, and even Wyschogrod *do* assume that the "truth" question (i.e., the question of whether saints have special insight into the nature of our true moral obligation to others) can be answered decisively. Melden, Coleman, and Wyschogrod assert, with varying degrees of conviction, that it is the saints who are enlightened in matters of self-other relations and we who are deluded (or, in the case of Wyschogrod, less "yielding"), while Urmson and the "commonsense" moral theorists insist that at some point other-regard that is "excessive" cannot at the same time plausibly be considered required. According to Melden, Coleman, and Wyschogrod, saints do what is plainly their duty; according to Urmson and subscribers to the standard view, saints supererogate. There are, to be sure, divisions within each camp. Melden and Coleman posit a double standard for saints and ordinary persons, while Wyschogrod sees the lives of saints as embracing the kind of life we would want to live. Similarly, Urmson can be distinguished from other thinkers (e.g., John Rawls) who, like him, deny the obligatory status of saintly actions, but do not set the standard of duty at a *minimal* level, beyond which *all* altruistic actions are labeled "supererogatory" by default. All of these thinkers, however, presume to know what life looks like from the saints' point of view, at least well enough to make judgments about how that perspective fares in comparison with our own. The approach of James is more humble, for it leaves to the future the at-present murky task of verifying saints' claims, thereby affording some flexibility to the developing moral agent who is exposed to saints and saintly narrative. James neither overconfidently likens the agent's destiny to that of the saints, nor forecloses on this outcome as a future possibility in exceptional cases.

Reaching a verdict on what I have called the "truth" question is in any case not what is most important when we consider the intersection of our lives with those of saints. For even if the saintly ideal does not seem true on its face, we must not fail to heed it, if only as a reminder that ordinary ethics alone sets an insufficient standard—a standard for which we should not ultimately settle. In this respect, saints' contributions to the real-world matters of political stability and social justice outweigh the dangers that they present to society by exposing themselves and others who follow them to the risk of exploitation. By treating the saintly ideal *as if* we were required to aspire to it—even granting the possibility, and even likelihood, that it is unrealizable—we expand the realm of what *is* altruistically realizable. As James remarks:

> It is not possible to be quite as mean as we naturally are, when they [i.e., saints] have passed over us. One fire kindles another; and without that over-trust in human worth which they show, the rest of us would lie in spiritual stagnancy. Momentarily considered, then, the saint may waste his tenderness and be the dupe and victim of his charitable fever, but the general function of his charity in social evolution is vital and essential.... In this respect the Utopian dreams of social justice in which many contemporary socialists and anarchists indulge are, in spite of their impracticability and non-adaptation to present environmental

conditions, analogous to the saint's belief in the existent kingdom of heaven. They help to break the edge of the general reign of hardness, and are slow leavens of a better order.[157]

One may draw a parallel between the passage from James that I just quoted and the following remark made by Taylor Branch, the esteemed biographer of King. Responding to a question posed by David Gergen, in which the interviewer asked Branch to describe what the early sixties meant to America, Branch stated:

> I think those years meant an America that enlarged freedom, when it didn't really think that it could, and discovered all kinds of optimism that had been kind of tamped down after World War II. . . . We were a much more provincial, narrow, and spiteful in many respects and divided country then than we are now. And it took a lot of courage and with the race issue and segregation having lived for a century after the Civil War, for people to believe that something good could happen. . . . And this is a story about ordinary people from all ranks . . . from presidents down to cripples, who took risks and risked their lives to enlarge freedom. [We] have inherited a much better country for it.[158]

Branch's remarks suggest that King's ethics are not only consistent with, but also importantly relevant to, ordinary morality. While it is the saint who takes the initial risk in prompting progress, the saint's unprecedented approach to real-world issues, such as social justice, sifts down into the masses and takes on a larger meaning.

There is nothing in this pragmatic observation with which Urmson would necessarily disagree. The standard view allows that extraordinarily virtuous people are of great moral value and can effect sweeping changes in the lives of those whom they encounter. Still, Urmson's assumption about the irrelevance of saintly ethics for establishing our "duty" has the effect of undermining the thrust of James's overall argument. This is because Urmson fears that the consequence of making saintly conduct substantively influential on the setting of moral requirement is that morality itself will come to demand too much. If this happened, causing us to fail to meet its requirements, we would inevitably lose respect for all of morality, including those "minimal" duties with which compliance by all is indispensable. Thus Urmson opines that believing saints' claims to be "doing only their duty" will have a detrimental effect on morality. James comes to the opposite conclusion. By acting *as if* saints speak the truth, both we and the morality to which we subscribe will be better off. A saintly ethic, while perhaps impossible to abide by in the present, is

relevant to ordinary morality by making it closer to the ideal. It is important to bear in mind that James, whose view is more moderate than that
of either Levinas or Wyschogrod, still carves out some conceptual space
for the category of supererogation. At no point does he deny that many
saintly acts are, from our point of view, above and beyond the call of duty.
He even uses the phrase "over-trust"—meaning an over-trust in human
response to goodness—to acknowledge the possibility that saints themselves may exaggerate both the nature of their moral responsibility and
their confidence in the potential for human beings to become better than
they are. Still, we have no reason to treat saints as poor guides to good
living. To the contrary, the more we find ourselves in their presence, the
less their actions will appear to *us* as either supererogatory or beyond our
reach. Indeed, saintly "excess" is most likely to appear excessive to those
who are already predisposed to regard the exhorting saint skeptically.
Conversely, to risk, to trust—to experiment, as Gandhi would have us
do—is to advance the frontiers of where we stand, in the present moment,
in terms of our moral and spiritual development, and thereby to lessen
the gap between there and where we might otherwise, ideally, like to be.

Characterizing Saints

In the first two chapters, I tentatively suggested that "duty" and "supererogation" may be variables rather than constants. According to this hypothesis, the more virtuous a person is, the more robust a sense of duty
that person has, and the smaller the range of supererogatory acts he or
she can perform. In the last chapter, citing the example of rescuers, I used
Lawrence Blum's term "noteworthily virtuous agents" to characterize
heroes, contending that as a result of their virtuous character, they had an
expanded, and continually expanding, sense of duty. Thus, I implied that
what was morally obligatory for the villagers of Le Chambon could be
considered supererogatory for others. I made this judgment, however,
with one central qualification: heroes, in addition to being extraordinary,
are *ordinary* persons. In excelling at being human rather than attempting
to transcend humanity altogether, they both affirm that they are mortal
and acknowledge their limitations. This qualification allowed me to rebut
Urmson's sweeping contention that a heroic morality is idealistic and
incapable of accommodating us as we actually are, as opposed to how we
would be in a perfect world. A central goal of the last chapter, then, was
to suggest that rescuers are moral exemplars, not only to be admired, but
also to be emulated by everyone in varying degrees. This finding is consistent with rescuers' self-understandings, in particular the claim that they
only did what "anyone in their shoes," who saw things as clearly as they
did, would have done. In making statements to this effect, rescuers offer

themselves as proof that it is indeed possible to overcome fear, even under the most trying of circumstances, in order to care for the helpless and thereby rise to a more elevated form of human self-fulfillment.

In this chapter, I have argued that saints, in contrast to heroes, are not ordinary, nor are they imitable in quite the same way that heroes are. Theirs is an excessive morality that begins from an already expanded sense of duty and extends to their total submission to the face of the Other. Saints are disposed to go beyond any robust sense of moral requirement, indeed to the very limit of what they can manage. While we can emulate heroes to a limited degree, it is unlikely that we would be able to make a saintly ethics of excess a requirement to which we *should* adhere. Although this does not mean that saints are wrong in describing their actions as morally obligatory, it does mean that Urmson is right to want to characterize the works of saints as supererogatory, insofar as that comment is made from the perspective of ordinary persons. At the same time, saints importantly remind us of what we are not yet, which is necessary to shake us out of a complacency to which we, as mortals, are naturally susceptible. This negative effect becomes a positive one over time as self-examination propels us to hope for a better age and strive toward higher standards individually. Saints are scarce in the world in a way that even heroes are not. This scarcity is reflected in their attitude toward other-regard. Whereas heroes perform considerable altruistic actions in *response* to a situation that morally requires their attention and action, saints *proactively* seek out others who might be in need anywhere.

Just how decisive this criterion of proactive altruism is for understanding the difference between heroes and saints becomes clear in the following proposed definition of "saints," which I now introduce in order to distinguish saints from heroes, and to move our understanding of saints beyond the Urmsonian conception. As was the case in my earlier definition of heroes, the criteria below are offered stipulatively; they do not constitute the necessary and sufficient conditions of sainthood. As such, they are not meant to cover exhaustively all of the possible characteristics that saints possess. I propose that saints are distinctive moral agents in that:

(1) They are, in addition to being *extraordinarily virtuous* (like heroes), *maximally* disposed to feel, desire, and act altruistically, to the extent that they substitute the welfare of others for their own.

(2) They have *no limits with regard to what is morally required of them.* As a result of their ability to see the interdependence of all things, saints, unlike heroes, do not think in terms of the categories of duty (including the concept of an expanding duty) or supererogation.

They acknowledge only their *responsibility* to others, which inten-
sifies the more they see that they are needed.

(3) They perform *considerable altruistic actions*, not as a *reactive* measure, but as a *vocation*. Saints devote their lives to seeking out their
beneficiaries. Since there will always be a surplus of others in need,
the duties of saints never end.

(4) They perform these actions without being deterred by concerns of
how costly they are. Because saints do not distinguish between the
needs of the Other and the needs of the self, it is misleading to say
that they overcome all inclination to self-interest, as Urmson claims.
Through engaging in their altruistic acts, saints achieve *self-fulfillment.*

(5) They are, unlike heroes, not both extraordinary and ordinary, but only
extraordinary. Saints embody an *ideal of character* that is not fully realizable by ordinary agents in the course of a lifetime. Nevertheless,
this ideal is worth heeding, for as William James suggests, it is one
that from afar can positively influence our own character development.

(6) They are visionaries, or to use Dorothy Day's term, "revolutionaries." As Percy Shelley once said of poets, saints are "the hierophants
of an unapprehended inspiration; the mirrors of the gigantic shad-
ows which futurity casts on the present."[159] Men and women before
their time, they introduce, enlighten, and compel us to expect more
from each other and from life than we have yet imagined.

These criteria conform to the two cases considered in this chapter. Flawed
though they were, Martin Luther King, Jr. and Dorothy Day threw aside
concerns for their own welfare in order to devote the whole of their lives
to the altruistic causes they deemed pressing, characterizing such devotion as a responsibility they had no choice but to fulfill. Moreover, these
aims were life-commitments, endless in nature, and proactively, not just
reactively, sought by these two figures. What made King and Day so
extraordinary was the consistency with which they waged their various
campaigns, day in and day out, without getting lost in the distractions
that occupy the rest of us. Finally, King and Day envisioned a new world
order, one they hoped to bring about through their example: a vision partially realized by King (a world of racial equality), and one still in its
infant stages, for which Day fought (a world bereft of poverty). As saintly
revolutionaries, both King and Day stood committed to making the world
a better place for those that would inherit it.

From the definition of saints offered above, it appears that Urmson is on firmer ground when he contends that saintly morality is beyond what we can, and therefore ought to, expect from ordinary persons, than he is when he makes the same claim in the case of heroes. The Urmsonian thesis is nevertheless only partially redeemed through reference to the example of saints. For while the ethics of excess is for us never fully realizable, it remains an ideal that both informs ordinary morality and narrows the distance between saints and the rest of us every time we aspire to it. Just as the category of the supererogatory vanishes for the saint, it begins to diminish for us as, through our exposure to saints, we take seriously the importance of those acts of charity and benevolence that are currently beyond our abilities. And even though we may not, and indeed may never, share the saint's way of looking at the world, the saint's virtue that stems from his or her special perspective *is* transferable. Just how virtue informs our conception of our moral duty is the topic of the next chapter.

NOTES

1. Caroline Walker Bynum, *Holy Feast and Holy Fast: The Religious Significance of Food to Medieval Women* (Berkeley: University of California Press, 1987), 7.

2. Hester G. Gelber, "The Exemplary World of St. Francis of Assisi," in *Saints and Virtues*, ed. John Stratton Hawley (Berkeley: University of California Press, 1987), 15–35.

3. St. Bonaventure, quoted in ibid., 17.

4. Saint Teresa of Ávila, *The Life of Saint Teresa of Ávila by Herself*, trans. J. M. Cohen (New York: Penguin Books, 1957), 33.

5. *Lives of Saints*, ed. Father Joseph Vann, O.F.M. (New York: John J. Crawley & Co., 1954), 363.

6. William James, *The Varieties of Religious Experience* (New York: Penguin Books, 1982), 250ff.

7. Pieper, Josef, *The Silence of St. Thomas: Three Essays*, trans. John Murray and Daniel O'Connor (New York: Pantheon Books, 1957), 19.

8. Hawley, "Introduction," in *Saints and Virtues*, xvi.

9. Joseph Dan, *Jewish Mysticism and Jewish Ethics* (Seattle: University of Washington Press, 1986), 115.

10. Owen Flanagan, *Varieties of Moral Personality: Ethics and Psychological Realism* (Cambridge: Harvard University Press, 1991), 4.

11. Ibid., 29.

12. These are not necessarily tradition-specific traits of saints but rather a more fully spelled out explication of Urmson's broad claim that saints overcome all "inclination, desire and self-interest." I make no metaphysical claims here about the "reality" that I postulate awakens saints, nor about the precise means by which they initially undergo self-transformation as a result of their exposure to this reality. I merely contend that saints' various worldviews (and their corresponding

222   MORALLY EXTRAORDINARY PERSONS

conceptions of "the Real") uniformly lead to what might be called a "saintly" ethos, according to which saints come to see themselves as subjects constituted by the other, totally devoted to the other's material and spiritual betterment.

13. In his own research on some of the devotional (*bhatki*) saints of north India, Hawley characterizes saintly conduct as representing a "morality beyond morality," which should not be expected to serve as an example for action in "this world." The *bhakti*, explains Hawley, establish their ethical community by reuniting disparate elements of traditional Hindu caste structure in the common praise of God, wherein a life of love and devotion comes to supersede the *dharma*, which is rendered moot in a world quelled of fear. The danger is that the adherent of *bhakti* values will leave the world rather than transform it, while nonetheless threatening through its influence to undo the adhesiveness of the *dharmic* glue necessary for society to function. See Hawley, "Introduction," *Saints and Virtues*, xvi; and Hawley, "Morality beyond Morality in the Lives of Three Hindu Saints," in *Saints and Virtues*, 66–72.

14. David Hugh Farmer, *The Oxford Dictionary of Saints*, 2d ed. (Oxford: Oxford University Press, 1987), 5.

15. In the Roman Catholic Church, "canonization" is the act of declaring a dead person a saint, an act that is typically preceded by beatification (the act of declaring the person to be among the blessed in Heaven) and by an examination into the life and miracles of the person. See Lawrence Cunningham, *The Meaning of Saints* (San Francisco: Harper and Row, 1980), 7, 48–59. See also Kenneth Woodward's comprehensive account of the historical and contemporary process of canonization in Woodward, *Making Saints: How the Catholic Church Determines Who Becomes a Saint, Who Doesn't, and Why* (New York: Simon and Schuster, 1990).

16. The "cult" of the saints refers to those early Christians who, having practiced the Christian virtues to an exceptional degree in spite of existing political or religious opposition, and having died into fullness of life with God, have been officially proposed by the church as models of Christian living and as intercessors for the faithful on earth. See Cunningham, *The Meaning of Saints*, 7–8. See also Peter Brown's classic, *The Cult of Saints: Its Rise and Function in Latin Christianity* (Chicago: University of Chicago Press, 1981).

17. Flanagan, for example, writes that although "saintliness is, in its original sense, a concept requiring some sort of spiritual identification, there has evolved a notion of a saint whose saintliness is not necessarily tied to any belief he or she has in divinity. The sorts of saints I have in mind are moral saints ... [who] exemplify some extraordinary moral trait or set of traits. But they are not candidates for official canonization since they do not perform miracles. Furthermore, they may be more than indifferent to matters of religious faith. They may reject belief in divinity. A moral saint could be a true believer. The point simply is that it is not necessary" (Flanagan, *Varieties of Moral Personality*, 1). Edith Wyschogrod, whose proposal will be under scrutiny in this chapter, also assumes a broader understanding of "saints" that at the same time de-emphasizes saints' religious backgrounds. She does not, for example, make theistic belief a necessary condition of sainthood, defining the saint as "one whose adult life in its entirety is

devoted to the alleviation of sorrow (the psychological suffering) and pain (the physical suffering) that afflicts other persons without distinction of rank or group or, alternatively, that afflicts sentient beings, whatever the cost to the saint in pain or sorrow." See Edith Wyschogrod, *Saints and Postmodernism: Revisioning Moral Philosophy* (Chicago: University of Chicago Press, 1990), 34.

18. J. O. Urmson, "Saints and Heroes," in *Essays in Moral Philosophy*, ed. A. I. Melden (Seattle: University of Washington Press, 1958), 199.

19. Cunningham, *The Meaning of Saints*, 7.

20. Mother Teresa, *In My Own Words* (New York: Gramercy Books, 1997), 1.

21. Robert Merrihew Adams, "Saints," *Journal of Philosophy* 81 (1984): 398.

22. James, *The Varieties of Religious Experience*, 212.

23. Ibid., 327.

24. Ibid., 357. James is a proponent of the view that saints can be depicted "universally," across all traditions and cultures. He writes: "The collective name for the ripe fruits of religion in a character is Saintliness. The saintly character is the character for which spiritual emotions are the habitual centre of the personal energy; and there is a certain composite photograph of universal saintliness, the same in all religions, of which features can easily be traced" (ibid., 271). James proceeds to mention four of these identifying features. They are: (1) the saint's awareness of being in a "wider" life than that of this world's mundane and selfish interests, which corresponds to his conviction in the existence of an "Ideal Power," or transcendent force of some sort; (2) a sense of "friendly continuity" with this Ideal Power as well as a desire to surrender to its control; (3) an overwhelming sense of joy and freedom that results from this surrender; and (4) a grand emotional shift in the center of the saint's being toward "loving and harmonious affections, towards 'yes, yes,' and away from 'no,' where the claims of the non-ego are concerned." These four conditions, James further specifies, lead to four practical consequences for saintly conduct, which are also universal in nature. They are "asceticism," "strength of soul" (i.e., the disappearance of fear and anxiety following the saint's new, blissful devotion to the Ideal Power), "spiritual purity," and "charity." It is this fourth attribute, "charity," which becomes of central importance in a "contemporary" understanding of saints. See ibid., 273–74.

These supposedly "universal" identifying features are arguably historically suspicious, particularly insofar as they promote a Protestant, theistic ontology (e.g., note terms such as "Ideal Power" and "surrender"). Nonetheless, the Jamesian claim that the saints are known by their "fruits" is plausible, for there is perhaps a common *ethos* that emerges from various saintly worldviews, namely, an ethos of complete other-regard. The ethos of other-regard need not be construed as *self-denying*. Indeed, as James observes, saints experience an overwhelming sense of "joy" and undergo a "blissful" devotion as part of their enlightened orientation in the world. Thus, while saints may transcend the pull of the ego and live an entirely selfless life, this does not mean that they do not also humanly flourish and achieve fulfillment.

25. Susan Wolf, "Moral Saints," *Journal of Philosophy* 79, no. 8 (1982): 419.

26. Ibid., 425.

27. Wolf also charges that as a result of their dedication to moral perfection, saints are deficient in being able to "enjoy the enjoyable life," "unattractive," and

so blindly committed to their moral cause that they inevitably come across as humorless and boring. See ibid., 422–26. Robert Adams refutes these charges, arguing that saints' characteristic passion makes them intriguingly quirky and often charismatic. See Adams, "Saints," 393ff.

28. Susan Wolf, for example, has argued in this way. See Wolf, "Moral Saints," 419, 421.

29. Wyschogrod relies especially on Levinas's volume, *Otherwise than Being or Beyond Essence*, trans. Alphonso Lingus (The Hague: Martinus Nijhoff, 1974).

30. Wyschogrod, *Saints and Postmodernism*, 33.

31. The assumption that there are experiences of *any* sort that are unmediated is contestable. In expositing Wyschogrod (and Levinas), I do not mean to give the impression that I accept uncritically their cognitive metaphysics.

32. Wyschogrod, *Saints and Postmodernism*, 33.

33. Levinas, *Otherwise than Being or Beyond Essence*, 58ff.

34. Urmson, "Saints and Heroes," 214.

35. Ibid.

36. Levinas, *Otherwise than Being or Beyond Essence*, 62ff. Levinas maintains that one must not think of our original condition as a state of sin. It is, on the contrary, an "original goodness" that emanates from the act of creation. Creatureliness is a "vulnerability" to the demands placed on it by the Other, which Levinas interprets as an affirmation of our innocence. For a more complete discussion, see Robert Gibbs, *Correlations in Rosenzweig and Levinas* (Princeton: Princeton University Press, 1992), 214–15.

37. Wyschogrod accepts the etymological definition of *theory* as "systematically organized knowledge applicable in a wide variety of circumstances, especially a system of assumptions, accepted principles and rules of procedure devised to analyze, predict, or otherwise explain the nature or behavior of a specified set of phenomena," with the caveat that theories involve contemplation and observation. That is, they involve cognition. According to Wyschogrod, theories—including moral theories—are patterned after the model of scientific understanding. They organize our way of ascertaining what is true by testing according to some mode of justification. This stipulative characterization of theories and moral theories will become a crucial reference point throughout the rest of this chapter. See Wyschogrod, *Saints and Postmodernism*, 127–29.

It is important to point out that in spite of her polemic against theorizing, Wyschogrod herself has what could loosely be called a moral theory, namely, that we understand and subsequently fulfill our responsibility to others by going out of our way to expose ourselves to saints and to saintly narratives. Thus, to accept at face value Wyschogrod's claim that her approach is "against theory" is somewhat misleading. It would be more precise to say that Wyschogrod is against a certain mode of liberal, post-Enlightenment theorizing in which rules and principles are employed to govern our interpersonal relations in a pluralistic setting. She is opposed to using *reason* as a main source of normative justification.

38. Ibid., 52.

39. Wyschogrod here refers to the approaches of Rawls and Gewirth, discussed later.

40. Wyschogrod, *Saints and Postmodernism*, 127.

41. Ibid., 44.

42. Ibid., 28, 243.

43. Ibid., 41–42.

44. Ibid., 150.

45. Ibid., xxiv, 63ff.

46. Ibid., xxiii.

47. While I characterize King, Day, and Mother Teresa as "saints," I remain aware that they also had flaws. Just as we should make every effort to call attention to the human being within heroes, such as the firefighters and rescue workers from September 11, we should also remain aware of the dangers of typologizing the saints we study. Take the example of Martin Luther King, Jr., whose virtue must be considered alongside flaws such as infidelity and plagiarism. While King's shortcomings can be considered negligible in the greater scope of his life and influence, they do attest to the oft-noted insight that saints, while maximally virtuous in some respects, nonetheless do not possess the full complement of virtues. See Flanagan, *Varieties of Moral Personality*, 9ff. For a discussion of King's extramarital affairs and plagiarism and their overall importance in King's life, see Michael Eric Dyson, *I May Not Get There with You: The True Martin Luther King, Jr.* (New York: The Free Press, 2000), 216–21 (on King's womanizing); and 139–51 (on his plagiarism). Dyson forces us to accept King with all his shortcomings and in the process allows us to see how these shortcomings do not diminish King's stature as perhaps the most important figure of the twentieth century. Even Mother Teresa, perhaps the most popularly hailed personage of our time, had her critics. Anne Sebba's biography, *Mother Teresa, 1910–1997: Beyond the Image* (New York: Doubleday Press, 1997), provides both a laudatory account of Mother Teresa's humanitarian work and a critical appraisal of her controversial views about abortion, rape, and the treatment of the handicapped, and of her association with dictators and her sometimes questionable ethical approach to fundraising. Sebba is thorough in her exploration of Mother Teresa's dedication to the poor and infirm, but she also captures the Albanian nun's conservative and often savvy approach to giving charity.

48. Martin Luther King, Jr., "I See the Promised Land," in *A Testament of Hope: The Essential Writings and Speeches of Martin Luther King, Jr.*, ed. James Washington (San Francisco: Harper Collins, 1986), 284–85.

49. William M. Ramsay, *Four Modern Prophets: Walter Rauschenbusch, Martin Luther King, Jr., Gustavo Gutiérrez, Rosemary Radford Ruether* (Atlanta: John Knox Press, 1986), 45–46. For a complete record of King's arrests, see Lerone Bennett, Jr., *What Manner of Man: A Biography of Martin Luther King, Jr.* (Chicago: Johnson Publishing Company, Inc., 1976), 243–45.

50. Frederick L. Downing, *To See the Promised Land: The Faith Pilgrimage of Martin Luther King, Jr.* (Macon, Ga.: Mercer University Press, 1986), 265.

51. Ibid. 274–75. Downing here refers to Martin Luther King Jr., as quoted in his father's autobiography. See the Reverend Martin Luther King, Sr., *Daddy King: An Autobiography* (New York: William Morrow, 1980).

52. See Stephen B. Oates, *Let the Trumpet Sound: The Life of Martin Luther*

226 MORALLY EXTRAORDINARY PERSONS

King, Jr. (New York: Harper and Row, 1982), 405; and David Lewis, *King: A Critical Biography* (New York: Praeger Publishers, 1970), 216ff.

53. Downing, *To See the Promised Land*, 269. Late in his life King became the victim of many smear campaigns, the most prominent of which was conducted by FBI director J. Edgar Hoover. Hoover, already annoyed at what he perceived to be King's rabble-rousing, and angry about King's alleged statements that the FBI had failed adequately to address violence against blacks in the South because many of its agents were Southerners, attacked King on November 18, 1964, calling him the "most notorious liar in the country." For more on this event and on King's tumultuous relationship with Hoover generally, see Lewis, *King: A Critical Biography*, 256–58; and Oates, *Let the Trumpet Sound*, 312–18. For a discussion of King's exchange with Hoover within the broader context of America's reaction to the freedom marches, see David J. Garrow, *Bearing the Cross: Martin Luther King, Jr., and the Southern Christian Leadership Conference* (New York: William Morrow and Company, 1986), ch. 7, esp. 360ff.

54. Downing, *To See the Promised Land*, 273.

55. King, *A Testament of Hope*, 279.

56. Ibid., 279–80.

57. Ibid., 286.

58. Ibid., 254.

59. Ibid.

60. Downing, *To See the Promised Land*, 271.

61. Ibid.

62. King, *A Testament of Hope*, 20.

63. Ibid.

64. Ibid.

65. Ibid., 284–85.

66. Ibid., 210.

67. Ibid., 256–57.

68. Lewis, *King: A Critical Biography*, 274–75. This day, which became known as "Bloody Sunday," shocked King, who first learned about it while in Washington, D.C., where he had gone to confer with President Johnson about the situation in Vietnam. King later became infuriated with Williams for acting on his own by proceeding with the march. This event prompted King himself to reflect on the danger of others following in his footsteps. See Oates, *Let the Trumpet Sound*, 348ff.

69. King, *A Testament of Hope*, 221–22.

70. Ibid., 222.

71. As William Robert Miller explains, the "purposiveness of suffering was a copiously recurrent theme in King's writings and speeches." Suffering was not understood by King to be "self-inflicted but voluntarily endured and embraced for the sake of one's integrity ... and for the other." King, in other words, converted suffering into an affirmative act, a positive manifestation of *agape*. See William Robert Miller, *Martin Luther King, Jr.: His Life, Martyrdom, and Meaning for the World* (New York: Weybright and Talley, 1968), 287.

72. Downing, *To See the Promised Land*, 270.

73. King, *A Testament of Hope*, 224.

74. Dorothy Day, *On Pilgrimage* (Grand Rapids, Mich.: William B. Eerdmans Publishing Co., 1997), 246–48.

75. The evidence that Dorothy Day eschewed any characterization that would construe her as a saint in her own life is abundant. See Day, *By Little and by Little: Selected Writings of Dorothy Day*, ed. Robert Ellsberg (New York: Orbis Books, 1999), 89–120, for examples based on her own testimony, as well as Kenneth Woodward's discussion of the debate over whether Day ought to have been canonized, in which the author recounts anecdotes of family and close friends to impart Day's own view of the matter, in Woodward, *Making Saints*, 32–33.

76. Robert Coles, *Dorothy Day: A Radical Devotion* (Reading, Mass.: Addison-Wesley Publishing Company, 1987), 11. Coles notes that in those days Day became consumed by her own moral outrage and started to worry that she might come across as an embittered, self-righteous person. These doubts indicate that Day was aware of how she might be perceived by others, and in particular of the mainstream mind-set that might not be prepared for the twin weights of her compassion and condemnation. That her fears about being misunderstood or resented did not, over the course of her life, lead her to change her views is a testament to the sincerity with which she thought them through.

77. William Miller, *Dorothy Day: A Biography* (San Francisco: Harper and Row, 1982), 428.

78. Dorothy Day, *The Long Loneliness: The Autobiography of Dorothy Day* (San Francisco: Harper San Francisco, 1997), 159. See also Coles, *Dorothy Day*, 11. Day's allusion to Pius XI may be contrasted with her admiration for Pietro da Morrone, a Benedictine monk who briefly became Pope Celestino V in 1294, before leaving the papacy after five months (the only pope ever to resign). Pietro da Morrone was deeply religious but ineffective as an administrator. Day would joke with her associates at the *Catholic Worker* that Pietro da Morrone was ironically *too much* like Christ to serve effectively as the leader of the church. Genuine saints, she held, could not live out the true meaning of their vocation within the constraining confines of the worldly church. As Coles notes, Day "thought of that brief papacy as a flash of heavenly light upon the church, upon mankind's religious history: how ill at ease, how out of place true virtue is in the world." See Coles, *Dorothy Day*, 146–47.

79. As cited by Coles, from his interview tapes, in ibid., 66–67.

80. From 1949 to 1951, Day became embroiled in a conflict with Cardinal Francis Spellman of New York City. Cardinal Spellman threatened to shut down the *Catholic Worker* after Day sided with the gravediggers of Calvary Cemetery, who had gone on strike against the Catholic Church, their employer. After Cardinal Spellman declined to negotiate with them, Day asserted in her column that "a Cardinal, ill advised, exercised so overwhelmingly a show of force against a handful of poor working men" (Coles, *Dorothy Day*, 81). As annoyed as Cardinal Spellman was by the public admonishment, he was even more rebuking of Day's relentless polemics against the recent war effort, for fear of the impression it would make on Catholic war veterans. Thus, in early March 1951 Monsignor Edward Gaffney, on behalf of the Archdiocese of New York, and at Cardinal Spellman's

228   MORALLY EXTRAORDINARY PERSONS

behest, asked Day to remove the term "Catholic" from the *Catholic Worker*. Day
and her coworkers denied the request. Day's response to Spellman and to the
church, which is highly pointed, if deferential, can be found in Day, *By Little and
by Little*, 334–37.

81. Coles, *Dorothy Day*, 71.
82. Day, *By Little and by Little*, 240, 343.
83. Ibid., 7.
84. Ibid.
85. Dorothy Day, *Loaves and Fishes* (Maryknoll, N.Y.: Orbis Books, 1997), 92.
86. Ibid.
87. Ibid., 84.
88. Dorothy Day, *Thérèse* (Springfield, Ill.: Templegate, 1979), vii.
89. Ibid., 72.
90. For a treatment of Day's application of Thérèse's "little way" and of the
"transposition" of this term from its original use in a setting among twenty
French nuns to that of New York City in the midst of the Great Depression, see
Leon J. Hooper, "Dorothy Day's Transposition of Thérèse's 'Little Way,'" *Theological Studies* 63, no. 1 (2002): 68–87.
91. Day, *By Little and by Little*, 110.
92. Day, *Loaves and Fishes*, 84–85.
93. Woodward, *Making Saints*, 32.
94. All three of these citations can be found in ibid., 32.
95. This is also Woodward's conclusion about Father Berrigan's view. Father
Berrigan's more extended remarks are quoted by Woodward in ibid., 35.
96. Ibid., 35.
97. Ibid., 36.
98. Robert Inchausti, *The Ignorant Perfection of Ordinary People* (Albany, N.Y.:
State University of New York Press, 1991), 70.
99. Ibid. (his emphasis).
100. I want to thank the anonymous reviewers of the *Journal of Religious Ethics*
for raising these objections in their evaluation of an article of mine that is in
progress on the role of exhortation in the writings of Dorothy Day and Martin
Luther King, Jr.
101. See Charles Taylor, *Varieties of Religion Today: William James Revisited*
(Cambridge: Harvard University Press, 2002), 115; and Nicholas Lash, *Easter in
Ordinary: Reflections on Human Experience and the Knowledge of God* (Charlottesville: University Press of Virginia, 1988), 1–64.
102. Day, *Loaves and Fishes*, 95, 97, 99.
103. Day, *By Little and by Little*, 149.
104. King, *A Testament of Hope*, 617.
105. Mother Teresa, *Total Surrender*, ed. Brother Angelo Devanada (Ann Arbor,
Mich.: Servant Publications, 1985), 54.
106. As Mark Taylor notes, the notion of "postmodernism" is not a unified
referent, and perhaps the only thing that can consistently be said about the term
is that it is defined as a response to "modernism." Modernism is widely thought
to begin with Descartes's inward turn to the human subject, in which the subject's

relation to otherness becomes mediated by, and ultimately reducible to, its relationship to itself. If we apply this understanding to the realm of ethics, then a modernist understanding of the moral task becomes the self's bid to overcome self-interest, where the "rules" or "laws" which govern the subject serve as the means by which this task is carried out. This is, in any case, how Wyschogrod sees modernism. In an alternative, postmodern framework of narrativity over law, self-interest is still overcome, but its overcoming is not the focus. Rather the overcoming of self-interest is the byproduct of the self's practice of responding unconditionally to the Other. Wyschogrod contrasts the rationality, unity, and totality of modernism to the "praxis," "difference," and "alterity" of postmodernism. As opposed to modern moral theory, which is organized around the single voice of reason, postmodern narratives are created by a multiplicity of saintly voices, whose messages cannot be predicted before hearing them. See Wyschogrod, *Saints and Postmodernism*, xv ff. and 75–80, for her treatment of the Cartesian account of the self. For a discussion of modernism as it relates to René Descartes, see Mark C. Taylor, *Altarity* (Chicago: University of Chicago Press, 1987), xxi–xxii.

107. Wyschogrod, *Saints and Postmodernism*, xxi.

108. Ibid., xiv. Wyschogrod assumes that humanity is threatened now more than ever before. The last century has witnessed the murder of millions of innocents during World War II and presently witnesses the unprecedented presence of nuclear, chemical, and biological weapons of mass destruction. In addition, conflicts that in former epochs remained local now have no guarantee of being contained, but perpetually threaten to balloon into full global war. The occurrence of mass death in our age has come to be seen as almost normal, and this is abetted by the fact that it is glamorized in popular culture and reported with regularity on television. In her book *Spirit in Ashes*, Wyschogrod characterized these phenomena under the collective referent, the "death event." In her view it is the single most important historical distinction of the postmodern age. The continuing threat of the "death event" makes the need for saints especially urgent in the contemporary world. See Wyschogrod, *Spirit in Ashes: Hegel, Heidegger, and Man-Made Mass Death* (New Haven: Yale University Press, 1985), 15–16.

109. Wyschogrod, *Saints and Postmodernism*, xvi.

110. Ibid., xxii, 3, 228, 249.

111. Wyschogrod, *Saints and Postmodernism*, 68–69. See also John Rawls, *A Theory of Justice* (Cambridge: The Belknap Press of Harvard University Press, 1971), 302ff.; and Alan Gewirth, *Reason and Morality* (Chicago: University of Chicago Press, 1978), 129–61. A critic might charge that in so characterizing Rawls and Gewirth, Wyschogrod treats them as straw men. The fact that theories based on principles of justice or a social contract assume that there is a *neutral ground* from which ethical decisions can emanate does not entail that such theories ultimately advocate a disguised form of *self-love*. While I appreciate that Wyschogrod may overstate the case against Rawls and Gewirth, I am still persuaded by her implicit claim that ethical approaches that give the self and the Other equal weight (e.g., an ethics of "equal-regard") inevitably end up not giving *enough* attention to the needs of others.

112. Wyschogrod, *Saints and Postmodernism*, 70. In response to this charge, Gewirth would likely reply that he does not lose sight of the distinction between the self and the Other, but that he simply identifies their interests. Wyschogrod could reply that to give the self and the Other equal consideration is to disadvantage the Other, for it is to assume that the needs of the Other can be known before the face-to-face encounter. To this rejoinder, I think Gewirth could counter that there *are*, in fact, material "needs" of *all* human beings, an awareness of which does not depend on any empirical discovery. We do not need to meet the Other, for example, to understand either the precariousness of the human condition or the importance of safeguarding the welfare and well-being of everyone. Food, shelter, and safety constitute universal needs. I think that at this point in the argument Wyschogrod would have to make a second argument, which she does, about why an altruism based on principles of reason is motivationally insufficient to prompt us to attend to the most needy and desperate in society. Having said this, I still think there is some force to Wyschogrod's epistemological point that altruism based on "theory" glosses over the radical nature of the Other's alterity, even if she exaggerates the case.

113. Levinas, *Otherwise than Being or Beyond Essence*, 64.

114. One may object that the Other surely suffers from common maladies like hunger, lack of shelter, and so forth. Wyschogrod could respond that the Other's particular predicament—and the way out of that predicament—will likely be specific to his or her unique situation and thus ought not to be predicted before the face-to-face encounter.

115. Wyschogrod, *Saints and Postmodernism*, xxiii.

116. Ibid., 33, 57.

117. Ibid., 85.

118. Ibid., 85–86.

119. Ibid. It is interesting to read these passages of Wyschogrod alongside Matthew 25, where very similar claims are made about the stranger.

120. Nicholas Rescher, *Unselfishness: The Role of the Vicarious Affects in Moral Philosophy and Social Theory* (Pittsburgh: University of Pittsburgh Press, 1975), 3ff., referenced by Wyschogrod, *Saints and Postmodernism*, 237.

121. Wyschogrod, *Saints and Postmodernism*, 237–38, quoting Rescher, *Unselfishness*, 5–6.

122. Wyschogrod, *Saints and Postmodernism*, 237–38.

123. Rescher, *Unselfishness*, 15.

124. Emmanuel Levinas, *Totality and Infinity: An Essay on Exteriority*, trans. Alphonso Lingus (Pittsburgh: Duquesne University Press, 1969), 215.

125. Wyschogrod, *Saints and Postmodernism*, 242.

126. Ibid.

127. Ibid., 147 (Wyschogrod's italics). I think that Wyschogrod, if pressed, would have to concede that according to saintly morality, saints are still concerned with their own necessities in the instrumental sense that they must meet them in order to continue giving to the Other. There is an assumption here that saints cannot become *as* destitute as the ones they help, lest they lose the capacity to render their

aid and assistance. But if one is a saint, he or she does not *think* about this practical constraint on his or her ability to give. The saint simply takes what he or she
absolutely needs to function without dwelling on it, and resumes his or her work
replenishing the Other.

128. Levinas, *Otherwise than Being or Beyond Essence*, 14.

129. Ibid., 64, 66–69.

130. Ibid., 76. Levinas calls the initial, primordial approach of the Other "an-
archic" in the sense that it signifies an ethical relationship before it can phenomenologically be described. Our awareness of the Other, for whom we are
responsible, precedes our rational or emotional *comprehension* of who the Other
is, let alone an explanation for why the Other is our burden. This radical disrup-
tion of thematization, in which the referent exceeds our capacity to put it into
words, occurs, according to Levinas, "in a past more profound than all that I can
reassemble by memory, by historiography ... in a time before the beginning"
(Levinas, *Otherwise than Being or Beyond Essence*, 88).

131. Levinas is at his most hyperbolic when describing the self's initial con-
frontation with the Other, in which the self is described as divesting itself of all
enjoyment and shelter, succumbing to the Other's command, which persecutes
the self with its gaze. An excellent analysis that brings clarity and contextualiza-
tion to the distinctive senses that Levinas gives to "accusation," "persecution," and
related terminology is presented by Robert Gibbs in *Correlations in Rosenzweig
and Levinas*, ch. 9.

132. According to Levinas, God exists in the face of the Other and is referred to
as the "trace." As Robert Gibbs writes: "For Levinas there is no gap between the
encounter with the other and the self-sanctification before God: the two moments
are entwined in the experience of the face of the other. While there clearly is a
self before I meet the other, that self is hollowed out, obsessed, inverted, extro-
verted, denucleated, and so on by the encounter.... Levinas calls this [infinite
process] ethics, but that is a translation of the 'Hebrew' term *sanctification*. The
infinity of the task is the trace of God who has been here" (Gibbs, *Correlations in
Rosenzweig and Levinas*, 187).

133. Just as Rudolph Otto claims in *The Idea of the Holy* that "the numinous" is
not taught, but rather awakened in us as an "a priori," so does Levinas postulate
the existence of an "a priori" in reference to our capacity to respond to the Other.
The numinous, in this sense, is horizontalized. Thus, while according to Otto we
are part of the genus *homo religioso*, for Levinas, we are hard-wired to be other-
regarding beings. The central question for each thinker is whether we will fulfill
our true essence. See Rudolph Otto, *The Idea of the Holy*, trans. John W. Harvey
(Oxford: Oxford University Press, 1958), 7, 112–16.

134. Wyschogrod, *Saints and Postmodernism*, 148.

135. Ibid., 150.

136. Ibid. "Throwness" is Heidegger's term for being thrown into the world
under circumstances not of our own choosing. It is, according to Heidegger and
other existentialists, a fundamental initial condition of our being-in-the-world.

137. Wyschogrod discusses yet another factor that precludes the notion of full

saintly realization, namely, the temporal nature of history, which traps all humans, saints and nonsaints, in its horizon. Since the outcome of immediate events is always unforeseeable, no potential saint can know whether the narrative of which he or she will form a part in the future will be a "saintly" one rather than a demonic one, or simply an indifferent one. In other words, sainthood is not simply a matter of agency; it is also a matter of historical contingency. Since in the course of real human history (as opposed to fiction), narrative cannot be brought to a close, hagiography is always susceptible to devolving into something less. Sainthood is in this sense dependent on the prior need, or lack, of the Other. One cannot will oneself to be a saint without these conditions being present. Such a view is consistent with the postmodern repudiation of a rationalistic ethics that begins with an autonomous, volitional self. See ibid., 150. Wyschogrod's discussion here relates to the broader issue of the role of luck in ethics. See Bernard Williams, "Moral Luck," in *Moral Luck: Philosophical Papers, 1973–1980* (Cambridge: Cambridge University Press, 1981), 20–39; and Martha Nussbaum, *The Fragility of Goodness: Luck and Ethics in Greek Tragedy and Philosophy* (Cambridge: Cambridge University Press, 1986), esp. 1–21.

138. Wyschogrod, *Saints and Postmodernism*, 256.

139. See, for example, ibid., 243.

140. Ibid., 29.

141. Ibid., 255.

142. On Wyschogrod's use of the term "death event," see note 108.

143. Again, see Jean Hampton, "Selflessness and the Loss of Self," in *Altruism*, ed. Ellen Frankel Paul, Fred D. Miller, Jr., and Jeffrey Paul (Cambridge: Cambridge University Press, 1993), 135–65; and William Galston, "Cosmopolitan Altruism," in Paul, Miller, and Paul, eds., *Altruism*, 118–34.

144. David Matthew Matzko, "Postmodernism, Saints and Scoundrels," *Modern Theology* 9, no. 1 (1993): 25.

145. Urmson, "Saints and Heroes," 210.

146. John Hick, *An Interpretation of Religion: Human Responses to the Transcendent* (New Haven: Yale University Press, 1989), 307.

147. A. I. Melden, "Saints and Supererogation," in *Philosophy and Life: Essays on John Wisdom*, ed. Ilham Dilman (The Hague: Martinus Nijhoff Publishers, 1984), 61–79.

148. Ibid., 77.

149. John A. Coleman, "After Sainthood?" in Hawley, ed., *Saints and Virtues*, 207, 212.

150. Ibid., 221.

151. James, *The Varieties of Religious Experience*, 358.

152. Ibid.

153. Ibid., 355.

154. Ibid.

155. Ibid., 357–58.

156. Ibid., 358.

157. Ibid., 358, 360. This view is articulated by Reinhold Niebuhr when he writes that we are creatures of "infinite possibilities that cannot be filled within the terms

of [our] temporal existence." See Reinhold Niebuhr, *The Nature and Destiny of Man: A Christian Interpretation*, 2 vols. (New York: Charles Scribner's Sons, 1949), 1:170. Elsewhere Niebuhr, echoing the sentiments of his predecessor, Ernst Troeltsch, writes: "The Kingdom is not of this world, yet its light illuminates our tasks in this world and its hope saves us from despair." See Niebuhr, "The Hitler-Stalin Pact," in *Love and Justice*, ed. D. B. Robertson (Philadelphia: Westminster, 1957), 80.

158. *Online Newshour: Martin Luther King, Jr. and Taylor Branch*, February 2, 1998. See www.pbs.org/newshour/gergen/february98/branch_2-2.html (last accessed on April 14, 2003).

159. Percy Bysshe Shelley, "Defense of Poetry," in *Norton Anthology: World Masterpieces*, vol. 2, ed. Maynard Mack (New York: Norton, 1995), 817.

PART III

Ordinary Persons and Moral Betterment

It does not matter how slow you go, as long as you don't stop.

—Confucius

Only those who will risk going too far can possibly find out how far one can go.

—T. S. Eliot

... lead me to the rock that is higher than I.

—Psalm 62

CHAPTER 5

Moral Development, Obligation, and Supererogation

The Thesis of Moral Development

If heroes are the products of their virtuous characters, if they really perceive vividly, while the majority perceives palely, the true nature of the responsibility to the other in need, then we should neither consider them to be falsely modest nor dismiss them as noncredible in terms of their potential to serve as moral guides for us. To the contrary, since their experience is continuous with ours, they have something important to say to us about what it means to be living among less-fortunate others. They know best what it means to humanly flourish, which includes an awareness of what it is to see and respond to those who are suffering. This is, in any case, an accurate reflection of heroes' way of seeing themselves in relation to us, a perception that we do not have the cognitive resources convincingly to contest from our nonheroic point of view.

Similarly, saints, while not "ordinary" in the way heroes are, can more plausibly be characterized as inspirational guides to good living than as purveyors of an unattainable ideal that lies at the periphery of morality. The enlightened consciousness of saints leads them to embrace a worldview in which the distinction between self and alter is transcended and which, as a result, leads them to engage in altruistic conduct that from a nonsaintly perspective must be judged as excessive. That such conduct appears to *us* as excessive, however, does not imply that saints are wrong to aver that they are bound to respond unconditionally to the call of the suffering. From our cautiously prudential perspective, *we* cannot determine whether saints are merely following their own personal aims and ideals or whether they are, in James's poetic limning, "slow leavens of a better order" without whom we would have no long-term model for our own progress.

The fact that we do not know what it is like to walk in heroes' and saints' shoes prior to approximating the heroic or saintly ourselves should give us pause before we label their altruistic deeds "above and beyond." There is no fixed boundary that separates supererogatory acts from morally obligatory ones. Our differing perceptions of the situations in which we find ourselves correspond to our differing moral particularities. Beyond the moral minimum, it is these perceptions that determine what we are required to do for others. This means that while we can arguably speak about universal, "rock-bottom" duties, such as the basic proscription against committing murder, or the obligation to allocate through taxation a small portion of our earnings to benefit society's least well-off, the distinction between those more demanding acts that are required and acts of supererogation is agent-relative.[1] Just where the distinction is drawn depends on the moral development of the agent. Gone, in such an account, is the supposition of the universalizability of duty in moral theory.[2]

So far this characterization of moral requirement has been offered speculatively, supported by the testimony of "heroes" and "saints" whose self-understandings differ from more conventional interpretations of their altruism. Heroes and saints contend not just that they have a basis for acting *as if* their "heroic" and "saintly" deeds are obligatory, but also that such deeds are *in reality* obligatory, every bit as morally binding as any other duty. But the defender of the standard view can respond to this contention by readily admitting that heroes and saints will remain unflinchingly committed to the view that what they do is obligatory. Indeed, Urmson would *expect* heroes and saints to reject his explanatory theory about them. That, after all, is their nature, as well as a testament to their moral fortitude. The fact that heroes and saints may be passionate in this regard does not in itself make their testimony any more convincing. Up until this point, then, the debate remains unresolved, leaving the defender of the standard view not yet satisfied. Counterexamples become compelling once they find support in a positive argument.

The purpose of this chapter is to construct this positive argument, and thereby to weave together the tantalizing implications of the previous chapters. This I will do through an appeal to neo-Aristotelian patterns of thought, and in particular to the insight articulated by certain virtue ethicists that our responsibility for others does not end with the avoidance of wrongdoing, but is continually borne in mind as part and parcel of our ongoing moral development.[3]

To this end, it seems appropriate finally to frame my hypothesis as a thesis, which can be stated as follows: Morality requires different things from different people at different times, as well as different things from the same person at different times. Precisely *what* morality demands of us at any one time depends on the particular pace at which we variously proceed toward the goal of moral betterment. What we have in *common* with each other is that we each ought, in our own distinctive ways, to dispose ourselves to become better people. This maxim, which is Aristotelian in nature, corresponds to the acquisition of virtue. As we become more virtuous,[4] we become increasingly capable of *perceiving* the true nature of our responsibilities toward others, and better able to harness the courage required for successfully *acting* responsibly. Thus, there is a direct relationship between moral development and the expansion of duty. This relationship has a bearing on how we are to be morally judged. In the standard view, we are evaluated according to the objectively characterizable actions we perform. By contrast, in the revised account, how we are morally judged depends ultimately on the degree to which we take seriously our underlying duty to improve our character. From now on, I will refer to this counterproposal to the standard view as the "thesis of moral development" and to its proponent as the "developmentalist."[5]

Relating an Ethics of Duty to an Ethics of Virtue: Three Distinct Types of "Ought"

There are two important prongs to the thesis of moral development. The first holds that as we acquire more virtue, the range of our positive duties expands beyond its initial level of minimal moral requirement. This implies that what the noteworthily virtuous person "ought" to do is more costly and quantitatively greater than what persons who possess only a mediocre level of virtue are morally required to do. The second fundamental idea is embodied in the teleological maxim that we each "ought" to be trying to improve ourselves throughout the course of our lives. Earlier, I conceived of this second "ought" as a meta-duty, not part of the range of first-order duties that increase with our level of moral development. This underlying "ought" of character development, or "meta-duty," in contrast to the "ought" that specifies our range of first-order duties, *is* a constant: we each, regardless of our stage of moral development, ought to be pushing beyond what we currently understand our range of first-order duties to be. There is also a third type of "ought" implied by the foregoing two claims, which, unlike the meta-duty to improve our character, also relates to an agent's range of first-order duties. This is the use of "ought" pertaining to minimal moral requirement, which specifies what *every* agent, regardless of his or her stage of moral development, is obligated to do (or not do) as a condition of his or her moral agency. This third, most basic type of "ought" is the only one acknowledged by Urmson as legitimate. It alone specifies the standard of conduct below which it is indispensable for us not to fall, lest morality as a whole become deprived of its regulating function in all human interaction.[6] This universal minimal standard is traditionally based on rules that apply to all agents qua agents.[7] In Urmson's account, only those maxims that make demands upon the moral capacities that everyone can be expected to possess can count as obligatory. According to the developmentalist, all three uses of "ought" morally constrain us. All three uses imply moral compulsion. In other words, we are morally culpable, or blameworthy, if we fail to do what we ought.[8]

Thus, according to the developmentalist, I am morally bound in three ways. I am morally bound not to fall below the moral minimum. Morality at this "thin," basic level applies to all agents regardless of how virtuous they are. Moreover, I am morally bound, again in the same way that everyone else is bound, to attempt to become more virtuous in my life. While the results of this effort will largely depend on my unique capacities and traits, including the trait that disposes me to harness other traits, I must continually put effort into bettering myself. This at the least entails questioning myself critically when I fall short of possibly attainable higher standards. This fundamental ought, or meta-duty, is Aristotelian in nature: I ought to aspire to incorporate virtue into my life for its own sake because it is suitable for good human living. Both the "ought" that applies to minimal moral requirement and the "ought" that bids me always to be improving my character are agent-neutral. They apply to all agents as such, independent of an agent's character. This is not the case with respect to the third kind of "ought," which varies from person to person. Once I begin to acquire more virtue, I become bound, for I am not already bound, to perform additional first-order duties that I formerly regarded to be a matter of supererogation and that still *are* instances of supererogation for other agents. This is the point at which morality "thickens" for me. As I become more virtuous, the range of my deontic duties expands. No longer do I regard minimal moral requirement as an adequate reflection of my duty. Moreover, at this stage of my development what I *ought* to do increasingly becomes a matter of what the fully virtuous person *would* do.[9]

One way to explain how these three kinds of "oughts" are connected is to clarify the relationship between deontic and aretaic ethics. Deontic moral theories make goodness of character conceptually dependent on right action. Conversely, aretaic moral theories make right action dependent on goodness of character. In the former, right or wrong action is determined without reference to moral character; in the latter, right or wrong action is determined in terms of moral character.[10] In deontic ethics my most important goal as an agent is to avoid wrongdoing by refraining from what is prohibited. This can be done by fulfilling both negative and positive duties. I am prohibited from killing, stealing, and so forth, just as I am prohibited from failing to save someone in dire jeopardy if doing so comes at little cost to myself. As long as I successfully manage to avoid what is prohibited, my job as a moral agent is complete; I cannot be judged as morally in the wrong according to any deontic criteria. By contrast, since judgments about rightness or wrongness in aretaic ethics stem from assessments about my character, if I want to avoid culpability, I must focus my attention on the kind of person I am (and am becoming).

Aretaic evaluations require us to probe into the nature of our capacity to dispose ourselves to feel, act, and desire in certain ways. We must ask ourselves questions that we can, but need not, consider from a deontic perspective. What is our thought process when we turn down requests to go above and beyond the call of duty? Do we dismiss such requests in our own mind, even though we might outwardly exert the effort to articulate a legitimate excuse, or do we feel a lingering sense of dissatisfaction with our perhaps too casual refusal to accommodate those who ask for our help? When we morally act, such distinctively aretaic questions force us to look beyond the actions themselves and introspectively examine ourselves. According to aretaic ethics, for example, there is no easy way in which I can say to myself, "I've done the right thing and now I'm finished," for, from an aretaic standpoint, I am never really morally off the hook.[11]

Returning to the different senses of "ought," it becomes clear that the duty associated with minimal moral requirement is the paradigmatic ought of deontic ethics, while the meta-duty to improve one's character—which is essentially an ought to *be* a certain sort of person—is an aretaic ought.[12] Characterizing the third kind of ought, which pertains to those more demanding duties that become morally binding once we acquire the requisite level of virtue, is a bit more tricky; for even though it is an ought that is agent-relative, it is every bit as obligatory as minimal moral requirement. For the noteworthily virtuous person, there is no difference in status between basic duties and more demanding altruistic acts that *become* duties. Both refer to specific *acts*, the performance of which is morally required. In this sense, it is accurate to characterize the third ought as a deontic ought. It can be contrasted with an aretaic meta-duty, which does not require us to perform specific acts.

Given the foregoing characterization of these three oughts, the thesis of moral development can now be restated as follows. We find ourselves in the world as agents who are from the start morally bound by certain minimal requirements.[13] These represent our initial set of deontic duties. But we also have an aretaic duty always to be improving ourselves. If we heed this aretaic duty, the scope of our deontic duties expands. What we formerly were justified in regarding as supererogatory becomes obligatory.[14] Deontic and aretaic concepts are thus importantly related to one another. Unlike other attempts in virtue theory to supplant an ethics of duty with an ethics of character, the developmentalist adopts an approach that seeks to combine both.[15]

Some Lingering Questions

To provide grounds for the thesis of moral development one must show that the aretaic meta-duty to improve our character actually exists. Where does the duty to become a better person come from? While the grounds for the thesis of moral development abound in theological contexts, little has been devoted in scholarship to providing a secular, pluralistic basis for such an approach. This makes sense. Religions often posit a notion of human fulfillment as consisting in a search for sanctification in which salvation and redemption, both teleological concepts, become the final goal of human existence.[16] By contrast, secular approaches in ethics tend to focus on ground rules, leaving to the discretion of particular agents different notions of future flourishing. In order to provide a secular basis for the thesis of moral development, the imperative to become better must spring from sources that arise within a secular moral tradition. I attempt to provide such a basis through reference to the ethical writings of Aristotle and various neo-Aristotelian scholars, both by emphasizing certain passages from the *Nicomachean Ethics* in which Aristotle recommends that we pursue the good by incorporating virtue into our own lives, and by connecting these passages to the stronger claim advanced by neo-Aristotelians that we ought always to be striving to improve our character. Subsequently, I attempt to explain how moral development expands the range of our first-order duties. Here, the argument becomes constructive and heads toward a proposal for integrating deontic and aretaic concepts into a unified normative theory.

Once the Aristotelian grounds for accepting the thesis of moral development are established, questions arise. Perhaps the most important of these pertains to whether or not the duty to improve our character is psychologically realistic, especially for those of us at lower levels of moral development. How do people who are not virtuous, and who are not initially disposed to be virtuous, change in order to live what is on the aretaic supposition a more fully human life? How can those who lack virtue even come to know what is virtuous in the first place? My initial response in answering these questions is to grant that many of us begin our journey in moral ignorance. Developmentalists need not make the strong claim that from the beginning of our moral lives we have full *knowledge* of an ideal of character about which, due to existing weaknesses in our character, we remain *able* only to do so much qua duty. Rather they may proceed from the more modest Aristotelian assumption that the aretaic maxim to improve our character is always *present* in our life and that the person totally oblivious to it, or only faintly aware of it, is dependent on his or her particular moral and religious traditions to make it apparent. It is true that in order to become virtuous we must initially allow ourselves to be persuaded by reasons held by virtuous persons themselves. But it is also possible that from a psychological perspective we are inclined, as human beings, to desire our character improvement for its own sake and that this inclination is sufficient to give us the initial momentum we need to move toward the goal of moral betterment.

Another set of questions that arise for the developmentalist pertains to whether the duty to improve our character ever ceases to be an overriding one in our pursuit of the good life. If the *telos* of moral development is to become more and more virtuous, is the thesis of moral development any different from antisupererogationist moral frameworks, such as thoroughgoing perfectionism (the view that we are required to cultivate our self-regarding and other-regarding qualities to the greatest degree possible) or consequentialism (the view that we are to do whatever we can to promote the realization of the overall good)? Developmentalists, who intend the thesis of moral development to be broadly applicable to ordinary moral agents, resist these associations. They want neither to dispense with the category of supererogation nor to see the intuition that we ought to aspire beyond the call of duty collapse into a rigorous, first-order deontic moral requirement. To work on improving oneself, developmentalists insist, is not the same as showing the results of one's improvement immediately.

This delicate middle position invites criticisms from two sides. Unqualified supererogationists will react to the thesis of moral development by objecting to its seemingly inconsistent acknowledgment of an "ought" that bears on us as a demand for improvement but is not immediately expressible in action. To such critics, an aretaic meta-duty that increases our range of deontic duties in the future comes uncomfortably close to violating the truism that "ought implies can," for it holds us at least weakly accountable to a standard of conduct that we may never be able to meet. Another set of criticisms emerge from antisupererogationists, who object to the developmentalist's view that there is a point, different for every agent, at which more demanding altruistic deeds are deemed optional. The objection here is that the "appeal to cost," normally relied upon by particular agents to justify the limiting of duty, is exaggerated.[17] Antisupererogationists extol developmentalists for problematizing moral complacency but criticize them for not following the logic of their thesis through to its natural conclusion, which they think requires them to dispense with the category of supererogation altogether.

Against both of these charges, the developmentalist shoulders the burden of defending a gradualist though morally demanding characterization of the imperative to be other-regarding. In the concluding section of this chapter, I consider responses to objections leveled against the developmentalist from those who defend conventional supererogationism and thoroughgoing antisupererogationism, and I discuss why the thesis of moral development is, in the final analysis, preferable to both approaches.

ARISTOTLE AND THE GROUNDS FOR THE ARETAIC META-DUTY

Living Well as Striving to Be Better

The propositions that we ought to incorporate virtue into our own lives and that persons who perform unusually self-sacrificial altruistic deeds, like heroes and saints, do so precisely *because* they incorporate virtue into their lives, are Aristotelian in nature. According to Aristotle, the fully virtuous person represents an ideal of character that functions to shape our motivations and organize our conduct. This ideal inspires us to acquire certain habits that enable good living.[18] By "good living" Aristotle means doing what is in accordance with what is excellent, or "fine," which we in turn come to know through portrayals of types of virtuous people.[19] One good example of this can be seen in Aristotle's description of the generous person. He writes:

> Actions expressing virtue are fine, and aim at what is fine. Hence the generous person as well (as every other virtuous person) will aim at what is fine in his giving and will give correctly; for he will give to the right people, the right amounts, at the right time, and all the other things that are implied by correct giving. He will do this, moreover, with pleasure or (at any rate) without pain.... If someone gives to the wrong people, or does not aim at what is fine, but gives for some other reason, he will not be called generous, but some other sort of person. Nor will he be called generous if he finds it painful to give; for such a person would choose wealth over fine action, and that is not proper to the generous person.... It is also very definitely proper to the generous person to exceed so much in giving that he leaves less for himself, since it is proper for a generous person not to look out for himself. However ... in speaking of generosity we refer to generosity that fits one's property.... Hence one who gives less (than another) may still be more generous, if he has less to give.[20]

Aristotle describes the virtue of generosity and prescribes its inculcation all at once. He does this, furthermore, through the very picture he paints of the generous person. We learn what generosity is by seeing *how* the generous person gives: pleasurably though not wastefully and without concern for his or her own state of wealth. Aristotle thus appeals to our human ability to recognize a virtue when we see it. But that is not all. To understand generosity in this way is, in effect, to become attracted to what is "fine" about it and subsequently to desire it for ourselves. By acquainting us with sketches of the fully virtuous person, Aristotle thereby paints a determinate portrait of the content of the end that is attained by living excellently, as correctly conceived by those who *have*, in fact, lived excellently.[21]

Thus, according to Aristotle, to know fully virtuous persons of one sort or another is at the same time to value their character states and to understand that we have some sort of duty to pursue those states for ourselves. This does not mean that we are required to perform the same deeds as they do, and, indeed, we may, given our current state of moral development, be unable to perform them. But it does mean that we do not have the luxury merely to *value* their virtuous character states, i.e., to recognize them as good but not necessary for ourselves. It is not enough simply to admire the virtuous; according to Aristotle, we must also be active in our pursuit of virtue. If we prize a particular virtue because we think highly of the actions that issue from its possession, then although we do not necessarily have to commit ourselves immediately to the performance of those actions, we must recognize the necessity of cultivating the virtue in question; otherwise, either our praise of it is insincere or our admiration is not a *moral* one.[22] To value or to accept particular virtues as good is at the same time to be motivated to become virtuous. It follows that *we* are to be praised or blamed on the basis of how earnestly we try to acquire those virtues that we find commendable in others. We cannot consistently hold the hero's bravery, the saint's selflessness, or other such virtues in our esteem without attempting to inculcate them in ourselves. Living by the basic rules alone is ultimately insufficient for living well. The fully virtuous person ought to be seen as an ideal of character that at the same time represents a blueprint for our own moral development.

Such an analysis is consistent with Aristotle's more general discussion of excellence and character. The virtues, he emphasizes, are dispositional. They are the way we exhibit our freedom and become different from how we currently are. As such, they reflect our most important choices. They are more than feelings such as desire, love, anger, and in general whatever implies pleasure or pain; or even capacities such as reasonability, lovingness, and other characteristics that enable us to have feelings.[23] Rather, virtues are *states* of character, "in respect of which we are well or badly off in relation to feelings."[24] Phrased in this way, it becomes clear that Aristotle maintains that being virtuous will require us to exercise the right kind of judgments about how we feel and how we should direct our capacities. If we are naturally compassionate, can we summon up the stern attitude necessary to admonish those who are inconsiderate? If we are brave, can we temper our eagerness to fight for the well-being of those weaker than us when a resolution could be reached through a more peaceful means? If we have a near infinite capacity to love our family, can we put such love in check when we are called upon to attend to the suffering stranger? These are all questions about our *state* of character, over which, unlike our natural capacities, we have control. We flourish when we assume responsibility for shaping ourselves. In this sense, virtue is tied to free will.

The acquisition of virtue, then, is an essential part of human flourishing, even if it does not represent the whole of it. However, there is more that needs to be said about becoming virtuous. While the maxim that we ought to incorporate virtue into our own lives is generally accepted by neo-Aristotelian scholars, there is a debate internal to the neo-Aristotelian camp about the *extent* to which this pursuit should occupy the attention of the fully flourishing human being. The dominant way of interpreting Aristotle's ethics over the past two decades has been to resist the claim that the fully flourishing agent ought, in the first instance, to be the other-regarding agent. This is a trend that is historically explained by comparisons drawn between Aristotelian ethics and the more impersonal, morally demanding frameworks of Kantianism and utilitarianism. Next to these alternatives, Aristotelian ethics has been characterized as relatively lenient. Susan Wolf, for example, argues that the agent who strives against limitations of time and energy to contribute to the overall human good misses out on essential "extra-curricular" aspects of living, which leads her to remark that her view "may be taken to support a more Aristotelian ... approach to moral philosophy" according to which esteemed moral agents, such as saints, ought to cease to retain the moral superiority that normative ethicists traditionally have bestowed upon them.[25] Wolf sharply contrasts the concepts of "saint" and "human being," maintaining that anyone aiming at good human living would be well-advised to eschew the ambition of trying to live a saintly life too.[26] The pursuit of virtue—especially as it pertains to the cultivation of other-regarding traits—is on the whole not the most important part of human flourishing. According to Wolf, flourishing more likely pertains to human happiness, consisting in the pursuit of personal projects and in the formation and sustenance of special relations.

There is a distinction here to be drawn between doing what a good human being would do and doing what is good *for* human beings.[27] Wolf, who argues that "moral ideals do not, and need not, make the best personal ideals,"[28] concludes that human flourishing corresponds to the latter. This conclusion mirrors one drawn by other neo-Aristotelians, such as Philippa Foot, who identify human flourishing with "natural goodness," or the goodness of living, individual beings in relation to their natural life forms.[29] For one who subscribes to such a view of flourishing, goodness resides in an interrelated set of general concepts such as reproduction, nourishment, love, security, and success, and not necessarily in other-regarding traits.[30] On this account, human happiness is both distinguished from and prized above moral betterment. Although moral betterment is not ruled out as a legitimate expression of the good, comfort and contentment are deemed to be the essential features of human flourishing. According to Wolf and Foot, we should therefore cultivate those traits with which we are already endowed, as well as those that are factually necessitated by our setting in the natural world.[31]

Such an account of human flourishing is not conducive to the developmentalist's project of deriving the aretaic meta-duty to improve our character from the Aristotelian maxim that we ought to pursue the good. In order to dispute the prevailing interpretation, the developmentalist must look more closely at *how* Aristotle recommends that we pursue the virtues; for, as we will see, the question of how to pursue the good is for Aristotle relevant to what goods, or traits, we ought to pursue. Wolf and Foot call attention to comfort and contentment as valuable features of human living, but Aristotle also talks about human striving. Thus, the question arises for the one who subscribes to an Aristotelian notion of the "good": should we work on acquiring merely those virtuous traits for which we already have a propensity, as well as pursuing a life that is conducive to our happiness, or should we also seek to become more benevolent, loyal, honest, and so on, regardless of what our particular strengths happen to be, because of the intrinsic value of these traits for any legitimate conception of human living?

Not only does Aristotle supply us with a clear response to this query, he turns out not to support the lenient view that has become dominantly expressed by Wolf, Foot, and others. Aristotle writes in the *Nicomachean Ethics* that we should "strain" ourselves to the greatest degree possible to perform "the finest actions," and implies that those who succeed in this endeavor are "welcomed and praised by everyone" for taking the pursuit of virtue seriously.[32] In telling us to strain ourselves, Aristotle does not merely mean that we ought to do the best we can to accentuate those traits that are already present in our character state; rather, he maintains that we ought to change from being one sort of person to being another. As various neo-Aristotelians such as David Norton and Nancy Sherman have noted, Aristotle enjoins aspirants of the virtuous life to exert effort to become what they currently are not, even if this means acquiring traits with which they are not naturally endowed.[33] According to Norton and Sherman, character improvement is for Aristotle a basic requirement. As human beings, we should recognize the possibilities for future human development rather than assume that we simply are as we appear to be at any particular moment in time. Elsewhere, Aristotle is even more explicit about his view of the non-static nature of human existence:

> We ought not to follow the proverb-writers, and "think human, since you are human," or "think mortal, since you are mortal." Rather, as far as we can, we ought to be pro-immortal, and go to all lengths to live a life that expresses our supreme element; for however much this element may lack in bulk, by much more it surpasses everything in power and value.[34]

Aspiration, Aristotle claims here, is essential to human nature and so it is essential to eudaimonistic living. Aspiration involves striving to become something different, something better. In a moral context, this means that we are responsible for doing the most we can to harness our capacity to help others. It is not enough for us to act in a consistently permissible manner, and seemingly trivial activities can have a significant impact on our overall evaluation as agents. Sherman considers a couple of examples intended to convey this sense of aspiration that are not captured by mere permissibility. She writes:

> I may act permissibly in refusing to participate in an important political poll for the thin reason that I would rather resume my conversation with my friend; or again omit no obligation when I rudely cut short a rights activist at the front door, explaining that I have a book to finish and a pot of beans overboiling on the stove. These specific actions of goodwill or generosity are not required; the omissions are permissible. But I do seem, nonetheless, to lack virtue *at such moments* and, in an Aristotelian sense, fail to do what is required of virtue.[35]

If I took seriously the Aristotelian maxim to incorporate virtue into my life, Sherman argues, then I would try to be more generous in making time for others, attempt to make donations to good causes within my means, and at least not behave callously when I decide that I am unable to give of myself in these respects. To the extent that I value the pursuit of virtue, but nonetheless manage to act only permissibly (and not virtuously), I am "akratic," or dispositionally deficient, a condition that is sufficient for my moral blameworthiness as an agent.[36] "If I consistently refuse my time or money for these sorts of solicitations, giving the reason that the pot is still boiling or the book is still on the back burner," writes Sherman, "then I am chronically akratic."[37] According to Sherman's reading of Aristotle, we are never allowed to step back from our "agent" status, which would afford us the luxury of relinquishing the ongoing consideration of our developing character. This does not mean that we cannot engage in leisure activities of seemingly negligible moral import. It does mean, however, that we must prepare ourselves continually for our moral betterment.

For Aristotle, then, morality is not only conterminous with human life; it pervades it at all times.[38] Wolf's dichotomization of human life into the moral and aesthetic spheres—in which one sphere is assumed to be emphasized frequently at the expense of the other, leading to the conclusion that good human living requires us to pay less attention to "moral" concerns and to give preference to personal projects and special relations[39]—can seemingly be refuted on Aristotelian grounds. Progress in one sphere positively impacts the chances of success in the other. We do not have the luxury of removing ourselves from social institutions by seeking refuge in the nonmoral domain of the private sphere.[40] We are at all times to pursue the good life, even in leisure, which inevitably entails our moral development.

It is by this logic that we can identify heroes and saints as who they are—as agents who retain their "heroic" or "saintly" character for the duration of their lives. This is unlike Urmson's portrayal of them as persons who act in a heroic or saintly manner on one or several occasions. Instead, heroes and saints are heroic and saintly because of their enduring character. There is stability in good character, for character transcends the classification of persons on the basis of one or a few acts. In terms of our own moral development, this means that *once* we reach certain plateaus, we are beholden to staying the kind of people we have become. The new horizons from such plateaus improve our moral vision, and we cannot ignore what we see by choosing to look away. Moral betterment is a progressive notion, and we tend not to morally "undevelop."[41] Thus, if we fail to maintain an already achieved level of virtue, it is most likely because we become complacent and *stop* playing an active role in shaping our own lives. As Aristotle remarks, while it is "originally open" to the person to pursue the virtuous life, once a certain character state has been acquired it cannot easily be discarded.[42]

Good character is also stable because the virtuous person acquires "continence." According to Aristotle, the "continent" person is the one who is determined to follow through on all of the commitments implied by his or her original project. He or she is the opposite of the "incontinent" person, who knows what constitutes the correct decision but acts on appetite instead.[43] As we become continent, we become obligated to act in conformity with whatever standards correspond to our developing character.

Continent people do not allow their initial purposes to devolve into a "take it or leave it" matter, regardless of the unpredictable obstacles that stand in the way of their eventual fruition. This phenomenology accounts for why heroes and saints report with such consistency that they had no choice but to act as they did. To have acted otherwise would have meant taking a deliberate step away from what they knew to be the finer path, which in turn would have constituted an implicit denial of their identity. Thus, what we are to do or not do cannot be considered apart from the series of decisions leading up to our actions. Our dispositions are not arbitrary. Our actions are predetermined by prior actions. As the neo-Aristotelian Julia Annas notes:

> Far from giving a rigid picture of the moral life, the [Aristotelian] picture emphasizes the way that our moral life is always in a process of development. Everything we do reflects the way we have acted and affects the way we will act. We are all the time faced with new and complex situations; how we deal with them reveals what we have become and affects what we are becoming. Even the stably honest person develops every time she acts honestly; every honest action reflects a determination to continue as she is, a determination that could be undermined by unfamiliar or complicated circumstances. If her honesty is indeed unchangeable, this results not from a lack of thought but precisely from continual thought about her honest actions.[44]

Like the devout believer who constantly has to reaffirm his or her faith by struggling against pangs of doubt, the moral agent whose moral development is significantly under way cannot become mechanical about the good habits he or she has acquired. The virtuous life is one of repetition. By looking at moral actions in snapshots, an act-based model of ethics has no basis for insisting on the repetitious nature of the agent's overall moral task. Annas suggests that Aristotelian ethics, by contrast, allows a broader view of morality in which the agent's horizon extends beyond the present. Indeed, the Aristotelian approach places

> an initial stress on one's life as a whole. When I wonder about where my life is going and whether I can change it, I am asking if my life as a whole might change direction. And when I ask whether I could acquire one of the virtues, I am not asking whether I could become generous *now*. Perhaps I could not bring myself to act generously, given the way my feelings and reactions have developed, or perhaps I could act generously but it would pain me to do so. So I cannot *now* be virtuous. But it is still up to me whether I become virtuous or not; for once I am convinced that

it is important to become virtuous, I can take steps to enable myself to act virtuously—by thinking harder before the appropriate occasion and consciously resolving to do so, for example.[45]

In this passage, Annas observes that in Aristotelian ethics contentment gives way to ambivalence. Virtue's work never ends. I can defend myself against judgments of wrongdoing when I turn down opportunities to act generously. However, if I take the pursuit of a good character seriously, I cannot escape the lingering sense of dissatisfaction that I should feel, at least occasionally, when I decline. This sense of dissatisfaction, argue neo-Aristotelians like Annas, is linked with a second-order duty we have to improve our character throughout our lives, in this case, by becoming more generous, or at least generous on more occasions.

If this interpretation of Aristotle's ethics is correct, then to fail to reject our tendencies toward complacency, tendencies that in the standard view we are encouraged, but not required, to correct, constitutes a self-betrayal. To act *only* as we deontically must is in the Aristotelian model to act in "bad faith."[46] According to Sartre, when I act in bad faith I engage in a self-deceptive refusal to admit to others and myself the full extent of my freedom. I avoid anxiety in making decisions, and thereby fail to choose certain courses of action that I know, or should ultimately come to know, are incumbent upon me.[47] To the defender of an Aristotelian approach, the standard view's proponents begin to resemble Sartre's waiter:

> All his behaviour seems to us a game. He applies himself to chaining his movements as if they were mechanisms, the one regulating the other; his gestures and even his voice seem to be mechanisms; he gives himself the quickness and pitiless rapidity of things. He is playing, he is amusing himself. But what is he playing? We need not watch long before we can explain it: he is playing at being a waiter in a café. There is nothing there to surprise us.[48]

People who cease to be self-critical—those who convince themselves that they act in good faith because they break none of the rules—only act *as if* they are people who live above reproach. They are temporarily responsible to their satisfaction, but they are not enthusiastic about their responsibility. In this sense they are like Sartre's waiter. If the waiter sticks to the beaten path throughout the course of the night, then his shift will come to an end without a hitch, but at some deeper level he is a hypocrite both in his character and in his conduct.

We should therefore not live in bad faith. We should take measures at various points in our life to improve our character. That we have an aretaic duty to become better people, however, constitutes only the first of the two prongs of the thesis of moral development. It is still a significant step to move from the acknowledgment that we must be vigilant about our character development to the conclusion that we ought to expand the range of our first-order deontic duties beyond the moral minimum. To reach this conclusion, it becomes necessary to elucidate the connection between aretaic and deontic ethics. The developmentalist does this by reexamining the concept of supererogation and by asking a straightforward question: Are there circumstances under which we can ever be found morally blameworthy for failing to go above and beyond the call of duty? Is qualified supererogation—the belief that supererogation is reducible to moral obligation on some level—an option for normative ethics? David Heyd thought there was no such possibility. But for the thesis of moral development to be true, it must be possible.

Virtue Ethics, Gregory Trianosky, and the Duty to Go beyond the Call of Duty

In 1986, Gregory Trianosky published "Supererogation, Wrongdoing, and Vice: On the Autonomy of the Ethics of Virtue."[49] The point of this essay was to establish possible grounds for moral wrongdoing in persons who failed to go above and beyond the call of duty. Trianosky's essay is pioneering because it was the first in contemporary ethics to make sense of the concept of supererogation within an aretaic moral framework, an ambition Heyd had boldly declared to be incoherent just four years earlier.[50]

It is traditionally held that we cannot ever be blamed for declining to go above and beyond. In his essay, Trianosky wonders why, if the traditional view is correct, we should so often be led to make excuses when we turn down others' requests to do more than obligation requires of us. If supererogation is truly optional, then from where does the need spring to defend ourselves against charges that we are in the wrong when we do not act supererogatorily? Trianosky considers what it would mean if the excuses we made *were* indicative of how we should morally act. Such excuses would then not be of a deontic nature, but would point to our desire to deflect negative moral judgments made about our character, motives, and attitudes. Trianosky uses the example of excuse-making as a springboard for developing his view that deontic concepts are inadequate to the tasks a moral theory should set for itself and the corresponding view that an ethics of virtue may have its own autonomous criteria for making moral judgments. In challenging Heyd, Trianosky hoped not only to expand the use of the concept of supererogation to virtue theory, but also to overturn ethicists' traditional reliance on deontic concepts for making moral evaluations.

Developmentalists, for whom virtue is the instrument of moral evaluation, heartily approve of Trianosky's first objective without, however, endorsing the second. This is because according to the thesis of moral development, aretaic *and* deontic concepts are interdependent. Developmentalists' use of Trianosky is thus primarily constructive. They have a stake in defending and making use of Trianosky's general thesis while seeking to draw a different conclusion from that thesis than the one drawn by Trianosky himself.

Trianosky's analysis begins with his reassertion of the fundamental feature of the standard view of supererogation, namely, that the failure to perform an act of supererogation is morally neutral and not blameworthy. Given this characterization, it would seem inappropriate to make excuses for our behavior when we fail to supererogate. Trianosky writes:

[I]t is plausible to think that blame for failure to perform is appropriate only when the act in question is obligatory and not when it is merely supererogatory. It is also plausible to think that there is an essential connection between *blame* and *excuse* of roughly this sort: excuses function essentially to deflect blame for failure to perform. Given these assumptions, it follows that ... no excuse is ever necessary for omitting to do what is merely good to do but not required.[51]

This passage employs the same reasoning as that of the standard view's most ardent proponent, David Heyd. Since acts of supererogation are by definition optional, there are no circumstances under which one can be blamed for failing to act supererogatorily. Yet, unlike Heyd, Trianosky moves directly to a discussion of a "certain phenomenon in our shared, common-sense morality which seems puzzling in light of this conclusion."[52] The phenomenon is this: throughout the course of our lives, we are sometimes asked to go above and beyond the call of duty by individuals who regularly do so themselves, and who would, were they in our shoes, undoubtedly perform the very act they are now asking us to perform. When we are asked, we often feel that we cannot simply deny the request without feeling as though we have fallen short of our responsibility, even though it is readily acknowledged that we are being asked to go above and beyond.

An extreme but poignant example of this phenomenon is Martin Luther King, Jr.'s appeal to his followers to place themselves in harm's way by taking up the cause of civil rights through nonviolent protests. As we recall, there was an awareness on King's part that such protests were not always successful and that those who chose to protest were susceptible to suffering violent outbursts directed at them by onlooking racists and even by the police. Despite the often-realized costs and the slow-to-be-gained benefits associated with marching and protesting, in his sermons King implored his listeners to follow him, fully aware of the morally demanding nature of his plea. The *puzzling* part of this phenomenon, according to Trianosky, is that when people refuse such requests, as they do the majority of the time, they consistently react by offering excuses for their decision. The reason for this seems simple enough: "We seem often to feel uncomfortable or even ashamed that we are unwilling to do more than is required of us ... [s]o much so, that we often make [an] excuse when it isn't even true."[53] According to the standard view we would be perfectly within our right politely to reject such requests. Yet, as it happens, we tend to feel uncomfortable when doing so. This is a striking, if frequent, reaction on our part given that our commonsense intuitions confirm the supererogatory nature of the deeds in question. After all, it is not as if we are faced with the prospect of trying to get out of performing imperfect duties (which are required but whose fulfillment can occur in any number of ways) when we make such excuses. Indeed, as Trianosky observes, those who solicit our help readily acknowledge that they are asking us to go above and beyond. They know, as we know, that we are not required to say yes. Yet they *implore* us to say yes, and they often count on the success of their attempts. Just as often we tend to feel the moral pressure of their requests. Is not the very *point* of calling something supererogatory to release us from this sense of moral compulsion?

Trianosky's solution to the puzzle is to locate the motivation for our excuse-making in a desire to deflect negative judgments about ourselves. These negative judgments do not stem from any wrongdoing per se, but pertain to a sense in which we are vice-ridden, either on a stable or occurring basis.[54] That is, he suggests that when I make excuses for why I refrain from going the extra mile, I do so either because I wish to deflect negative judgments about my enduring *character*, or because I want to draw attention away from a flaw in my *motivational structure* on some particular occasion.[55] In both cases, I want to avoid negative aretaic moral judgments; for while my failure to act supererogatorily does not expose me to deontic criticism, if I am not careful about how I articulate my refusal, then I will open myself up to the charge that I am acting from a less than virtuous, or even vicious, motive. If I repeatedly excuse myself, then I become vulnerable to being accused of having a vicious character. Trianosky's point seems to be that I am often quick to make excuses for why I cannot go above and beyond the call of duty on a particular occasion because when I am asked by those who themselves would help were they in my position, I recognize in myself the feeling of indifference and am dismayed by this reaction. I do not desire to help others in the way I am being asked. Moreover, I am not disposed to attain such a desire, whereas it is clear to me that others, including the person making the request, do not have the same aretaic shortcomings. I thus seek to obscure from others what I either discover or already know to be a major flaw in my motivational structure, if not my character.[56] As this becomes habitual, the more I notice the frequency with which I decline to go above and beyond, the more my lack of motivation to improve my character becomes apparent, and the more I will implement excuses.

If instances of excuse-making of this sort are legitimate indicators of flaws in our character and motivational structure—and they seem to be— then purely deontic criteria are in and of themselves incomplete as a means of rendering moral judgments. Our tendency to offer excuses when we fail to go above and beyond the call of duty is a signal that even we ourselves believe that we ought to be continually morally improving. Hence there is a sense in which we are blameworthy if we live our lives without trying to do so. Yet, if we consulted deontic criteria alone in making moral judgments, we could never be found blameworthy in this respect.

Trianosky thinks that the looseness of fit between wrongdoing and vice follows directly from this observation. Prominent defects in an agent's motivational structure may go unnoticed from a deontic point of view, but this does not mean we should accept the agent's character as morally adequate. Trianosky explains:

> [I]f this defect in motivational structure reflects a standing trait, then the agent may well also be guilty of a certain *hypocrisy*. Imagine that his concern for the well-being of others regularly vanishes when his obligations come to an end, to be replaced by a disposition to coldly calculated self-interest. Then we may reasonably suspect that what altruistic concern he seems to display in fulfilling his obligations is itself really a sham. In all likelihood, real concern for others is not defined by the same boundaries that define our obligations. Conscientious such an agent may be. But, we suspect, he is conscientious as the Pharisees described in the New Testament were conscientious. He swerves not one jot from what the law requires, but has no real human concern in his heart. This hypocrisy is also a vice, a genuine defect of *character*, which might be revealed in— and perhaps only in—the consistent refusal to do what is beyond duty.[57]

In this passage Trianosky demonstrates how someone who "conscientiously" never fails to do his or her duty, but who at the same time *consistently* does not go above and beyond, is a hypocrite and thus warrants a negative moral judgment. He reasons that since there is no provision in deontic ethics to characterize such a person, deontic ethics must be defective. Trianosky takes the example of the stereotypical "Pharisee" as incontrovertible evidence that judgments about character are autonomous from, and in fact may be more telling than, judgments about the rightness or wrongness of an agent's actions. His analysis is compatible with the self-understanding of heroes and saints, at least as heroes and saints have been characterized in this book, as noteworthily virtuous persons. Heroes and saints are at their core the opposite of the person who "swerves not one jot from the law" but who lacks "real human concern." Their altruism is not motivated by a calculation based on self-interest. It springs from the need of the Other. Since we identify heroes and saints, the most morally righteous among us, by their heroic and saintly character, not by their deeds alone, it would seem that virtue is a much more powerful instrument than conduct, in terms of making moral judgments.

Does this mean that we should dispense with deontic criteria altogether in favor of adopting an autonomous aretaic moral theory? According to the developmentalist, we should not. The developmentalist wagers that Trianosky's important insight—that good character, not right action, is necessary to overcome moral complacency—just as likely supports as it belies an ultimately demonstrable connection between the deontic and aretaic spheres. Trianosky argues that since deontic concepts are insufficient as a means of assessing the overall goodness of an agent, they ought to be replaced by aretaic ones, and he is right that an exclusive reliance on deontic concepts induces moral complacency. But aretaic concepts, which are necessary and distinct from deontic ones, can also *inform* our original assumptions about rightness and wrongness and ultimately lead us to alter our conception of what is deontically required. Trianosky's complaint about deontic ethics is that it is conceivable that a moral agent could be deontically superlative and simultaneously failing from an aretaic point of view. This is supported by the observation that people sometimes exhibit vice when they are technically guilty of no deontic wrongdoing. By contrast, in aretaic ethics the fully virtuous person, whose nature precludes him or her from ever regarding the deontic moral minimum as sufficient, does not seem to be lacking *either* from a deontic or an aretaic point of view. Trianosky thinks this comparison between the fully virtuous person and the deontic exemplar demonstrates the superiority of an ethics based exclusively on aretaic criteria.

But what is it to become more virtuous? Trianosky himself gives us a clue when he ties virtue to one's willingness to go beyond the call of duty. If we want to be virtuous we should not act like stereotypical Pharisees, who fulfill only a specified set of duties over the span of their lives. Fully virtuous persons, who presumably *become* virtuous over time, tend not to make the same rigid distinctions as the deontically superlative agent between duty and supererogation. What this suggests is that the more virtuous we become, the less strenuously we are inclined to insist on the existence of optional, praiseworthy deeds that exceed duty. Now, Trianosky invokes this tendency as evidence that the overall *telos* of morality is aretaic, whereby one's "duty" comes to signify what the fully virtuous person would do were he or she in the agent's shoes. In contrast, the developmentalist is inclined to interpret the same phenomenon as pointing to a modification within the deontic sphere that corresponds to our improvement in character. We may fully agree with Trianosky when he remarks that one's willingness to go above and beyond is a sign of virtue. But over a lifetime, the virtue that enables one to be willing to do so catalyzes a reassessment of just what *is* considered going above and beyond the call of duty and what *is* considered part of duty. We still need the deontic *concepts* of duty and supererogation, in other words, to be able to identify our moral responsibilities at each successive stage of development. This is *how* our "duty" is ultimately known from an aretaic point of view. On a concrete level, what the fully virtuous person considers to be his or her duty—meaning what the fully virtuous person "would do"—is understood by the less virtuous person to be part of the supererogatory.

Just as deontic concepts are not in and of themselves adequate for providing us with the tools for making important moral judgments, as Trianosky rightly charges, so is it the case that an aretaic *telos* requires the retention of the deontic concepts of duty and supererogation as a yardstick to which agents may refer in order to measure their distance from the fully virtuous person. One advantage of retaining both deontic and aretaic concepts in moral theory, as opposed to adopting a purely aretaic moral theory, is that the actions of a virtuous person do not become "self-justifying."[58] The deontic concepts of duty and supererogation allow one to come to a determination about right action that does not rely on the potentially ambiguous notion of "what a virtuous person would do." Given that there is *some* acknowledged boundary between duty and supererogation by which an impartial standard of minimal moral requirement is originally determined,[59] there will always be an additional reference point *besides* our predictions of how a virtuous person would act to determine what ought to be done. And as one undergoes moral development, one can continually reassess what constitutes right action by taking note of the way the boundary between duty and supererogation has shifted from its initial position. Critics of virtue ethics frequently worry that it is "structurally unable to say much of anything" about what people ought to do.[60] The developmentalist's modified ethics of virtue, which incorporates deontic concepts, is not susceptible to such a charge, although it is still based on the Aristotelian idea that character is foundational.

Taking a stance against "eliminatism," the view that an ethical theory based entirely on character can do all the work of ethics,[61] does not imply that the virtues have a secondary status. With Trianosky, the developmentalist maintains that right action, when it is action beyond the moral minimum, is conceptually derived from certain antecedently specified character traits. These are the traits exhibited by progressing moral agents. They are not merely ideals embodied by the fully virtuous exemplar, which we should strive to heed as much as we can.[62] They are normatively guiding traits, directly informing us of what our moral duties are in the present. In this way, the developmentalist embraces a theory of virtue that envisions a mutually reciprocal relationship existing between states of character and action, in which character gives us knowledge of the right course of action (duty) while the performance of right acts reinforces our good character (virtue).[63]

Duty and Virtue in Jewish and Christian Thought and Scripture

This way of conceiving of the relationship between duty and virtue within a virtue theory generally is, not surprisingly, present in the basic tenets of Hebrew and Christian scripture. In both Judaism and Christianity, the ideal of character to which humans are meant to conform is God, in whose image humans are made (Genesis 1:27). In the Jewish tradition, this doctrine is confirmed in traditional verses from the Torah such as "Ye shall be holy, for I the Lord your God am holy" (Leviticus 19:2); "now, Israel, what doth the Lord thy God require of thee ... but to walk in all his ways and to love Him ..." (Deuteronomy 10:12; 28:9); and "Righteousness, righteousness shalt thou pursue" (Deuteronomy 17:20). The passage from Leviticus goes on to introduce a list of traits that include issues of moral concern (e.g., charity, justice, honesty, kindness to the disadvantaged).[64] These are essentially cast as virtues expressible in commands, which no pre-specified set of duties can fully encompass. The Ten Commandments are indispensable as a specification of what is minimally required, and they lead people in the direction of right living, but they are incomplete when judged from the perspective of Jewish ethics. In this light, the character traits that Jews are enjoined to cultivate in Leviticus and Deuteronomy become ones that inform them of the additional moral requirements for which they also may come to be accountable. As Menachem Kellner explains:

> Fully aware ... that no specification of legal obligations can cover every moral dilemma, the rabbis of the Mishnah and Talmud rely on a number of broad spectrum Biblical commands ... and on the *obligation* to go beyond the letter of the law in fulfillment of God's will—to demand

supererogatory behavior from Jews. Such a demand may be justified on the grounds that one never fully satisfies the obligation to imitate God.[65]

The "broad" commands, as well as the obligation to act *lifnim mishurat hadin*, are essentially commands to imitate God, the ideal being, and so they are commands to act virtuously. Virtue, in turn, here measured by the Jew's success in his or her attempt to follow in God's path, is the instrument through which right living is attained. Hence Moses Maimonides remarks at the end of *The Guide of the Perplexed* that moral excellence is reflected in right conduct attained through the cultivation of the divine traits of loving-kindness, justice, and righteousness.[66]

The relationship between virtue and duty understood to be present in the thesis of moral development is similarly emphasized in Christian ethics. The Gospel of Matthew, for example, focuses on an internalization of righteous action that calls attention to both dispositions and character states, as well as right conduct.[67] As Joseph Kotva notes:

> Matthew ... presumes a connection between the internal and the external: one's conduct (the external) flows from and reflects one's inner character (the internal). Thus, good or evil fruit is the manifestation of a good or evil tree (3:8, 10; 7:15–20; 12:33); and people will render account at the judgment for every careless word because such words manifest the true character of one's disposition and heart (12:34–37). . . . Even Jesus' activities of healing and feeding the crowds are portrayed as flowing from the disposition or emotion of "compassion" (14:14; 15:32; 20:34; cf. 9:36).[68]

We are reminded of Trianosky's remark about the Pharisee who lacks authenticity because he follows the law for appearance's sake without caring about the law's larger purpose. Matthew does not dispense with rules and actions. While the law remains necessary, however, it remains morally relevant only insofar as it makes reference to the attitude that justifies it. External action and internal disposition are equally necessary for the tree to grow and bear good fruit. This interpretation of the relationship between duty and virtue in the Book of Matthew reflects James Keenan's summary of how goodness and rightness function in contemporary Thomistic Christian thought. "Goodness," Keenan writes,

> is descriptive of the first and most formal movement in a person. Unlike earlier approaches, goodness is not a judgment consequent to action, but a judgment antecedent to action. Rightness, on the other hand, concerns whether one's life and actions attain what is necessary for the protection

and the promotion of values. As attaining pertains to rightness, striving
pertains to goodness.... Goodness moves one to strive for rightness.
Badness is failing to move oneself.[69]

Goodness has antecedent priority over rightness, though rightness is
indispensable in its own right insofar as it serves as a vindication of what
is in fact good about the virtues. Like Kotva, Keenan emphasizes the
example of the Pharisees, who, while "right-doing," were judged to fall
short because they lacked the aretaic *motivation* to do right that comes
from a striving "pure heart."[70] However, it is right action, as the fruit of
goodness, that provides for the attainment of a stable, value-laden existence within which it becomes ever more possible to strive.

The presence of both deontic and aretaic concepts in scripture and Jewish and Christian thought gives momentum to the project of the developmentalist, if for no other reason than that a clear picture of how duty and
virtue can interrelate is offered in two long-standing traditions. Over and
against models based exclusively on rules, principles, and actions, or models based purely on dispositions and feelings, a virtue ethics that incorporates deontic concepts like duty and supererogation is able to reflect on both
the external and the internal qualities of human action. Beyond the level
of minimal moral requirement, it is true that the kind of virtue ethics
which the developmentalist favors does not equally stress action and character. Duty, at advanced stages of moral development, is derived from character. However, going with the metaphor expressed in Matthew, it is only
through the expression of character *in* action that we can see how well the
tree has, in fact, grown and what sort of growing it still has left to do.

In this section, I have located the normative grounds for the aretaic
meta-duty to improve our character in Aristotle's ethics and have demonstrated the connection that can be shown to exist between the aretaic and
deontic spheres. I have yet to show whether or not the thesis of moral
development is psychologically realistic. How does moral development
work for agents who, from the start of their moral existence, are "devel-
opmentally challenged" insofar as their character is concerned? In the next
section, I offer suggestions for how to go about acquiring the moral virtues, even when their acquisition seems unlikely.

PSYCHOLOGICAL REALISM AND THE THESIS OF MORAL DEVELOPMENT

Acquiring the Virtues

One of the strengths of Urmson's essay "Saints and Heroes" is its sensitivity to the necessity of constructing an ethics that takes into account
human psychology. We can only be morally required to perform actions

that are within the scope of what we reasonably can be expected to do. Not all moral theories attempt to show the relevance of psychology to considerations of what we ought to do. Some look for justifications for rightness and wrongness, goodness of character, and other normative concepts in "moral reason," thereby assuming that it is the agent's responsibility to adapt his or her conduct to whatever requirements have been sanctioned by the theory in question. According to this view, ethics is understood to be autonomous in the sense that it "provides ideals of agency that do not reflect actual psychological realities or existing human practices."[71] Urmson, to his credit, rejects as untenable the prospect of a moral theory whose motivational structure current or future members of our species empirically are not likely to adopt. If ethics is *completely* independent of human psychology, it remains only theoretically realizable. But ethics must be more. It must "work" for those to whom it is meant to apply.

In holding this view, Urmson finds himself in conflict with classical thinkers like Immanuel Kant, who wrote in the *Groundwork of the Metaphysics of Morals*: "The ground of obligation must be looked for, not in the nature of man nor in the circumstances in the world in which he is placed, but solely *a priori* in the concepts of pure reason."[72] The charge is that Kant's view is psychologically unrealistic because it assumes that edicts of moral reason will override our commonsense intuitions about what we are likely to be able to do for others when the two come into conflict. When such conflicts arise, a de jure endorsement of the moral law is often met with a de facto erosion of it. Urmson makes this point concretely by taking two examples from history:

> [T]he prohibition laws asked too much of the American people and were consequently broken systematically; and as people got used to breaking the law a general lowering of respect for the law naturally followed; it no longer seemed that the law was something that everyone could be expected to obey. Similarly in Britain gambling laws, some of which are utterly impractical, have fallen into contempt as a body.[73]

Reflection on these examples leads Urmson to conclude that regardless of what moral reason is said to dictate, if one were to represent an excessively demanding act as part of what is morally required, "the effect would be to lower the urgency and stringency that the notion of duty does in fact possess."[74] Urmson's point underscores the importance of not neglecting the way in which motivation and psychology impact the field of ethics.[75] The question is: what, exactly, constitutes "excessively demanding"?

According to Urmson, it is unreasonable ever to expect anyone to achieve more than the moral minimum. The issue is whether this view cedes too much to the idea that human nature poses limits on moral requirement. A more moderate view than Urmson's is raised by Owen Flanagan, who argues that almost every contemporary moral tradition can be adapted to close the gap between reason and motivation as long as it respects the following metaethical principle:

> Principle of Minimal Psychological Realism (PMPR): Make sure when constructing a moral theory or projecting a moral ideal that the character, decision processing, and behavior prescribed are possible, or are perceived to be possible, for creatures like us.[76]

PMPR is intended as a *constraining* feature of any good moral theory; duties must be considered real options, or by definition they cannot be required for human beings. At the same time, PMPR does not preclude requirements from being morally demanding or even realizable by agents at some future date.[77] Urmson takes the truism that ethics must not neglect human nature to be a justification for the equation of duty with minimal moral requirement. However, PMPR permits moral theories to be more demanding than minimal moral requirement. But how much more demanding? Can PMPR, for example, accommodate the thesis of moral development, which is based on the stringent Aristotelian maxim that we ought always to be improving our character?

One advantage of the developmentalist's Aristotelian approach when compared with other morally demanding alternatives is that it proceeds from the bottom up. Our motivation for acting in this or that way does not depend on demands imposed on us by "morality," construed as an objective, external imposition. Rather, it derives from our unique set of strengths and capacities and our general desire to see these traits flourish to the greatest extent possible.[78] This feature of Aristotelian ethics has on occasion been positively incorporated into the moral frameworks of non-Aristotelian theorists, such as John Rawls. In *A Theory of Justice*, Rawls generates the principles of justice, and he then asks whether they are the sole constraining features of morality and, drawing upon Aristotle's *Nicomachean Ethics*, determines that there are psychological reasons to pursue our life plans that are consistent with the principles of justice.[79] To this end, he introduces the "Aristotelian Principle," which states that "other things being equal, human beings enjoy the exercise of their realized capacities (their innate or trained abilities), and this enjoyment increases the more the capacity is realized, or the greater its complexity."[80] The Aristotelian Principle is a principle of motivation that expresses a "psychological law":

[T]he principle implies that as a person's capacities increase over time (brought about by physiological and biological maturation, for example, the development of the nervous system in a young child), and as he trains these capacities and learns how to exercise them, *he will in due course come to prefer the more complex activities that he can now engage in which call upon his newly realized abilities.* The simpler things he enjoyed before are no longer sufficiently interesting or attractive.... As we witness the exercise of well-trained abilities by others, these displays are enjoyed by us and arouse a desire that we should be able to do the same things ourselves. We want to be like those persons who can exercise the abilities that we find latent in our nature.[81]

According to Rawls's reading, Aristotle maintains that human beings actively seek a level of achievement that dynamically moves beyond the level to which they are currently accustomed. When activities do not satisfy the Aristotelian Principle our participation in them will make us feel uncomfortably bored with our lives. In order to maintain our self-respect we must work continually toward our future progress.[82] Others who are at more advanced levels of accomplishment spur us on by their example.[83]

Rawls helpfully lays bare the process of how we change from one sort of person to another according to Aristotle's view. We become our future selves after exposure to the possibility of changing is revealed by others who already possess the traits we desire; subsequently, we struggle to cultivate such traits ourselves. In other words, we discover whether we can possess the qualities that virtuous persons have by actually trying out their way of life. The virtues, Aristotle observes,

we acquire, just as we acquire crafts, by having previously activated them. For we learn a craft by producing the same product that we must produce when we have learned it, becoming builders, e.g., by building and harpists by playing the harp; so also, then, we become just be doing just actions, temperate by doing temperate actions, brave by doing brave actions.[84]

According to Aristotle, the habituation of a virtue, while slow going over a period of time, is in every instance initiated by a deliberate decision on the part of the agent to begin. We are to "plunge right in," so to speak, although our doing so may initially come as an uncomfortable shock. As we get better at those activities at which we are initially unskilled, we become more inspired to pursue new levels of achievement. In turn, our accomplishments renew our desire to continue striving. Like the novice mountain climber who cannot begin to appreciate the task ahead of him before taking the first step, and who continues to remain in the dark before finally getting a glimpse at the precipice, we must initially "feel our way" with respect to becoming better people, guided by what we hear by way of advice from sources we regard as trustworthy. And, just as the mountain climber becomes inspired upon reflecting mid-journey on his evident progress, leading him to climb at an even faster pace, we come to recognize our increasing capacity to be virtuous, leading us also to become more committed to the moral task of which we were once only vaguely aware.

To be sure, there is discomfort, and perhaps even pain involved in the initial stages of progress. However, such discomfort or pain has a way of abating as a beginner advances. We may reflect upon another example drawn from the realm of athletics in order to bring the psychological state of the beginning moral agent into further clarity. Consider the person who is out of shape, who has heard it said that she ought to get into shape, and who, as a result, decides one day to take a run. Very likely, she will not enjoy her first experience either while running or shortly afterwards, when her muscles will be stiff and sore. But later, when she reflects upon her accomplishment, she will feel a certain degree of satisfaction, and her next run will likely be a more rewarding experience. In the same way, the initial unpleasantness of trying to change—either our physical condition or the state of our moral character—while almost always an obstacle to the beginner, should not be considered an insurmountable obstacle. Indeed, we can *expect* to experience this kind of unpleasantness whenever we wish to change ourselves in some fundamental way. But, after a time, we can also expect such unpleasantness to give way to a kind of satisfaction. Predictions about how much we can change should not be based on initial impressions of how difficult change will be. In order to claim legitimately that we have failed at one activity or another, we must at least have been trying in earnest over an extended period. However, a sustained effort to succeed will likely produce positive results.

At this point, the critic may be inclined to ask how the defender of the thesis of moral development can mount an appeal to those who do not wish to ascend the mountain in the first place. What does one say to the person who has no desire to begin to improve him- or herself? The Aristotelian model works best for those who have already determined that they are going to be practitioners of virtue, in spite of their degree of inexperience. However, it apparently gives little directive to beginners deprived of good examples after which to fashion their desires, dispositions, and actions. In this case, beginners do not even know who the virtuous are, let alone why they should be recognized as people to be emulated. This may be true even if the virtuous go out of their way to make themselves available to the thoroughly nonvirtuous; for the nonvirtuous are not prepared to accept virtuous persons' reasons for acting the way that they do. Beginners must be able to grasp *some* of the virtuoso's reasons, runs this objection, even if this consists in the mere recognition that the virtuoso has something valuable to teach them. This problem is complicated by the consideration that the more accustomed people become to living nonvirtuous lives, whether through chance circumstances of birth and upbringing or by choice, the harder it will be to convert them later on. If an Aristotelian ethic, which claims to be so broad in scope as to account for human nature itself, also makes an appeal to natural or circumstantial advantages that some agents enjoy over others, then how can it work ubiquitously, as it is intended to do? Julia Annas, a staunch defender of the Aristotelian approach, raises essentially the same question in her discussion of virtue. According to Aristotle's position, she writes,

> the virtuous know that they are doing the right thing because this judgment can be defended by, and explained to, the virtuous and aspirants of virtue. But, while the virtuous can encourage and defend one another, it seems that they have little to say to the non-virtuous, the person who rejects their judgments or does not accept their examples as fixing the content of particular virtues. The criterion of right action thus turns out to be defended in a way that looks circular. This action is the right thing to do, we are told, because it is what a virtuous person would do; and the virtuous person is the person with the disposition to do just this kind of thing. So on this position the virtuous seem to have nothing seriously to discuss with the non-virtuous: the virtuous person seems already precluded from accepting the non-virtuous person's challenge on an action.... [Although] once one has developed habits of judgment and feeling, these will all go on as mutually reinforcing one another, as we have seen, it becomes a mystery how the non-virtuous person could ever become 'converted' to the life of virtue, which to the person who has developed in a different way would seem to have no appeal.[85]

How do thoroughly nonvirtuous persons become virtuous enough to recognize that they need to acquire virtue? Do we not already have to *be* virtuous to *become* more virtuous? Aristotle himself rhetorically asks this question, acknowledging the charge of circularity that the critic might be inclined to raise against his own position:

> [S]omeone might raise this puzzle: "What do you mean by saying that to become just we must first do just actions and to become temperate

we must first do temperate actions? For if we do what is just or temperate, we must already be just or temperate."[86]

Buttressing this sentiment, Aristotle states elsewhere that if we are to do what is just or temperate, we must at least consider justice and temperance to be qualities we want to develop in our character. He explains:

[F]or actions expressing virtue to be done temperately or justly (and hence well) it does not suffice that they are themselves in the right state. Rather, the agent must also be in the right state when he does them. First he must know (that he is doing virtuous actions); second, he must decide on them, and decide on them for themselves; and third, he must also do them from a firm and unchanging state.[87]

Those who decide for the first time to incorporate a virtue such as justice or temperance into their own lives have a lot to fulfill. They must be propelled by the foreknowledge that they seek the good, they must know what is intrinsically worthy about this pursuit, and they must take the objective seriously, by not being too quick to give up on it. In short, it looks as though the beginner must not treat the endeavor as a beginner, but as someone advanced enough to meet at least these necessary criteria. What, if any, resources are at the beginner's disposal to become more advanced even if becoming more advanced is a desire that is not available to the beginner him- or herself?

An Aristotelian answer to this query lies in the reflection that human beings are interdependent, vulnerable creatures whose individual acquisition of any kind of skill depends on the society in which such a skill would ultimately be practiced. The Aristotelian grants that agents at beginning stages of development have no choice but to rely on the shared views of others for guidance. They must take certain things on faith alone. While over time, the development of a virtue will involve the testing and adjusting of what they are told to do by the various authorities to which they appeal, the burden of appealing to such authorities in the first place, which requires at least the attributes of humility and initiative, rests on their shoulders alone. Beginners must trust. They must know themselves to be beginners, and they must initially look elsewhere for help in elevating themselves. The value of tradition and community is that it fulfills this function.

This response, however, requires further refinement; for, assuming that beginners *do* decide to trust others to help them reform their character, the critic may still ask how they will eventually become their own person, with their own, individually developed set of dispositions, attitudes, and beliefs.

Becoming virtuous involves forging a distinctive identity and not merely parroting the actions and attitudes of a mentor. How do moral agents at beginning stages of moral development, who are required to rely on their mentors so thoroughly, manage to escape the trap of blind mimesis?[88]

According to the thesis of moral development, after the initial movement of trust, in which we acknowledge that we need the help of others more virtuous than us, we can very quickly come to agree with or dissent from whatever advice we receive. Thus, practitioners of virtue at an intermediate stage may well, in the process of their ongoing development, revise or reject some of the initial judgments they accepted when first learning to be virtuous. It is true that beginners proceed from certain givens about what is right to do, which must be taken on faith alone. Nevertheless, in the process of development they will come to acquire the capacity for reflection that enables them to adopt a critical attitude toward these givens and all other judgments about actions; if and when they should decide to part company with the initial consensus, they can give reasons for so doing.[89]

The journey toward virtue can thus be explained in three stages. The first stage consists of an initial act of trust in which beginning moral agents esteem and subsequently try to emulate someone whom they identify as more virtuous than they are. This initial stage of mimesis is followed by a gradual habituation process in which beginners acquire virtue. During this second stage beginners become proficient at their mentors' skills, and in the process they discover and become inspired by the fact that they are morally capable of doing more than they might have initially thought. In the final stage, developing moral agents may engage in reasoned reflection, subjecting their current set of beliefs to scrutiny and, potentially, to revision. It is in this latter stage that moral agents acquire some distance from the virtuosi who serve as their mentors. The third stage does not pick up precisely where the second stage ends. Following the initial act of trust, in which beginners make the decision to change through the help of others more advanced, the next two stages of habituation and reasoned reflection work in a dialectical fashion. As developing agents become more virtuous, they acquire the insight that will enable them to regard their moral progress self-critically, which in turn equips them to choose their path of development more precisely.

There will always be a sense in which the initial act of mimesis, when beginning moral agents make their movement toward the virtuoso, is and remains an act of sheer trust. The beginner must depend on the virtuoso until he or she becomes experienced. However, since any given virtuoso presumably represents a consensus of authoritative voices, most likely the beginner will only vaguely be pointed in the right direction. Whereas

Aristotle places a lot of emphasis on trusting the right authorities while we are young,[90] his point can be broadened to suggest that our moral traditions can continue to have a positive influence on us throughout our lives.

It seems, then, that the beginner who lives in a community whose values are informed by a particular moral or religious tradition has the resources to advance beyond his or her current level of moral development. There is another reason that the beginner is not faced with a hopeless task, however—a reason which is related to the nature of the virtues themselves. We pursue the virtues, Aristotle repeatedly argues, because they are intrinsically good. They are "choiceworthy" in themselves, apart from any advantage they bestow upon us.[91] We are able to identify the kind of people we admire on the basis of whether or not they possess these traits *because* of the kinds of beings we are. What Aristotle implies here is that by virtue of human nature we are naturally disposed to know what is virtuous. We are, but for exceptional cases, born with the capacity not only to recognize bravery, generosity, compassion, benevolence, and other virtues, but also to understand intuitively why they are valuable. For this reason, the beginning moral agent is slightly ahead of the game when compared with, for example, a person learning to play chess, or a practitioner of some other craft. We are all, Aristotle posits, endowed with the propensity to develop our character.[92]

Thus, unless those at beginning stages of moral development stubbornly refuse to do so, they have enough resources at their disposal within their community to get started on their journey toward betterment. Although manifested variously from individual to individual, the pursuit of the good is a thoroughly public affair. It is no secret, for example, that we ought to strive to become virtuous, and thereby other-regarding. The major unknown that faces us at the outset is just *how* other-regarding we will ultimately be able to become.

This final consideration leads us to raise another set of issues about the morally developing agent's journey. These pertain to the expert rather than to the beginner. So far, I have asked whether or not the thesis of moral development is too demanding to be considered psychologically realistic, and I have determined that it is not. But what does this conclusion imply in terms of our *ongoing* development? Does it continue forever? Does it halt? Do striving agents reach natural endpoints, beyond which it is truly infeasible to expect them to develop any further? If not, then what distinguishes the developmentalist from the perfectionist who requires the pursuit of the maximal development of all human capacities, or from the consequentialist who requires the pursuit of the overall good generally?

The Thesis of Moral Development as Distinct from Perfectionism and Consequentialism

The developmentalist's view that what is right requires ongoing reference to our developing character invites comparisons to positions that lie at the opposite extreme of moral minimalism. In maintaining that the category of supererogation is used too readily by moral minimalists, defenders of the kind of Aristotelianism suggested above, who put so much emphasis on virtue, can be accused of overcorrecting in the other direction by making the search for the good never-ending and all-encompassing. Can we meaningfully differentiate the thesis of moral development from maximally demanding moral approaches, such as perfectionism or consequentialism?

Perfectionism, as it will be understood here, is the position that what is ultimately good is the pursuit of the elements of an ideal, or "perfect," human life, that is, a life that completely realizes those human characteristics that are both exceptional and essential.[93] According to perfectionism, it is "objectively" good for us to pursue ideals; it is good regardless of whether we happen to desire it. There can be no sense in which we are *too* ambitious with respect to becoming better.[94] Perfectionism aims at the maximization of the achievement of human excellence in all of our intellectual and moral faculties.[95]

Consequentialism is similar to perfectionism in its impartialist endorsement of an "objective" moral standard, but it modifies the emphasis the perfectionist places on self-regard. Specifically, consequentialism holds us morally responsible for performing whatever actions lead to the best overall results. In the realization of this objective, it does not acknowledge limits to the number, kind, or severity of altruistic sacrifices that an agent might be obliged to make. The pursuit of the overall good reigns supreme. An individual's interests count as one vote and are given equal weight to those of all other agents.

Notwithstanding their respective differences (e.g., perfectionism is broader than consequentialism insofar as it promotes the harnessing of nonmoral as well as moral virtues), two important commonalities distinguish both of these approaches from the thesis of moral development. First, unlike the thesis of moral development, both perfectionism and consequentialism are agent-neutral insofar as they identify an "objectively" good "final end," a goal that applies invariably to each agent. In perfectionism, the goal is to become an excellent, well-rounded individual who possesses a balanced mix and abundance of the intellectual and moral virtues. In consequentialism, the goal is to routinize our actions so that they will always produce the best results in terms of the overall good. The developmentalist's approach, by contrast, is agent-relative: what I must do will always take into account the fact that it is I, and not someone else, who is the agent. This consideration will tend to limit what I am required to do (either for myself or for others). Second, both perfectionism and consequentialism are *maximizing* moralities: the theories require us to work as hard as we can until we have achieved the greatest perfection or until we have realized the greatest good. Again, by contrast, the thesis of moral development requires only that we devote ourselves to our continual improvement. Both the maximizing models and the more gradualist model of moral development require us to strain ourselves to expand the range of our moral capabilities. However, success on the one hand pertains to how far progress is made on an absolute scale, while success on the other is measured in terms of incremental improvements. Ideals, in the developmentalist's view, importantly retain their "ideal" status, and success is measured not in the binary terms of whether or not the most or the best has been done, but against the perception we have of our own potential to improve. To return to the example of the mountain climber, for the developmentalist, the point is not to get to the summit but to continue climbing. It is true that the summit itself for each climber is ultimately the same; moral agents in each model advance toward the same goal. Nevertheless, only in maximizing moral theories is each climber judged by how far he or she falls short of the top. By contrast, the developmentalist recognizes that, due to human finitude, the top is out reach for most people. In our earnest attempts to become better climbers, we are not infinitely trainable.[96]

The contrast between these two ethical models serves to highlight a major supposition of developmentalists, namely, that moral development is a gradual process. The "higher flights" of morality, as Urmson called them, can only be attained by climbing step by step, and each climber has a different starting point. The prospect of getting to the top of the mountain is not the focus so much as getting to the next plateau. According to the developmentalist, we *all*, no matter what our natural capacities, have the same potential to flourish. To be sure, the person who makes the most of the least warrants more esteem than the underachiever born with talents that in the first instance place him or her objectively closer to the fully virtuous person.[97]

The developmentalist's gradualist view of moral ascent thus diverges sharply from the consequentialist's demand that everyone everywhere begin immediately to promote the overall good. Developmentalists allow that there may be agent-specific reasons that exempt particular persons at particular times from making certain sacrifices. Consequentialists make no such provision. An example might help to clarify the difference between the two schools of thought. Take the case of two girls, one who has been spoiled by the excessive materialism of her parents, and another who has been reared to appreciate the importance of sharing with others. While both the developmentalist and the consequentialist (and not the unqualified supererogationist) would argue that it is to some degree incumbent on each girl to share her large bag of cookies with her hungry classmates, only the developmentalist would contend that the burden to do so is not shared by the two girls equally. This is because the developmentalist thinks that it is morally relevant that the two girls have been brought up differently, and furthermore thinks that how the girls have been reared impacts their respective moral capacities, which in turn affects what is morally required of them. In this example, the spoiled girl labors under the handicap of lacking virtuous guidance from her parents. Specifically, she has not been sufficiently trained in matters of generosity and friend-making. These are virtues that the girl who is not spoiled does possess, and whose possession makes easier for her the performance of altruistic actions like that of sharing with others. According to the developmentalist, the circumstance of the spoiled girl's morally disadvantaged background should mitigate against the inclination to judge her negatively when we notice the resistance she displays upon being asked to give away some of her cookies. It is likely that over time she will come to learn through experience what is good about sharing with others. This will happen when people point out to her *that* she is selfish and proceed to explain to her *what is wrong* with selfishness. If at this point she does not attempt to dispose herself to become less selfish, which will result in her failure to *be* less selfish, she becomes morally blameworthy in a way she was not before. The means by which the consequentialist engages in a moral evaluation of the two girls is, by contrast, much simpler. It depends strictly on the actions that each girl takes, each time she takes them, and it makes no concessions for the circumstances that incline one girl to act differently from the other.

    To clarify the developmentalist's view a little further, we may turn from the relatively benign example just mentioned to the far more serious and controversial one discussed in chapter 3. According to consequentialism, bystanders and rescuers shared exactly the same duty to save the Jews from Hitler (provided that both had an equal opportunity to rescue). By contrast, according to the thesis of moral development, rescuers, whose virtuous character enabled them to perceive the overriding moral urgency of rescuing more vividly than bystanders could, arguably had a duty to rescue, thereby putting themselves and their families at great risk, while bystanders did not. While developmentalists suggest, against minimalists, that we should not simply understand the phenomenon of rescuing as an instance of supererogatory behavior, they also maintain that, given the great costs involved, rescuing became one's duty, strictly obligatory as all moral duties are, only for those who had the requisite amount of virtue to be able to perceive it as such and to act on that perception. Developmentalists reason in the following way. Although there were compelling reasons that bystanders ought to have intervened on behalf of Jews, these reasons were outweighed from the bystanders' point of view by the costliness of rescuing and the risk in which rescue efforts potentially placed their families. Lacking the virtuous insight to be able to perceive the *overriding* moral urgency of rescuing, bystanders were caught in a moral conflict, forced to deliberate about the extent to which costs to family and self were to take priority over the benefits to a recipient who was a stranger. The greater these costs in the scenario, the more compelling were the bystanders' reasons to regard rescue efforts as supererogatory. Righteous gentiles, whose virtuous perception and courage enabled them legitimately to maintain the irrelevance of such costs to the question of whether they were morally required to rescue, had an equally compelling case for regarding their conduct as obligatory. We might pause to notice the seemingly controversial claim that is being made on behalf of the developmentalist. Indeed, it appears that what is being suggested is that bystanders were justified in not intervening in Hitler's widespread campaign to eliminate the Jews from Europe, which, if true, would imply that well-known Holocaust theologians, such as Elie Wiesel, are wrong to have suggested that bystanders engaged in morally culpable behavior.

Such a conclusion, however, would be hastily drawn. The thesis of moral development does not let bystanders off the hook; it is simply subtler than maximalist positions such as consequentialism with respect to how it dispenses blame among bystanders for their inaction. In claiming that bystanders lacked rescuers' capacity to see and to act on the overriding moral nature of the claim placed on them by the faceless, destitute Jewish Other, the developmentalist does *not* at the same time claim that bystanders were released from the obligation of *disposing* themselves to become the kind of people who could come to possess this capacity over time. Indeed, the majority of bystanders, who were not as virtuous as rescuers, presumably could see through exposure to rescuers in proximity to them that if they *were* more virtuous then they would become better equipped to act rightly, in this case by intervening on behalf of Hitler's helpless victims. Given the further premise that we each have, in our various situations, a duty to improve our character, such bystanders would, on the developmentalist's account, incur blame if they failed to make an effort to be the kind of person for whom the activity of rescuing would become more of a viable option.[98] While the moral minimalist or commonsense theorist would regard the act of rescuing as supererogatory, and the consequentialist would regard the same act as obligatory, the developmentalist would evaluate the act of rescuing as supererogatory for some and morally obligatory for others, depending on who is performing (or not performing) the act, and on what one's attitude is with respect to its performance.

Consequentialism is more morally demanding than an ethics based on moral development in terms of its assessment of our obligations in the present situation. In consequentialism, any duties we might have in the future, we also have in the present. Since consequentialist views do not acknowledge the category of the supererogatory at all, there is also no conception of a changing border that separates acts of duty from acts of supererogation. In this sense, consequentialism is maximally stringent and rigidly antisupererogationist. It makes no allowance for the subjective particularities of different agents.

Having distinguished an Aristotelian approach to conceiving the relationship between duty and supererogation from that advocated by the moral minimalist and the antisupererogationist, the next task is to defend it against potential criticisms from both sides. This, in essence, amounts to an explicit defense of qualified supererogationism.

CRITICISMS AND RESPONSES

Defending the Thesis of Moral Development against the Charge of Idealism

The legacy of Urmson's "Saints and Heroes" was to give ethics an empirical dimension. At present, it is widely agreed that only an ethics that incorporates moral psychology into its conception of what it requires of us can avoid what the philosopher and psychologist Mark Johnson has called a "tyrant's morality": a morality of "absolute standards that we impose on ourselves and others, without any attention to whether people could actually live up to such standards, apply them to real situations, and improve life by means of them."[99] The category of supererogation has become a way for normative ethics to make room for its self-consciously empirical character. The category creates a way to classify especially onerous actions as morally optional.

Conventional supererogationists believe that the only way to *guarantee* that morality does not become self-defeating is to construct it in such a way that its demands are reasonably within reach of all. They would allege that the thesis of moral development is idealistic due to its insistence on the adoption of a moral *telos* whose nature is to venture beyond, for purposes of redefining, what is "reasonable." While there may be some flexibility about where to set the boundary between duty and supererogation, once the bar is finally declared fixed within the conventional view, it will come to represent the standard that people are used to, inclining them to interpret attempts to alter it as an impingement on their basic rights and liberties. The more minimal the standard, argue the defenders of this view, the less likely people will be to engage in a revolt against morality as a whole, and the more tenable small adjustments to the fixed standard will prove to be, if they should become necessary. Ongoing adjustments of the kind suggested by the developmentalist are ruled out due to the psychological strain they would impose upon the majority of persons.

Thus, traditional supererogationists tend to resort to two kinds of empirical appeals to human motivational psychology to justify their moral minimalism. First, they compensate for human fallibility and self-interest by setting the standard of moral requirement low enough so that the demand to comply with it will not deter the majority of those agents presumed to be incapable of exceeding a mediocre standard. (This move is understood to be realistic rather than pessimistic.) Second, they take into account the way human beings tend to manage their expectations by characterizing this standard as a constant. By always knowing in advance exactly what will be morally required of us, our conceptions of our unfettered freedom to pursue projects and to develop special relations will be kept intact. According to this logic, the idea that our duty expands as we morally develop is motivationally inefficacious. It prompts us to resent morality as a whole. By regarding the performance of especially demanding altruistic deeds as morally valuable without making them required, minimalists can still encourage us to become better people without putting the vital normative concept of duty in jeopardy.

Minimalists thus wager that the imposition of excellence on mediocre agents will simply serve to make more difficult their already tenuous relationship to morality. The developmentalist counter-wagers that human beings are naturally inclined to pursue the good insofar as they are able. In response, minimalists grant that in some particular cases, the Aristotelian Principle will persuade agents away from moral mediocrity; however, they maintain that on the whole these cases are exceptional and are empirically outweighed by the far more prominent realities of human nature, such as our selfishness and desire to do as we wish in the private sphere. They would contend that those who subscribe to the thesis of moral development underestimate the propensity of human beings to interpret the maxim to better themselves as an unwelcome burden, or to become frustrated by the prospect of failing under the weight of this burden. At this point in the argument the developmentalist has a decisive response.

In holding up aspiration as central to human nature, the developmentalist does not deny that the demands of morality can be strenuous, perhaps at times even seemingly impossible. Indeed, one of the best ways for us to test whether we are pushing ourselves is to ask ourselves if we *do* feel frustrated or want to quit. The developmentalist simply denies that this frustration and occasional desire to give up is as detrimental to every agent as the minimalist assumes it is. The minimalist wins the argument only if such frustration indicates a failure on the part of the developmentalist to recognize what is *impossible*. But not only is such frustration not necessarily indicative of impossibility, it is a condition of possibility. The minimalist is in error in assuming that an agent's despair over the difficulty of his or her acting virtuously *now* invariably counts as evidence against his or her being likely to change in the future.[100] In fact, human psychology would seem just as likely to suggest the opposite: the more elusive a goal seems at first, the more seduced I am by the prospect of its accomplishment. As Martha Nussbaum argues, it is the nature of human beings to move in the direction of transcendence, without transcending fully.[101] Humans lie between the beasts, who *are* constrained not to advance beyond their definable limits, and the gods, whose freedom from these limits renders the aspiration for virtue moot. In contrast to both the beasts and the gods, humans are a dynamic species. It is precisely the foreknowledge that they *could* fail or succeed that compels them to test how far the upper bounds of (im)possibility can be stretched.[102] Such testing is, in effect, human striving for excellence. Human limitation thus impels rather than thwarts the pursuit of human excellence.[103]

In addition to criticizing the minimalist's acknowledgment of only the binary options of limitation (e.g., of ordinary persons) and transcendence (e.g., of heroes and saints), the developmentalist may also call into question the minimalist's assumption of a rather narrow view of "possibility." Altruistic acts that lie beyond an agent's *present* capacities are not treated by the minimalist as real possibilities. By contrast, the developmentalist makes a distinction between altruistic actions that are too demanding in the present, but can become less so over time, and conduct that is of such a sacrificial nature, such as the saint's "ethics of excess," that it ought always to be regarded as above and beyond for anyone who is not a saint. According to the developmentalist, "possibility" connotes the possibility for *fulfillment* in the future and the possibility for *improvement* in the present. The acknowledgment of an aretaic "ought" that bears on us as a demand for improvement, but does not immediately express itself in action, does not contradict the moral truism that "ought implies can." This is because according to "ought implies can" we are only ever required to perform those deeds that we are at any present moment able to perform.[104]

Supererogationists working within a purely deontic framework, like David Heyd, would object on the grounds that the developmentalist is being inconsistent in saying as much. On the one hand, the developmentalist requires us to change, presumably by doing things we previously did not; on the other hand, this requirement does not match up in a one-to-one correspondence with specific actions that can be construed as duty.[105] Yet, in floating this criticism, such thinkers fail to appreciate the strong temporal link between acquiring a virtuous character and reenvisioning the nature of one's (deontic) responsibilities. Virtue, according to Heyd and others, is either a function of the degree to which an agent performs right action, or is unrelated to right action altogether. In other words, in Heyd's view, virtue never *determines* right action. However, if the developmentalist is right that over the long run the more virtuous we are, the clearer perception we will have of what is morally required of us, then the developmentalist is justified in subscribing to a broad understanding of "possibility" that bases what is fulfillable in terms of the agents we can *become*. Once virtue is shown to bear on duty, the idea that the full scope of our duty can be measured by looking at isolated moments in time becomes less plausible.

In leaving room for a category of supererogation, the developmentalist acknowledges the existence of altruistic good deeds that can at the present moment be considered too demanding to make obligatory. The developmentalist simply denies that the existence of the category of supererogation can be used as an excuse for failing to exert the effort to go beyond the minimum. More generally, the developmentalist wishes to curb the tendency in traditional supererogationism for agents to act indifferently about a morality that exists beyond the moral minimum. The idea of an aretaic meta-duty to which we are accountable forces each of us individually to test the full extent of what lies within the realm of moral possibility, without making obligatory actions that lie beyond this realm. Since this "ought" of character does not obligate us to perform deeds that are for the moment beyond our capacities, the developmentalist fully respects the maxim "ought implies can" and thus cannot be charged with promoting an idealistic morality.

Defending the Thesis of Moral Development against
the Charge of Leniency

In holding out for options in morality, the developmentalist ensures that we will not be alienated by a moral theory that makes unreasonable demands. But if the developmentalist always requires us to become more virtuous, and morality as a whole pervades human living as much as the developmentalist indicates, then to what extent are moral options *really* available for us to exercise? This is a question that the antisupereroga-tionist hopes the developmentalist will ask. In dialogue with the devel-opmentalist, the antisupererogationist could reason in the following manner: "Since you maintain that the nature of our duties increases as we improve our character, would it not also be the case that the whole set of supererogatory acts of an advanced moral agent comes, over time, to be regarded as required? And if this is the *telos* of an aretaic ethic, then is it not spurious to suggest a gradualist approach, especially since you are ultimately speaking to those of us who are, in effect, already disposed to become better people?" Although both the antisupererogationist and the developmentalist share the concern that the existence of moral options can devolve into moral complacency, only the former wants to dispense with them entirely. Though initially attracted to the developmentalist's rigorous stance against minimalism, the antisupererogationist charges that the developmentalist sells out at the critical point by allowing agents to decide for themselves when they have done all they can do for others, given their stage of moral development. Such a criticism is made, fur-thermore, by appealing to the developmentalist's own way of reasoning. If our duties increase as we become more virtuous, as the developmen-talist maintains, then is it not also true that eventually the whole category of supererogation vanishes for advanced moral agents? And if this much is true, is it not then the case that the foundation of the *ultimate* moral "ought"—what it is ultimately morally right to do—would be based on some final end, which we may call the overall good? Indeed, remarks the antisupererogationist, the force of the developmentalist's own teleological logic compels the developmentalist to do away with the category of mer-itorious nonrequired good acts, at least with respect to advanced agents.

The antisupererogationist's challenge does not end here. Even in antic-ipation of a satisfactory explanation of how the category of supererogation is *consistent* with the thesis of moral development, the antisuperreroga-tionist will still want to hear a good argument from the developmentalist for why it is also *valuable* within a moral framework. The antisuper-erogationist imagines that even the supererogationist who is not a mini-malist, including the developmentalist, will contend that when someone performs an altruistic act that is not morally required and benefits another, he or she is acting out of genuine concern for the person being helped, a motive which affects the quality of the act itself. In this vein, we may recall Heyd's "positive" justification for the category of supererogation:

The decision to act beyond what is required is free not only from legal or physical compulsion, but also from informal pressure, the threat of moral sanctions, or inner feelings of guilt. It is purely optional. Such a freedom allows for the exercise of individual traits of character and for the expression of one's personal values and standards of moral behaviour. Being purely optional, the supererogatory act is spontaneous and based on the agent's own initiative. Not being universally required (of everyone in a similar situation), supererogatory action breaks out of the impersonal and egalitarian framework of the morality of duty—both by displaying individual preferences and virtues, and by allowing for some forms of favouritism, partial and unilateral treatment of someone to whom the agent wishes to show some concern. . . . These characteristics of supererogatory behaviour are valuable partly because some types of virtuous behaviour can be realized only under conditions of complete freedom and would be stifled under a more totalitarian concept of duty. Supererogation is necessary as providing an opportunity to exercise certain virtues.[106]

Supererogation, far from psychologically deterring us from acquiring virtue by condoning moral complacency, actually becomes an enabling condition of its pursuit, or, as the antisupererogationist has anticipated, so it might be argued. But the antisupererogationist has a response: Why should we assume that by acting from duty we will not *also*, just as eagerly and genuinely, desire the well-being of those who benefit from our acts of altruism? Shelly Kagan presses this point into service:

> [T]here is no good reason to believe [the supererogationist's] claim. The existence of a moral requirement, and indeed the recognition of this requirement, is perfectly compatible with acting out of direct concern for the relevant individuals. Neither the existence of such concern nor the motivational force of such concern need be reduced by the realization that there is in fact a morally decisive reason to provide the aid in question.[107]

Kant articulates this view even more strongly: acting from duty, he avers, is the most compelling of all human motivations. When we act so as to conform our own actions to the moral law, we engage in a profound act of human freedom. "What essentially distinguishes a duty of virtue," writes Kant in *The Doctrine of Virtue*, is that "external compulsion" is impossible; such a duty is "based only on free self-constraint."[108] It has not yet been made clear, then, that supererogation is intrinsically valuable, so much so that we ought to insist on its existence at the expense of possibly failing to heed otherwise morally decisive reasons to act altruistically. The antisupererogationist's two criticisms are met by showing that (1) the concept of supererogation is, in fact, still *consistent* with the developmentalist's approach to ethics, notwithstanding its teleological nature, and furthermore that (2) it is *valuable* within such a framework.

The problem of consistency speaks to the objectives that are claimed on behalf of the developmentalist. While the *telos* of an ethics based on moral development is to become a fully virtuous person, this *telos* is not, nor is it meant to be, *realized* for the majority of agents, contrary to the antisupererogationist's assumption that the developmentalist thinks otherwise. The fully virtuous person is, on the developmentalist's account, an *ideal of character* for whom the concept of supererogation admittedly becomes obsolete. The point of speculating about ideally virtuous persons, however, is not to get us to emulate them immediately, but rather to motivate us to become more critical with respect to our own moral progress. Saying that we ought to decrease the range of actions that we consider to be above and beyond is not the same as saying we all ought to become moral saints. Now, as long as we are *not* moral saints, there will always be some distance that separates us from the fully virtuous person. This distance can be measured in terms of noting which of those altruistic deeds that we regard as supererogatory, moral saints regard as required. Unlike moral saints, when we are faced with the opportunity to conduct ourselves altruistically, we may, depending on the deed in question and our current level of moral development, regard such conduct as required or supererogatory. What we are in every case *obligated* to do, however, is to reflect both upon the decision at which we arrive and upon the decision-making process itself. This becomes especially true when we choose not to perform an action that we currently consider to be above and beyond. If moral saintliness lies beyond our reach, we cannot ever, according to the developmentalist, say to ourselves "this is something that a saint, and not someone like me, would choose to do," as a way of dismissing the option from our minds. When it comes to especially demanding altruistic deeds—deeds that fully virtuous persons would simply perform *without* questioning themselves—we must at least remain ambivalent about the matter—that is, if we are taking our moral development seriously. It is in this respect that the acknowledgment of the category of supererogation does not, in and of itself, become tantamount to moral leniency.

Thus, the category of supererogation itself proves to be consistent with an ethics based on moral development, even though it recognizes that the precise relationship between duty and supererogation is always in flux. Regardless of the unique stage of moral development that each of us attains, there will always be certain deeds that are beyond our capacity to perform. The identification of these deeds as supererogatory at a particular time in our lives is consistent with the Aristotelian idea that, not having achieved perfection of our character, we ought to try to be improving it. In addition, it serves to clarify *which* of those deeds that the ideally virtuous person would perform have the potential to become real possibilities for *us* in our own, not-too-distant future. In this sense, the category of supererogation serves as a reminder of how we could otherwise be rather than as an excuse for doing only the moral minimum.

The concept of supererogation is, furthermore, one that the developmentalist can argue is *valuable*. The developmentalist grants Kagan's point that "the existence of a moral requirement, and indeed the recognition of this requirement, is perfectly compatible with acting out of a direct concern for the relevant individuals." However, the developmentalist further points out to Kagan that just because concern is *compatible* with requirement does not mean the two will always coincide. They may not, and they are *unlikely* to overlap in an approach to morality, such as Kagan's, that does not emphasize the importance of "growing into" one's acceptance of more duties. The concept of supererogation serves as a way of ensuring that what Kant calls "free self-constraint" has a way to blossom in each particular agent.

Moreover, it is hard to see how the developmentalist could retain the concept of an ideal, which is a crucial source of motivation for our moral betterment, without the category of supererogation. It is hard to see how *particular* agents would relate to ideals without the flexibility of moral options, which are denied in the kind of strong universalism inherent in antisupererogationism. The philosopher Margaret Urban Walker has remarked upon this point:

> That there is particularity in our moral positions rests on the fact that human beings (within all but the catastrophic reaches of experience) are the kinds of beings who deeply care about, find meaning and identity, in certain sorts of structures and features of their lives, even if in quite different *versions, combinations,* and *weighings* of these elements.... Particulars should be accorded *moral* relevance at all only if and to the extent that they play an important role in supporting and enhancing our *moral competence.* Moral competence is our ability to act in ways consistent with the constraints [that] values and principles impose on us morally. It is, minimally, the capacity to acknowledge consistently that certain values and principles do so constrain us.... [But] there is a significant kind of moral competence which goes beyond the minimum, moral self-definition in its *strong* form.... [T]he exercise of strong moral self-definition consists in making and acting upon irreducibly

particular moral judgments. By requiring implicit universality, universalism denies the possibility of strong moral self-definition.[109]

A benefit of the concept of supererogation is that it allows us morally to
define ourselves in Walker's "supra-minimal" sense. Defining ourselves
in this manner is a prerequisite for character development. Walker's point
rings true on an intuitive level: when we are exposed to saints, like King
or Day, we do not simply decide to be like them; rather, we focus on
particular features of their character, weigh those features against our
own, and then decide how character modification in our own particular
case is most likely to be successful. While antisupererogationists are right
to claim that it is perfectly consistent for an altruistic action motivated by
duty to be fully desired by the agent, they fail to appreciate the alienating
potential of "duties" that come across as too onerous, and that are justified for reasons other than that of an agent's own choosing. While it is not
impossible for the duty-abiding agent to self-sacrifice for the greater good
out of an earnest desire to do so, even if this is a desire based on reason,
it remains unlikely that agents will come to be motivated by reason alone.

There is also an important pedagogical function of the concept of
supererogation. The developmentalist takes into account that we make
decisions to improve our character gradually. On one occasion we decline
an act of supererogation, but a sense of dissatisfaction lingers with us for
having done so; on a subsequent occasion, we may be less likely to decline,
or we may even come to regard the act as required. But however we think,
whatever we do, it is crucial that it has occurred to us that we have had
the option to consent or refuse. It is through this freedom to decide either
way that we existentially become aware of what it feels like to say "no"
while part of us wants, at the same time, to say "yes." This kind of ambivalence is both morally instructive and critical for our changing. At this
point, the antisupererogationist might be inclined to reply that the developmentalist's aretaic meta-duty to improve our character is *itself* a moral
requirement that impinges on us from the outside. And if this is the case,
then the developmentalist will confront the same issues that have been
raised against the antisupererogationist with respect to motivation, specifically, that moral *concern* and moral *requirement* will not necessarily coincide. This point is well taken. It is true that the aretaic meta-duty *is* a
constant, which applies to all agents as such, regardless of their capacities,
social contexts, and circumstances of birth and upbringing. However, the
developmentalist may reply that *this* kind of duty—to improve our character—is inherently much more flexible than any duty that pertains to
specific actions. In this sense it might be reinterpreted as an *imperfect*

duty, one whose fulfillment can proceed in an infinite variety of ways. According to the developmentalist, agents can be aware of their development at varying paces and levels of intensity; what they cannot do is become complacent with the current state of their character. The concept of supererogation, which allows agents some leeway to pick and choose their own "character battles," is conducive to this broad kind of objective—hence its normative value.

The thesis of moral development endorses a view of morality that is sufficiently realistic in terms of human psychology, and which at the same time does not succumb to moral leniency. Furthermore it captures the heart of Aristotle's important observation that we ought to strive against our limitations to the greatest degree possible, without attempting to transcend human nature altogether. This is an observation that is all but neglected in purely deontic ethical approaches. Within religious traditions this observation takes on a prophetic dimension. There is *value* in our feeling morally compelled to do more than what is defined as required, because we are presumed to be creatures created in likeness to the creator, whose essence is to be approximated, if not realized, through human effort. "Yet they seek me daily, and delight to know my ways, as if they were a nation that did righteousness and did not forsake the ordinance of their God," proclaims the prophet Isaiah (58:2). On the supposition that humans are made in the image of something higher, it follows that we are profoundly unfinished, self-questioning beings—works in progress, whose nature it is to become something other than we currently are, within the limits of what we can, in fact, become. Sometimes, as the prophet Isaiah predicts, the search seems futile and in actuality meets without much more success. "Therefore justice is far from us, and righteousness does not overtake us; we look for brightness, but we walk in gloom. We grope for the wall like the blind, we grope like those who have no eyes; we stumble at noon as in the twilight, among those in full vigor we are like dead men" (Isaiah 59:10). The one who conducts the search easily is searching for the wrong things. Such is the nature of authentic human striving. In this prophetic view of human existence, in which finitude is constituted as a given, anxiousness and dissatisfaction become constructive human attributes, prized over other traits such as contentment, comfort, and self-assurance. In this respect, the proponent of the thesis of moral development, for whom the activity of striving plays such a key role, finds in his or her religious counterpart a philosophical ally. They each explore and seek to give credibility to the notion that there is something valuable, instructive, and humanly true about remaining restless with respect to what one has so far morally achieved in life.

I have begun with what might be called a contemporary, "common-sense" picture of the moral agent and have sought to revise this view with reference to insights that emerge from the ethics of virtue. While this effort may be characterized as a debate among participants that come from within a particular secular moral tradition, it is one that is influenced by, and has important ramifications for, those outside its immediate circle. Indeed, the relevance of the thesis of moral development is far-reaching for thinkers working in secular and religious ethics alike. In the final chapter, my aim is to show how this is so in the specific cases of two important twentieth-century theologians, Abraham Heschel and Paul Tillich, both prophetic thinkers in their own right.

Notes

1. An "agent-relative" reason is one that appeals to this or that particular person, while an "agent-neutral" reason pertains to the impersonal point of view, which applies to all agents, as such. On the distinction between the two terms, see Samuel Scheffler, *Human Morality* (Oxford: Oxford University Press, 1992), 103–5.

2. Here I adopt J. L. Mackie's sense of "universalizability" as a test of acceptability according to which any maxim that would qualify as universalizable would do so for any agent: (1) under any relevantly similar set of circumstances; (2) regardless of differences in our abilities, resources, or circumstances of birth and upbringing; and (3) regardless of personal preferences, ideals, or values. Mackie sees these three criteria as tests for asking whether or not one could put oneself in the place of another in adopting a particular maxim. Since I am proposing that heroes and saints have more of an *ability* to perceive their duty than ordinary persons—a violation of the second criterion—I would hold that duty is not in all cases universalizable in Mackie's sense. See J. L. Mackie, *Ethics: Inventing Right and Wrong* (New York: Penguin Books, 1977), 90–92. An example of a weaker sense of "universalizability" that *could* apply to the duties of heroes and saints is that of uniform treatment within a specific class. Onora O'Neill adopts this usage. See Onora O'Neill, *Towards Justice and Virtue: A Constructive Account of Practical Reasoning* (Cambridge: Cambridge University Press, 1996), 125.

3. Many virtue ethicists have observed a difference between "ancient" and "modern" ethics. The contrast is drawn in roughly the following way. In modern ethics moral duty is conceived minimalistically, in that only those negative maxims that serve to prevent the infringement of basic human rights and those positive maxims that are needed to secure the most minimal levels of cooperation and equity in society can qualify as obligatory. In ancient ethics, by contrast, what we ought to do corresponds to our development of virtue, which is expansive and ongoing and may require us to do more for others than we otherwise would in a rules-based morality. In *Quandaries and Virtues*, Edmund Pincoffs makes this observation explicit, asserting that what distinguishes modern morality from

classical morality is that the former is built on the "Hobbesian truism" that morality is a societal construct intended to protect and preserve the interests of everyone. Without rules and minimal universal norms, human lives would become unbearable. According to the "Hobbesian truism," morality is what prevents social anarchy. This being the case, there is not the same necessity in modern morality as in ancient morality for the virtues, the development of which is not necessary for the maintenance of an ordered society. See Edmund Pincoffs, *Quandaries and Virtues: Against Reductivism in Ethics* (Lawrence: University Press of Kansas, 1986), 58ff.

The political theorist David Norton takes Pincoffs's insight as his point of departure. Since a successful "modern" model requires the observance by nearly everyone of rules that are both easily understood and acknowledged as authoritative, Norton notes, "the rules must be very straightforward, and acting in accordance with them must require very little in the way of developed moral character." Norton thinks this requirement explains the "tendency of modern modes of normative ethics—contractarianism, deontology, utilitarianism, intuitionism, ideal observer theory, agent theory—" to rely on overly simple "rules of the sort as, 'Do not lie,' 'Do not steal,' 'Keep your promises,' 'Do not commit murder,' etc., and to introduce exceptions and complications with great reluctance." See David Norton, *Democracy and Moral Development* (Berkeley: University of California Press, 1991), 41–42. As the classical counterpart to the "Hobbesian truism," which Pincoffs discusses, Norton counterposes the Socratic truism, which is the proposition "that any person may in the course of his or her life encounter one or more ultimate tests in which to pursue the course of life that he or she has chosen to live at the risk of life or well-being (Socrates, *Apology*: 'This is the truth of the matter, gentlemen of the jury: wherever a man has taken a position that he believes to be best, or has been placed by his commander, there he must I think remain and face danger, without a thought for death or anything else, rather than disgrace.')" (ibid., 42).

Pincoffs and Norton probably draw the contrast between ancient and modern ethics too simply. Not only can virtues accommodate rules, but it is also arguably the case that the two concepts should not be dichotomized in the first place. Conversely, an ethics of rules need not be based on Hobbesian self-interest, as many "moderns" allow for the intrinsic value of moral goodness in their view. It is not my purpose here to enter into these historical debates. In making my appeal to virtue ethics I wish merely to appropriate the positive insight from thinkers like Pincoffs and Norton that our responsibility to others does not *end* with the observance of rules whose main purpose it is to admonish us against any wrongdoing.

4. By using phrases like "as we become more virtuous" or "as we acquire virtue," I mean "as we ascend to a higher *level* of virtue," e.g., become more benevolent, more courageous, and more insightful ·with respect to determining the nature of our positive duties, all at once. To be virtuous, in this understanding, is to be more skillful, or practiced, in these regards. That these virtues are all related to one another in this respect is something that I assume while readily acknowledging exceptions to the rule (e.g., one could be courageous without being benevolent). One thinker who deals thoroughly with the questions of how the presence

of one kind of virtue impacts another, whether there can be conflict among the virtues, and whether we can speak of the "virtues" (plural) in the first place is Lee Yearley. See Yearley, *Mencius and Aquinas: Theories of Virtue and Conceptions of Courage* (New York: State University of New York Press, 1990), esp. 13–17.

5. The "thesis of moral development" is different from Lawrence Kohlberg's well-known theory that there are six different stages of development through which all individuals pass as they move into moral maturity. See Lawrence Kohlberg, *Essays on Moral Development:* Vol. I, *The Philosophy of Moral Development: Moral Stages and the Idea of Justice* (New York: Harper and Row, 1981). Kohlberg's theory is principally Kantian in nature, while my thesis is heavily influenced by neo-Aristotelian patterns of thought, drawing especially on the work of Julia Annas, David Norton, Nancy Sherman, and Iris Murdoch. See Julia Annas, *The Morality of Happiness* (Oxford: Oxford University Press, 1993); Norton, *Democracy and Moral Development*; Nancy Sherman, "Common Sense and Uncommon Virtue," in *Midwest Studies in Philosophy XIII—Ethical Theory: Character and Virtue,* ed. Peter French, Theodore E. Uehling, Jr., and Howard K. Wettstein (Notre Dame, Ind.: University of Notre Dame Press, 1988); Nancy Sherman, *The Fabric of Character: Aristotle's Theory of Virtue* (Oxford: Clarendon Press, 1991); and Iris Murdoch, *The Sovereignty of Good* (New York: Routledge and Kegan Paul, 1970).

6. J. O. Urmson, "Saints and Heroes," in *Essays in Moral Philosophy,* ed. A. I. Melden (Seattle: University of Washington Press, 1958), 211.

7. There have been various ways of grounding universal rules in the history of ethics. Urmson, for his part, focuses primarily on principles that can be derived from Kantian and utilitarian theories. Intuitionists, in contrast to Kantians and utilitarians, contend that there are no overarching principles that ground universal rules, claiming more strongly that such rules are immediately justified. It is important to note that in both cases, however, there is a presupposition of universal truth and universal justification. In introducing the concept of supererogation, Urmson does not seek to overturn this strong sense of moral universalism. He simply wishes to limit the range of actions that can be considered morally required. In contrast to Urmson and his predecessors, one may assume that there is consensus on universally applicable rock-bottom duties without resorting to the further grounding level of principles or intuitions. That is, one may maintain that we can have cross-cultural normative consensus—minimal moral requirement—without universal justification. This approach to grounded universal norms is also introduced by Sumner B. Twiss and Bruce Grelle in "Human Rights and Comparative Religious Ethics: A New Venue," *The Annual of the Society of Christian Ethics* 15 (1995): 31–33; and by Abdullahi Ahmed An-Na'im in "Towards a Cross-Cultural Approach to Defining International Standards of Human Rights: The Meaning of Cruel, Inhuman, or Degrading Punishment," in *Human Rights in Cross-Cultural Perspectives,* ed. Abdullahi Ahmed An-Na'im (Philadelphia: University of Pennsylvania Press, 1992), 20.

8. Here I am invoking "ought" in its prescriptive usage. For a discussion of the distinction between prescriptive and other linguistic uses of "ought," see R. M. Hare, *Moral Thinking: Its Levels, Methods, and Point* (Oxford: Clarendon Press, 1981), 22–24.

9. This familiar statement of the "ought" of virtue ethics can be traced back to Aristotle himself. See Aristotle, *Nicomachean Ethics*, trans. Terence Irwin (Indianapolis: Hackett Publishing Company, 1985), 1107a1–2. Good expositions of this passage can be found in Rosalind Hursthouse, "Virtue Theory and Abortion," *Philosophy and Public Affairs* 20 (1991): 225; Linda T. Zagzebski, *Virtues of the Mind: An Inquiry into the Nature of Virtue and the Ethical Foundations of Knowledge* (Cambridge: Cambridge University Press, 1996), 235; Philippa Foot, "Virtues and Vices," in Foot, *Virtues and Vices* (Berkeley: University of California Press, 1978), 4; and Gregory W. Trianosky, "Virtue, Action, and the Good Life: Toward a Theory of the Virtues," *Pacific Philosophical Quarterly* 68 (1987), 126, 139.

10. Thus, in deontic moral theories, judgments about character presuppose an assessment of the rightness or wrongness of the acts an agent performs. Conversely, in aretaic moral theories, an action is considered right or wrong if it is one that a person who is virtuously motivated, and who understands a situation in the way that a virtuous person would understand it, would do or would not do in similar circumstances. In the former, agents distinguish themselves by what they do. In the latter, agents distinguish themselves by their level of virtue; rendering a judgment about what they do is a *function* of that virtue. See Zagzebski, *Virtues of the Mind*, 232–35.

11. Sherman, "Common Sense and Uncommon Virtue," 99.

12. The phrase "aretaic ought," which I also refer to here as an "aretaic meta-duty," is a term of art; for, strictly speaking, it is deontic, as I have defined "deontic" and "aretaic." Its object, not its basis, is virtue. The very notion that there can be a sense of duty in a virtue ethic is a controversial one. William Frankena, for example, argues that *any* aretaic ethical theory, in contrast to all forms of deontic ethics, cannot accommodate the quasi-legalistic concept of an "ought" as its primary morally motivating force, including even an overarching (meta-) duty to improve our character. See Frankena, "The Ethics of Love Conceived as an Ethics of Virtue," *Journal of Religious Ethics* 1, no. 1 (1973): esp. 25–29. Frankena claims that an aretaic ethics is "actuated not by a sense of duty, but by a certain other disposition, motive or what have you, e.g., by a straightout desire or concern for the good of others as such (not as something one ought to feel or promote)" (ibid., 29). He contends that in an aretaic ethics, virtue is activated not by duty, but by a good motive such as generosity or sympathy (which are virtues themselves). Accounting for the justificatory force lying behind this kind of motive is a problem Frankena thinks that anyone who attempts to construct an autonomous aretaic ethics must confront. He does allow that an aretaic ethics could make deontic concepts *secondary* to (i.e., conceptually derivable from) already cultivated dispositions.

13. Even Aristotle acknowledges that certain basic actions are required or forbidden independent of motive or character, such as the proscription against murder, theft, and adultery. See Aristotle, *Nicomachean Ethics*, 1134a15–22, 1136a9–25.

14. While I focus primarily on the expansion of positive duty, it is conceivable to suggest that as I become more virtuous, I develop more negative duties as well. With the acquisition of virtue, certain offensive acts, perhaps categorized as permissible according to deontic criteria (e.g., Roderick Chisholm's example of

maliciously informing on a colleague) now become prohibited. See Chisholm, "Supererogation and Offence: A Conceptual Scheme for Ethics," *Ratio* 5 (1963): 1–14.

15. While almost all virtue ethicists agree that character is essential for determining right action, the varieties of virtue ethics abound, and a virtue ethic need not dispense with deontic language entirely. For a discussion of the varieties of virtue ethics, see Justin Oakley, "Varieties of Virtue Ethics," *Ratio* 9 (1996): 128–52. In his article, Oakley distinguishes among six different kinds of claims of virtue ethics. The first of these is the predominant one that (a) an action is right if it is what an agent with a virtuous character would do under similar circumstances. The others are, in order: (b) goodness is conceptually prior to rightness; (c) the virtues are irreducibly plural intrinsic goods; (d) the virtues are objectively good; (e) some intrinsic goods are applicable to the particular agent who is performing them; and (f) acting rightly does not require that we maximize the good. Oakley also contrasts nonconsequentialist virtue ethics from three kinds of consequentialist virtue ethics: (i) character-utilitarianism, (ii) Aristotelian perfectionism, and (iii) satisficing perfectionism (the view that we ought to promote virtue to a level that is "good enough"). For an excellent example of a non-Aristotelian, "satisficing" virtue ethics, see Michael Slote, *From Morality to Virtue* (New York: Oxford University Press, 1992); and Michael Slote, *Goods and Virtues* (Oxford, Clarendon Press, 1983).

16. Hence Joseph Kotva argues for a virtue ethic out of Christian sources that proceeds from the common Christian claim: "Jesus is our true nature or end." From such a maxim it follows that the Christian should try to become *better* by attempting to live as Jesus did. The aretaic meta-duty to become better is thus implied in an imperative of sanctification, which calls for ongoing growth in all aspects of the Christian's character. See Joseph Kotva, Jr., *The Christian Case for Virtue Ethics* (Washington, D.C.: Georgetown University Press, 1996), 37–38, 86.

17. Shelly Kagan expresses this view in *The Limits of Morality* (Oxford: Oxford University Press, 1989), 231ff.

18. Aristotle, *Nicomachean Ethics*, 1098a16–18.

19. Ibid., 1116b2, 1119b16, 1121a1. For Aristotle, moral goodness (i.e., virtue) and happiness are separate but equally indispensable parts of the overall good of flourishing. Thus, it is not implausible to assume that the ideally flourishing human will be, among other things, fully virtuous. For further explication of Aristotle's views about the overlap between self-flourishing and other-regard, see Annas, *The Morality of Happiness*, 257ff.

20. Aristotle, *Nicomachean Ethics*, 1120a23–1129b5.

21. John McDowell, "Deliberation and Moral Development in Aristotle's Ethics," in *Aristotle, Kant, and the Stoics: Rethinking Happiness and Duty*, ed. Stephen Engstrom and Jennifer Whiting (Cambridge: Cambridge University Press, 1996), 22–23.

22. Elizabeth Pybus, "Saints and Heroes," *Philosophy* 57 (1982): 197.

23. Aristotle, *Nicomachean Ethics*, 1105b29–1106a13.

24. Ibid., 1105a26. Lee Yearley has defined the virtues similarly. They are, he writes, "a group of related and relatively well-defined qualities that most individuals in a group think reflect admirable characteristics." A virtue (singular),

288 ORDINARY PERSONS AND MORAL BETTERMENT

then, would be a "disposition to act, desire, and feel that involves the exercise of judgment and leads to a recognizable human excellence or instance of human flourishing. Moreover, virtuous activity involves choosing virtue for itself in light of some justifiable life plan." See Yearley, *Mencius and Aquinas*, 13.

25. Susan Wolf, "Moral Saints," *Journal of Philosophy* 79, no. 8 (1982): 433.

26. For example, Wolf quotes George Orwell's observation, "Many people genuinely do not wish to be saints, and it is probable that some who achieve or aspire to sainthood have never felt much temptation to be human beings" (ibid., 436, note 4).

27. Oakley, "Varieties of Virtue Ethics," 133.

28. Wolf, "Moral Saints," 435.

29. Philippa Foot, *Natural Goodness* (Oxford: Clarendon Press, 2001), 4–5, 26–27.

30. Ibid., 36. Also see Foot, "Virtues and Vices," 4–5.

31. Foot, *Natural Goodness*, 37.

32. Aristotle, *Nicomachean Ethics*, 1169a6–8.

33. See Norton, *Democracy and Moral Development*, 3; and Sherman, "Common Sense and Uncommon Virtue," 98–102. Both Sherman and Norton read into the *Nicomachean Ethics* an imperative for character improvement. For Norton, this implies moral improvement in the sense of becoming more altruistic. Sherman's view is closer to that of Foot and Wolf. For her, character improvement can mean moral improvement, but need not always. Virtue, she states, "casts a wider net" than the attributes of benevolence and kindness.

34. Aristotle, *Nicomachean Ethics*, 1177b35 ff.

35. Sherman, "Common Sense and Uncommon Virtue," 98.

36. Ibid., 98. See also Aristotle, *Nicomachean Ethics*, 1151a3–b25.

37. Sherman, "Common Sense and Uncommon Virtue," 98–99.

38. David Norton, "Moral Minimalism and the Development of Moral Character," in *Midwest Studies in Philosophy XIII—Ethical Theory: Character and Virtue*, ed. Peter A. French, Theodore Uehling, Jr., and Howard Wettstein (Notre Dame, Ind.: University of Notre Dame Press, 1988), 187.

39. Consider the following passage from "Moral Saints":

Even if we could provide a sufficiently broad characterization of the range of positive ways for human beings to live . . . I think there are strong reasons not to want to incorporate such a characterization more centrally into the framework of morality itself. For, in claiming that a character trait or activity is morally good, one claims that there is a certain kind of reason for developing that trait or engaging in that activity. Yet, lying behind our criticism of more conventional conceptions of moral sainthood, there seems to be a recognition that among the immensely valuable traits and activities that a human life might positively embrace are some of which we hope that, if a person does embrace them, he does so *not* for moral reasons. (Wolf, "Moral Saints," 434)

Wolf suggests that morality can contaminate nonmoral traits in roughly the same way that Kant is worried that duty done from any motive, other than out of reverence for the moral law (e.g., duty done out of inclination), is impure. It is *Wolf's* view and not necessarily Aristotle's that the moral and the nonmoral spheres should be separated (and given separate weight) in this fashion.

40. This neo-Aristotelian view can be compared with Kotva's characterization of a virtue ethics within a Christian context. Kotva writes:

[B]ecause virtue theory focuses on the movement toward a human *telos*, toward the best life for human beings to live, no aspect or action is exempt from moral concern. Because our choices influence the kind of people we become, every voluntary human act is morally relevant and susceptible to moral scrutiny. Indeed, the range of morally relevant concerns is even greater than this. Every institution and every human practice affects the kind of people we become. So even institutions and practices invite moral attention. (Kotva, *The Christian Case for Virtue Ethics*, 37)

41. Of course, we can become debilitated in one way or another, in which case we might cease to be responsible for that of which we were formerly capable. An agent could develop Alzheimer's disease, for example, making him or her understandably less attentive to the concerns of others than he or she might once have been. I could be so traumatized by an experience in war that I withdraw from others later in life. Additionally, it is conceivable that we can be led away gradually from our good dispositions for no good reason at all—for example, when we are simply susceptible to a weakening resolve in one respect or another. Note the *passive* nature of the character development in each of these cases, however. According to Aristotle, all things being equal, we will tend not to *opt* to devolve morally if we acknowledge the worthiness of pursuing the morally good life in the first place. Once I get a glimpse of how I ought to be due to my enhanced vision, a function of my increased level of virtue, I do not unlearn or "un-see" that to which I have been exposed.

42. Aristotle, *Nicomachean Ethics*, 1113b5 ff. The same is true of viciousness, which is hard to discard once we have habituated ourselves to it. See ibid., 1114a29.

43. Ibid., 1152a17. "Akrasia" is translated into "incontinence" in English.

44. Annas, *The Morality of Happiness*, 52.

45. Ibid., 56.

46. Jean-Paul Sartre, *Being and Nothingness*, trans. Hazel E. Barnes (London: Methuen and Co. Ltd., 1969), 59.

47. One might be inclined to object to my allusion to Sartre in connection with my discussion of this Aristotelian conception of moral irresponsibility. Sartre, the critic avers, refers to "bad faith" as a way of explaining how human beings try to evade the burden of freedom, whereas Aristotle is concerned merely with weakness of character. In response I would suggest that in failing to do more than what is deontically required of me, I am guilty of a kind of voluntary ignorance, in which I engage in order to evade the initially daunting burden of trying to morally improve. In effect, I allow myself to follow the easy path by believing that behaving in a merely permissible manner is morally adequate. An example of a thinker who relates the distinct concepts of akrasia and self-deception is Lloyd

Steffen. See Lloyd Steffen, *Self-Deception and the Common Life* (New York: Peter Lang, 1986), 234–46.

48. Sartre, *Being and Nothingness*, 59. While in this passage Sartre is technically talking about confusing myself with my roles, one could apply this insight to the realm of morality. If I live only up to the minimally morally permissible, i.e., by avoiding wrongdoing, then I can be said to be fulfilling a role as a morally good agent without putting sufficient thought into what it actually *means* to be morally good.

49. Gregory Trianosky, "Supererogation, Wrongdoing, and Vice: On the Autonomy of the Ethics of Virtue," *Journal of Philosophy* 83 (1986).

50. David Heyd, *Supererogation: Its Status in Ethical Theory* (Cambridge: Cambridge University Press, 1982), 7, 32ff.

51. Trianosky, "Supererogation, Wrongdoing, and Vice," 26.

52. Ibid., 27.

53. Ibid., 27–28.

54. Ibid., 29.

55. Ibid. Trianosky implies that in making such excuses, I seek *both* to deflect the impression that my character is flawed (either on a permanent or occasional basis), even if it is not flawed in this respect, *and* to hide the flaw from others when it is actually present. He does not spend much time on this distinction, however. This raises an interesting question: To what extent am I blameworthy at all in the former case, in which my excuses are motivated only by the objective of making sure others do not form the wrong impression of me? Am I really wrong from an aretaic point of view if I seek merely to ensure that others do not come to the *incorrect* conclusion that I have shirked my responsibilities? Indeed, is it not possible that excuses intended to deflect negative aretaic judgments when I decline to go above and beyond the call of duty merely constitute insurance against these (false) judgments? I think Trianosky might respond that our discomfort cannot always be explained by this more benign interpretation. According to Trianosky, our immediate move to make excuses is, *at the very least*, an indication that we are not confident either about our current level of virtue or about our current perception of what moral duty entails. This observation is borne out if we consider the case of heroes and saints, whose character precludes them from making excuses for what they will be unable to do.

56. We are aware of our shortcomings even when we are alone. "[I]n the privacy of our own conscience," writes Trianosky, "we are sometimes hesitant to refrain from what is supererogatory because of what we think that choice would say *to ourselves* about the depth and sincerity of our moral commitment" (ibid., 30, note 5). For more on the self-consciousness of our aretaic shortcomings, see Thomas E. Hill, Jr., "Ideals of Human Excellence and Preserving Natural Environments," *Environmental Ethics* 5 (1983): 211–24.

57. Trianosky, "Supererogation, Wrongdoing, and Vice," 33–34 (his emphasis).

58. Oakley, "Varieties of Virtue Ethics," 137.

59. Such a standard will admittedly vary across moral and religious traditions, but will, over time, come to be expressed in universal norms over which there is cross-cultural consensus.

60. See, for example, Robert Louden, "On Some Vices of Virtue Ethics," in *The Virtues: Contemporary Essays on Moral Character*, ed. Robert B. Kruschwitz and Robert C. Roberts (Belmont, Calif.: Wadsworth Publishing Company, 1987), 70.

61. Gregory Pence, "Virtue Theory," in *A Companion to Ethics*, ed. Peter Singer (Oxford: Basil Blackwell, 1993), 254.

62. The view that some personal moral ideal *is* what guides one's decision making is expressed in Antonio Cua, *Dimensions of Moral Creativity* (University Park: Pennsylvania State University Press, 1978); Pincoffs, *Quandaries and Virtues*; and Julius Moravcsik, "On What We Aim At and How We Live," in *The Greeks and the Good Life*, ed. David J. Depew (Fullerton: California State University, 1980). This view is discussed by Trianosky in "What Is Virtue Ethics All About?" in *Virtue Ethics: A Critical Reader*, ed. Daniel Statman (Washington, D.C.: Georgetown University Press, 1997), 51.

63. Daniel Mark Nelson interestingly argues that it is through prudence that we articulate the norms that ought to guide us. In other words, according to Nelson, *prudence* is primary and originally governs deontically right action. See Daniel Mark Nelson, *The Priority of Prudence: Virtue and Natural Law in Thomas Aquinas and the Implications for Modern Ethics* (Pennsylvania: Pennsylvania State University Press, 1992), esp. 1–26.

64. Menachem Kellner, "Jewish Ethics," in Singer, ed., *A Companion to Ethics*, 85.

65. Ibid., 86.

66. Moses Maimonides, *The Guide of the Perplexed*, vol. 2, trans. Shlomo Pines (Chicago: University of Chicago Press, 1963), 630–38 (chs. 53 and 54). In chapter 54, Maimonides writes that the perfection of the moral virtues "consists in the individual's moral habits having attained their ultimate excellence. Most of the *commandments* serve no other purpose.... But this species of perfection is likewise a preparation for something else and not an end in itself. For all moral habits are concerned with what occurs between a human individual and someone else" (ibid., 635). Just as the commandments induce the cultivation of divine attributes—loving-kindness, justice, and righteousness—these traits are ultimately expressible in other-regarding actions. The closing chapters of the *Guide* are based on Maimonides' explanation of Jeremiah (9.23), where the command to imitate God's beneficence, judgment, and justice appears explicitly. The explanation results in a full-blown virtue ethic in which God's attributes come to be regarded as a model for human conduct. See Raymond L. Weiss, *Maimonides' Ethics: The Encounter of Philosophic and Religious Morality* (Chicago: University of Chicago Press, 1991), 169ff.

67. Kotva, *The Christian Case for Virtue Ethics*, 105.

68. Ibid.

69. James F. Keenan, S.J., *Goodness and Rightness in Thomas Aquinas's Summa Theologiae* (Washington, D.C.: Georgetown University Press, 1992), 15.

70. Ibid., 16–17.

71. Owen Flanagan, *Varieties of Moral Personality: Ethics and Psychological Realism* (Cambridge: Harvard University Press, 1991), 24.

72. Immanuel Kant, *The Groundwork of the Metaphysics of Morals*, trans. H. J. Paton (New York: Harper and Row, 1964), 57. Flanagan argues that this passage is not indicative of Kant's overall view, which is more compatible with human psychology than it may initially appear to be. See Flanagan, *Varieties of Moral Personality*, 27–28.

73. Urmson, "Saints and Heroes," 212.

74. Ibid.

75. Echoing Urmson, Michael Stocker argues that in order for moral theories to be effective, we must be able to live by them, lest they strike us as some foreign imposition that we are unlikely to heed. In other words, it is not enough for a framework to give *reasons* for following a "moral" course of action. It must provide *motives* for our wanting to abide by those reasons. This is a standard by which, according to Stocker, most modern moral theories tend to fail. However, Stocker also argues that if we did base altruistic motives on moral reasons, then we would lose something central to the way we enter into relationships with others, namely, the "first-person" relevance of our perspective to those actions and attitudes that represent the activities promoted by social interaction. Thus, concludes Stocker, there is an inherent "schizophrenia" in most modern moral theories. See Michael Stocker, "The Schizophrenia of Modern Ethical Theories," *Journal of Philosophy* 73 (1976): 453–66.

76. Flanagan, *Varieties of Moral Personality*, 32.

77. Realizable possibilities occur along a continuum. There are possibilities that I can actualize right now because they require little transformation in the person that I currently am, which can be contrasted with others that would require much more time and effort and "might make me a very different sort of person—recognizably continuous with the person I was before, but perhaps with different core aims, a slightly different bearing, and perhaps even different friends." See ibid., 40–41.

78. The *source* of the value of these traits, however, is separate from our desiring them. Developmentalists' overall view of the pursuit of virtue and human flourishing commits them to an "objective theory of human good," which is the view that flourishing is a matter of having certain goods in one's life, goods that all human beings ought to have, objectively speaking. See Shelly Kagan, *Normative Ethics* (Boulder, Colo.: Westview Press, 1998), 39.

79. See Flanagan, *Varieties of Moral Personality*, 112ff.

80. John Rawls, *A Theory of Justice* (Cambridge: The Belknap Press of Harvard University Press, 1971), 426.

81. Ibid., 427–28 (my emphasis).

82. Ibid., 440.

83. According to Rawls, the Aristotelian Principle is confined to the good life, which is to be distinguished from what constitutes moral obligation. I use Rawls here only for the limited purpose of explicating Aristotle's own understanding of how human beings improve and change from one sort of person into another. I think that it is significant that a liberal Kantian, such as Rawls, capably makes such an observation and uses it for constructive purposes.

84. Aristotle, *Nicomachean Ethics*, 1103a31–b2.
85. Annas, *The Morality of Happiness*, 110.
86. Aristotle, *Nicomachean Ethics*, 1105a18–22.
87. Ibid., 1105a26–34.
88. For an example of an account of ethics that *is* based entirely on the phenomenon of mimesis, see William Schweiker, *Mimetic Reflections: A Study in Hermeneutics, Theology, and Ethics* (New York: Fordham University Press, 1990).
89. Annas, *The Morality of Happiness*, 114.
90. Aristotle, *Nicomachean Ethics*, 1104a25. The reliance upon the moral upbringing of children in his ethics, which presupposes the right sort of education, makes Aristotle somewhat susceptible to charges of elitism. Good character is dependent on the right kind of apprenticeship. But what about the child who lacks the benefit of worthy influences? For a good exposition of just how important the rearing of children is in Aristotle's ethics, see Alasdair MacIntyre, *Dependent Rational Animals: Why Human Beings Need the Virtues* (Chicago: Open Court Press, 1999), 70ff.
91. Aristotle, *Nicomachean Ethics*, 1097b20.
92. Aristotle defends two very broad assumptions upon which the thesis of moral development relies, which I here accept without entering into debate. The first is that virtue is essential for human flourishing, and the second is that we are naturally disposed to be virtuous (and to have particular virtues). One might say that, according to Aristotle, we are "homo virtuoso" in the sense that everyone is born with the dormant capacity to flourish by means of becoming virtuous. While the especially careful scholar may have the impulse to shy away from some account of human nature, it is difficult not to make some reference to it in this book given the frequency with which the concept appears in the *Nicomachean Ethics*.
93. Kagan, *Normative Ethics*, 40. Of course, as Kagan points out, even within a broadly perfectionist approach there is room for substantial debate over what qualifies as either "exceptional" or "essential" for the good human life. However, whatever traits perfectionists decide will have to be included on such a list, they would all agree that such traits are to be completely realized, now, in the present.
94. Thus, as opposed to most theological doctrines, there is seldom any recognition in perfectionism of human finitude.
95. Thomas Hurka, *Perfectionism* (Oxford: Oxford University Press, 1993), 5. Moral perfectionism is not the equivalent of radical other-regard. According to Hurka, perfectionism actually favors self-regard *over* other-regard, which he claims is one of its strengths. Hurka writes:

Not only is perfectionism attractive but its study also points to defects in current moral philosophy. On this view now dominant among moral philosophers, morality concerns only acts that affect other people. It tells us not to frustrate others' desires or interfere with their freedom but says nothing about what we or they should choose for ourselves. Perfectionism strongly rejects this view. It has an ideal for each human—that she develop her nature—and it may criticize her for failing to achieve it. (It may also criticize her for failing to help others, but this is not the only criticism it can make.) In my view, its acceptance of *self-regarding duties* is a great strength in perfectionism. (Ibid., 5)

96. In this sense, the developmentalist's ethic may be considered *weakly* perfectionist. The summit remains the *telos,* but not necessarily the immediate goal, of the mountain climber. See my discussion of perfectionism within the context of secular and theological ethics in the Introduction.

97. Aristotle says this explicitly in his discussion of the generous person. See note 20.

98. Not all bystanders were the same, and thus some are more blameworthy than others. For a discussion of various kinds of bystanders and their moral responsibility during the Holocaust, see David Jones, *Moral Responsibility in the Holocaust: A Study in the Ethics of Character* (Lanham, Md.: Rowman and Littlefield, 1999), 213–17. It is important to note, incidentally, that in presenting this particular case, I assume that rescuers are not *less* virtuous than bystanders for neglecting, or at least de-emphasizing, the importance of special relations as a consequence of their choosing to rescue. In my view, the objection that rescuers lacked virtuous insight because they put their families at risk goes only so far, for ultimately the burden falls on the critic to offer reasons why he or she doubts the judgment of the rescuer. By what standard could one know that rescuers were not justified in overriding prima facie duties of special relations in saving the Jews from Hitler? While there is no decisive way to say for sure, we arguably may be more persuaded by the testimony of rescuers who articulate with confidence and clarity that they *knew* they did the right thing in rescuing Hitler's victims (and thereby putting their families at risk) than we are by bystanders who often equivocated about the positives and negatives of rescuing given the empirical realities they faced.

99. Mark L. Johnson, "How Moral Psychology Changes Moral Theory," in *Mind and Morals: Essays on Cognitive Science and Ethics,* ed. Larry May, Marilyn Friedman, and Andy Clark (Cambridge, Mass.: MIT Press, 1996), 49.

100. Of course, the developmentalist would have to make sure not to *overstate* what is, in fact, possible for an agent in the future. The point is that frustration in and of itself is not an indicator of impossibility.

101. See Martha Nussbaum, *Love's Knowledge: Essays on Philosophy and Literature* (Oxford: Oxford University Press, 1990), esp. ch. 15.

102. Ibid., 371–77.

103. Ibid., 378.

104. That we lack the virtue to be required to perform one act or another does not mean that we do not see that more would be required of us *if* we were more virtuous. We do not know specifically *what* would be required of us, only *that,* indeed, more would. Or, going with my earlier metaphor, we can look up the mountain and always know we should be looking up the mountain, without being able to envisage where our next place on the mountain will be, or what the view will be once we get there. Note that I assume here that it is *true* that "ought implies can." Not all moral theorists would agree with me, however. Someone who does

not take this maxim for granted might suggest that one could *know* what one ought to do without having the *strength of character* to do it. One's knowledge of what is right could out-step one's ability to do the right thing. And if this is so, would not this fact challenge the assumption that "ought implies can"? In response, I would reaffirm that when we become more virtuous, we acquire moral insight and moral ability all at once. That is, we move to a higher *level* of virtue. Thus, if I *know* what I ought to do, I also at least know that it is morally required of me to acquire those virtuous skills that would enable me to do it, and thus to work to dispose myself accordingly. To not be able to do what I know I ought to do thus becomes, at least according to the thesis of moral development, a *morally culpable lack of ability*. If I know what I am morally required to do, then with enough effort, I can dispose myself to do it.

105. Heyd, *Supererogation*, 141.

106. Ibid., 175.

107. Kagan, *The Limits of Morality*, 239.

108. Immanuel Kant, *The Doctrine of Virtue: Part II of the Metaphysics of Morals*, trans. Mary J. Gregor (Philadelphia: University of Pennsylvania Press, 1964), 41.

109. Margaret Urban Walker, "Moral Particularity," *Metaphilosophy* 18 (1987): 175–76.

CHAPTER 6

Human Striving and Creative Justice

The duty to go beyond the call of duty, which I have defended through
the modification of a certain secular moral tradition, has implications
beyond the context in which it has primarily been discussed in this book.
As I have noted throughout, it is a concept that also figures prominently
in Jewish and Christian thought (not to mention the thought of other
religious traditions). Specifically, its appearance within a religious setting
induces practitioners to seek the *telos* of moral betterment beyond the
ways in which they are already commanded by law to perform good acts.

According to the standard view, supererogation is something that is
perceivable primarily from the outside, by those who are themselves not
inclined to perform supererogatory acts. In "Saints and Heroes," Urmson
states explicitly that supererogation, exemplified by the performance of
heroic and saintly acts, is best identified by those who are not heroes or
saints. His argument is that only ordinary persons possess the objectivity
from which to put extraordinarily virtuous acts in their proper perspective. In Urmson's view, it is society that calls attention to the heroic or
saintly status of heroes and saints; heroes and saints are not in a position
to judge what is required of them, much less deny the praise lavished on
them when they are (described as) going above and beyond.

I have argued that such a contention is shortsighted because it fails to
recognize the possibility that one of the marks of a virtuous agent is the
capacity for that agent to discern among different levels of moral compulsion that emerge from within him or herself.[1] Indeed, it is possible that
heroes and saints *do* recognize that the rules of a society do not require
them to perform the onerous altruistic acts for which they become
known, but also realize that duty encompasses, but is not exhausted by,
society's rules. Duty is additionally determined by what sort of person one

is, for it is informed by one's convictions and by the commitments that one undertakes. In other words, duty, as I have noted throughout, is a function of both law and character.[2] Duty is not a static yoke but an ever-expanding "ought" that doubles back on itself. The otherwise seemingly paradoxical phrase "duty to go beyond the call of duty" calls attention to an internal sense of supererogation, according to which one engages in self-critical assessment in order to set one's other-regarding ambitions in tandem with the pace of one's moral development.

To the extent that the aretaic meta-duty of character development insists on our ongoing self-scrutiny, it resembles a central normative message of the theologically oriented figures periodically visited throughout these chapters, namely, that the human mission is one of moral betterment, of becoming, over time, what we are not quite yet. In this chapter, I explore head-on two concrete cases of the acknowledgment of the duty to go beyond the call of duty in the ethical proposals of two twentieth-century religious thinkers: Abraham Heschel, the Jewish theologian, ethicist, and civil rights activist, and Paul Tillich, the Christian existentialist and theologian. Upon examining the ethical writings of Heschel and Tillich, it becomes clear that the duty to go beyond the call of duty is not a new concept, and certainly not one that can be gleaned only through engaging in a retrieval of Aristotelian ethics, but rather one that is already alive and well in a religious setting, evident upon reflecting on what these two thinkers have to say about the nature and purpose of human existence. If the thesis of moral development can be shown to be present in the concrete cases of these two religious thinkers, then secularists and religionists alike will have further grounds for accepting the developmentalist's admittedly strong claim that the underlying duty of character improvement is one that is incumbent upon us all.

Heschel and Tillich can be characterized as qualified supererogationists. Both recognize a minimum level of moral requirement that should be built upon over time. Moreover, both paint a picture of the developing moral agent by discussing the virtues that such an agent should exhibit, which can be contrasted with the picture of the duty-fulfilling agent described in the standard view. Finally, both thinkers recognize the importance of our awareness of finitude, thereby laying grounds for the sort of self-questioning and introspection that is, in their accounts and in the account of the developmentalist, required for good human living.

Abraham Heschel and Human Striving

One of the underlying motivations of this book has been to provide a revised model in normative ethics for thinking about when and in what sense we should assume responsibility. What are the circumstances under which it is appropriate to feel moral compulsion? My answer to this question has been to stand in favor of a relatively demanding sense of moral requirement, suggesting, along with most virtue theorists, that ethics is as much about *being* a certain sort of person as it is about *doing* certain things. When we encounter the starving refugee or the elderly neighbor whose car is stuck in a snowy driveway, one of the most instructive resources to consult before deciding how we will react is our own sense of what being human entails. This is especially true if we understand "being human" not only to include, but also to emphasize, helping others in their time of need. One problem commonly exhibited by proponents of the standard view is that they provide an algorithm for deciding what is morally required and not required of us in particular situations without giving sufficient treatment to the question of what is intrinsically meaningful about helping others in the context of the human situation. In the exclusively deontic view, if we choose not to perform some especially demanding altruistic action, it is only the potential recipient, and not we ourselves, who fails to benefit from the missed opportunity. In an approach that makes duty dependent on character, by contrast, striving beyond minimal moral requirement is tantamount to living a meaningful life. Whereas in the standard view self-regard and other-regard stand in an inverse relationship, in the revised view the two coincide, altruistic sacrifices representing a key facet of self-fulfillment more broadly considered.

The idea that concern for the other and the personal quest for meaning are directly linked constitutes the basic tenet upon which Abraham Heschel's ethical philosophy is built. Heschel, a Jew exiled from Poland following the rise of Hitler, came to the United States in 1940 to teach at the Hebrew Union College and later at the Jewish Theological Seminary. His aim, in the words of one interpreter of his work, was to "shock modern man out of his complacency and awaken him to that spiritual dimension fading from the contemporary consciousness."[3] For Heschel, the central task of the modern age was for human beings to recapture a personal awareness of God and other people by feeling the presence of God "within and beyond things and ideas," and by coming to terms with both their dependence on God and God's dependence on them.[4] In *Between God and Man*, Heschel laid out the nature of this partnership between the deity and the human subject:

We must continue to ask: What is man that God should care for him? And we must continue to remember that it is precisely God's care for man that constitutes the greatness of man. To be is to stand for, and what man stands for is the great mystery of being His partner. God is in need of man.[5]

The fully human life is one in which we are not mere onlookers in society. Human beings cannot be satisfied with accepting what is given. Rather, they must be proactive by conducting themselves in a way that shows they are worthy of God's love and care, by seeking out those of God's creatures who are in distress, and by becoming outraged by those who react with indifference to the anguish of others. This is what it means to share in God's work, to be "His partner."

Additionally, however, human beings affect God, who generates a "prophetic sympathy," and who, along with other human beings, "needs to be needed."[6] According to Heschel, God depends on human beings to carry out His designs on earth. Within the context of Judaism, this relationship can be described as chosenness. The Jewish covenant with God imposes a mutual responsibility on both the human being and God that makes life harder for Jews without making them superior to others. Thus, according to Heschel, the Jew must always do more than uphold minimal norms and pursue basic values. Heschel writes: "There is a price to be paid by the Jew. He has to be exalted in order to be normal. In order to be a man, he has to be more than a man. To be a people, the Jews have to be more than a people."[7] To be human is to be more than human. It is to try to see beyond our current horizons, aware that the place from which we look, wherever we are, will not give us a clear view of what we are trying to see. Human finitude does not give us an excuse for maintaining the status quo. Quite to the contrary, it propels us toward what is infinite.

This sentiment is reflected in Heschel's understanding of Jewish law. The practitioner of Halakhah who has too exaggerated a concern for legality and discipline is guilty of "religious behaviorism."[8] Like Maimonides, Heschel emphasizes "not the awareness of being commanded but the awareness of Him who commands; not of a yoke we carry but of a will we remember; the awareness of God rather than the awareness of duty."[9] Duty, understood as merely command, is empty law, which cannot possibly accommodate God's present, active will. "Religious behaviorism," which Heschel is against, is placing emphasis upon the law without making any attempt to ascertain the good that lies behind every requirement. While observance of the law does require an enduring and stable obedience, the purpose of the law is always to transcend the constraining features of the commandments that comprise it in order to provide a pattern of living appropriate to God's presence.[10] In Heschel's approach the commandments transform rather than limit human existence. Living a life based on commitment to Torah enables Jews not only to come closer to God but also to flourish as human beings, whose essence is to live, think, and act in the image of God. A life lived in God's image, which entails more than rote obedience to Halakhic law, is a life lived well.

This interpretation of what Jewish observance consists in resembles a "virtue ethic" insofar as it conceives of what the Jew "ought" to do in terms of the Commander rather than the command. The Jew, in other words, ought to do what the fully virtuous person—who in Heschel's view arguably becomes God Himself—would have him do. Whereas mere awareness of being commanded has the potential to result in completion of the moral task, an awareness of "Him who commands" imposes upon the human subject the feeling that one is never quite morally finished. In Heschel's view, human beings who live well exist in a state of anxious flux, continually strengthening their bond with God, ever ready to answer for what God, the Commander, may require of them next. Elsewhere Heschel likens this readiness to answer to being "responsible."[11]

In his short book *Who Is Man?*, Heschel develops his own ethics of virtue. He announces at the outset of the book that he is concerned with the "totality of man's existence," with the question of "what we are in the light of an intuitive expectation or a vision of what man ought to be."[12] Being human, according to Heschel, involves more than just existing as a human being. It involves knowing who one is, where one is destined, and how one will get there, all of which are questions of self-knowledge. Thus, "being human" confers upon the human being basic responsibilities. We should never become comfortable with the current state of our character. Heschel argues:

> Man is not free to choose whether or not he wants to attain knowledge about himself. He necessarily and under all circumstances possesses a degree of such knowledge, preconceptions, and standards of self-interpretation. The paradox is that man is an obscure text to himself. He knows that something is meant by what he is, by what he does, but he remains perplexed when called upon to interpret his own being. It is not enough to read the syllables of a text written in a language which one does not understand, to observe and to recount man's external behavior, important and necessary as such an enterprise is. Man must also interpret them in terms larger than his inner life. . . . Sensitivity to one's own behavior, the ability to question it, to regard it as a problem rather than as a structure consisting exclusively of irreducible, immutable, and ultimate facts, is an essential quality of being human. . . . Self-understanding can hardly be kept strictly within the limits of description of facts, since the self itself is a compound of facts and norms, of what *is* as well as a consciousness of what *ought* to be. The essence of being human is value, value involved in being human. . . . Thus the root of self-understanding is in the awareness of the self as a problem; it operates as

a critical reflection. Displacement of complacency, questioning the self, in acts and traits, is the primary motivation of self-understanding.[13]

We are from the beginning of our moral existence finite creatures meant to discover who we are and probe the nature of our limitations and possibilities. Through the process of self-discovery we become critical questioners capable of asking what it means to *be* human beings. This process involves developing ourselves both in terms of what we do (our acts) and who we are (our traits). Our developmental nature is what distinguishes us from the animals:

> It is a fatal illusion to assume that to be human is a fact given with human being rather than a goal and an achievement. To animals the world is what it is; to man this is a world in the making, and being human means being on the way, striving, waiting, hoping. Neither authenticity of existence nor the qualities of being human are safe properties. They are to be achieved, cultivated, and protected.... To be human we must know what humanity means and how to acquire it. Our being human is always on trial, full of risk, precarious. Being human is an opportunity as well as a fact.[14]

By using the term "opportunity" Heschel means something specific. We do not know what we are ultimately capable of and thus cannot predict before the fact what will be required of us. There is no "facticity" with regard to the human subject.[15] Our world is never what it is, per se. It is "a world in the making," a problem in need of fixing. As Heschel explains:

> Human living is not simply being here and now, being around a matter of fact ... it is being in a dilemma, being cross-examined, called upon to answer. Man is not left alone. Unlike the being of all other beings, man knows himself as being exposed, challenged, judged, encountered. To be human is to be a problem.[16]

The problem of being human cannot be solved, because the problem is the essence of humanity itself. We exist in motion, never standing still.

The articulation of these sentiments should by now be familiar. Indeed, the developmentalist insists that when we have an opportunity to help someone in need but arrive at the conclusion that we lack the wherewithal on that occasion to perform the required sacrifice, we ought not simply to walk away from the episode with indifference. Our judgment of our responsibility in a situation ought not to constitute the *final* judgment.

Rather, by the developmentalist's reckoning, we should remain humble and wonder about whether the things we fail to do are things we should try harder to do the next time. It is this lingering sense of dissatisfaction that stays with us as we abide current moral obligations which forms the kernel of a righteous character. In Heschel's prophetic view such dissatisfaction is what causes us to expand our sense of duty:

> To insist that I *must* be only what I am now is a restriction which human nature must abhor. The being of a person is never completed, final. The status of a person is *status nascendi*. The choice is made moment by moment.[17]

As we "become human" we also modify our initial sense of who we are and how we ought to be. These modifications, in turn, impact what our duties will be in the future. That we exist as unfinished, as "non-final,"[18] then, represents a major point of convergence between Heschel's ethics and that of the developmentalist.[19]

For Heschel, the duty to become different pertains to a requiredness that is part of the terms of our existence as God's created subjects. Since there is an original purpose with which we are endowed, not being our own creators, we have an original duty to fulfill God's commandments. Heschel insists on the temporal priority of this duty over being.[20] "Man's will," Heschel comments, "cannot be separated from his ought to be."[21] Heschel refers to this ought as an "indebtedness" which is present from the very beginning of human existence, and which constitutes human essence:

> Man cannot think of himself as human without being conscious of his indebtedness.... To eradicate it would be to destroy what is human in man. *The sense of indebtedness, although present in the consciousness of all men, is translated in a variety of ways: duty, obligation, allegiance, conscience, sacrifice.*[22]

The idea that human existence is one and the same with human obligation is a far cry from the unqualified supererogationism posited in the standard view, in which human beings are postulated in the first instance to be free from any other-regarding constraints other than those minimally necessary for society to function. In Heschel's view, duty, or indebtedness, is not an imposition but the essence of the human condition. It is not easily defined. It consists of searching and questioning. We reconcile our own experience with God's will by continually asking ourselves questions that probe our level of moral seriousness. Do we live our lives in such a way as to help others in their time of need? Are we committed to living a fully human life? Clearly, the vigilance and self-critical posture that is present in the developmentalist's view of responsibility finds expression in the theology and ethics of this modern Judaic thinker.

PAUL TILLICH AND CREATIVE JUSTICE

Like Heschel, the German-born American Christian thinker Paul Tillich bases his theology and ethics on what he perceives to be the disturbing separation of human existence from human essence and of man from God. Tillich calls this predicament, which has become especially problematic in the modern era, "estrangement," and he refers to the moral and theological task that it poses as the "ultimate concern," which is a concern to be reunited with the divine and, consequently, with human essence itself.[23] As with Heschel, Tillich sees human beings as born into the world free, but also as responsible for their self-fulfillment. In the Christian's case, this search culminates in reunion with Jesus. Rather than emphasizing Jesus as an important historical figure who brought about great social and ethical reform, Tillich interprets him as "The Christ," the bearer of the creative power, or "New Being," capable of overcoming estrangement by helping humans to reconcile their existence with their essence.[24] Tillich explains this reconciliation through his interpretation of the familiar normative concepts of love and justice.

Both Tillich's elucidation of love and justice and Heschel's virtue-based ethics are compatible with the thesis of moral development.[25] As does the developmentalist, Tillich interprets concepts like "duty" and "justice" in an expandable, non-deontic fashion. However, like Heschel, Tillich casts morality as an essentially theological enterprise that is revealed in the encounter between the divine and the human subject.[26]

The nature of Tillich's conception of moral requirement emerges in the two texts that provide the clearest and most succinct statement of his ethics: *Morality and Beyond* and *Love, Power, and Justice*.[27] Tillich clarifies at the outset of *Morality and Beyond* that he is interested in repudiating the arguments of two kinds of opponents: "moralists" for whom the ethic of *agape* has become an oppressive burden, and secular ethicists (whom Tillich calls "relativists"), who, in ignoring the foundational role of grace, cannot help but fail to account for the basis of any moral requirement.[28] Tillich explains that these two positions can be overcome by reestablishing the relevance of freedom and grace to morality. This, in turn, is a process of identifying the moral imperative—the foundational "ought" of human existence—in the quest for us to become what we essentially are, as creatures who exist both in union with God and as "participants" in our world.[29] For Tillich, the moral act is a "self-realization of the centered self" that is at once both liberating, insofar as it represents the actualization of human potential, and unconditionally binding, insofar as humans cannot choose to conduct themselves otherwise without contradicting who they essentially are.[30] Participation becomes a reflection of self-actualization.

When we participate we take a stand. We adopt an affirming or critical stance in matters pertaining to the world. Such initiative requires courage. We must be proactive by supporting causes and movements that are righteous and by attempting to thwart injustice, wherever we may encounter it. It becomes apparent that for Tillich morality does not consist merely of working within certain rules. Morality is considerably broader in scope. It is, at its foundation, a matter of who we are and are becoming and not simply a matter of what we do.

This conception of morality is teleological, in both a self-regarding and an other-regarding sense. As we self-actualize, that is, as we strive toward a particular ideal of character, we "participate in eternity."[31] Tillich retrieves and makes positive use of the term "eudaimonia" in order to make his point:

> Wherever this state of participation is reached, there is *eudaimonia*, fulfillment under the guidance of a "good daimon," a half-divine power. To reach this goal is an unconditional imperative. And since the practical virtues are the precondition for fulfillment through participation in the divine, they also have unconditional validity.... The word [eudaimonia] means fulfillment with divine help, and consequent happiness. This happiness does not exclude pleasure, but the pleasure is not the aim, nor is happiness itself the aim. It is the companion of fulfillment, reached together with it.[32]

The theological dimension of eudaimonia is related to its moral dimension; for by exercising the "practical virtues," Tillich essentially means loving agapistically. *Agape* is the crucial ethical-religious concept in Tillich's teleological framework, and Tillich also calls it the source of all moral demands.[33] That *agape* is the source of all moral norms, however, does not mean that it is the equivalent of an overarching rule that we can use to predict, before the fact, what might come to qualify as morally required. As Tillich explains:

> An unchanging principle, it nevertheless always changes in its concrete application. It "listens" to the particular situation. Abstract justice cannot do this; but justice taken into love and becoming "creative justice" or *agape* can do so. *Agape* acts in relation to the concrete demands of

the situation—its conditions, its possible consequences, the inner status of the people involved, their hidden motives, their limiting complexes, and their unconscious desire and anxieties. Love perceives all these—and more deeply the stronger the *agape* element is.[34]

It is the very nature of *agape* not to specify in formulaic fashion the set of rules and norms that may be required of particular agents. Quite to the contrary, *agape* requires different things from people, depending on their capacities and the particular situations in which they find themselves. "Creative justice" is justice and love in one. It is a justice that is appro- priately molded for each new situation, that is, a "listening" justice that transcends the fixed standards of "conventional morals."[35]

Tillich takes up the theme of creative justice in *Love, Justice, and Power*, where he contrasts it with proportional or *tributive* justice. Tributive jus- tice is that which protects us from being taken advantage of, while *creative justice* is a higher level of justice that is neither formulable nor even expressible and, as such, is more appropriate for our self-realization of the "centered self."[36] Tributive justice is more certain in what it requires. Tillich writes:

> It is a calculating justice, measuring the power of being of all things in terms of what shall be given to them or what shall be withheld from them. I have called this form of justice tributive because it decides about the tribute a thing or a person ought to receive.... Distributive justice gives to any being the proportion of goods which is due to him; retrib- utive justice does the same, but in negative terms, in terms of depriva- tion of goods or active punishment. The latter consideration makes it clear that there is no essential difference between distributive and retrib- utive justice. Both of them are proportional and can be measured in quantitative terms. In the realm of law and law-enforcement the tribu- tive form of justice is the norm.[37]

Tributive justice corresponds to the implementation of "duty" in the standard view. It protects us from having our rights violated and ensures that we get what we deserve in terms of the goods that are owed to us. Tributive justice is the justice of desert. Because anything done in excess of the minimal standard of desert is beyond the scope of tributive justice, it alone cannot promote the teleological goal of self-realization, and it may even be the case that the strict use of tributive justice will prevent the attainment of this goal. Tillich thus notes that there may be cases in which there is a need to supplement, and even at times supplant, tributive justice:

They include all trespass of the positive law in the name of a superior law which is not yet formulated and valid. They include struggles for power which are in conflict with indefinite or obsolete rules.... They include all those events in which justice demands the resignation of justice, an act without which no human relation and no human group could last.[38]

In such instances tributive justice by itself becomes a contravention of justice. Since one can be unjust "even if one is legally right,"[39] prudential, or "jurisprudential,"[40] models of moral requirement will sometimes have to yield to a transforming, or creative, justice.

Creative justice is more flexible than tributive justice, and so it is better able to deal with life's real situations, especially insofar as broad structures of power come to rearrange society's more important norms that are thought to be stable. Since creative justice is dynamic, it cannot be identified in definite terms. As Tillich notes, tributive justice is "never adequate" to creative justice because it "calculates in fixed proportions. One never knows *a priori* what the outcome of an encounter of power with power will be."[41] Creative justice, by contrast, takes nothing for granted. It exists to keep in check those structures of power upon which tributive justice relies. It challenges hierarchy and aims at unity. This raises an interesting question, analogous to the one asked by the critic who worries that virtue ethics is structurally unable to say much of anything about what people ought to do. If creative justice works not through calculation but through response, then how can we come to recognize the conditions for its application? Tillich himself addresses this question:

> What is the criterion for creative justice? In order to answer this question one must ask which is the ultimate intrinsic claim for justice in a being? The answer is: Fulfillment within the unity of universal fulfillment. The religious symbol for this is the kingdom of God.[42]

The *telos* of creative justice is the "ought" that directs us to realize our essence. This ought lies beyond the more definite ought that corresponds to the rules of society, our obedience to which is no less demanding than that which would be required of us in the kingdom of God, where we exist together in full human fellowship. Just as we saw Owen Flanagan (another Christian thinker) do in order to elucidate his understanding of saints-as-exemplars, Tillich refers to the case of the righteous from the Jewish tradition, the *tzaddikim,* as those persons whom we admire in "the Biblical literature of both testaments," in order to clarify creative justice. Tillich calls the *tzaddikim* the "just ones" who subject themselves to the divine orders according to which everything in nature and history is created and moves. But this subjection is not the acceptance of commandments as such, . . . it is the loving obedience to him who is the source of this law. Therefore, the concept of the [*tzaddik*] unites subjection to the law with piety towards him who gives the law. . . . As in its application to man, so in its application to God justice means more than proportional justice. It means creative justice and is expressed in the divine grace which forgives in order to reunite. God is not bound to the given proportion between merit and tribute. He can creatively change the proportion, and does it in order to fulfill those who according to proportional justice would be excluded from fulfillment.[43]

God transcends proportion and goes beyond the rules for the higher purpose of administering true justice. It is through grace that we have the means to exercise the same ambition. This we do when we exceed the lower standard. On such occasions justice becomes true justice, which is a "form of reuniting love."[44] Tillich's distinction between the law and the source of the law is similar to the one that Heschel draws between the commandment and the Commander. We cannot choose only to follow tributive justice, for as we seek fulfillment through attempting to live a life in union with God, that which constitutes the narrower sense of justice changes. Tributive justice expands, while still remaining qualitatively distinct from, creative justice. It is necessary but not sufficient to explain moral requirement. It is the beginning of justice. Love, on the other hand, "does not do more than justice demands," but is "the ultimate principle of justice. Love reunites; justice preserves what is to be united."[45] Love, in other words, redefines justice at a lower level, even as justice at its highest level becomes synonymous with love.[46]

In Tillich's ethics, love and justice coincide. At the same time, by seeing love and justice as distinct normative concepts Tillich is able to express two standards of moral requirement. Were they the same concept, he would be recommending a version of religious "moralism" (in which *agape* is manifest as a divine command, or law), which he is against. By the same token, if love were considered completely optional, and justice, by contrast, required, Tillich would have no way of insisting on the kind of moral compulsion that is properly felt by human beings in search of their "centered-self."

Tillich's endorsement of creative justice as the natural successor of minimal morality, of course, depends on a prior, theologically governed proposal for overcoming estrangement. For Tillich, it is the "Christ," or creative power, through whose grace we gain the means to become participants with God. As participants, we acquire the wherewithal to lean in the direction of the divine ideal. This is the bridging of human existence and essence, which is also the fulfillment of human existence. Without grace, the human remains in exile, with no avenue for deliverance from estrangement. Yet the normative message in Tillich's thought—that we are finite but also free beings in need of self-realization—has relevance beyond the prophetic narrative in which it is revealed in his Christian, theocentric schema. The recognition of a *telos* toward which all human beings are oriented and the repudiation of stasis that such an orientation provokes are both observations about the human condition that arguably take on a universal dimension.[47] While developmentalists and prophetic religionists may debate over whether God's assistance is required to bridge the gap between human essence and existence, in both cases there is the basic recognition of the incompleteness of the human subject in the present moment.

Tillich's distinction between the two levels of justice is analogous to the double standard of moral requirement that was found to be present in the examples of *lifnim mishurat hadin* and the Second Love Commandment considered at the end of chapter 2. In each case, the interpreter conveys the value in feeling morally compelled to go beyond a standard already required by duty, locating that value in the elastic, expansive nature of character development. Such an analysis confirms the reflexive nature of virtue for the developing moral agent. To try to incorporate virtue in one's life is already to exhibit virtue. Conversely, in order to exhibit virtue, one must be committed to seeking it.

CONSCIENCE

The prophetic thought of Heschel and Tillich explicitly raises from a religious perspective an issue that has been given primary consideration in this book, namely, the issue of the extent to which we should be motivated by a moral ideal. For Heschel, this ideal is reflected in the emulation of God through acting responsibly; for Tillich, it comes in the imperative to expand one's existing sense of justice by heeding the norm of *agape*. What responsibility and creative justice involve is not always clear. What is morally required of us in any one moment depends on the particularity of that situation. What is required of us over time presupposes a string of fluid, contextually sensitive judgments. Ultimately, according to both Heschel and Tillich, "right action" is derived from an assessment of how we should be in light of a certain picture of human flourishing. They suggest that we should see ourselves as *responding* beings, anxious about what is going on around us and attentive to what we will go out of our way to do as we find ourselves participants in the world. Will we make an effort to combat evil when it is in our midst? Will we do so even when we bear no direct guilt for its advent? In the prophetic mind-set, we ought to be vigilant, scrutinizing onlookers, ready at a moment's notice to become voicers and actors. Morality as a whole makes this demand on us even in our private lives.

Being humanly responsible is acknowledging that we do not have the luxury of retreating into our private lives where we can bask in the comfort of moral neutrality and stasis. Responsibility is the antithesis of complacency. Thus, Heschel proclaims, "merely to be human we must be more than human." Not to be more is to be less. In saying this, Heschel reminds us to be self-critical, watchful, and ethically ill-at-ease, even when we are not in the wrong. At the same time, according to Heschel and Tillich, being responders is not enough for living a fully human life. We must become the kind of people who are *able* to respond when a response is called for. This is a question of how to live, what dispositions and habits to acquire. It is not a matter of merely deliberating on what to do or not do. Criticizing primarily the descendents of the Kantian tradition, Heschel writes:

> Modern thinking has often lost its way by separating the problem of truth from the problem of living, cognition from man's total situation. Such separation has resulted in reason's isolationism, in utopian and irrelevant conceptions of man. Reflection alone will not procure self-understanding. The human situation is disclosed in the thick of living. The deed is the distillation of the self. We can display no initiative, no freedom in sheer being; our responsibility is in living.[48]

We are responsible for who we are as well as for what we do. And who should we be? The answer provided by Heschel and Tillich is tied to their convictions about what is most meaningful about human life, namely, the search for and eventual union with God, which culminates in the acquisition of virtue, in the form of mercy, compassion, and loving-kindness. To live with God is to walk in His ways, which taken as commandment, becomes a commandment of character development. The answer to the question "Who should we be?" that is provided by the developmentalist, while not couched in theological language, is nearly the same. We should be responsible in living, both responsible for ourselves and for our own development, and responsible for the welfare and well-being of others. Responsibility implies vigilance. It implies watching out for our character, directing it in ways that will resist the temptation to succumb to nondeliberate, unreflective living.

This vigilance over who we become and for whom we watch out is, both in a secular and a religious context, human *answerability*, the trait that, when we finally discover it in ourselves, leads us not merely to be in the world, but to have an effect on it as it affects us. We might think of answerability as the human faculty of "conscience." In *Morality and Beyond*, Tillich characterizes conscience as an uneasiness with oneself that induces the self to turn inward. He invokes the culminating epiphany of Shakespeare's Richard III: "Oh coward conscience, how dost thou afflict me.... Is there a murderer here? No. Yes, I am. Then fly. What, from myself?" (*King Richard III*, Act V, scene 3).[49] Conscience defends the self against self-contradiction by refusing it the convenience of tolerating existing defects in character. The turn inward is a movement of self-judgment, and, if necessary, self-condemnation. While the process of serious introspection can be painful, moral action springs from conscience. It causes the self to fight for outcomes other than the ones that would otherwise unfold around it by default. It is arguably conscience that the Huguenots of Le Chambon possessed and that bystanders lacked in their respective defiance and acceptance of the Führer's law. In conscience, we ask ourselves: "What more is there left for me to do? What have I *missed*?" To ask these questions is to live in good faith. By asking them we do not leave our situation in life as we find it. Like the developmentalist, Heschel and Tillich problematize the status quo by insisting that to be is always to be more. "To be human is to be a problem," Heschel writes. To live humanly is to live a life morally ever on the hook. In conscience we remain attuned to our humanity. Conscience furnishes us with our integrity, even as it calls us back to self-analysis from an enjoyed respite. Through this process, we undergo moral development. To be sure, it is a labor-intensive process, although, if Heschel and Tillich are right, it is not something to lament.

NOTES

1. The political theorist John Tomasi also criticizes Urmson along these lines. See Tomasi, "Individual Rights and Community Virtues," *Ethics* 101 (1991): 526.

2. Along these lines, Tomasi distinguishes between "justice-duty" and a more fundamental, second-order "character-duty." See ibid., 527.

3. Robert M. Seltzer, *Jewish People, Jewish Thought: The Jewish Experience in History* (New York: MacMillan Publishing Company, 1980), 753.

4. Abraham J. Heschel, *Man Is Not Alone* (Philadelphia: The Jewish Publication Society of America, 1951), 116.

5. Abraham J. Heschel, *Between God and Man: An Interpretation of Judaism*, ed. Fritz A. Rothchild (New York: The Free Press, 1959), 75. The passage is quoted by Seltzer in *Jewish People, Jewish Thought*, 755.

6. Heschel, *Man Is Not Alone*, 109; quoted by Seltzer in *Jewish People, Jewish Thought*, 754.

7. Abraham J. Heschel, *The Sabbath* (New York: Harper and Row Torchbook, 1966), 64; quoted by Seltzer in *Jewish People, Jewish Thought*, 756.

8. Heschel, *Between God and Man*, 86.

9. Ibid., 125.

10. Arnold Eisen, "A Re-Reading of Heschel on the Commandments," *Modern Judaism* 9, no. 1 (1989): 20–21.

11. Heschel specifies that to be "responsible" is to have "the capability of being called upon to answer, or to make amends, to someone for something, without necessarily being directly connected with or involved in a criminal act." See Abraham J. Heschel, *Moral Grandeur and Spiritual Audacity*, ed. Susannah Heschel (New York: Farrar Straus Giroux, 1996), 220. Heschel here invokes the old prophetic teaching that while not everyone is guilty of evil, all are responsible. Since evil is everywhere, we can predict neither what our responsibility will entail nor how much will be demanded of us. There is no telling what God, "the Commander," may require of us at any point in time.

12. Abraham J. Heschel, *Who Is Man?* (Stanford: Stanford University Press, 1965), 4–5. I first became aware of this text as an exemplary instance of Heschel's association with virtue ethics by reading Joseph Woodill's *The Fellowship of Life: Virtue Ethics and Orthodox Christianity* (Washington, D.C.: Georgetown University Press, 1998), esp. 1–10. Interestingly, Woodill devotes this volume to exploring the possibilities for a virtue ethic out of the sources of Orthodox Christianity.

13. Heschel, *Who Is Man?*, 6–12.

14. Ibid., 41–42.

15. Ibid., 40.

16. Ibid., 104–5.

17. Ibid., 41.

18. Ibid., 41–42.

19. Heschel also indicates, like the developmentalist, that we acquire the resources for improving our character through our exposure to others who need us and whom we need for our moral education. He observes a communal component to the acquisition of virtue, writing: "Man in his being is derived from, attended by, and directed to the being of community. For man *to be* means *to be with* other human beings. His existence *is* coexistence. He can never attain fulfillment, or sense of meaning, unless it is shared, unless it pertains to other human beings" (ibid., 45). Because we need examples to follow, the pursuit of virtue will always occur within a specific community or tradition. This does not mean that we should ape the patterns of conduct exhibited by those responsible for our moral education. Rather, we should create new standards as we follow established ones.

20. Ibid., 97.

21. Ibid., 98.

22. Ibid., 109 (my emphasis). Heschel's exposition of "indebtedness" resembles that of Emmanuel Levinas. Both Heschel and Levinas speak of an original debt that can never fully be erased. Also, by using terms like "duty" and "sacrifice," Heschel implies, as does Levinas, that we repay our debt by performing other-regarding acts. Still, there are notable differences in their approaches. First,

for Heschel our indebtedness arises as part of our covenant with God at the very moment of our creation, whereas for Levinas, while it may be a trace of God who initially "commands," our debt to the other issues directly from the face of the other. Second, Heschel's ethics resembles Aristotelian patterns of thought, while Levinas's does not. By this I mean that in Heschel's account there is an ever-present emphasis on what is possible. Human beings are "unfinished" and develop in the direction of a *telos*, which is simultaneously the acquisition of virtue and union with God. According to Levinas, by contrast, we are all already necessarily bound to be maximally devoted to the other. Thus, with Levinas there is a notice-able absence of discussion about what is *possible* in favor of what is *necessary*.

23. Paul Tillich, *Systematic Theology, Volume II: Existence and the Christ* (Chicago: University of Chicago Press, 1967), 45; Tillich, *The Courage to Be* (New Haven: Yale University Press, 1952), 47, 82.

24. Tillich, *Systematic Theology, Volume II*, 79ff.

25. For an example of someone who argues that Tillich's religious philosophy is consistent with virtue ethics, see Glenn Graber, "The Metaethics of Paul Tillich," *The Journal of Religious Ethics* 1, no. 1 (1973): 113–33.

26. Paul Tillich, *Morality and Beyond* (Louisville: Westminster John Knox Press, 1995), 14, 23, 64.

27. Paul Tillich, *Love, Power, and Justice* (Oxford: Oxford University Press, 1960).

28. Tillich, *Morality and Beyond*, 13–14.

29. Ibid., 21; see also Tillich, *The Courage to Be*, 89–91.

30. Tillich, *Morality and Beyond*, 21–23.

31. Ibid., 29.

32. Ibid.

33. Ibid., 42.

34. Ibid.

35. Ibid., 42–43.

36. Tillich, *Love, Power, and Justice*, 63–64. Tillich also talks briefly about a level of justice even more basic than tributive or creative justice, namely a "justice based on the power of a thing's being," by which Tillich means the right of a being (whether it be a tree or a human) to self-actualize into its intended state (ibid., 63).

37. Ibid., 64.

38. Ibid., 65.

39. Ibid.

40. See chapter 1, note 37. The "jurisprudential" paradigm is one whose sub-ject matter is taken to be individual duties and rights and whose maxims pertain only to what must be done and what must not be done. According to the philoso-pher Loren Lomasky, a morality based on the jurisprudential paradigm lacks the resources to ask how one ought to live one's life, what traits of character one ought to develop, and the like. See Loren Lomasky, "Justice to Charity," *Social Philoso-phy and Policy* 12, no. 2 (1995): 33.

41. Tillich, *Love, Power, and Justice*, 64.

42. Ibid., 65.

43. Ibid., 65–66.

44. Ibid., 66.

45. Ibid., 71.

46. The relationship that Tillich describes between love and justice is similar but not equivalent to Reinhold Niebuhr's conception of love fulfilling yet negating justice (in German, expressed by the verb "aufheben"). See Niebuhr, *An Interpretation of Christian Ethics* (San Francisco: Harper and Row, 1935), 80. Both thinkers see love and justice as aspects of the same reality; however, only Niebuhr recognizes a sense in which they are fundamentally opposed to one another. For Tillich the higher form of creative justice is a form of love, while for Niebuhr the two concepts remain irreducibly distinct from, while also existing in a dialectical relationship with, one another. See also Niebuhr, *The Nature and Destiny of Man: A Christian Interpretation*, vol. 2 (New York: Charles Scribner's Sons, 1949), 246.

47. To be sure, they are noted even by the most important secular deontologists of our time. See, for example, my discussion of Rawls's explication of the Aristotelian Principle, in chapter 5.

48. Heschel, *Who Is Man?*, 94.

49. See Tillich's discussion of conscience in chapter 4 of *Morality and Beyond*.

The Banality and Contingency of Good and Evil

SOCRATES: But we ought to consider more carefully, for this is no light matter: it is the question, what is the right way to live?

—Plato, *The Republic*

In one of the more striking claims to have emerged since the Holocaust, Hannah Arendt contended that Adolf Eichmann, the bureaucrat chiefly in charge of administering Hitler's final solution, "was not Iago and not Macbeth, and nothing would have been farther from his mind than to determine with Richard III 'to prove a villain.'"[1] Arendt characterized Eichmann as a cog in the machinery of the Third Reich, no more or less than a slave to his circumstances. Her thesis was that since Eichmann saw himself as doing his duty in carrying out Hitler's will, he, and by extension others like him, had virtually no appreciation for the gravely criminal nature of their evil actions. The implication was that even the most ordinary, law-abiding person could unwittingly perpetrate the worst of crimes under the right set of circumstances.

Arendt's coverage of Eichmann's trial initially appeared in a string of *New Yorker* articles that were later published together in *Eichmann in Jerusalem: A Report on the Banality of Evil*. One of the things Arendt observed in her weekly installments was that Eichmann's role in the death of thousands, while methodical and diligent, was carried out without the motive of hatred or spite.[2] However devastating, his crimes were, as the subtitle states, "banal." The extermination of the Jews was policy. Eichmann did his job. His evil lay not in an explicit agenda, but in the uncritical, thoughtless acceptance of that job.

Arendt's observations about Adolf Eichmann also confirmed something else: the humanity of the villain. During the trial in Jerusalem, Arendt reported the testimony of half a dozen psychiatrists who certified him as "normal,"[3] and Eichmann himself revealed in more than one spontaneous utterance that he was a man capable of sentiment, affection, and even humility. For all the times he came across as pathetic and small, it would be inaccurate to characterize him as a calculating psychopath. Quite to the contrary: Eichmann's evil was caused by the fact that he *didn't* think, in precisely the same way that so many of us fail to think in life. It is just that in *those* circumstances, not thinking led to catastrophic results.

Arendt depicts Adolf Eichmann as an ordinary person who nevertheless committed great evil because of the manner in which he had habituated himself to performing evil deeds. Eichmann was not *born* the villain he so manifestly became. This is important. It means that the evil in whose advent Eichmann played such an instrumental role was not only banal, the byproduct of exposure to an ordinary set of circumstances, such as those in wartime when underlings act out of obedience. If Arendt is right, then Eichmann's participation in evil was also *contingent*. Considered as an outcome of human agency, it constituted but one possible result. According to Arendt's thesis, it is imaginable that in some other possible world Eichmann could have turned out to be benign, or perhaps virtuous.

Following the appearance of *Eichmann in Jerusalem*, Arendt became the target of considerable criticism for having characterized Eichmann as thoughtless but not morally wicked.[4] By her lights, Eichmann's indifference rather than his malevolence made him a doer of evil. This claim is controversial in two respects. First, it implies that the Eichmanns of the world are more ubiquitous than we might expect. If evil is understood to be part of the everyday—if evil is the norm and not the exception—then it is not eradicable. Evildoers cannot be vanquished the way monsters easily identified as monsters can be. Second, and more seriously, the claim implies that we are not that different from Eichmann. We are not who we would like to think we are, namely, creatures perhaps prone to conventional and occasionally more serious types of sin, but who are nevertheless immune to the kind of moral pestilence that overtook the Nazis when they set out to eliminate an entire race. In one fell swoop, Arendt dispelled myths about the existence of real-life Billy Budds and Claggarts. As human beings, we have the capacity to point in both directions. Arendt's conclusion was disconcerting, for it suggested that evil is something that for us becomes unexpectedly possible, contingent on the circumstances (both within and outside our control) that give rise to its advent, as well as contagious among those in proximity to those already in its grip. In simply endeavoring to capture and characterize the human being in Eichmann, Arendt opened the door for a chilling moral hypothesis: in this life we enjoy no guarantee against becoming certain sorts of people. Who we become, and the moral legacy we leave behind, are from the moment we are born yet to be determined.

In a sense, it is a version of Arendt's thesis for which I have argued in this book. Our futures are and remain morally contingent. We are not born good or evil, we become so. There are differences between the two theses, to be sure. The biggest of these pertains to the application of the concepts of banality and contingency to evil and, alternatively, to the good. According to Arendt's thesis, ordinary people can find themselves in a situation in which their actions become destructive simply by following the path of least resistance. Evil, in this sense, afflicts them as a privation; that is, it is the *absence* of concern, community, and goodness.[5] By contrast, according to the developmentalist, ordinary people come to perform good acts by spoiling inertia and assuming command of their lives (taking into account, of course, that they are limited and that not everything in life is within their control). Whereas both evil and good are "banal" in the sense that they can become the norm for the conduct of almost anyone, the banality of good is not simply a matter of circumstance but also one of decision, effort, and repetition. Goodness is banal as training for something is banal. With respect to both the acquisition of evil and the acquisition of good, what seemed formerly beyond the sphere of possibility slowly becomes a reality. However, while evil and good are both contingent states, in the case of the latter, agency is more primarily the moving force.

Arendt's critics were in fact outraged that she seemed to be letting Eichmann off the hook by not holding him sufficiently accountable for his own actions. If Eichmann was no more than an instrument of a design for which he was not the architect, then how much accountability does he bear for the final product? Here the critics' point is worth considering. Arendt seems to imply that part of Eichmann's culpability was bad moral luck. Eichmann's indifference, combined with the pressure that was brought to bear on him by his superiors, led to his crimes. But if this is so, then can we really say that Eichmann himself was "evil" rather than a victim of circumstance, albeit one served by his own apathy? It is precisely here where the thesis of moral development can be utilized to explain agent accountability in moral theory. To be sure, the assignment of blame in the thesis of moral development *begins* by calling attention to the kind of neglect that ensues the very moment when we fail to take up the personal goal of moral betterment. For the developmentalist, accountability is not a *result* but a *condition* of being in the world. Indeed, according to the thesis of moral development, we stand a fair chance of becoming Eichmanns ourselves if we do *not* make the assumption that we are, from the start, accountable for our character.

These differences notwithstanding, it is important to realize the overarching implication of Arendt's thesis for morality. Because of the contingency of human participation in evil and good, there is no guarantee at the beginning of our life as to how we will turn out. In addition, there is no predicting the situations in which we will find ourselves, including the moral dilemmas we will have to confront. Precisely what we are accountable for, and to whom we are accountable, are variables unveiled in the thick of living. Leading a human life assures us of this. Responsibility, in this sense, *attaches* to banality. If evil and good are not necessary outcomes, then we always bear some of the responsibility for our participation in evil and good. One of the subtleties of Arendt's observations about Adolf Eichmann's self-understanding rests in this conclusion. At the trial in Jerusalem, Arendt characterizes Eichmann as if he were discovering himself, and all he had apparently become, for the first time. Arendt, for her part, puts us on notice. Eichmann is not the unknowable, monstrous other. He is a possible future self. Simply dichotomizing, constructing binaries for our moral convenience, amounts to lazy, inadequate moral judgment. And just as we do not have the luxury of assuming that there are no circumstances under which we could do what Eichmann did, neither can we reasonably contend that what the hero or saint does is more than we could do. The banality and contingency of good and evil confirm the fundamentally proactive nature of morality.

Arendt arguably overstates the extent of Eichmann's self-deception, and even if she doesn't, the critic could still challenge her conclusion about the extent to which evil is always banal; for whether or not Eichmann was a cog, Hitler and others in his circle were surely not. There are moral monsters in this world. Indeed, the Holocaust itself, notwithstanding the smallness in stature of many who facilitated it, is every bit as radically evil as it is banally so. Yet Arendt is not suggesting that a lack of malevolent intention in any way lessens Eichmann's responsibility for what took place under his watch. Quite to the contrary, in fashioning evil as a privation, as a "lack" to begin with, she emphasizes the need to *form* intentions and aims in the moral life. We are responsible for what we do and what we do not do. For all the controversy it generated, Arendt's thesis is to be valued for the way it puts us on guard by clarifying the inevitably momentous nature of our decisions and of our indecision. Our moral standing is the product of habits we acquire and of our failure to develop others.

Training for the Good Life

A moral existence is one of training for something. It is an existence of setting goals and then trying to achieve them. For all of their insistence on the value inherent in voluntary, rational action, Urmson and Heyd fail to call attention to the contingency of our moral character, the idea that who we ultimately become is a radically undetermined notion from the perspective of who we are in the present. While Urmson and Heyd acknowledge variances among the moral traits that people possess, they take for granted the presence or absence of these traits in particular persons. This assumption leads them to place little emphasis on the proactive side of morality. Indifference, a privation in its own right, is in their view not commendable, but it is acceptable as long as it is not additionally supported by wrongdoing. In this respect, Urmson, Heyd, and other defenders of the standard view veer from the question that centrally occupied Socrates: What is the best kind of life for a human being to live? In *The Republic*, this is a question posed not merely to special or extraordinary sorts of human beings, such as heroes or saints; it constitutes the appropriate point of departure for everyone, from the saint on down to the scoundrel. If Socrates is right, then extraordinary things are eventually to be expected of ordinary people. While what morality requires of us remains proportional to what our character enables us to do, we have a responsibility to work on our character in order to increase our moral capabilities.

Our conventional moral assumptions and our justice system furnish us with little inducement to conduct Socrates' inquiry. In our society, moral expectation is the outgrowth of an assessment of a character that we inherit, and which, we presume, we cannot do very much about. We consider it a noteworthy accomplishment for morality if it is able to convince us to uphold the bare minimum. This attitude, which can be characterized as pessimistic or realistic, depending on one's perspective, is the natural byproduct of a society that puts liberties first and last. If we deem that the attitude is realistic, then we believe, with most commonsense theorists, that where we set the bar in terms of moral demandingness bears a great deal on how effective morality will be. Moral realists of this sort wager that restricting the liberty *not* to pursue a life of noteworthy moral achievement will produce a society in which individuals are on the whole less served by morality than they would be if morality bound them more minimally. The price of prioritizing individual liberties over other goods, of course, is that we forgo opportunities to put ourselves in a position to offer our assistance to others whom we *might* be able to help, for the insistence on preserving individual liberties goes hand in hand with relinquishing any mandate to morally strain ourselves.

Yet such is the price that the vast majority of neo-Enlightenment thinkers of the twentieth century have been willing to pay. This is so because of the profound importance our culture assigns to the value of liberty. John Rawls, arguably the most prominent of the contemporary, neo-Enlightenment thinkers, distinguishes the highest good of liberty from other social benefits, to be restricted only for the sake of liberty itself. In *A Theory of Justice*, Rawls flatly asserts that in "favorable" conditions, i.e., conditions that approximate the equal distribution of justice among all parties, "the desire for liberty is the chief regulative interest that the parties must suppose they will have in common. . . ."[6] Liberty supersedes other goods because without it, any led life would be humanly deficient. Rawls's qualification of this judgment is important. Liberty is something that is ultimately to be prized among all parties "in due course,"[7] once societies have been sufficiently developed to allow for the equal enjoyment of benefits by all of their members. The liberty of some persons can be curtailed in order to bring about those conditions in society in which liberty will be enjoyed by all. Yet this qualification does not change the fact it is liberty that is ultimately prized as the good most intrinsically valuable for human flourishing. Clearly there are others, including some quoted extensively in this book, who demur. Martin Luther King, Jr., for one, offers an explicitly contrasting view of human flourishing:

> All men are interdependent. Every nation is an heir of a vast treasury of ideas and labor to which both the living and the dead of all nations have contributed. Whether we realize it or not, each of us lives eternally "in the red." We are everlasting debtors to known and unknown men and women. . . . In a real sense, all life is interrelated. The agony of the poor impoverishes the rich; the betterment of the poor enriches the rich. We are inevitably our brother's keeper because we are our brother's brother. Whatever affects one directly affects all indirectly.[8]

According to King, it is not only an enduring but also a propitious feature of human nature that we are connected in this way, entering this world "in the red," as he puts it. Our interdependence and interrelatedness transcend the historical disparity between rich and poor, provider and provided for. Human communities are not constituted to be seeking a time when they will no longer depend on one another, for interdependence is implied by human nature. According to King, our dignity lies in the mutual furtherance of our lot and that of others. While Rawls and King both emphasize the dissolution of societal economic disparity, for King, the arrival of that improved future time does not in any way change the inherent nature of our co-ownership of each other's fortunes and miseries.

To side with King is to appreciate that a morality based exclusively on the value of liberty threatens to be one that keeps us from one another more than it brings us together. This will almost certainly happen if "liberty" is thought to entail the unfettered right to choose not to morally strain ourselves. A juridical model of morality concerned with the avoidance of wrongdoing directs us to protect the social order, but it fails to foster social connection. The upshot is a lawsuit-saturated society bereft of Good Samaritans—in short, a society in moral crisis.

I have polemicized against a dominant view in contemporary secular ethics that sees the realm of the morally required as significantly narrower in scope than the realm of the morally good and locates virtue primarily in the latter. Such a view, I have argued, fails to take seriously not only the moral perceptions of especially virtuous persons, like heroes and saints, but also the view of those ordinary persons who wish to understand ethics in relation to such figures. Supererogation is a critical concept for normative ethics, in both secular and religious contexts, for it serves as the measure between the present and the future, between how we actually are and how we could possibly be. The concept of supererogation enables us not to dismiss moral ideals as unrealizable and as having no relevance to how real people ought to live and conduct themselves. In working from an initial supposition that ideals are above and beyond, we are afforded the flexibility to pursue them at our own pace, without lapsing into the false view that their pursuit represents a futile endeavor. Antisupererogationists impose certain standards of moral conduct on all agents right from the beginning of their moral existence. In doing so, they do not make sufficient allowance for the key observation about human nature—apropos in both the religious and the secular realms—that virtue is gradually acquired through the practice and repetition of good habits. Having said this, it is important also to acknowledge that the concept of supererogation has potentially destructive consequences for morality, particularly if it is invoked as an unconditional exoneration from performing demanding altruistic deeds. Unqualified supererogationists who hold this view are explicit in their severance of ideals from real-world morality. There is nothing in their view that suggests we should ever move beyond the status quo. There is no imperative to change. Moral development is optional.

However, if the developmentalist is right, then the concept of supererogation connotes more than moral optionality, for it is a concept that forces us to recognize a multi-tiered array of true representations of how we ought to act at different stages in our lives. Qualified supererogationism, by its very nature, keeps us attuned to the world of others. It forces us to take note not only of the other who needs our help, but also of those few moral virtuosi especially skilled at devoting themselves to the other's betterment. To the extent that such virtuosi become our mentors, moral ideals become increasingly accessible. Regardless of whether the moral virtuosi we encounter become our mentors, at the very least their existence stands as a challenge to the ways in which we become accustomed to conceiving our responsibility in society. Such exemplars are not simply anomalies. When we encounter them, we are forced to ask ourselves how well we are living our lives, as well as whether we ought to exercise a choice or a series of choices that for them is no longer an option.

Admittedly, even the developmentalist must grant that we never know before the fact how much we will be able to morally develop, and consequently how much we will be able to redefine for ourselves what is "duty" and what is "above and beyond." Yet neither were those whom we might call heroes and saints sure of their capacity to evolve into exemplary moral agents before actually doing so, much less able to predict their heroic and saintly status during the time when they knew themselves to be no more than ordinary men and women.

NOTES

1. Hannah Arendt, *Eichmann in Jerusalem: A Report on the Banality of Evil* (New York: The Viking Press, 1965), 287.

2. Ibid. Arendt documents Eichmann's repeated claims to have neither harbored hatred for the Jews nor displayed ill will toward his victims. Arendt considers that this was in part due to Eichmann's personal relationship with Jews. Not only did he himself have a Jewish mistress from Linz, there were Jews in his family. See ibid., 30ff.

3. Ibid., 25ff.

4. As Charles T. Mathewes observes, by Arendt's thesis nearly anyone, and not merely a Satanic *Übermensch*, could have acted as Eichmann did. See Mathewes, *Evil and the Augustinian Tradition* (Cambridge: Cambridge University Press, 2001), 166ff. Much has also been made of Arendt's remark that the Jews did not do enough in their own defense and may have even cooperated in their own slaughter. See Arendt, *Eichmann in Jerusalem*, 117–18. One of the best critiques of Arendt along these lines is articulated by Richard Wolin, "The Ambivalence of German-Jewish Identity: Hannah Arendt in Jerusalem," *History and Memory* 8 (1996): 9–34.

5. Evil construed as a "privation," or absence of the good, is an Augustinian formulation, which Arendt adopted. For more on Arendt's Augustinian characterization of evil, see Mathewes, *Evil and the Augustinian Tradition*, 165–71.

6. John Rawls, *A Theory of Justice* (Cambridge: The Belknap Press of Harvard University Press, 1971), 545.

7. Ibid.

8. Martin Luther King, Jr., *A Testament of Hope: The Essential Writings and Speeches of Martin Luther King, Jr.*, ed. James Washington (San Francisco: Harper Collins, 1986), 626.

Bibliography

Adams, Robert. "Saints." *Journal of Philosophy* 81 (1984): 392–401.
————. "Vocation." *Faith and Philosophy* 4 (1987): 448–62.
Ahad Ha'am. *Essays, Letters, Memoirs—Ahad Ha'am*. Translated by Leon Simon. Oxford: East and West Library, 1946.
An-Na'im, Abdullahi Ahmed. "Towards a Cross-Cultural Approach to Defining International Standards of Human Rights: The Meaning of Cruel, Inhuman, or Degrading Punishment." In *Human Rights in Cross-Cultural Perspectives*, edited by Abdullahi Ahmed An-Na'im, 19–43. Philadelphia: University of Pennsylvania Press, 1992.
Annas, Julia. *The Morality of Happiness*. Oxford: Oxford University Press, 1993.
Anscombe, G. E. M. "Modern Moral Philosophy." *Philosophy* 33 (1958): 1–19.
Aquinas, Thomas. *Summa Theologica*, I.II, Question 108; II.II, Question 184. Translated by Jordan Aumann, O.P. New York: MacGraw-Hill Book Co., 1947–48.
Arendt, Hannah. *Eichmann in Jerusalem: A Report on the Banality of Evil*. New York: The Viking Press, 1965.
Aristotle. *Nicomachean Ethics*. Translated by Terence Irwin. Indianapolis: Hackett Publishing Company, 1985.
Atfield, Robin. "Supererogation and Double Standards." *Mind* 28 (1979): 481–99.
Badhwar, Neera Kapur. "Friendship, Justice, and Supererogation." *American Philosophical Quarterly* 22 (1985) 123–32.
————. "Altruism Versus Self-Interest: Sometimes a False Dichotomy." In *Altruism*, edited by Ellen Frankel Paul, Fred D. Miller, Jr., and Jeffrey Paul, 90–117. Cambridge: Cambridge University Press, 1993.
Baechler, Jean. "Virtue: Its Nature, Exigency, and Acquisition." Translated by John W. Chapman. In *Virtue: Nomos XXXIV*, edited by John W. Chapman and William A. Galston, 25–48. New York: New York University Press, 1992.
Baron, Marcia. "Kantian Ethics and Supererogation." *Journal of Philosophy* 84 (1987): 237–62.
Barry, Curtis. "The Supererogatory, the Foolish, and the Morally Required." *Journal of Value Inquiry* 15 (1981): 311–18.
Batchelor, John. *Lord Jim*. London: Unwin Hyman, 1988.

Beauchamp, Tom L., and James F. Childress. *Principles of Bioethics*. 4th ed. Oxford: Oxford University Press, 1994.

Becker, Gary. *The Economic Approach to Human Behavior*. Chicago: University of Chicago Press, 1976.

Benedict, Philip. *The Huguenot Population of France, 1600–1685: The Demographic Fate and Customs of a Religious Minority*. Philadelphia: Transactions of the American Philosophical Society, vol. 81. part 5, 1991.

Bennett, Lerone, Jr. *What Manner of Man: A Biography of Martin Luther King, Jr.* Chicago: Johnson Publishing Company, Inc., 1976.

Blum, Lawrence A. *Friendship, Altruism, and Morality*. London: Routledge and Kegan Paul, 1980.

———. *Moral Perception and Particularity*. Cambridge: Cambridge University Press, 1994.

Brandt, Richard. "Blameworthiness and Obligation." In *Essays in Moral Philosophy*, edited by A. I. Melden, 3–39. Seattle: University of Washington Press, 1958.

Brown, Peter. *The Cult of the Saints: Its Rise and Function in Latin Christianity*. Chicago: University of Chicago Press, 1981.

Browning, Christopher. *Ordinary Men*. New York: Harper Collins, 1992.

Bynum, Caroline Walker. *Holy Feast and Holy Fast: The Religious Significance of Food to Medieval Women*. Berkeley: University of California Press, 1987.

Calvin, John. *Institutes of the Christian Religion*, vol. 1. Edited by John T. McNeill. Translated by Ford Lewis Battles. Philadelphia: The Westminster Press, 1960.

Campbell, Joseph. *The Hero with a Thousand Faces*. New York: Pantheon Books, 1949.

Camus, Albert. *The Fall*. Translated by Justin O'Brien. New York: Vintage Press, 1991.

———. *The Plague*. Translated by Stuart Gilbert. New York: Vintage Press, 1991.

Card, Claudia. "On Mercy." *Philosophical Review* 81 (1972): 182–207.

Carney, Frederick S. "The Role of Rules in Law and Morality." *Southwestern Law Journal* 23 (1969): 438–53.

———. "On Frankena and Religious Ethics." *Journal of Religious Ethics* 3, no. 1 (1975): 7–25.

Chisholm, Roderick. "Supererogation and Offence: A Conceptual Scheme for Ethics." *Ratio* 5 (1963): 1–14.

Chisholm, Roderick, and Ernest Sosa. "Intrinsic Preferability and the Problem of Supererogation." *Synthese* 16 (1966): 321–31.

Coleman, John A. "After Sainthood?" In *Saints and Virtues*, edited by John Stratton Hawley, 205–25. Berkeley: University of California Press, 1982.

Coles, Robert. *Dorothy Day: A Radical Devotion*. Reading, Mass.: Addison-Wesley Publishing Company, 1987.

Conrad, Joseph. *Lord Jim*. New York: Doubleday, 1922.

Cua, Antonio. *Dimensions of Moral Creativity*. University Park: Pennsylvania State University Press, 1978.

Cunningham, Lawrence. *The Meaning of Saints*. San Francisco: Harper and Row, 1980.

Dan, Joseph. *Jewish Mysticism and Jewish Ethics*. Seattle: University of Washington Press, 1986.

Dancy, Jonathan. "Supererogation and Moral Realism." In *Human Agency—Language, Duty, and Value: Philosophical Essays in Honor of J. O. Urmson*, edited by Jonathan Dancy, J. M. E. Moravcsik, and C. C. W. Taylor, 170–88. Stanford: Stanford University Press, 1988.

———. "Intuitionism." In *A Companion to Ethics*, edited by Peter Singer, 411–20. Oxford: Basil Blackwell, 1993.

Davis, Nancy. "Contemporary Deontology." In *A Companion to Ethics*, edited by Peter Singer, 205–18. Oxford: Basil Blackwell, 1993.

Day, Dorothy. *Thérèse*. Springfield, Ill.: Templegate, 1979.

———. *By Little and by Little: Selected Writings of Dorothy Day*, edited by Robert Ellsberg. Maryknoll, N.Y.: Orbis Books, 1992.

———. *Loaves and Fishes*. Maryknoll, N.Y.: Orbis Books, 1997.

———. *The Long Loneliness: The Autobiography of Dorothy Day*. San Francisco: HarperSanFrancisco, 1997.

———. *On Pilgrimage*. Grand Rapids, Mich.: William B. Eerdmans Publishing Company, 1997.

Demmer, Klaus. *Shaping the Moral Life: An Approach to Moral Theology*. Edited by James Keenan. Translated by Roberto Dell'Oro. Washington, D.C.: Georgetown University Press, 2000.

DeNicola, Daniel L. "Supererogation: Artistry in Conduct." In *Foundations of Ethics*, edited by Leroy Rouner, 149–66. Notre Dame, Ind.: University of Notre Dame Press, 1983.

Dickens, Charles. *Works of Charles Dickens: A Tale of Two Cities and Sketches by Boz*. New York: The Kelmscott Society, 1904.

Diefendorf, Barbara. *Beneath the Cross: Catholics and Huguenots in Sixteenth-Century Paris*. Oxford: Oxford University Press, 1991.

Dombrowski, Daniel A. "Back to Sainthood." *Philosophy Today* 33 (1989): 56–62.

Donagan, Alan. *The Theory of Morality*. Chicago: University of Chicago Press, 1977.

Donne, John. *Devotions upon Emergent Occasions*, XVII. Edited by Anthony Raspa. Montreal: McGill-Queens University Press, 1975.

Dostoevsky, Fyodor. *The Brothers Karamazov*. Translated by Andrew H. MacAndrew. New York: Bantam Books, 1970.

Downing, Frederick L. *To See the Promised Land: The Faith Pilgrimage of Martin Luther King, Jr.* Macon, Georgia: Mercer University Press, 1986.

Driver, Julia. "The Suberogatory." *Australasian Journal of Philosophy* 70 (1992): 286–95.

Dyson, Michael Eric. *I May Not Get There with You: The True Martin Luther King, Jr.* New York: The Free Press, 2000.

Eisen, Arnold. "A Re-Reading of Heschel on the Commandments." *Modern Judaism* 9, no. 1 (1989): 1–33.

Engstrom, Stephen, and Jennifer Whiting, eds. *Aristotle, Kant, and the Stoics: Rethinking Happiness and Duty*. Cambridge: Cambridge University Press, 1996.

Erlanger, Philippe. *St. Bartholomew's Night: The Massacre of Saint Bartholomew*. Translated by Patrick O'Brian. Westport, Conn.: Greenwood Press, 1960.

Farmer, David Hugh. *The Oxford Dictionary of Saints*, 2d ed. Oxford: Oxford University Press, 1987.

Feinberg, Joel. "Supererogation and Rules." In *Ethics*, edited by Judith Jarvis Thomson and Gerald Dworkin, 391–411. New York: Harper and Row Publishers, 1968.

Feldman, Fred. *Doing the Best We Can*. Dordrecht, Holland: D. Reidel, 1986.

Fishkin, James S. *The Limits of Obligation*. New Haven: Yale University Press, 1982.

Flanagan, Owen. *Varieties of Moral Personality: Ethics and Psychological Realism*. Cambridge, Mass.: Harvard University Press, 1991.

Flew, R. N. *The Idea of Perfection in Christian Theology: An Historical Study of the Ideal for the Present Life*. New York: Humanities Press, 1968.

Fogelman, Eva. *Conscience and Courage: Rescuers of Jews during the Holocaust*. New York: Anchor Books, 1994.

Foot, Philippa. *Virtues and Vices*. Berkeley: University of California Press, 1978.

———. *Natural Goodness*. Oxford: Clarendon Press, 2001.

Frankena, William K. "The Ethics of Love Conceived as an Ethics of Virtue." *Journal of Religious Ethics* 1, no. 1 (1973): 21–36.

———. "Conversations with Carney and Hauerwas." *Journal of Religious Ethics* 3, no. 1 (1975): 45–62.

Friedman, Philip. *Their Brothers' Keepers*. New York: Holocaust Library, 1978.

Fuchs, Josef. *Human Values and Christian Morality*. Dublin: Gill and MacMillan, Ltd., 1970.

Galston, William A. "Cosmopolitan Altruism." In *Altruism*, edited by Ellen Frankel Paul, Fred D. Miller, Jr., and Jeffrey Paul, 118–34. Cambridge: Cambridge University Press, 1993.

Garrow, David J. *Bearing the Cross: Martin Luther King, Jr. and the Southern Christian Leadership Conference*. New York: William Morrow and Company, 1986.

Gauthier, David. *Morals by Agreement*. Oxford: Oxford University Press, 1986.

Gelber, Hester G. "The Exemplary World of St. Francis of Assisi." In *Saints and Virtues*, edited by John Stratton Hawley, 15–35. Berkeley: University of California Press, 1987.

Gellately, Robert. "'A Monstrous Uneasiness': Citizen Participation and Persecution of the Jews in Nazi Germany." In *Lessons and Legacies: The Meaning of the Holocaust in a Changing World*, edited by Peter Hayes, 178–209. Evanston: Northwestern University Press, 1991.

Gert, Bernard. *Morality: A New Justification of the Moral Rules*. New York: Oxford University Press, 1988.

Gewirth, Alan. *Reason and Morality*. Chicago: University of Chicago Press, 1978.

Gibbs, Robert. *Correlations in Rosenzweig and Levinas*. Princeton: Princeton University Press, 1992.

———. *Why Ethics?: Signs of Responsibilities*. Princeton: Princeton University Press, 2000.

Gilleman, Gérard. *The Primacy of Charity in Moral Theology*. Translated by William Ryan and André Vachon. London: The Newman Press, 1959.

Gilligan, Carol. *In a Different Voice: Psychological Theory and Women's Development*. Cambridge, Mass.: Harvard University Press, 1982.

———. "Moral Orientation and Moral Development." In *Women and Moral Theory*, edited by Eva Feder Kittay and Diana T. Meyers, 19–33. Savage, Md.: Rowman and Littlefield Publishers, 1987.

Glover, Jonathan. *Humanity: A Moral History of the Twentieth Century.* New Haven: Yale University Press, 1999.

Gordon, Lewis. *Bad Faith and Antiblack Racism.* Atlantic Highlands, N.J.: Humanities Press, 1995.

Gourevitch, Philip. *We Wish to Inform You That Tomorrow We Will Be Killed with Our Families: Stories from Rwanda.* New York: Picador USA, 1998.

Graber, Glenn. "The Metaethics of Paul Tillich." *Journal of Religious Ethics* 1, no. 1 (1973): 113–34.

Gushee, David P. *The Righteous Gentiles of the Holocaust: A Christian Interpretation.* Minneapolis: Fortress Press, 1994.

Halberstam, David. *Firehouse.* New York: Hyperion Books, 2002.

Hale, Susan C. "Against Supererogation." *American Philosophical Quarterly* 28, no. 4 (1991): 273–85.

Hallie, Philip. *Lest Innocent Blood Be Shed: The Story of the Village of Le Chambon and How Goodness Happened There.* New York: Harper and Row, 1979.

Hampton, Jean. "Selflessness and the Loss of Self." In *Altruism,* edited by Ellen Frankel Paul, Fred D. Miller, Jr., and Jeffrey Paul, 135–65. Cambridge: Cambridge University Press, 1993.

Hare, John E. *The Moral Gap: Kantian Ethics, Human Limits, and God's Assistance.* Oxford: Clarendon Press, 1996.

Hare, R. M. *Freedom and Reason.* Oxford: Oxford University Press, 1963.

———. *Moral Thinking: Its Levels, Methods, and Point.* Oxford: Clarendon Press, 1981.

Häring, Bernard. *The Law of Christ,* vol. 2, translated by Edwin G. Kaiser. Westminster, Md.: Paulist Press, 1963.

Hart, H. L. A. *The Concept of Law.* London: Oxford University Press, 1976.

Hauerwas, Stanley. *Character and the Christian Life.* San Antonio: Trinity University Press, 1975.

———. "Obligation and Virtue Once More." *Journal of Religious Ethics* 3. no. 1 (1975): 27–44.

———. *Against the Nations: War and Survival in a Liberal Society.* Minneapolis: Winston Press, 1985.

Hawley, John Stratton. "Introduction: Saints and Virtues." In *Saints and Virtues,* edited by John Stratton Hawley, xi–xxi. Berkeley: University of California Press, 1987.

———. "Morality beyond Morality in the Lives of Three Hindu Saints." In *Saints and Virtues,* edited by John Stratton Hawley, 52–72. Berkeley: University of California Press, 1987.

Heschel, Abraham J. *Man Is Not Alone.* Philadelphia: The Jewish Publication Society of America, 1951.

———. *Between God and Man: An Interpretation of Judaism.* Edited by Fritz A. Rothchild. New York: The Free Press, 1959.

———. *Who Is Man?* Stanford: Stanford University Press, 1965.

———. *The Sabbath.* New York: Harper and Row Torchbook, 1966.

———. *Moral Grandeur and Spiritual Audacity.* Edited by Susannah Heschel. New York: Farrar Straus Giroux, 1996.

Heyd, David. *Supererogation: Its Status in Ethical Theory.* Cambridge: Cambridge University Press, 1982.

———. "Moral Subjects, Freedom, and Idiosyncrasy." In *Human Agency—Language, Duty, and Value: Philosophical Essays in Honor of J. O. Urmson,* edited by Jonathan Dancy, J. M. E. Moravcsik, and C. C. W. Taylor, 152–69. Stanford: Stanford University Press, 1988.

———. "Supererogation and Ethical Methodology: A Reply to Mellema." *Philosophia* 24 (1994): 183–89.

———. "Obligation and Supererogation." In *Encyclopedia of Bioethics,* edited by Warren T. Reich, vol. 4, 1833–38. New York: Macmillan, 1995.

Hick, John. *An Interpretation of Religion: Human Responses to the Transcendent.* New Haven: Yale University Press, 1989.

Hill, Thomas, Jr. "Self-Respect Reconsidered." *Tulane Studies in Philosophy* 31 (1982): 129–37.

———. "Ideals of Human Excellence and Preserving Natural Environments." *Environmental Ethics* 5 (1983): 211–24.

Hinman, Lawrence M. *Ethics: A Pluralistic Approach to Moral Theory.* 2d ed. Fort Worth: Harcourt Brace College Publishers, 1994.

Homer. *The Odyssey.* Translated by W. Shrewing. Oxford: Oxford University Press, 1980.

Hook, Brian S., and R. R. Reno. *Heroism and the Christian Life: Reclaiming Excellence.* Louisville: Westminster John Knox Press, 2000.

Hooper, Leon. "Dorothy Day's Transposition of Thérèse's 'Little Way.'" *Theological Studies* 63, no. 1 (2002): 68–87.

Horne, James. "Saintliness and Moral Perfection." *Religious Studies* 27 (1991): 463–71.

Hudson, W. D. *Modern Moral Philosophy.* Garden City, N.Y.: Doubleday & Co., 1970.

Humberstone, I. L. "Logic for Saints and Heroes." *Ratio* 16 (1974): 103–14.

Hume, David. *An Inquiry Concerning the Principles of Morals.* Edited by Charles W. Hendel. New York: Liberal Arts Press, 1957.

———. *A Treatise of Human Nature.* Edited by L. A. Selby-Bigge and P. H. Nidditch. Oxford: Clarendon Press, 1978.

Hurka, Thomas. *Perfectionism.* Oxford: Oxford University Press, 1993.

Hursthouse, Rosalind. "Virtue Theory and Abortion." *Philosophy and Public Affairs* 20 (1991): 223–46.

Inchausti, Robert. *The Ignorant Perfection of Ordinary People.* Albany: State University of New York Press, 1991.

Jacobs, Louis. "Greater Love Hath No Man . . . The Jewish Point of View of Self Sacrifice." In *Contemporary Jewish Ethics,* edited by Menachem Marc Kellner, 175–83. New York: Sanhedrin Press, 1978.

———. "The Relationship between Religion and Ethics in Jewish Thought." In *Contemporary Jewish Ethics,* edited by Menachem Marc Kellner, 41–57. New York: Sanhedrin Press, 1978.

James, William. *The Varieties of Religious Experience: A Study in Human Nature.* New York: Penguin Books, 1982.

Johnson, Mark L. "How Moral Psychology Changes Moral Theory." In *Mind and Morals: Essays on Cognitive Science and Ethics*, edited by Larry May, Marilyn Friedman, and Andy Clark. Cambridge, Mass.: MIT Press, 1996.

Jones, David. *Moral Responsibility in the Holocaust: A Study in the Ethics of Character*. Lanham, Md.: Rowman and Littlefield Publishers, 1999.

Jones, L. Gregory. *Transformed Judgment: Toward a Trinitarian Account of the Moral Life*. Notre Dame, Ind.: University of Notre Dame Press, 1990.

Kagan, Shelly. "Does Consequentialism Demand Too Much?: Recent Work on the Limits of Obligation." *Philosophy and Public Affairs* 13 (1984): 239–54.

———. *The Limits of Morality*. Oxford: Oxford University Press, 1989.

———. *Normative Ethics*. Oxford: Westview Press, 1998.

Kamm, Frances Myrna. "Supererogation and Obligation." *Journal of Philosophy* 82 (1985): 118–38.

Kant, Immanuel. *The Doctrine of Virtue: Part II of the Metaphysics of Morals*. Translated by Mary J. Gregor. Philadelphia: University of Pennsylvania Press, 1964.

———. *The Groundwork of the Metaphysic of Morals*. Translated by H. J. Paton. New York: Harper and Row, 1964.

———. *The Critique of Practical Reason*. 3d ed. Translated by Lewis White Beck. New York: MacMillan Publishing Company, 1993.

Kaufmann, Walter. *Nietzsche: Philosopher, Psychologist, Antichrist*. 4th ed. Princeton: Princeton University Press, 1974.

Keenan, James F. *Goodness and Rightness in Thomas Aquinas's Summa Theologiae*. Washington, D.C.: Georgetown University Press, 1992.

———. "Virtue Ethics: Making a Case as It Comes of Age." *Thought* 67, no. 265 (1992): 115–27.

Kellner, Menachem. "Jewish Ethics." In *A Companion to Ethics*, edited by Peter Singer. Oxford: Blackwell Publishers, 1993.

King, Martin Luther, Jr. *A Testament of Hope: The Essential Writings and Speeches of Martin Luther King, Jr.*, edited by James M. Washington. San Francisco: Harper Collins, 1986.

King, The Reverend Martin Luther, Sr. *Daddy King: An Autobiography*. New York: William Morrow, 1980.

Kittay, Eva Feder, and Diana T. Meyers, eds. *Women and Moral Theory*. Savage, Md.: Rowman and Littlefield Publishers, 1987.

Kohlberg, Lawrence. *Essays on Moral Development: Vol. I, The Philosophy of Moral Development: Moral Stages and the Idea of Justice*. New York: Harper and Row, 1981.

Kolm, S. C. "Altruism and Efficiency." *Ethics* 94 (1983): 18–65.

Korsgaard, Christine. "From Duty and for the Sake of the Noble: Kant and Aristotle on Morally Good Action." In *Aristotle, Kant, and the Stoics: Rethinking Happiness and Duty*, edited by Stephen Engstrom and Jennifer Whiting, 203–36. Cambridge: Cambridge University Press, 1996.

Kotva, Joseph, Jr. *The Christian Case for Virtue Ethics*. Washington, D.C.: Georgetown University Press, 1996.

Lash, Nicholas. *Easter in Ordinary: Reflections on Human Experience and the Knowledge of God*. Charlottesville: University Press of Virginia, 1988.

Lauritzen, Paul. "Moral Prerogative or Religious Duty?" *Journal of Religious Ethics* 15, no. 2 (1987): 141–54.

Levinas, Emmanuel. *Totality and Infinity: An Essay on Exteriority.* Translated by Alphonso Lingus. Pittsburgh: Duquesne University Press, 1969.

———. *Otherwise than Being or Beyond Essence.* Translated by Alphonso Lingus. The Hague: Martinus Nijhoff, 1974.

Lewis, David. *King: A Critical Biography.* New York: Praeger Publishers, 1970.

Little, David. "The Law of Supererogation." In *The Love Commandments: Essays in Christian Ethics and Moral Philosophy,* edited by Edmund N. Santurri and William Werpehowski, 157–81. Washington, D.C.: Georgetown University Press, 1992.

Little, David, and Sumner B. Twiss. *Comparative Religious Ethics: A New Method.* San Francisco: Harper and Row, 1978.

Lomasky, Loren E. "Justice to Charity." *Social Philosophy and Policy* 12, no. 2 (1995): 32–53.

Louden, Robert. "On Some Vices of Virtue Ethics." In *The Virtues: Contemporary Essays on Moral Character,* edited by Robert B. Kruschwitz and Robert C. Roberts, 66–80. Belmont, Calif.: Wadsworth Publishing, 1987.

Luther, Martin. "Treatise on Good Works." Translated by A. T. W. Steinhauser. In *Works of Martin Luther,* vol. 1, edited by Henry Eyster Jacobs, 173–286. Philadelphia: Muhlenberg Press, 1943.

———. *Martin Luther: Selections from His Writing.* Edited by John Dillenberger. New York: Doubleday, 1962.

MacIntyre, Alasdair. *A Short History of Ethics: A History of Moral Philosophy from the Homeric Age to the Twentieth Century.* London: Routledge and Kegan Paul, 1966.

———. *After Virtue.* 2d ed. Notre Dame, Ind.: University of Notre Dame Press, 1982.

———. *Whose Justice? Which Rationality?* Notre Dame, Ind.: University of Notre Dame Press, 1988.

———. *Dependent, Rational Animals: Why Human Beings Need the Virtues.* Chicago: Open Court Press, 1999.

Mackie, J. L. *Ethics: Inventing Right and Wrong.* New York: Penguin Books, 1977.

Maimonides, Moses. *The Guide of the Perplexed.* 2 volumes. Translated by Shlomo Pines. Chicago: University of Chicago Press, 1963.

Margolis, Howard. *Selfishness, Altruism, and Rationality.* New York: Cambridge University Press, 1981.

Mathewes, Charles, T. *Evil and the Augustinian Tradition.* Cambridge: Cambridge University Press, 2001.

Matzko, David Matthew. "Postmodernism, Saints and Scoundrels." *Modern Theology* 9, no. 1 (1993): 19–36.

McDowell, John. "Deliberation and Moral Development in Aristotle's Ethics." *Aristotle, Kant, and the Stoics: Rethinking Happiness and Duty,* edited by Stephen Engstrom and Jennifer Whiting, 19–35. Cambridge: Cambridge University Press, 1996.

McGoldrick, Patricia. "Saints and Heroes: A Plea for the Supererogatory." *Philosophy* 59 (1984): 523–28.

McNamara, Paul. "Making Room for Going Beyond the Call." *Mind* 105, no. 419 (1996): 415–50.
Melden, A. I., ed. *Essays in Moral Philosophy.* Seattle: University of Washington Press, 1958.
———. "Saints and Supererogation." In *Philosophy and Life: Essays on John Wisdom,* edited by Ilham Dilman, 61–79. The Hague: Martinus Nijhoff Publishers, 1984.
Mellema, Gregory. *Beyond the Call of Duty: Supererogation, Obligation, and Offence.* Albany: State University of New York Press, 1991.
———. "Must We Do the Best We Can?" *Philosophy Today* 36 (1992): 39–43.
———. "Supererogation, Blame, and the Limits of Obligation." *Philosophia* 24 (1994): 171–82.
———. "Is It Bad to Omit an Act of Supererogation?" *Journal of Philosophical Research* 21 (1996): 405–16.
Mill, John Stuart. *Utilitarianism.* London: Longmans, Green, and Co., 1907.
Miller, William. *Dorothy Day: A Biography.* San Francisco: Harper and Row, 1982.
Miller, William Robert. *Martin Luther King, Jr.: His Life, Martyrdom, and Meaning for the World.* New York: Weybright and Talley, 1968.
Monroe, Kristen Renwick. "John Donne's People: Explaining Differences between Rational Actors and Altruists through Cognitive Frameworks." *Journal of Politics* 53, no. 2 (1991): 394–433.
———. *The Heart of Altruism: Perceptions of a Common Morality.* Princeton: Princeton University Press, 1996.
Monroe, Kristen Renwick, Michael C. Barton, and Ute Klingemann. "Altruism and the Theory of Rational Action: Rescuers of Jews in Nazi Europe." *Ethics* 101 (1990): 103–22.
Moore, G. E. *Principia Ethica.* Cambridge: Cambridge University Press, 1968.
Moravcsik, Julius. "On What We Aim At and How We Live." In *The Greeks and the Good Life,* edited by David J. Depew, 198–235. Fullerton: California State University Press, 1980.
Moseley, Edwin. "Christ as Tragic Hero: Conrad's *Lord Jim.*" In *Religion and Modern Literature: Essays in Theory and Criticism,* edited by G. B. Tennyson and Edward E. Ericson, Jr., 220–32. Grand Rapids, Mich.: William B. Eerdmans Publishing Company, 1975.
Mother Teresa. *Total Surrender.* Edited by Brother Angelo Devanada. Ann Arbor, Mich.: Servant Publications, 1985.
———. *In My Own Words.* New York: Gramercy Books, 1997.
Murdoch, Iris. *The Sovereignty of Good.* London: Routledge and Kegan Paul, 1970.
Nagel, Thomas. "The Limits of Objectivity." In *The Tanner Lectures on Human Values,* vol. 1, edited by Sterling McMurrin, 77–139. Cambridge: Cambridge University Press, 1980.
———. *The View from Nowhere.* Oxford: Oxford University Press, 1986.
Nelson, Daniel Mark. *The Priority of Prudence: Virtue and Natural Law in Thomas Aquinas and the Implications for Modern Ethics.* University Park: Pennsylvania State University Press, 1992.
New, Christopher. "Saints, Heroes, and Utilitarians." *Philosophy* 49 (1974): 179–89.

Newman, Louis. "The Quality of Mercy: On the Duty to Forgive in the Judaic Tradition." *Journal of Religious Ethics* 15, no. 2 (1987): 155–72.

———. "Law, Virtue, and Supererogation in the Halakhah: The Problem of
'*Lifnim Mishurat Hadin*' Reconsidered." *Journal of Jewish Studies* 60, no. 1
(1989): 61–88.

———. "Ethics as Law, Law as Religion: Reflections on the Problem of Law and
Ethics in Judaism." *Shofar* 9, no. 1 (1990): 13–31.

Niebuhr, Reinhold. *Moral Man and Immoral Society.* New York: Charles Scribner's
Sons, 1932.

———. *An Interpretation of Christian Ethics.* San Francisco: Harper and Row, 1935.

———. *The Nature and Destiny of Man: A Christian Interpretation,* 2 vols. New
York: Charles Scribner's Sons, 1949.

———. *Love and Justice.* Edited by D. B. Robertson. Philadelphia: The Westminster Press, 1957.

Nietzsche, Friedrich. *Thus Spoke Zarathustra: A Book for None and All.* Translated
by Walter Kaufmann. New York: Penguin Books, 1978.

Norton, David. "Moral Minimalism and the Development of Moral Character."
In *Midwest Studies in Philosophy XIII—Ethical Theory: Character and Virtue,*
edited by Peter A. French, Theodore Uehling, Jr., and Howard Wettstein,
180–95. Notre Dame, Ind.: University of Notre Dame Press, 1988.

———. *Democracy and Moral Development.* Berkeley: University of California
Press, 1991.

Novak, David. *Jewish Social Ethics.* Oxford: Oxford University Press, 1992.

Nussbaum, Martha. *The Fragility of Goodness: Luck and Ethics in Greek Tragedy
and Philosophy.* Cambridge: Cambridge University Press, 1986.

———. *Love's Knowledge: Essays on Philosophy and Literature.* Oxford: Oxford
University Press, 1990.

———. "Aristotle on Human Nature and the Foundation of Ethics." In *World,
Mind, and Ethics: Essays on the Ethical Philosophy of Bernard Williams,* edited
by J. E. Altham and Ross Harrison, 86–131. Cambridge: Cambridge University
Press, 1995.

Nygren, Anders. *Agape and Eros.* Translated by Philip S. Watson. Philadelphia: The
Westminster Press, 1953.

Oakley, Justin. "Varieties of Virtue Ethics." *Ratio* 9 (1996): 128–52.

Oates, Stephen B. *Let the Trumpet Sound: The Life of Martin Luther King, Jr.* New
York: Harper and Row, 1982.

Ogletree, Thomas W. *The Use of the Bible in Christian Ethics.* Philadelphia:
Fortress Press, 1983.

Oliner, Samuel P., and Pearl M. Oliner. *The Altruistic Personality: Rescuers of Jews
in Nazi Europe.* New York: Free Press, 1988.

O'Neill, Onora. *Constructions of Reason: Explorations of Kant's Practical Philosophy.* Cambridge: Cambridge University Press, 1989.

———. *Towards Justice and Virtue: A Constructive Account of Practical Reasoning.*
Cambridge: Cambridge University Press, 1996.

Otto, Rudolph. *The Idea of the Holy.* Translated by John W. Harvey. Oxford:
Oxford University Press, 1958.

Outka, Gene. *Agape: An Ethical Analysis*. New Haven: Yale University Press, 1972.

Paldiel, Mordecai. *Sheltering the Jews: Stories of Holocaust Rescuers*. Minneapolis: Fortress Press, 1996.

Paul, Ellen Frankel, Fred D. Miller, Jr., and Jeffrey Paul, eds. *The Good Life and the Human Good*. Cambridge: Cambridge University Press, 1992.

————. *Altruism*. Cambridge: Cambridge University Press, 1993.

————. *Virtue and Vice*. Cambridge: Cambridge University Press, 1998.

Pence, Gregory. "Virtue Theory." In *A Companion to Ethics*, edited by Peter Singer, 249–58. Oxford: Basil Blackwell, 1993.

Peterfreund, Sheldon. "Supererogation and Obligation." *The Personalist* 56 (1975): 151–54.

Pieper, Josef. *The Silence of St. Thomas: Three Essays*. Translated by John Murray and Daniel O'Connor. New York: Pantheon Books, 1957.

Pincoffs, Edmund. *Quandaries and Virtues: Against Reductivism in Ethics*. Lawrence: University Press of Kansas, 1986.

Pope, Stephen J. *The Evolution and the Ordering of Love*. Washington, D.C.: Georgetown University Press, 1994.

Pritchard, Michael S. "Self-Regard and the Supererogatory." *Tulane Studies in Philosophy* 31 (1982): 139–51.

Proudfoot, Wayne. *Religious Experience*. Berkeley: University of California Press, 1985.

Pybus, Elizabeth. "Saints and Heroes." *Philosophy* 57 (1982): 193–200.

————. "A Plea for the Supererogatory: A Reply." *Philosophy* 61 (1986): 526–31.

Radcliffe, Dana. "Compassion and Commanded Love." *Faith and Philosophy* 11, no. 1 (1994): 50–71.

Ramsay, William M. *Four Modern Prophets: Walter Rauschenbusch, Martin Luther King, Jr., Gustavo Gutiérrez, Rosemary Radford Ruether*. Atlanta: John Knox Press, 1986.

Rawls, John. *A Theory of Justice*. Cambridge, Mass.: The Belknap Press of Harvard University Press, 1971.

Raz, Joseph. "Permissions and Supererogation." *American Philosophical Quarterly* 12 (1975): 161–68.

Reaman, G. Elmore. *The Trial of the Huguenots in Europe, the United States, South Africa, and Canada*. Baltimore: Genealogical Publishing Co., 1972.

Reeder, John P. "Beneficence, Supererogation, and Role Duty." In *Beneficence and Health Care*, edited by Earl Shelp, 83–108. Dordrecht, Holland: D. Reidel, 1982.

————. "Forgiveness: Tradition and Appropriation." *Journal of Religious Ethics* 15, no. 2 (1987): 136–40.

————. "Foundations without Foundationalism." In *Prospects for a Common Humanity*, edited by Gene Outka and John P. Reeder, Jr., 191–214. Princeton: Princeton University Press, 1993.

————. "Extensive Benevolence." *Journal of Religious Ethics* 26, no. 1 (1998): 47–70.

————. "What Is a Religious Ethic?" *Journal of Religious Ethics* 25, no. 3 (1998): 157–81.

Rescher, Nicholas. *Unselfishness: The Role of Vicarious Affects in Moral Philosophy and Social Theory*. Pittsburgh: University of Pittsburgh Press, 1975.

Roberts, Robert C. "What Emotion Is: A Sketch." *Philosophical Review* 97, no. 2 (1988): 183–209.

Rorty, Richard. *Contingency, Irony, and Solidarity.* Cambridge: Cambridge University Press, 1989.

Ross, C. D. *The Right and the Good.* London: Oxford University Press, 1973.

Rowe, Christopher. "Ethics in Ancient Greece." In *A Companion to Ethics,* edited by Peter Singer, 121–32. Oxford: Basil Blackwell, 1993.

Saint Teresa of Ávila. *The Life of Saint Teresa of Ávila by Herself.* Translated by J. M. Cohen. New York: Penguin Books, 1957.

Salmon, J. H. M. *Society in Crisis: France in the Sixteenth Century.* New York: St. Martin's Press, 1975.

Santurri, Edmund N., and William Werpehowski, eds. *The Love Commandments: Essays in Christian Ethics and Moral Philosophy.* Washington, D.C.: Georgetown University Press, 1992.

Sartre, Jean-Paul. *Being and Nothingness.* Translated by Hazel E. Barnes. London: Methuen and Co. Ltd., 1969.

Sauvage, Pierre. *Weapons of Spirit.* Documentary film. Los Angeles: Friends of Le Chambon, 1989.

Scheffler, Samuel. *Human Morality.* Oxford: Oxford University Press, 1992.

Schmidtz, David. "Reasons for Altruism." In *Altruism,* edited by Ellen Frankel Paul, Fred D. Miller, Jr., and Jeffrey Paul, 52–68. Cambridge: Cambridge University Press, 1993.

Schneewind, J. B. *The Invention of Autonomy: A History of Modern Moral Philosophy.* Cambridge: Cambridge University Press, 1998.

Schumaker, Millard. *Moral Praise.* Edmonton: St. Stephen's College, 1977.

———. *Supererogation: An Analysis and Bibliography.* Edmonton: St. Stephen's College, 1977.

Schweiker, William. *Mimetic Reflections: A Study in Hermeneutics, Theology, and Ethics.* New York: Fordham University Press, 1990.

Sebba, Anne. *Mother Teresa, 1910–1997: Beyond the Image.* New York: Doubleday Press, 1997.

Seltzer, Robert M. *Jewish People, Jewish Thought: The Jewish Experience in History.* New York: MacMillan Publishing Company, 1980.

Shelley, Percy Bysshe. "Defense of Poetry." In *Norton Anthology: World Masterpieces,* volume 2, edited by Maynard Mack. New York: Norton, 1995.

Sherman, Nancy. "Common Sense and Uncommon Virtue." In *Midwest Studies in Philosophy XIII—Ethical Theory: Character and Virtue,* edited by Peter A. French, Theodore Uehling, Jr., and Howard Wettstein, 87–114. Notre Dame, Ind.: University of Notre Dame Press, 1988.

———. *The Fabric of Character: Aristotle's Theory of Virtue.* Oxford; Clarendon Press, 1991.

Shue, Henry. "Solidarity among Strangers and the Right to Food." In *World Hunger and Morality,* 2d ed., edited by William Aiken and Hugh LaFollette, 113–32. Upple Saddle River, N.J.: Prentice Hall, 1996.

Sidgwick, Henry. *The Methods of Ethics.* 7th ed. Chicago: University of Chicago Press, 1962.

Singer, Peter. ed. *A Companion to Ethics.* Oxford: Basil Blackwell, 1993.
———. "Famine, Affluence, and Morality." In *World Hunger and Morality,* 2d ed., edited by William Aiken and Hugh LaFollette, 26–38. Upper Saddle River, N.J.: Prentice Hall, 1996.
Slote, Michael. *Goods and Virtues.* Oxford: Clarendon Press, 1983.
———. *Beyond Optimizing: A Study of Rational Choice.* Cambridge, Mass.: Harvard University Press, 1989.
———. *From Morality to Virtue.* New York: Oxford University Press, 1992.
Smart, J. J. C., and Bernard Williams. *Utilitarianism: For and Against.* Cambridge: Cambridge University Press, 1973.
Spohn, William. "The Recovery of Virtue Ethics." *Theological Studies* 53, no. 1 (1992): 60–75.
Stace, W. T. *Religion and the Modern Mind.* Philadelphia: J. B. Lippincott, 1952.
———. *Mysticism and Philosophy.* New York: St. Martin's Press, 1960.
Statman, Daniel, ed. *Virtue Ethics: A Critical Reader.* Washington, D.C.: Georgetown University Press, 1997.
Steffen, Lloyd. *Self-Deception and the Common Life.* New York: Peter Lang, 1986.
Sterba, James. "Can A Person Deserve Mercy?" *Journal of Social Philosophy* 10 (1979): 11–14.
Stocker, Michael. "The Schizophrenia of Modern Ethical Theories." *Journal of Philosophy* 73 (1976): 453–66.
Stout, Jeffrey. *Ethics after Babel: The Language of Morals and Their Discontents.* Boston, Beacon Press, 1988.
Sutherland, N. M. *The Huguenot Struggle for Recognition.* New Haven: Yale University Press, 1980.
Taylor, Charles. *Sources of the Self: The Making of the Modern Identity.* Cambridge, Mass.: Harvard University Press, 1989.
———. *Varieties of Religion Today: William James Revisited.* Cambridge, Mass.: Harvard University Press, 2002.
Taylor, Mark C. *Altarity.* Chicago: University of Chicago Press, 1987.
Tec, Nechema. *When Light Pierced the Darkness: Christian Rescue of Jews in Nazi-Occupied Poland.* Oxford: Oxford University Press, 1986.
Thomas, Laurence. *Vessels of Evil: American Slavery and the Holocaust.* Philadelphia: Temple University Press, 1993.
Thomson, Judith Jarvis. "A Defense of Abortion." In *The Problem of Abortion,* 2d ed., edited by Joel Feinberg, 173–87. Belmont, Calif.: Wadsworth Publishing, 1984.
Tillich, Paul. *The Courage to Be.* New Haven: Yale University Press, 1952.
———. *Love, Power, and Justice.* Oxford: Oxford University Press, 1960.
———. *Systematic Theology, Volume II: Existence and the Christ.* Chicago: University of Chicago Press, 1967.
———. *Morality and Beyond.* Louisville: Westminster John Knox Press, 1995.
Tomasi, John. "Individual Rights and Community Virtues." *Ethics* 101, no. 3 (1991): 521–36.
Trianosky, Gregory. "On the Obligation to Be Virtuous: Shaftesbury and the Question: Why Be Moral?" *Journal of the History of Philosophy* 16 (1978): 289–300.

———. "Supererogation, Wrongdoing, and Vice: On the Autonomy of the Ethics of Virtue." *Journal of Philosophy* 83 (1986): 26–40.

———. "Virtue, Action, and the Good Life: Toward a Theory of Virtues." *Pacific Philosophical Quarterly* 68, no. 2 (1987): 124–47.

———. "What Is Virtue Ethics All About?" In *Virtue Ethics: A Critical Reader*, edited by Daniel Statman, 42–55. Washington, D.C.: Georgetown University Press, 1997.

Troeltsch, Ernst. *The Christian Faith.* Translated by Garrett E. Paul. Minneapolis: Fortress Press, 1991.

Twiss, Sumner B., and Bruce Grelle. "Human Rights and Comparative Religious Ethics: A New Venue." *The Annual of the Society of Christian Ethics* 15 (1995): 21–48.

Urmson, J. O. "Saints and Heroes." In *Essays in Moral Philosophy*, edited by A. I. Melden, 198–216. Seattle: University of Washington Press, 1958.

Vann, Father Joseph, ed. *Lives of Saints.* New York: John J. Crawley & Co., 1954.

Walker, Margaret Urban. "Moral Particularity." *Metaphilosophy* 18 (1987): 171–85.

Walzer, Michael. *Thick and Thin: Moral Argument Home and Abroad.* Notre Dame, Ind.: University of Notre Dame Press, 1994.

Waters, Tony. *Bureaucratizing the Good Samaritan: The Limits of Humanitarian Relief Operations.* Boulder, Colo.: Westview Press, 2001.

Weiss, Raymond L. *Maimonides' Ethics: The Encounter of Philosophic and Religious Morality.* Chicago: University of Chicago Press, 1991.

Werpehowski, William. "*Agape* and Special Relations." In *The Love Commandments: Essays in Christian Ethics and Moral Philosophy*, edited by Edmund N. Santurri and William Werpehowski, 138–56. Washington, D.C.: Georgetown University Press, 1992.

Williams, Bernard. *Moral Luck: Philosophical Papers, 1973–1980.* Cambridge: Cambridge University Press, 1981.

———. *Ethics and the Limits of Philosophy.* Cambridge, Mass.: Harvard University Press, 1985.

Wilson, Robert. *Conrad's Mythology.* Troy, N.Y.: The Whitston Publishing Company, 1987.

Withrobe, R. "It Pays to Do Good, but Not More Good Than It Pays." *Journal of Economic Behavior and Organization* 2 (1981): 201–13.

Wolf, Susan. "Moral Saints." *Journal of Philosophy* 79, no. 8 (1982): 419–39.

———. "Above and Below the Line of Duty." *Philosophical Topics* 14, no. 2 (1986): 131–48.

Wolgast, Elizabeth. *The Grammar of Justice.* Ithaca, N.Y.: Cornell University Press, 1987.

Wolin, Richard. "The Ambivalence of German-Jewish Identity: Hannah Arendt in Jerusalem." *History and Memory* 8 (1996): 9–34.

Woodill, Joseph. *The Fellowship of Life: Virtue Ethics and Orthodox Christianity.* Washington, D.C.: Georgetown University Press, 1998.

Woodward, Kenneth. *Making Saints: How the Catholic Church Determines Who Becomes Saints, Who Doesn't, and Why.* New York: Simon and Schuster, 1990.

Wyschogrod, Edith. *Spirit in Ashes: Hegel, Heidegger, and Man-Made Mass Death.* New Haven: Yale University Press, 1985.

―――. *Saints and Postmodernism: Revisioning Moral Philosophy.* Chicago: University of Chicago Press, 1990.

―――. *An Ethics of Remembering: History, Heterology, and the Nameless Others.* Chicago: University of Chicago Press, 1998.

Yearley, Lee H. *Mencius and Aquinas: Theories of Virtue and Conceptions of Courage.* Albany: State University of New York Press, 1990.

―――. "Recent Work on Virtue." *Religious Studies Review* 16, no. 4 (1990): 1–9.

Yoder, John. *The Politics of Jesus.* Grand Rapids, Mich.: Eerdmans Press, 1972.

―――. *The Priestly Kingdom: Social Ethics as Gospel.* Notre Dame, Ind.: University of Notre Dame Press, 1984.

Zagzebski, Linda T. *Virtues of the Mind: An Inquiry into the Nature of Virtue and the Ethical Foundations of Knowledge.* Cambridge: Cambridge University Press, 1996.

Index

accountability, 36, 111–12, 309–10, 316–17
activism, 85, 102n20, 190–91, 220, 309
Adams, Robert, 84
After Virtue (MacIntyre), 34–36, 101n4
agape, 95–96, 187–88, 191, 303–5
Aggadah, 104n43
Ahad Ha'am, 86–87
Alyosha (*The Brothers Karamazov*), 85
Annas, Julia, 250–51, 265
Anscombe, Elizabeth, 28–29n32, 64n3
anti-supererogationism: consequentialism as, 33, 37; demanding nature, 56–57, 65n10, 320; qualified supererogation and, 92–93; vs. thesis of moral development, 243, 273, 277–81
Arendt, Hannah, 314–17, 321n2, 321nn4–5
aretaic ethics: deontic theories and, 67n19, 240–42, 253, 256–60, 286n10, 286n12; duty and virtue, 10–11; religious ethics and, 12–18, 258–60, 287n16, 311n12, 312n25; supererogation, 66n17, 252–57; types, 287n15. *See also* Aristotelian ethics; thesis of moral development
Aristotelian ethics: child-rearing, 293n92; hero's humanity and, 118–19; moral irresponsibility, 289n47; in thesis of moral development, 242–52, 279, 296–97; as type of aretaic ethic, 287n15; virtue acquisition, 239–40, 262–68, 293n92. *See also* neo-Aristotelian ethics
asceticism, 87–88, 174–77, 223n24

aspiration, 118–19, 247–48, 263–64, 275, 282, 297–303
autonomy. *See* free will

Bad Faith and Antiblack Racism (Gordon), 164n94
Barton, Michael, 144
Beneath the Cross (Diefendorf), 162n70
Between God and Man (Heschel), 298–99
Biblical law, 93–96, 104n43, 258–60, 299. *See also* law in society
"Bloody Sunday", 226n68
Blum, Lawrence, 78–79, 82, 115, 148, 151–52, 169n124
The Brothers Karamazov (Dostoevsky), 85
Brown, Peter, 88–89
Bynum, Caroline Walker, 87–88
bystanders: conduct evaluation of, 167–68n115, 168n116, 271–73, 294n98; excuses for inaction, 57, 252–55, 290n55; heroes' view, 139–44, 147, 149, 163–64n94

Campbell, Joseph, 157n3
Camus, Albert, 26, 82–83, 102n14, 123–27, 160n54
canonization of saints, 179, 196–97, 222n15
Carney, Frederick, 64n6
Carton, Sydney (*A Tale of Two Cities*), 120–23, 127, 159n37
Catherine of Siena, Saint, 87–88
Catholicism: canonization of saints, 179,

196–97, 222n15; Huguenots
persecution, 133–36, 162n70, 162n72,
162–63n81; response to poverty,
192–94. *See also* Christianity
The Chambonnais, 131–41, 161–62n63,
162–63n81, 163nn84–85. *See also*
Huguenots
charity, 54, 96–100, 105n52, 223n24
Christianity: duty, 96–100, 258–60;
heroism, 110–11, 160n54; on secular
ethics, 45–46; virtue, 105n52, 258–60;
virtue ethics and, 12–18, 287n16. *See
also* Catholicism; religious ethics;
righteous gentiles
Coleman, John, 212–16
"Commission for the Designation of the
Righteous", 160–61n58
commonsense morality. *See* ordinary
morality
communal solidarity, 116, 119, 124–26,
140, 160n54. *See also* moral
communities
complacency, 6, 57, 92, 140, 251, 277
Conrad, Joseph, 120–23, 127, 159n38
conscience, 241, 281–82, 308–10. *See also*
excuses for inaction
consequentialism, 33, 37, 168–69n119,
243, 269–73, 287n15
context of altruism, 110, 114, 298, 308. *See
also* moral communities
cost of altruism: in deontic ethics, 55,
57–58; heroes' view, 46, 51, 75, 129–30,
145; in ordinary morality, 37–38, 42,
45; for righteous gentiles, 129–30, 145;
saints' view, 3–4, 46, 51, 75, 174–75,
220
courage, 11, 111, 128, 173
creative justice, 58–59, 86–87, 305–8,
313n46
The Cult of the Saints (Brown), 88–89

Day, Dorothy: about, 191–97,
227–28nn75–80; activism, 85, 102n20;
as a revolutionary, 220; self-
examination provoked by, 3–7; on
suffering, 88; as "world" saint,
197–200
Demmer, Klaus, 14–17

deontic moral theories: aretaic theories
and, 67n19, 240–42, 253, 256–60, 286n10,
286n12; duty, 54–59, 67–68n22,
240–42, 246, 278, 280; evaluative
sphere and, 79–81; other-regard,
41–42, 54–59; self-regard, 54–59,
73n80, 298; supererogation, 54–59,
72–73n74, 252–57; Urmson's reform
of, 40–43
Dependent Rational Animals (MacIntyre),
293n90
developmentalists. *See* thesis of moral
development
Dickens, Charles, 120–23, 127, 159n37
Diefendorf, Barbara, 133–34, 162n70
The Doctrine of Virtue (Kant), 278
Dostoevsky, Fyodor, 85, 201
duty: in deontic ethics, 54–59, 67–68n22,
240–42, 246, 278, 280; heroes'
expanded view, 144–48, 152–53; in
minimalist ethics, 54–59, 91–92; *vs.*
obligation, 27n8; in ordinary morality,
36–44, 61–63, 67nn20–21, 79–81; in
religious ethics, 58–59, 93–100,
258–60; role duties, 27n8, 51, 69n44,
75, 114; in thesis of moral development,
238–42, 296–97; *vs.* virtue, 10–11,
61–63, 90–91

Eichmann, Adolf, 314–17, 321n2
Eichmann in Jerusalem (Arendt), 314–15,
321n4
Enlightenment ethics, 34–35, 42. *See also*
neo-Enlightenment ethics
equal-regard, 202–3, 229n111
estrangement, 298, 303, 307–8
"ethics of excess", 7–8, 22, 183, 200–211
Evil and the Augustinian Tradition
(Mathewes), 321nn4–5
excuses for inaction, 57, 252–55, 290n55.
See also conscience
exhortations, 5, 7–8, 192, 196, 228n100,
253–54

The Fall (Camus), 26
The Fellowship of Life (Woodill), 311n12
feminism, 15, 24, 29n41, 37, 210
firefighters, 112–14, 157n14